BREAKING WITH MOSCOW

Arkady N. Shevchenko

March 1978.

BALLANTINE BOOKS • NEW YORK

To my wife, Elaine

Library of Congress Catalog Card Number: 85-5204

ISBN 0-345-30088-2

This edition published by arrangement with Alfred A. Knopf, Inc.

Manufactured in the United States of America

First International Edition: August 1985
First U.S. Edition: January 1986

"Part autobiography, part spy thriller, part primer on the workings of ordinary Soviet society, part treatise on how the cumbersome Soviet government works and part sententious lesson for the American future. In all these respects, it is valuable.... The book rings true."

Robert Finn
Cleveland Plain Dealer

"For 20 years, Arkady N. Shevchenko was where no other defector or spy has been—attending meetings of the politburo, the ruling leadership of the Communist Party, working in the offices of Soviet Foreign Minister Andrei A. Gromyko, and serving as the senior Russian official at the United Nations, where he had access to some of his Government's most sensitive cable traffic.... His anecdotes are replete with confirmation of Western fears of Soviet leaders as power-hungry liars and cheats, yet as very cautious men. His inside portraits of those gray men... are often revealing and important."

Leslie H. Gelb
New York Times Book Review

"Many of Shevchenko's revelations challenge years of Western 'expert' interpretations, and have profound and sobering implications. But *Breaking With Moscow* is more than a sweeping review of personalities and events.... Compellingly written, this book addresses with urgency the most profound issues of our time. It is vital reading, not only for the architects of American foreign policy, but for anyone truly concerned with peace in our time."

Robert Bidinotto
The Boston Herald

"His memoir (written in a surprisingly literary, sprightly English) has the intrigue and intellectual adroitness of a spy thriller–cum–political philosophy primer. On a personal level, Mr. Shevchenko is very appealing.... Highly readable, especially the author's close-up cameos of top Soviet leaders."

Betsy Kline
Kansas City Star

PREFACE

It is not my purpose in this memoir to instill feelings of hostility in Americans toward the Soviet people, or to complicate in any way efforts to promote peace. The world has enough madmen trying to do that. What I want is to share with the reader my experiences under the Soviet system; to tell the truth about it as I lived it; to inform the public of Soviet designs, and to warn of the dangers they present to the world. In so doing I hope also, in however small a way, to help the Soviet people eventually find their way to liberty.

The U.S.S.R. cannot be erased from the earth or removed from its position at the center of power in the modern world. The survival of mankind may depend upon temperate relations between the Soviet Union and the United States. Both possess unprecedented power to exterminate or to save humanity. Each measures the other's intentions largely in terms of its own particular assumptions and outlook; and the misunderstandings that, not surprisingly, arise could result in disastrous confrontation. Thus, it is vitally important for the West to know as accurately and as completely as possible the thinking and attitudes of those who make policy in the Kremlin.

The first part of this book is entitled "The Reluctant Spy" —a title that reflects my feelings about my secret cooperation with the U.S. government. Spying is widely regarded as a less-than-honorable profession; spying for a country other than one's own is, in most cases, an extreme expression of disloyalty. But I have never regarded myself as a spy in the true sense of the word, nor have I felt that I betrayed my people or my country. I have always loved Russia and I

v

always will. For a relatively short time in my life I worked with the U.S. government to help it better comprehend the objectives and actions of the Soviet regime—a regime I knew well and had grown to hate. That regime, and the system that props it up, is what I "betrayed."

Since the book deals with some subjects that are sensitive and current, a few names have been changed and certain sources have not been identified. I do not want to hurt anyone—Soviet or American—whom I respect and who might suffer if his real name were mentioned.

This book has been written for the general public. I have tried to explain many things as clearly and simply as possible, something that was often not easy to do, given the complex nature of international relations. I must stress, in this connection, the absolute impossibility of covering fully in a single volume either my personal experiences or every important aspect of the situation and problems of the Soviet Union. It is my intention in the future to do more formal and scholarly studies concerning the U.S.S.R. and the United Nations.

I WANT TO EXPRESS MY DEEPEST APPRECIATION TO THOSE who helped me write this book. First of all, to my wife, Elaine, whose prodigious assistance and encouragement never failed me. It may sound like a cliché, but it is also the simple truth, to say that without her this work would never have been completed. Although I had published several books and many articles in the Soviet Union, I found it very difficult to write an "American" book. The style and approach suitable for Soviet readers are quite different from what is customary in the English-speaking world, and it was only after several false starts that I finally discovered the key that "turned the lock." Through it all, Elaine remained patient and enthusiastic.

I also owe sincere gratitude to my dear friend, William Geimer, whose steady support, wisdom, and judgment were invaluable. In moments of discouragement and setback, Bill was there to put Elaine and me back on track each time.

I greatly appreciate the help of my editor, Ashbel Green,

and the contributions of others who have assisted me in this effort.

My deepest satisfaction in writing this book came from being able, for the first time in my life, to express myself free of anyone's control or the necessity of remembering what was politically or ideologically acceptable. The United States has given me refuge and a new life, but this has been its greatest gift.

Arkady N. Shevchenko
October 1984

FOREWORD

Since the original publication of my memoir there have been further changes in the Soviet leadership. In February 1985, Konstantin Chernenko died and Mikhail Gorbachev was selected as the new leader. Andrei Gromyko relinquished his post as Foreign Minister and has become titular head of state. Because of these events, for this edition I have added some material about the new leader and possible trends in Soviet policy.

Arkady N. Shevchenko
September 1985

PART ONE

THE RELUCTANT SPY

1

I SWORE AT MYSELF. LOCKED IN BUMPER-TO-BUMPER traffic in the middle of New York's Queensboro Bridge, I poured out my anger in Russian invective, cursing myself for not anticipating the traffic jam, exasperated at the prospect of disruption of my carefully laid plans.

I gripped the steering wheel as though my willpower could lift my car out of the crawling procession. Any New Yorker would know enough to avoid this lemming-like rush out of Manhattan on a Friday night, and I felt almost a native, having lived there for many years. Tonight of all nights I couldn't be late, not for this critically important meeting.

I had prepared for it calmly, checking and rechecking timing and details. But now an uneasy feeling of possible failure rose in me. What if the man I was to meet didn't wait for me? What if he thought the whole arrangement had been a trick? Would I ever be able to contact him again?

Then another doubt arose: Was my secret safe? Suppose I had been betrayed and was heading into a trap? Was there another car lurking in the traffic with me, behind me, following me?

For anyone brought up and educated in the Soviet Union, it was natural to feel paranoia; there, self-preservation makes suspicion of everyone's motives second nature.

In my normal New York life I was routinely watched, sometimes constantly, sometimes intermittently. This evening, I hoped, the surveillance had slacked off. But the uncertainty was unnerving. I had to find out if I was being tailed but there was no way I could. The traffic was too dense to let me identify any single car in the mass of headlights in my rearview mirror.

If anyone *was* watching, he would, so far at least, have nothing unusual to report. Arkady Nikolaevich Shevchenko, Soviet diplomat, United Nations bureaucrat, was merely following his weekend routine, heading for the run-down Long Island mansion in Glen Cove where the Soviet Mission to the United Nations provided a country hideaway for its top functionaries. What the watchers did not know, I hoped, was that tonight there was good reason to track me. I was on my way to a secret meeting with a United States official who was waiting for me back in Manhattan. But I had to reach him with no one following me. My chauffeur, who was somewhere beginning his weekend, was a KGB shadow. So was my top personal assistant in the thirty-fifth-floor office I had occupied since the spring of 1973 as United Nations Under Secretary General for Political and Security Council Affairs. So were, I knew, other men who periodically appeared around me.

I had lived under shadows for years, but that didn't make them any easier to take. I had learned to coexist with the KGB, as almost every Soviet does, accepting their threats and intrusions throughout my life and work. But finally, this evening, I was going to try to escape them for good.

To do so successfully, however, my intentions had to remain secret a while longer. I had to be certain that the Soviets suspected nothing of my plans, and that the Americans would be willing to help me implement them promptly. Now, out on the Long Island Expressway, as the traffic thinned out, a fresh wave of anxiety came over me and I picked up speed.

To any other driver the car I spotted behind me would seem just an ordinary, late-model Buick sedan, but this one was the favorite model, make, and color of my colleagues at the Soviet Mission. The head of the KGB in New York, the *rezident*, drove one. Its presence might mean nothing. Perhaps the driver was an ordinary commuter. But it could be a Soviet surveillance car.

I had to know if it was a tail. I began to weave from lane to lane, drawing curses and horn-blaring from other drivers. I sped up, then slowed down, but still the Buick hovered behind me, five or six car lengths back. Speeding up to sixty, seventy, seventy-five, my thoughts blurring as the car raced along, I came up fast on Exit 39, the turnoff to Glen Cove. Barely braking, I swung my car hard across the right-hand lane onto the exit ramp, into the darkened back road where, should the Buick follow, I would know I was in trouble. It did not. The chase had been imaginary. For a moment, relief flooded through me.

A siren wailed behind me and a red light pulsed in my rearview mirror. But my pursuer was not the KGB, just a Nassau County policeman who had observed my wild driving.

I apologized and decided not to invoke diplomatic immunity: Displaying my credentials might avoid a traffic ticket, but would involve a long dispute with him. Some fellow Soviet might come by and see us. The time might be noted. Someone might wonder why I was stopped only a few miles from Glen Cove at seven o'clock but did not appear there until several hours later. I could not afford to take such a chance. At that point I was impatient to get back to Manhattan. I accepted the officer's tongue-lashing and the summons with no objection.

IT HAD ALL BEGUN SOME WEEKS BEFORE IN MY OFFICE AT the United Nations. There I made my final decision to break with the Soviet system.

Many of my UN colleagues regarded me as a hard-liner, an orthodox guardian of Soviet interests in the Secretariat who would not hesitate to bend the rules in favor of the U.S.S.R. There was good reason for such an evaluation. Bowing to pressure from Moscow and from Yakov Malik, the Soviet Ambassador to the UN, was essential in my job, and the common knowledge that I was an experienced Soviet administrator who was inclined to extend his own power and control wherever possible also contributed to that image. More than twenty years' immersion in the values and goals of the Soviet system and association with its leaders had made a deep imprint on me. That environment had shaped me into a kind of clockwork mechanism running automatically, not easy to stop.

As my disaffection from the Soviet system and what it represented developed, however, I was able occasionally to lend discreet support to ideas or measures contrary to Soviet desires, and, whether in large matters or small, I took increasing

5

satisfaction in putting my hand in as such opportunities presented themselves. But I doubted whether the Americans were aware of that. My reputation, I thought, might weaken their confidence in my sincerity. They would probably probe for motives, and they would not be easily satisfied with explanations of frustration or discontent. I thought they would be interested in hearing me out, but on the other hand, détente was in full bloom. Would the United States be willing to harbor me at the risk of dimming even slightly détente's rosy glow? The Soviets would likely accuse the United States of spoiling the climate between Moscow and Washington. One individual, after all, no matter what his position, is not really worth that much in the great affairs of nations.

The Americans might also think I was playing some kind of game, or worse, that I had gone mad. Perhaps they would suspect that I was a drug user, or that I was an alcoholic whose pickled brain no longer functioned.

Although I was uncertain how the Americans would view my prospective defection, I had no doubt about the Soviets' reaction. If they found me out, they would ship me home to a grim future, or perhaps no future at all. Defections of chess champions or artists are one thing; defection from the ranks of the political elite is quite another.

I had argued with myself round and round, and every question or conclusion seemed to emphasize the danger of my position. Nevertheless, the disgust I now felt for the system I served and for myself in abetting it, combined with hope for a new life, impelled me into approaching the Americans. I decided to sound them out indirectly and unofficially. But how? The answer came accidentally, like so many things in life.

Several weeks before that traumatic Friday, I had run into an old American acquaintance in a UN corridor. We knew each other both professionally and socially. He had always struck me as intelligent and open by nature. I also was aware that he had connections in Washington. I decided on the spot that he was my opportunity. I told him there was something I wanted to discuss in confidence and asked him if he could go for a lunchtime walk the next day.

When we met at the lobby door of the UN headquarters, it was pouring rain. We canceled our plans but discovered that we were both attending the same diplomatic dinner the follow-ing week.

In a corner of our host's suburban residence, I drew my friend aside. "I have something unusual to ask you," I said abruptly. "I've decided to break with my government and I want to know in advance what the American reaction would be if I asked for asylum."

He gaped at me in amazement. "What? Are you serious, Arkady?" he asked.

"I'm completely serious." He looked stunned.

"I wouldn't joke about something like this," I repeated.

Trying to maintain a casual appearance, I asked him if he could get a preliminary reading for me before I did anything, whether he could check with Washington discreetly and get word back to me.

His astonishment subsided and he thought for a few mo-ments.

"Look, we've known each other a long time," he said, "and of course I'll try to help you. But my involvement must remain secret. I don't want anyone to know I had anything to do with this. I'm going to Washington next week. I'll make inquiries for you, but let's not be seen together again, not even in a restaurant."

We agreed to stage a chance encounter in the UN library, where we would not talk, but only exchange written mes-sages.

Some days after his return from Washington, I entered the library at the arranged hour and found my friend casually leafing through a book in an otherwise empty part of the ref-erence section. He saw me and then slipped a piece of paper into the volume he was holding, closed the book, and replaced it on the shelf. After he left, I retrieved the book and withdrew the paper. "A man is coming from Washington specifically to meet with you. It is my feeling that you will be welcome, and I hope you will be reassured by your talk with him."

The note directed me to go to a bookstore not far from the UN building the next day at about two-thirty. My friend and the man from Washington would be waiting there. I was not to talk to them, but merely to memorize the stranger's face. The following afternoon at three-thirty, on another note in the library, my friend would leave an address where I would meet the man. I should write on that paper what time would be convenient for me, and my friend would convey the message. "After that, you are on your own. Destroy this note."

The next afternoon I arrived at the bookstore a little early. It was a small shop, convenient for the purpose of the rendezvous. Tall, library-like book stacks filled the center of the room. The store employees could not see who might be among the corridors of books.

I spotted my friend. His companion was tall and squarely built, with an open look about him. As we pretended to browse among the shelves we exchanged glances. I turned to leave the store. A copy of John le Carré's novel *The Spy Who Came In from the Cold* caught my eye, and the irony of the afternoon scene, a clandestine meeting such as occurs in so many films and books, inspired me to buy it.

At three-thirty the next day I went again to the UN library and found my friend placing another slip of paper in a different book. On the paper I found an address which I memorized. I then wrote: "This Friday night between 8 and 9."

On Fridays, I usually dismissed my chauffeur for the weekend and drove the car myself. My wife, Lina, routinely went out to Glen Cove after lunch on Fridays, and since the UN normally was busy at the end of the week, she would not expect me until very late. My drive to Long Island would seem routine right up to the last minute. I planned to double back to the city once I was sure no one had followed me.

I left the library, returned to my office, and began to ponder my meeting with the man from Washington. Who was he? What would he have to say? Did he have any authority to make decisions? What could I do to convince him that my motives were honest? What might he ask me to do to prove myself?

Those and other questions ran through my mind over and over. What I wanted was asylum, and protection both from Soviet efforts to reclaim me and from KGB hit men. But I half expected a noncommittal reaction, some vague promise to pass along my request to higher authorities in Washington.

DRIVING MORE CALMLY, I RETURNED ALONG BACK ROADS TO the Grand Central Parkway, over the Triborough Bridge, and found a parking space on a dark street on the upper East Side. I hailed a taxi and took it to a corner in the East Sixties. I was about ten minutes late. I hurried down an empty side street and descended the steps of an ordinary brownstone.

The man who answered the doorbell introduced himself as Bert Johnson. He had a firm handshake and wore a well-cut conservative dark suit.

"I've been waiting for you," he said. "Come on upstairs."

Johnson was businesslike but hospitable. He offered me a drink. I asked for scotch. We sat down on a sofa in a comfortably furnished library, its walls filled with books and paintings, but the pleasant surroundings did nothing to ease my tension.

I looked at him closely, searching his face for a clue to what kind of man he was. His manner was easy and natural. He showed neither surprise nor distrust.

He seemed to be waiting for me to get down to the business which brought us together. But even after so much private rehearsal I could not, for a while, find the words to begin.

"I'm not here on impulse. And this isn't something I just decided to do in the last few days," I said at last.

He nodded quietly and somehow the gesture distressed me.

"The idea of escaping has been growing in me for years and I'm ready to act and now I ask for your help," I continued.

Johnson nodded again. I could see that I would get no guidance from him. I would have to proceed on my own.

"I'm telling you that I have decided to break with my government," I blurted.

His nodding reaction was certainly natural, for he already knew what I was going to say. But I grew more uneasy. I suddenly realized that what bothered me was that he wasn't bombarding me with questions and arguments regarding my motivations as I had anticipated. I stopped in a pause that seemed to yawn for hours. Johnson did not try to fill the silence.

I started again. I tried to explain the process by which my convictions had become clear to me. My lack of expertise in English had never seemed so important before; now my head ached with my efforts to express myself properly. I attempted to stress that I was no longer a Soviet in spirit, and no longer

9

could be a part of the Soviet world. I told him of the intolerable situations where I often had to act like an idiot at the UN, defending a Soviet position while at the same time pretending to act objectively, as I was obliged to do, as Under Secretary General. My reasons seemed so weak that I tried again from another angle.

I told Johnson that in the beginning I was full of hope. I bragged to him how fast my career had moved, and boasted that I had friends, people I had been to school with and liked, in positions of influence, and that some of us once thought we might make a difference, might be able to help open up the Soviet system.

Johnson simply sat there and let me ramble. Only later did I understand that at that moment he (and the U.S. government) was not really interested in researching my motivations. Rather, it was his job to make a suggestion that would test me not by words but by deeds. I tried to calm down, to sound more pragmatic, less idealistic.

"It isn't money or comfort," I said. "I get all the benefits of being a Soviet ambassador. My wife and I have a good apartment in Moscow filled with fine things; we have anything we want. We have a dacha, a country place, in one of the best areas outside Moscow. We have plenty of money, *plenty*. It's not that at all," I repeated. "It's that in exchange I have to be as obedient to the system as a robot to his master—and I no longer believe in the system."

I told him that our telephones were always tapped, that the KGB was constantly watching me, often following me, that the Party was always after me to do political work which had nothing to do with my job as a diplomat but which intruded into my own and others' personal lives. I was required to be a propagandist for them, to parrot whatever they wanted me to say at meetings and encourage others to think the same way. But, most distasteful of all, I was compelled by the Party to be a moral watchdog over my fellow Soviets in New York. I detested the hypocrisy that this entailed; I wanted instead to work for what I believed in and was interested in; I wanted to do something valuable with my life.

Johnson listened in silence. Then he asked me whether I had informed my wife about our meeting. I said I had not, but that

I intended to do so. I could see that Johnson was pleased with my answer, but he made no further remark.

Finally, I made my request. What I meant to do was defect openly and speak out for myself. I needed protection and I did not want to be controlled.

"I want to work and write and live without any government telling me what to do or say. Will your government let me do that?"

Johnson stood up and walked to the bar in the corner of the room. "I don't know about you, but I'm going to have a double. How about you?" he said.

The tone of his remark made all the difference. It was friendly; he seemed to understand my tensions. He was suddenly a human being, not an institution or court before which I had to justify myself. I quickly accepted his offer. We stood at the bar while he poured scotch and soda. He raised his glass to touch mine. For the first time that night we both smiled.

Back on the couch, he lit a cigarette. "Okay," he said, leaning back. "First of all, I'm authorized to offer you the protection you asked for. If you're ready to defect, we're ready to welcome you, to help you, to receive you right now if that's what you want."

"It's exactly what I want," I interjected.

"We know a lot about you," he continued. "We've followed your career for a long time, so I have to ask if you're really sure about this. If you have any doubts, you should tell me now. Once this goes forward, neither of us can stop it."

"I've made up my mind."

He said that in the United States I wouldn't have any special privileges of the kind I had become used to as a member of the Soviet upper class. No car and driver, no government-supplied home. None of the luxuries that the Soviet government showered on its favored bureaucrats.

"All those things you take for granted—we don't supply them," he reiterated. "Could you really give them up?"

"Yes, I can. I know what is important to me in life." I had a sudden urge to laugh. I had the surreal feeling that I was in some sort of marriage ceremony, a wild contrast to my emotions of two minutes before.

Johnson sipped his drink and put it down on the table in front

11

of us. He looked at me a moment and then said, "You realize that if you live openly there will always be a risk to your life."

I knew quite enough about the KGB's long arm and memory. I wondered why Johnson said this: was he trying to discourage me from defecting instead of reinforcing me in my decision? I began to be apprehensive.

Johnson broke into my thoughts: "A minute ago you said you wanted to do something worthwhile. Do you think that defecting is the only way you can do this?"

"Well . . ." I hesitated. "By defecting I can contribute a great deal."

"There's no doubt about that," he said. "But think about how much you could do if you stayed where you are a little while."

"What do you mean?"

He described the initial excitement in Washington when it was learned that I wanted to defect. Everyone realized what a blow this would be to the Soviets. And they were ready to help me if that's what I wanted. But there had been other ideas too. Would I consider staying on as Under Secretary General for a while? There was a lot of information I could provide from that vantage point if we worked together. I could help them find out more about Soviet planning and intentions, about the leadership's thinking. Besides, he pointed out, I would need time to get my family ready for the eventual defection.

I felt something like a chill cross my chest.

"That is to say, you want me to be a spy," I said.

"Well, not exactly," he replied. He thought for a few seconds and continued: "We wouldn't have to call it spying. Let's say from time to time you could provide us with information at meetings like this."

I didn't know what to say. The proposal had thrown me off my bearings. "What you're asking me to do is extremely dangerous," I said finally. "I don't have any training for that sort of thing."

He took another swallow of scotch. "Please think about it," he said quietly.

I looked at him closely. His manner was not threatening or pressuring, but it was clear what he wanted from me. I was not prepared to hear it; I needed time to digest the idea. Almost automatically I told Johnson I would think it over.

That satisfied him and seemed to conclude the meeting. I got up to leave.

"When can we talk again?" he asked.

"Next Friday would be the best time for me. Is there a way to reach you, a telephone number?" I asked.

He gave me a number to memorize. I repeated it several times to fix it in my mind. We shook hands and I left, once again to journey through Manhattan and out to Long Island, this time with a curious mixture of relief and dread.

2

DRIVING BACK TO LONG ISLAND, I FORGOT MY EARLIER PRE-occupation with a KGB shadow. At first I didn't really think about the substance of the conversation. I was speculating on the impression I had made on Johnson.

I chided myself for the clumsy articulation of my thoughts and feelings. I had been unable to express precisely the layers of reasons, feelings, and emotions built over so long a time. I was no Einstein who could synthesize complex phenomena at one stroke. But I took some comfort in the thought that we would talk again; I would have more than one evening to explain my reasons.

At least Johnson must accept that my decision had nothing to do with money. The Americans were aware of the privileged life of the Soviet elite, and if they knew a lot about me they probably knew that I was a rich man and would probably never be as rich in the United States as I had been in the Soviet Union. Furthermore, I had not tried to make any deal to trade my knowledge for money.

Then I began to dwell on Johnson's ominous proposition

that I become a spy. At first I couldn't quite grasp the idea. It was too fantastic to imagine myself in such a business. Like most others, I considered spying a dirty game or at best a less than honorable profession. Even those who had turned against their governments for political reasons were often viewed skeptically. Their protestations seemed inadequate to explain motives so strong that they could uproot one from his family, his country, his place in the universe.

But what could one expect from one's fellow man for confessing oneself as a spy? The only excuse for spying is tied to the moral value of the cause for which it is undertaken. But it is not easy to prove—even to yourself—that your purpose is virtuous. On many occasions I would find that the morality of spying was one of the most difficult things to demonstrate.

I had long felt distaste for the world of spying and deceit. It was something I didn't like to think about. I was well aware of the dangers. I vividly remembered the public trial in 1963 of Colonel Oleg Penkovsky, who was shot immediately afterward. Almost without exception, spies—sooner or later—were caught, even the best, such as Colonel Rudolf Abel during the 1950s. Moreover, I was no adventurous James Bond type. Nor did I have any training for spying.

I began to regret not having turned away Johnson's suggestion immediately. Why did I give him grounds for believing that I did not strongly oppose the idea? I should have rejected it right away instead of saying I would think it over.

Like many Slavs, in a corner of my soul I am fatalistic and superstitious. I wondered why at crucial moments the most important things always seemed to go wrong. Now I was playing a dangerous form of Russian roulette.

Breaking with my government was a way out of hopelessness and frustration. Open defiance of the Soviet system would be an honorable course. But a secret life inside it . . . wasn't that just another form of the deceptions I wanted to leave behind? Could I possibly be a spy? Could I continue in work I had hated for years and in addition take on an even more undesirable job, becoming lonelier than ever in a hostile camp? I didn't know, and no one could help me.

In a state of depression exacerbated by exhaustion, I reached Glen Cove about midnight. As I had expected, Lina found nothing out of the ordinary in the hour. She was sympathetic when I told her I was too tired to eat or drink; I just wanted to go to bed.

I could not sleep, however. I kept asking myself: Had I done the right thing after all or had I acted too hastily? No. I had to put an end to my mental double life. I had reviewed the arguments pro and con, time and again, searching my motives, my beliefs, the structure of my life.

I was torn by contradictory feelings. I was worried about my family. I dreaded leaving my native land forever. I realized the difficulties of adjusting to a new culture. But despite my anxieties, I also looked forward with hope and anticipation. I had seen enough to understand both the bright and dark sides of American society, and for me the bright one was overwhelming. I had waited long enough. If I had been alone and free to decide my fate without regard for anyone else, I would have left the Soviets years before. But I was not alone; I had my family to consider: my wife, to whom I had been married since I was twenty-one; my son Gennady and my daughter Anna.

The hardest thing would be to tell Lina what I had determined to do. From the first days of our marriage, her abiding dream had been to see me in the top echelons of power in the Soviet Union. It would be a nightmare for her to hear me suggest that we start over in a country she neither understood nor cared about. But for the safety of all of us, I couldn't discuss anything with her before my plan to defect was approved by the Americans. She might accidentally give us away in conversation. Worst of all, she might not agree with me and might deliberately attempt to prevent my leaving the Soviets. She was used to having her way and was quite capable of going to Gromyko or the KGB *rezident* and telling him that I was not well or that I was too tense and exhausted from overwork, and suggesting we should return to Moscow for a time. Even if we were not sent home, it would bring me to their attention in ways I did not want.

But I felt if I could persuade her that she would be safe and comfortable, I had a chance of inducing her to join me. And if I could have Lina, I could get my darling Anna, the brightest spot in my heart. The time was not too distant when she would have to return to Moscow to continue her education—the Soviet school in New York went through only the first eight grades, and no exceptions were made, not even for children of high functionaries.

Gennady was another problem. He was in Moscow, an adult. He was also married, a further complication. I could arrange for a short vacation in New York for him, as I had done before when he had spent a summer as a student intern at the UN. But I knew I had no moral right to force on him any decision about his future, and if he did not wish to leave the Soviet Union, I might never see my son again.

But Lina and Anna were now in New York and I was determined to try to have them with me. The thought of losing them was so painful I couldn't face it. Wait a bit more, postpone it a little longer. I figured I had at least several weeks before the final break. It seemed like a lot of time.

The atmosphere at Killenworth, as the Glen Cove estate was known before the Soviets bought it, was conducive to meditation and reflection. That weekend I welcomed the peace and quiet.

The morning after my meeting with Johnson I was unusually quiet. Lina questioned my odd mood and was irritated by my silence. I said I was preoccupied with some difficult documents I had to approve in the coming week, and took a pile of papers out of my briefcase and put them on the table. But my thoughts were very far from the UN.

I knew I was already a "defector." That word, so familiar in the West, does not exist in Russian. This is, as the Soviets say, not accidental. Contemporary Russian has only two words for people who leave the Soviet Union: "traitor" and "emigrant"; and in the eyes of the Soviet authorities the two are synonymous. Both are used to describe persons who have betrayed their motherland, the Soviet people, everything dear and loved, irrespective of their reasons for wanting to leave the country. Consequently, I too had difficulty with the term. I felt I had to "break with the Soviet system, its ruling regime," rather than "defect." I didn't want to be a defector. That expression conjured up a picture of a man with no country. I would always love my native land and the people of whom I am a part, and I would never believe I had betrayed them. I wanted to cut my ties with the regime and the system, not with my countrymen. I wanted Johnson to understand this distinction. I would emphasize it in my next talk with him.

Neither was I a "dissident," another hardly translatable word in Russian. Of course, "dissent" in its conventional meaning is part of the Russian language, but the expression "dissident" has traditionally had only a religious connotation, not a political meaning. Recently, it has come to refer to an *inakomyslyashchy*, or "a person who thinks differently, or someone who does not think like me," a rather vague way of describing people like Sakharov, Solzhenitsyn, or Bukovsky. But I had never fought my government the way dissidents did. On the contrary, I served it loyally and as well as I could for many years.

For others, nonetheless, I would be a defector, and I thought more and more about what might happen to me. I wondered also about the motivations and fates of other defectors, particularly those from the Soviet Union. I would undoubtedly encounter some of the same difficulties they had.

I knew that many of them were unhappy. Some had had family tragedies or had met unexpected misfortunes which led to bizarre behavior. Others had difficulty making a living or were unable to practice their professions in their new lives. Worst off of all, it seemed to me, were those whose motives were suspected, like KGB officer Yuri Nosenko, or Grigory Bessedovsky, the former chargé d'affaires at the Soviet Embassy in Paris who defected long before World War II. I am still puzzled as to why the plight of political defectors is so much harder than that of artists or writers, whose motives for defecting are always taken on faith. If limitation of artistic freedom is considered a valid justification for defection, then why are those deprived of the dignity of being conscientious in their government jobs not given the same credence?

As much as possible, I wanted to avoid repeating the mistakes of other defectors—something I would later discover was not always easy. I was sure of one thing: I would never agree to a life of anonymous misery stuck away in a safe house, swapping one prison for another. I could alter my appearance or change my name, but I would never have another identity in my own mind.

I had originally believed that defectors did not follow a pattern. Some had been persecuted or repressed in the Soviet Union; some felt that their security or their lives had been threatened; some had money, drinking, or love problems. Others' ambitions or careers were thwarted. Some looked as if they were psychologically unstable, frustrated people who did not fit in anywhere.

But my experience in the U.S.S.R. led me to conclude that beneath the multiplicity of reasons there was a common denominator. At bottom, it was the Soviet system that pushed its subjects to desperation, curtailing their freedoms or forcing them to act against their convictions.

Why was I being driven out? To all appearances it was illogical. I should not have had any real reason to hate or even dislike the Soviet system. It had given me its best: a high position in the ruling class, complete financial security, privileges, and the prospect of still further advancement. To an outsider's eye, it could only seem that I had a happy, contented life. In Soviet terms, I had it made. Why had I in the end come to Johnson?

My childhood and youth were a time when the system began to shape me into what is called a "normal and healthy Soviet man." I did not suffer during the Stalinist period; on the contrary, I had everything I could want and, indeed, everything went as well as it possibly could until my father's death in 1949. Even afterward, things weren't so bad. As a student in Moscow I had a room, and if there were many times I had no money in my pocket, I had plenty of hope. I found great happiness when I met Lina, when we married, and when our son was born. In the not-too-distant future, I would be graduating from the prestigious diplomatic institute with many opportunities ahead of me.

Occasionally, one or another dark side of Soviet life irritated me or aroused indignation at the gap between theory and practice, between words and deeds. But there were always sufficiently convincing explanations for all the shortcomings: the Soviet Union was the brave land where a golden age was being built, and the new is never born without struggle and errors that are the result of human nature. I and my fellows were taught to think schematically; to speak in formulas without reflection or vacillation; to accept on faith all that the Communist Party taught and all that it represented. My teachers insisted that we be models and examples, that we strive to be superior in the socialist ideal so we could occupy worthy positions as had our parents, our brothers and sisters, aunts and uncles, friends and acquaintances, and, finally, many other equally respected members of the "multinational collective of Soviet society."

Of course, in every family there may be a black sheep. It is necessary to educate them, to correct them, and if necessary to punish them. It was inculcated in us to rise, to ascend to ever-higher positions, to guarantee oneself and one's family personal well-being and security. But one was not supposed to shout about it. The *narod* (the people) would regard such a person as an immodest and unprincipled careerist and not a "genuine Leninist." The genuine Communist should project himself as one whose only care is the happiness of the masses.

Like almost all my friends and classmates, I was molded by this teaching. We were proudly convinced that in time we would assume the leadership of our country to carry on the construction of Communism. My wife as well as my friends and comrades thought the same way: one has to get what one can and hold out.

And I did.

Cramming in the institute until I was exhausted, participating in boring, endless, and useless Komsomol (the Young Communist League) assignments consumed a great deal of time. But I performed dutifully. It led up the path to the middle-class elite from which I had come, and was a stepping-stone toward higher dreams. I held out. But just as a termite bores into a tree and leaves it a husk, so all of this drained conscience and integrity from me and my comrades.

Khrushchev's unmasking of Stalin, in his secret speech at the Twentieth Party Congress in 1956, wounded me deeply, almost destroying my faith in the Soviet system as if it had been a house of cards, and it brought me to a crossroads. All that had been sacred for me before—the genius of Stalin, the infallibility and vision of the Party, its justness, its concern for the fate of the people and the country—seemed false. Our world seemed to have been stood on its head. It was difficult to comprehend and still more difficult to explain the atrocities committed under Stalin.

We were all reassured that the guilty had been found and punished and that such things would never happen again. Then Khrushchev loosened the harness on daily life, art, literature, and promised a golden age. Dazed and reeling from the upheaval, people hailed him and we grasped at the promise as we would cling to a boulder in a whirlwind. The "thaw" took place. This breath of fresh air blew not only inside the country but also in foreign policy. All the same, I could get no precise or clear grasp of how Stalinism could have happened. Khrushchev had never acknowledged the full extent of the terror, much less the fact that the Party and its entire system bore responsibility for it. This did not mean that I did not continue to look for an explanation. But the passage of time, the events and enthusiasms of youth, and simply the living of life for the time being pushed my thoughts about it to the back of my consciousness.

I believed in Khrushchev. Inspired by him, I came to the Ministry of Foreign Affairs in 1956. The apparent beginning of progress in disarmament negotiations drew me in. Khrushchev, with whom I had the good fortune to become acquainted and to work, seemed a man, not a god like Stalin. I took it as a sign of hope.

Then, late that same year, Soviet tanks smashed Hungarian freedom. But it didn't seem to be Khrushchev's fault! Molotov, Malenkov, and Kaganovich still dominated the Politburo. However, in 1957, Khrushchev threw them out. Now, I thought, he will lead us toward better things, toward positive changes. Perhaps not as quickly and directly as I would like, but, as they say, one builds a house brick by brick.

There was another world I had an inkling of from books and newspaper articles, from my courses at the institute, and from what I had learned from others who had been there. The West was as enigmatic to me as the U.S.S.R. was to Americans. Judging from what I had been able to glean, the West appeared both attractive and repulsive, both prospering and decaying. I saw it for myself in 1958 when I spent several months in New York. More than anything else I was struck by the openness of American society. It was evident even though my short visit to the United States took place under the strictest supervision of the KGB. I had read and heard a lot about the American freedoms, half believing and half doubting. At home in the U.S.S.R., everything was just the reverse of what I saw in the United States. All was under lock and key in the most literal sense—our mouths, newspapers, television, literature, art, travel out of the country. We had to keep our own thoughts locked up if they differed with official opinion. Khrushchev loosened the reins, yes, but in no way removed them.

As I rose in the diplomatic service and became more mature, I acquired a deeper understanding of Soviet society, the functioning of the bureaucratic apparatus, and the life of the elite. The fragmented mosaic of facts, of reports about this or that practice in the Foreign Ministry, of our foreign policy actions, and of what stood behind them began to fall into place, fleshing out the picture ever more clearly to me.

But there were many parts and details that were shadowy. The Cuban adventure, the Berlin Wall, propaganda campaigns about disarmament instead of negotiations, the economic mess at home, the unfulfilled promises, the rebirth of the "cult of personality," or idolatry of the leader—this time for Nikita Khrushchev—the "thaw" which proved to be a false spring, all this led to disappointment; again to a loss of faith.

So I had become part of the stratum that tried to portray itself as fighting what it coveted. While criticizing the bourgeois way of life, its only passion was to possess it; while condemning consumerism as a manifestation of philistine psychology, a result of poisonous Western influence, the privileged valued above all else the consumer goods and comforts of the West. I was not immune. The gulf between what was said and what was done was oppressive, but more oppressive still was what I had to do to widen the gap. I tried to remember everything I ever said, and what others had told me, because my survival and success depended greatly upon that. I pretended to believe what I did not, and to place the interests of the Party and the state above my own, when in fact I did just the opposite. After

21

I had lived that kind of life for years, I began to see Dorian Gray's real picture in my shaving mirror.

I smiled and played the hypocrite not only in public, at Party meetings, at meetings with acquaintances, but even in my own family and to myself. Every politician or diplomat must feign to one degree or another for the common cause or in the interests of his country—and at times for not such good causes. But to dissemble in everything, always and everywhere, having lost faith in what you are doing—not everyone can stand up under this. To be compelled to act in such a way is like forcing a deeply religious individual to live among militant atheists, not only constraining him to reject God but insisting that he curse Him and the Bible every step of the way.

Not all of my colleagues managed to sustain such a life. Some left politics altogether; some became taxi drivers or drank themselves to death; some of them went mad and some committed suicide.

Most of them, however, simply abraded their scruples and lived as best they could with the callused remains of their integrity. They became inveterate cynics who ceased to distinguish good from evil, devoting themselves entirely to their careers for personal gain and to preserve the dictatorship of the elite to which they belonged.

But the vacillating ones also continued to serve the Soviet system, keeping their doubts to themselves, creeping along in a double life for various reasons: fear of hurting their families, an overall attachment to their country, and uncertainty that there were any better alternatives. I belonged to this group. To remain a member of the upper class it was not enough to lie and pretend. One also had to fight for survival or be thrown down. After years spent among the elite I finally got my fill of its venality and coarseness. That life is unbelievably ugly. Indeed, it even promotes personal betrayals. For the elite they are a necessary part of life. Suspicion and intrigue have become a high art. If Machiavelli were alive and living in Moscow today, he would be a student, not a professor.

In the sixties, after my disillusionment with Khrushchev and his fall, however, cautious hope revived in me. There was new leadership. At that time I didn't know the new man leading the

Kremlin and, again, I thought there might be a chance for positive change. At the same time, another element entered my life. I became more closely acquainted with Americans while working at the Soviet Mission to the UN in New York. For several years I had plenty of opportunity to compare the two different systems and two different ways of life. Many things Americans took for granted appealed to me. I envied their freedom to think, speak, and write, their freedom to act and work. I wanted to work with my heart behind my work. I began to realize then that I would never have such opportunities in my native land.

I didn't idealize American society—I saw its failings and understood that many émigrés had found hard lives and sadness here. But the positive aspects of this muscular, forthright society were far more numerous than the negative ones, and could in no way be compared with the situation in the U.S.S.R. I knew I was not alone in my thinking. A few close friends revealed to me similar feelings. I experienced déjà vu as I heard the same anxieties I had had in my own youth expressed by some of the young diplomats recently graduated from my institute.

Still, I had not completely lost my faith in the Soviet system and had no intention of defecting. But my heretical thoughts eroded my confidence that the Soviet way was best. Cracks appeared, like those on the surface of a frozen pond, becoming longer and more numerous, but not yet deep enough to break the ice.

More than anything else, two events propelled me toward defection. Ironically, they were both promotions. In 1970, Gromyko appointed me his personal political adviser. Before that, I had been only a spectator of high politics. Then I discovered what went on behind the scenes, how the system really worked and what were its unwritten laws. I saw the Soviet leaders as they were, not as they wanted to be seen.

I sat at the same table with Brezhnev, Gromyko, and other members of the Politburo, and I learned a great deal about the men who were the masters of the Soviet Union. I saw how easily they called vice virtue, and just as easily reversed the words again. How their hypocrisy and corruption had penetrated the smallest aspects of their lives, how isolated they were from the population they ruled.

Gromyko, for example, had not set foot in the streets of Moscow for almost forty years. Almost all the others were no different. In the gilded, stale, and silent Kremlin corridors a museum has been ensconced, a museum of ideas, visible but fossilized as a fly in amber. Those who have made their careers preserving these relics have tried to force the Soviet people to believe in a social system based on utopian myth. For them, the rigid application of Marxist-Leninist ideology has always been the fundamental *raison d'être* for keeping power in their hands. Some of them, it is true, like the late Mikhail Suslov or Boris Ponomarev, genuinely believed in Soviet dogmas; for them, ideological doctrine was more than a matter of public lip service and a cover for self-interest. But as for Brezhnev and some of his other colleagues, while they understood very well the importance of ideology, they could barely comprehend Marx's *Capital* or Lenin's *Materialism and Empirocriticism*.

The Kremlin was the last place on earth where one might expect directness, honesty, and openness. The falsity of these men was everywhere, from their personal lives to their grand political designs. I watched them playing with détente. I saw them building unprecedented military strength, obviously far beyond the needs of defense and security, at the expense of the Soviet people. I heard them express, with cynical jokes, their willingness to suppress freedom among their allies. I witnessed their duplicity with those who follow the Soviet line in the West or in the Third World, extending even to participation in conspiracies to kill "unsuitable" political figures of other countries. They avidly sought hegemony and were infected with the imperialistic sickness of which they accused others—first, to widen the U.S.S.R.'s zone of influence in the world and, second, to find ways to appease their insatiable desire for expansion.

Despite much-touted programs to provide the people with "the highest living standard in the world," Soviet economic experts admitted privately that the gap in consumption between the Soviet Union and the West, which was narrowed in the 1960s under Khrushchev, widened under Leonid Brezhnev.

What these self-directed politicians had achieved was nuclear "overkill" potential, inedible by the population.

In many respects my years as Gromyko's adviser were as revealing to me as Khrushchev's disclosures about Stalin. My feelings came into sharper relief after my appointment as Under Secretary General of the UN in 1973. Earlier, when I had been in the United States, my position had been solidly partisan with regard to the interests of the Soviet Union, and I had spent most of my time with my countrymen. Now I became part of the UN Secretariat, which functioned on principles completely at odds with those of the Soviet system. Whatever the values or weaknesses of the UN, and despite the fact that my government continued to consider me a Soviet ambassador rather than an international civil servant, my work in the Secretariat expanded my philosophical horizons. I could see as clearly as if I were reading an architect's blueprint the striking contrast between the two systems.

Many features of the Soviet regime are well known. But I finally realized that the divinity before which the Kremlin rulers bowed was their own power and the maximal satisfaction of their personal requirements and those of the privileged upper class. These requirements had no limit, from the acquisition of foreign automobiles to whole nations outside the Soviet bloc.

The old men of the Brezhnev Politburo had settled into an intensely conservative pattern in domestic policy, in which they feared and would not tolerate any change or new ideas; they liked the reassurance of familiar slogans repeated and repeated until even they believed them. It gradually became clear to me that the Soviet system, at least in its most essential elements, could not change or develop in the foreseeable future. The elite will not permit anything that undermines its power, and it has power enough to prevent anything it opposes from happening. It was possible that new Soviet leaders, groomed by Brezhnev and his colleagues as their successors, would bring a new style and tempo, some reforms, but hardly any substantial change in the system itself.

Brezhnev's vanity was gargantuan and he was happy to nurture his own "cult of personality." His immodest behavior and the marks of undeserved distinctions and honors which he awarded himself were disgusting to many; in his love for praise, medals, and honorary posts he surpassed even Khrushchev. His sycophants, however, never blushed as they referred to him as "the great toiler; the man of legend," even though it was plain to all who knew him that he was a man of limited intellect and ability. A well-known quotation from Marx once came to mind: "Hegel says somewhere that all great events and personalities in world history reappear in one fashion or another. He forgot to add: the first time as tragedy, the second as farce." It is the latter designation that I am confident history will attach to Brezhnev and his fellow travelers.

To strive for more and more and ever more of the same became too much. I had no further expectations of contributing anything usefully positive in my life's work even if I were to climb higher. And the prospect of living as a mental dissident while maintaining the posture of a bureaucratic "yes man" in practice was terrible to contemplate. A future of trying to outwit my fellow members of the elite for a bigger piece of the cake, of permanent shadowing by the KGB and permanent nagging by the Party, was insupportable. As I approached the pinnacle of influence, I found it a desert. By continuing to serve the Soviet regime I would be helping to support and promote what I hated.

I considered resigning from my position and joining the ranks of the open dissidents to fight the regime inside the country. But I realized I would spend the rest of my life in jail or in a mental institution and would accomplish nothing more than irritating the authorities. I knew too much for the government to let me remain at large at home or to exile me to the West.

I was young, measured by Soviet standards of achievement, but I was also middle-aged; I would not be as flexible as a young immigrant who could absorb much faster than I the characteristic tones and patterns of U.S. society. Still, others older than I had done it and many seemed to have made a successful transition. I had hopes that I could too.

At the same time, my reflections stirred feelings of unease. I began to regret the way I had approached the whole thing from the very beginning. Perhaps I should have stated my intentions directly to the American Ambassador to the UN, John Scali. I knew him rather well, and I felt sure he would not have suggested to me that I become a spy. Scali was anything but a friend of the Soviets, although he maintained diplomatic tact in all exchanges I observed.

The Soviet ambassador at the time, Yakov Malik, returned Scali's dislike, and behind his back would spitefully call him "the American Himmler" because of a physical resemblance he saw in Scali to the Gestapo chief. I couldn't see any such likeness myself, but Malik took pains to point it out to his fellow Soviets, and he never tired of telling us that it was a good thing Scali did not have a free hand, for that "devil would love to wring our necks." Nonetheless, no matter how Scali might feel about Malik, I felt fairly confident he would be willing to help me, and I almost decided to go to him, and to tell Johnson to forget the whole thing.

Gradually, I realized that this was idle speculation. Even if I had approached Scali in the beginning, the CIA might have become involved anyway. They could still have tried to persuade me to become a spy. I might still have found myself in the same dilemma.

As I thought over my options, I came to the conclusion that I would decline Johnson's proposition. The prospect of living in the netherworld of intrigue, even if for a brief period, seemed too much for me. And, frankly, I was afraid of the danger. I would tell Johnson that I sincerely, even desperately, wanted to defect but that I could not become a spy. If they refused to accept me on those terms, I would simply continue as Under Secretary General of the UN and attempt to seek out another country, one that would accept me unconditionally.

Then the awful thought came to me that I really had no choice in the matter. If they wished, they could force me to do it. The KGB had repeatedly warned Soviet diplomats that if we deviated from its prescribed rules of behavior the CIA or FBI would not miss the opportunity to tape or film us. Perhaps the KGB was right; I had no way of knowing. If it was true, the Americans could prove to the Soviets that I was a traitor. They could blackmail me. I knew that the world of espionage had its own rules, and suspected that the KGB had no exclusive claim on ruthlessness.

I realized I was trapped.

3

THE FOLLOWING WEEK I WAS IN TURMOIL, SWINGING FROM one decision to another. To my surprise, I slowly began to reconcile myself to Johnson's proposal. If our places had been reversed, I knew I would do my utmost to try to use him as an opportunity to penetrate the Soviets at a high level. But although this seemed logical and natural as an abstract proposition, I was still uneasy at being the man involved.

The more I reflected on the idea, the more I was able to find positive aspects in it: I could gain time to prepare myself. Time would enable me to make a better case with Lina, to persuade her to my view. We could make practical arrangements for our new lives in America by bringing some of the things we loved from our Moscow home. Furthermore, I thought, to work for the Americans for a while would be the most effective way of dissipating any doubts they might have about my honesty and sincerity. The Americans could grant me political asylum, all right, but I figured they were under no obligation to do more than that for me, and I would need protection for quite some time as well as help in getting settled. After the debriefings, they might throw me away like a squeezed lemon. I hoped for more than that.

I resolved to prove myself not in words but in deeds. After all, my original plan had been to help the United States by exposing the secrets of the Soviet regime and speaking out against it; I wanted to help the West. Here was a way to do it in spades.

The arrangements for my next meeting with Johnson seemed simple, but when the time came to make the confirming phone call, I suddenly found the mechanics daunting. I could not phone from my home, from the Mission, from my UN office. All those lines were monitored. I could use a pay telephone, but that seemed too risky. A Soviet colleague might see me and wonder what I was up to, why I wasn't using my office phone.

Friday morning, as I sat in a UN committee meeting, I listened with only half an ear to the diplomats' talk, my mind preoccupied. Finally I remembered the telephones the UN provided for the delegates' convenience on the main floor. Even if those lines were tapped, my conversation would be short, my voice unidentifiable. When the session broke for lunch, I joined my colleagues and walked with them to the North Delegates' Lounge. That huge hall, whose bar and comfortable chairs draw diplomats for both serious and trivial talk throughout the working day, is well supplied with telephones. It would be perfectly natural for me to use one as though I were simply checking with my office for messages. Nonetheless, I could not shake off an anxiety that mounted as I scanned the lounge. Others were using the telephones and I had to wait.

I decided to take my chances in another place, the corridor that runs behind the podium of the General Assembly. There was no bar here to attract a crowd. Two telephones sat on separate tables about six feet apart, and one of them was already taken. The man speaking into it was a stranger whose English carried a heavy Spanish accent. A Cuban? Did he recognize me? I stood indecisively for a moment, and then took what seemed to me like an enormous plunge. I sat down and dialed the number. It rang twice before a woman answered.

"Hello," she said. No other identification.

"This is Andy. I'll be on time tonight."

"That's fine," came her reply. "I'll tell him."

I hung up. The Latin American—as I had decided he was —was still deep in his own conversation. If he had noticed mine, he gave no sign. Still, to be on the safe side, I called my office in case I had been observed and the observer checked on me later on.

The day wore on routinely, but apprehension continued to cloud my perceptions. One of my Soviet assistants walked into my office unannounced; I was startled, but all he wanted was my permission to leave early, to lengthen his weekend by a few hours. I probably surprised him with my quick assent. My only thought, however, was to get rid of him.

My appointment at the East Side town house was for between eight and ten o'clock that night. It was close to eight when I finished supper at home and proposed to Lina that she join me for a walk. It was a safe offer to make; she liked to walk in the country but not in the city. When she went shopping, it was with a purpose. I liked to browse; she liked to buy. That evening, as I expected, she chose to stay home.

Out on the street, I tried to look like a casual pedestrian. I gazed at shopwindows, pretending an interest in men's clothing stores while my real concern was to detect if anyone was following me. A few blocks down Third Avenue I went into a delicatessen I often patronized, bought a package of Finn Crisp crackers and a bottle of Perrier water, and came out with my parcel and with a stronger feeling that no one was shadowing me. Nevertheless, I walked further down the avenue, past the side street where Johnson waited, turned right onto another quiet crosstown street, right again on Lexington Avenue, and then quickly right again back toward Third Avenue and the brownstone.

I hurried along the pavement, glad of the trees that lined it but also worried that behind any one of them, invisible to me, might be some KGB agent observing me and my destination. In the brownstone's doorway it seemed an eternity until Bert Johnson answered my ring and let me in.

"It's good to see you," he said as he closed the door. "Everything okay?"

"Yes . . . and no," I answered. "I don't think anyone saw me, but I don't really know."

Johnson told me to relax and led me to an elevator at the back of the entrance hall, a creaking, old-fashioned wooden machine that groaned its way to the second floor. As we rode up to the library, I noticed that his appearance had changed. Instead of the dark business suit of the week before he wore casual clothes and his shirt was open. Where he had been reticent and formal, he was now affable, easygoing.

His attitude helped me to calm down as well, and I agreed

30

with pleasure when he proposed that we call each other by our first names. I liked that American custom, which is followed in Russia only between close friends or relatives. As we sat down on the sofa, I expected him to put the question I had been thinking about for a week. I still was not sure exactly how best to approach it.

Instead, Johnson began by asking about my health. I admitted I was exhausted. I told him that my workload at the UN was heavy, and that the Mission had been after me more than usual lately, always wanting something. He expressed sympathy; he asked whether I took any exercise, whether I had any vacation plans.

Why didn't he get to the point? I fidgeted slightly as I told him that I had had little vacation, that the meetings in the Security Council had been wearing, that I was tired. "Besides," I said, "since we talked, I haven't thought of anything else."

"Well, what have you been thinking?" He wouldn't ask the question directly.

I began to question Johnson about the nature of his proposal, and at the same time said I wasn't sure I could do what he wanted. I reiterated that I had never belonged to the KGB and I did not know their techniques, had no training. Furthermore, I'd be taking a terrible chance; I would probably be caught before I got started. I hoped he would let me off the hook; he didn't.

Johnson said that Washington was aware that I had no KGB connections, that his government trusted my sincerity. He touched a nerve. Of all things, good or bad, that anyone could say about me, that was a point about which I wanted no mistake.

"But I think you're exaggerating," he continued. "You're letting your imagination run away with you." He stressed that the Americans had no intention of involving me in dangerous operations, and that they did not want me to follow people around or steal and photograph documents. They would never ask me to do anything that would require the kind of maneuverings people read about, with secret drops for material and all kinds of fantastic gadgets.

31

What they desired was information to which I already had access. They wanted to know about policy matters, political decisions, and how those decisions were reached. They welcomed material that came from my background, my contacts, my work.

"You've worked closely with Gromyko and a lot of others. You know what they're thinking about and what's going on behind the scenes in Moscow and in the Mission here. You can help us understand what the policies are, how they're made, and who makes them."

I protested that I already intended to give that knowledge to American government specialists, so it wasn't necessary for me to stay in my present position any longer for that purpose.

Johnson interrupted me: "Wait a minute, let me finish. There's another angle to all this: your own motivation. You convinced me last week that there's nothing impulsive or selfish about your decision. If you wanted wealth and security, you'd stay with the Soviets, but if you really want to fight them we can help you do it in the most effective way."

I told Johnson that my special position in New York had disadvantages as well as benefits. I had freedom to go anywhere and meet with anyone without getting permission, but that also made me more exposed. The KGB had to watch me because my safety was their responsibility. Although the agents could not limit what I did or where I went, they were always suspicious because their first instinct was to trust no one. I said I didn't see how I could meet Johnson on a regular basis because I didn't know how I could shake them.

He sensed that my unease was real and tried to reassure me, repeating that he would not ask me to take foolish risks. He emphasized that I would avoid establishing a set pattern or routine for contacting or meeting him, that I would use various telephones when calling, and that I would make no change from my usual habits.

His words were reassuring but they still did not address the core of my doubts. I could spot most, but not all, KGB when I was under surveillance. I had no idea whether they had followed me on the street, even tonight. I asked Johnson if he had people who could check whether the KGB showed any special interest in what I did and where I went.

He promised to organize a special detail right away. He said he would let me know immediately if there were any signs of trouble, and assured me that the Americans would move in if necessary.

I was grateful for this attitude, but I knew that every time I entered the Mission I would remember that I could be held captive inside it and forced to fly directly home to Moscow. Just that year, I had seen a junior diplomat hustled out of New York with no chance to save himself.

The victim had been a Mission official who had been arrested by the New York police for a drunk-driving episode that had included a quarrel with a bus driver. The Soviet claimed, probably to protect himself, that the arrest had been a provocation, that the Americans had used the incident to try to recruit him. Whether or not the Mission security men believed him, as soon as the city police released him to Soviet custody, he was put under what amounted to arrest inside the Mission and shipped home on the next Aeroflot flight.

I told Johnson about this episode, tame indeed compared to what I was contemplating, to underscore my worry that something similar could happen to me. "I go to the Mission almost every day. Once I'm inside, there is nothing any government on earth could do if the Mission detains me. They could invent any pretext for holding me or for sending me back to Moscow. A sudden heart attack, a stroke, anything. They have used such excuses over and over."

"But there are things we can do," Johnson insisted. He said there really wasn't much danger that they would kill me inside the Mission. I was too well known for them to risk that kind of disappearance; my wife would raise a storm; the United Nations would ask embarrassing questions. I agreed that the Soviets wouldn't want those kinds of things to be aired in public.

"If they did try to take you back to the Soviet Union, they'd have to get you through Kennedy Airport," he continued. "There we can step in and make sure you're leaving of your own free will." He told me I should always let them know when I would be taking a trip myself, and especially whenever I was going to Kennedy. He asked me whether I went there to meet people coming from Moscow on the regular Aeroflot flight.

I told him I went there frequently to welcome delegations or important visitors or just to greet friends. Johnson said that they wanted to know in advance when I was going, if possible. American agents routinely watched those flights, and they would receive particular instructions about me. They would go on special alert if I appeared unexpectedly.

"If that happens and you're in trouble, you should make a sign of some sort, raise your right hand, and we'll know you need help," he said.

Johnson was completely businesslike in discussing this contingency, but I pictured myself being shuffled, heavily drugged, by a squad of KGB men through the airport lounge, unable to make any sign of distress at all. I tried to repress the fantasy as he went on.

"Besides, we would be alerted if you stayed in the Mission for an unusual length of time. But we should have an emergency arrangement to contact you. Is there an American doctor that you see regularly?"

There was the dentist, but my wife used him more than I did. There was a dermatologist I had seen several times during my assignment in the sixties. I gave Johnson his name.

"Would it be unusual for him to ask you to come in for an appointment?"

"No, not really. He's done it before to remind me that I'm due for a checkup," I replied. "My secretary knows he's my doctor."

"Okay. Then if you get a message that he's phoned, call me immediately. It should be a good way to warn you if something goes wrong."

Johnson was now clearly assuming that I would accept his proposition, and he was right. I had no real resistance. He probably sensed that I felt I had no choice.

"Look," he said, "why don't you try it for a while? I know you can do it. You'll find it easier than you think. Don't worry, we're not going to put you in danger." He paused. "Okay?"

"All right. For a while."

"Good." He smiled. He repeated his advice not to change my normal routine. "As long as you keep to your habits, you won't create any suspicion."

I looked at my watch. It was close to ten o'clock. We made arrangements for our next meeting the week after next.

Tuesday, twelve days ahead, was clear, assuming no emergency arose at the UN. Johnson suggested that we try to get together in the middle of that day rather than at night, to vary the schedule. I promised to confirm the meeting by telephone on Monday, but added that if I did not come Tuesday, Johnson should wait for me again on Wednesday around lunchtime.

We had talked so much about procedures that we had neglected substance. What kind of information should I bring?

Johnson said I would be the best judge of what was important and of how much time to give to any subject, but that it would help to have a basic pattern. He suggested I start with the most recent cables received in the Mission, the date, the time they were sent, the text as fully as I could get it.

I was startled. What did he mean, the full text of cables? One minute he was reassuring, concerned for my safety, minimizing the dangers I would have to confront. Next he was asking me to risk my neck. To copy a code cable inside the Soviet Mission would invite almost certain detection.

"I can't do that," I protested. "We aren't even supposed to make notes on what we read in the code room, just the gist, not the actual language. And you said I shouldn't take photos or have any compromising materials on me."

He quickly responded that they did not expect full copies, just whatever I could remember of the important messages.

I didn't want Johnson to expect too much from the cables that came to the Mission, and I explained the limits on information received there. He assured me that the lack of immediacy would not be a major drawback.

"The big developments will stick out a mile," Johnson said, "you'll spot them right away." What might be of more interest to Washington might be difficult for me to identify at first. Something that seemed completely routine to me because it was so familiar might be absolutely novel to them. I should try to read as if I were seeing the information for the first time. I must try to think of its value to outsiders, what it might reveal to someone without my background and experience.

Johnson particularly wanted me to be on the lookout for nuance, new shades of meaning signaling a change in policy or indicating debates on certain issues. I must have looked skeptical, for he reassured me that, although I might not think so now, it would come very naturally after a while and that my worries were more the product of my imagination than of reality.

At home Lina was awake but incurious. I mumbled something about my walk having made me thirsty, poured myself a glass of Perrier, and settled into my chair, pretending interest in a book. My mind, however, was on my conversation with Johnson. I had begun it uncertain as to where it would end. Yet with the decision made, I felt a surge of anticipation. I would strike this bargain with the Americans to win my freedom and gain their assistance in my campaign against the Soviet regime. But I was impatient to start anew, and I wanted a quick passage through that interim existence.

I did not realize at the time that I had overlooked a crucial point. I had put no limit on the length of my secret service. I had entered a shadow world without defined boundaries, and assumed that a matter of months would be long enough to prove my sincerity. But years of anxiety were before me and the danger which I first thought I could not face became, for all that time, my constant companion.

4

THE FOLLOWING MONDAY MORNING I WAS DUE AT THE MISsion for the regular nine o'clock staff meeting. Yakov Malik loved these gatherings whether or not there was any business to discuss. They were a bureaucratic device he had learned long ago from Stalin, who would bring all his associates together just to see what their eyes told him.

Would Malik sense some change in me? I searched my face as I shaved for a sign that might give me away but my expression appeared normal. I took the routine walk of two blocks from my apartment building to the Mission, where the uniformed American policemen at the door greeted me cheerfully.

The Soviet guards behind their bulletproof glass door inside the building also smiled a welcome as they pressed a button to open the inner door for me. But I barely returned their salutation. In the elevator to the sixth floor, I felt uneasy among the other passengers.

I entered Malik's office half imagining that some unseen X-ray machine would sound an alarm announcing to everyone that Shevchenko had become an American spy.

Malik's office was a specially designed secure room, double-walled with an air space through which low music played constantly. His soundproofed lair was a proud piece of KGB handiwork, but it had a major flaw: it was so poorly ventilated that it could be suffocating if many people were in it for any length of time. But apparently there was enough air for Malik. Meetings in the "murder chamber," as his staff called the room, sometimes lasted for hours.

Inside, top Mission personnel were milling around chatting. I shook hands and said good morning as if everything were as usual. As I took my place at the massive conference table which extended from Malik's desk, my nervousness persisted. I bent over my newspaper pretending to be absorbed in it. Malik came in and took his chair.

I had never cared for Yakov Malik. After he replaced Fedorenko in 1968, I worked as his subordinate for two years. When I returned to New York in 1973 with a rank equal to his, he could not adjust to the change in status. Tall and trim, distinguished-looking even when his gray hair began to thin, Malik treated his subordinates with contempt, especially when they failed to understand the machine-gun clatter of his speech or when they ventured to offer opposing views. Malik considered himself a figure worthy of reverence, a kind of Kremlin regent in the UN. People were afraid of his power, and he was happy to feed their fear. He would often subject his young assistants and other diplomats to long bouts of petty and abusive scolding for "insufficient zeal," one of his regular complaints. In a gesture of exaggerated weariness, he would throw his arms out on his desk as he lectured them. "What can I do with you? And what could you do without me?" he would sigh. "You're as blind as a mole. I don't know when I'll be able to teach you how to work!" His self-important, derisive attitude toward those of lower rank or social standing was typical of the Soviet ruling class.

The staff meeting that morning was routine; the talk, dull. Malik was in an unusually good mood. Sometimes when I was silent at these gatherings, he would gibe heavy-handedly: "Aha! Shevchenko doesn't speak. Shevchenko has nothing to add. Well, we know why. He and his people take it easy sitting at their desks drinking coffee until it's time to go out for a long lunch. Hard workers. Ah, yes."

That day, however, he didn't bother to taunt me. For a change, he did not try to drag out the meeting when it was clear the agenda was light and easily dealt with. But as he dismissed the rest of the staff, he turned to me.

"Arkady Nikolaevich," he said, "could you stay just a minute?"

My apprehension rose, but all he wanted was that I review two draft cables on disarmament matters coming up on the UN schedule. His staff had prepared them, but he wanted to be reassured of their accuracy. He often made such requests of me.

"Will you just look them over?" he asked. "I'm sorry to keep you, but it's a bit urgent and I'd like to send them out today."

He was affable. I was obliging. Most of all, I was relieved. I left his office and went up to the seventh floor, to the *referentura*, the special code and communications unit, where the drafts were waiting. As I stretched my left hand up to the button hidden behind the light fixture outside the unmarked outer door, I shivered slightly. But my hand was steady now.

It shook when I had taken a cup of tea before the staff meeting, but now I was in control again, feeling as though I had survived a great test.

In answer to my ring, a buzzer sounded, freeing the door to open as I pushed. I entered the familiar small antechamber and reflexively deposited my briefcase on a shelf and stood in front of the peephole that was the only opening in the heavy steel door that led into the inner, soundproofed suite. An armed guard swung the portal back and admitted me. At another door, the top half of which was a bank teller's window, I asked the duty officer for the cables Malik wanted me to approve. He brought me the ledger books in which the drafts were written out, and I quickly checked them over, changing only a few phrases, initialing them, and hurrying out with the promise that I would come back that evening to catch up on the cable traffic.

In my car on the way to the UN I reflected on the Mission and what it meant in terms of the task Johnson had given me. I had rarely thought about the code cable reading room and the system of controls over the material in it except as an annoyance. Now I examined the setup in my mind, and realized that the rules I was going to break existed for only one reason: absolute security. The arrangements had been established to control the flow of information, to ensure its secrecy, to frustrate curiosity—or espionage.

It was also a perfect manifestation of the paranoia that governs so much Soviet behavior. If the controls hamper diplomatic communication and result in restricting rather than disseminating valuable information, or if they complicate economic management inside the U.S.S.R., that is a secondary consideration. Control and secrecy are top priorities, ensuring obedience based on ignorance or, where essential, on the carefully calibrated sharing of knowledge.

The *referentura* was a fortress. Entrance to it was a complicated undertaking. It would be impossible to leave if anyone suspected a breach of security. Similarly stringent controls applied alike to incoming and outgoing cables. Both had to be written out by hand into special ledgers with numbered pages. It was against the rules to prepare a draft message outside those premises or to take a copy of one out of the room. All the Mission records having anything to do with coded communications, therefore, were kept behind the double doors on the seventh floor, hard to reach, difficult to use, but completely secure. To eliminate the slightest possibility that the sounds made by the striking keys could be monitored and deciphered to reveal the secret code, the use of typewriters was forbidden in composing cables. Monitoring would in any case have been virtually impossible within the *referentura*, which was soundproofed like Malik's office, but the KGB always thought it better to overdo than not do enough. Moreover, I was certain that hidden peepholes let security men watch us in the cubicles as we read.

Following my meeting with Johnson I made a special effort to read the cable traffic with a fresh eye. At first, I found little I thought Johnson would consider valuable intelligence.

There were several cabled instructions on low-grade UN matters, a number of "circular" messages—reports from other missions which the Foreign Ministry routinely shared in whole or in part with posts dealing with related matters—but not much of real substance.

As our next meeting approached, I wondered what Johnson would think when I produced such a small catch. Would he simply grill me until I reported something sensational? And how long might that take? I did not intend to spy for very long.

It was Johnson's idea to set our first working session for a lunch hour. But he was safe inside his town house; I was the one out on the street in broad daylight, exposed and jumpy.

Crowds in big cities are supposed to be the perfect shelter, a mass of indifferent bodies into which fugitives can melt and vanish. But I felt that if anyone could achieve invisibility in that herd, it would be a professional with his eyes on my back.

Thin sunshine and a noticeable chill made most people walk briskly that day. I moved more slowly, twice turning to look in a shopwindow when I saw Soviets from the UN staff going in the same direction. They were probably bound for the inexpensive cafeteria in the Mission, and paid no particular attention to me.

Still, when I turned into the side street and could see the familiar entrance, I decided on a last-minute evasion. I walked quickly down the block, well past Johnson's doorway, looked up at the house numbers, pretended to be confused, and then turned around to head back for Third Avenue. As far as I could see, my charade had drawn no interested spectators. The few other people on the pavement seemed oblivious to me. None of the faces I searched looked familiar or embarrassed by my gaze. I rang the town-house bell.

Johnson opened the door almost immediately. "Were you lost?" he asked. "I saw you go by a minute ago."

I explained what I had done and why. He chuckled. "You're learning."

We didn't talk much that day. I watched Johnson's face closely when I told him that my hours of reading in the code room had been fruitless.

"Don't worry, Andy. I understand all that," he said. "This isn't some hit-and-run act for us or for you."

The words were reassuring but somewhat vague, giving me the impression that this might go on longer than I had thought. It occurred to me that Johnson might not know precisely what he might be able to learn from me. It was as though he were playing for time. I knew the feeling: I had often experienced it at negotiations when I went into a meeting without clear instructions, with nothing to do but repeat clichés and await developments. But I dismissed the thought. Instead, I interpreted the American's attitude to mean that he was still testing my sincerity.

I could hardly blame him. If our roles were reversed I would be extremely cautious too. Johnson said that there were many important matters they wanted to talk about beyond current information from code cables, but there was no time now. He proposed that we take care of several formalities.

"I need to take your picture and your fingerprints," he said. I was surprised. "What for?"

"It's just for the files so others will know that you are who you say you are if you ever need to prove your identity and I'm not around."

I posed with my jacket on and off, full face and profile, smiling and serious. As he worked, Johnson put another question to me.

"Would you mind if other people joined us? Not today, but at another meeting? Some of my colleagues want to know who other Soviets are at the Mission and in the Secretariat. What their real jobs are."

"You mean the KGB? That could take a lot of time. There are hundreds of them, plus military intelligence agents."

"The FBI wants to make sure it's watching the right people," Johnson said. "You could help a lot by identifying as many as you can."

I agreed to his request. I had no qualms about identifying the KGB in New York. They were no friends of mine. I divided them into two categories: nuisances and threats. It would be a pleasure to reveal what I knew about them. And I could demonstrate my good faith by helping to penetrate the Soviet espionage establishment.

Meanwhile, my duties as Under Secretary General and my work for the Mission continued to occupy me. Business at the United Nations is perhaps most active in its lobbies and bars. The North Delegates' Lounge is the largest of such rooms. Its main decoration is a huge tapestry, a gift from the People's Republic of China, which depicts the Great Wall.

This enormous artwork dominates the lounge with very bright colors. I have never seen it fail to strike any newcomer. I have always felt that the tapestry is an allusion to China's greatness, its long, eventful history and its rich, ancient culture. I also think that it stands as a kind of reproach to those who for so long tried to exclude China from the UN.

It was an accident that China became the topic of my first substantive political conversation with Johnson. Looking back, however, it seems somehow fitting that we, a Soviet and an American, should begin a long association with this subject.

Our discussion was sparked by a cable from Vasily Tolstikov, the Soviet Ambassador in Peking, a message that the Foreign Ministry had sent on to some missions as guidance on the current status of Sino-Soviet relations. The cable also contained a new reminder of the necessity to exert every effort to collect information about China. No scrap was too small to be overlooked, particularly if there was any hint of a possible move against the Soviet Union. Any nuances in the balance of power in China were also to be particularly noted. There was nothing sensational in Tolstikov's analysis, but I guessed that Johnson would be as interested in anything concerning China as in material concerning the Soviets. I was not mistaken. His eyes brightened when I mentioned Tolstikov.

"What else was in the cable? Do you remember who signed it and what its date was?" he asked.

I answered his questions, but emphasized that most of Tolstikov's reports were of such turgid length and superficiality that the real experts in the Foreign Ministry laughed at his prose and moaned at his lack of insight. His latest cable was no exception. It was so full of orthodox Soviet diatribes against Mao Tse-tung that the classified report could have appeared in the Soviet press as a standard polemic for public consumption.

"This is the safety-in-repetition technique," I joked to Johnson. All an ambassador had to do was rewrite a few editorials from the latest *Pravda* as a political assessment and throw in some local color. That way he reassured everyone that the truth was exactly what the orthodox members of the Politburo thought it was.

I added that Soviet diplomats in China were often unable to evaluate subtleties of potential importance or to alert Moscow to the alignments that were taking shape. That was the reason I thought he should know about this cable. Tolstikov was all but admitting that his main sources of information in Peking were other foreigners and diplomats—and not very high-level ones at that. He had practically no access to reliable Chinese informants.

Although the cable did not contain information of high importance, we talked about it a long time that evening. When I left Johnson and stepped out onto the sidewalk, I saw that it had rained heavily. New York's millions of lights cast a pinkish glare on low, heavy clouds. I was tired; I had delivered a lengthy monologue, but this time there had been real rapport between us. In high spirits I took a deep breath of the rain-washed air.

5

I READ THE CODE CABLES AND OTHER SECRET MATERIAL ARriving from Moscow via diplomatic pouch. In addition, officials from the Central Committee, the Foreign Ministry, and other branches of government and academic institutions, including friends from the embassy in Washington, visited New York. I was also following events and gossip in Moscow through the "pocket post"—the stream of private letters carried back and forth by individual diplomats and other travelers to avoid the mandatory opening and checking by the KGB censors.

I kept Johnson up to date on what was going on in the Kremlin, particularly regarding the Brezhnev-Kosygin frictions over the future course of Soviet-American relations, about Moscow's instructions to Ambassador Anatoly Dobrynin in Washington, details of Soviet policy, and the political rationale for many plans and events in various parts of the world. I told him about the Soviet positions on arms-control negotiations—SALT and others—including fallback provisions contained in the instructions. I told him of specific Soviet plans for continuing the fight with movements in Angola that did not accept Moscow's role there. From officials in Moscow involved in economic matters, I passed on the information that the original oil fields in the Volga-Ural region on the Ob River would soon decline and that in several years the Soviet Union would have difficulty expanding oil production in the smaller, less accessible fields. Of course, I briefed Johnson regularly about the goings-on in the Mission. However, I could not spend much time with him without raising KGB suspicions. Gradually, delivering information grew tedious, and I became restless and impatient.

By the end of 1975, I still had found no way to disclose to either Lina or Anna the new life I was planning for us. I had

44

been working hard and the strain was heavy. I needed a rest, a change of scene and climate. I had to get Lina away from New York and into a setting where I could bring her to share my feelings and join my plans. We left Anna with friends at Glen Cove and flew to Florida to see in the New Year, and, I hoped, to begin a new kind of life.

At the Hotel Carillon in Miami we swam, slept, and relaxed. The weather was beautiful; the ocean warm and soothing. Away from the Mission and the clandestine meetings, I felt my tensions dissolve. In New York, KGB agents almost certainly monitored our apartment, as they had at Glen Cove, but in Miami they could not have had enough time to install listening devices in our room. Even if the KGB had sent agents to keep watch on us, they must have kept their distance. I sensed no surveillance, only the comfort of freedom.

On New Year's Eve I took Lina to a small Italian restaurant not far from our hotel. It was a cozy place, the kind we both enjoyed, and in our quiet booth I started the conversation I had been rehearsing to myself for days.

"Isn't it wonderful here?" I began.

"It is," Lina agreed. "I, we, have had a very good time."

"Yes, and what's so awful is that it's almost over. We have to go back to New York, back to face Malik, the KGB, and all those Party leeches. I'm tired. I've realized it down here and I don't know how much longer I can stand it."

Lina looked at me with concern.

"I mean it," I continued. "We ought to think seriously about the future, whether we should go back to Moscow, where I can find work that is less of a strain. Or maybe we can figure out something else."

"What are you talking about?" Lina was alarmed. Even my cautious hint upset her. "We have to stay in New York as long as possible. Do you think we can get all the things we like in Moscow? Perhaps you've forgotten that rubles alone won't do it. Let me remind you that even Politburo members don't have access to the kinds of things we have in New York. We'll never get them if we're stuck in Moscow."

"But we already have everything, Lina. A fine apartment, a dacha, beautiful furniture. There's money in the bank, and you've got jewels, furs, clothes. What more do we need?

People are already jealous of us. There's been gossip. You know that."

"You really are a coward, Arkady," she exploded. "All the *nachal'niki* [bosses] use their time abroad to get rich, to buy things. Fedorenko did it when we first worked in New York. Malik does it now. What do you think Lidiya Dmitriyevna and I do when Gromyko brings her to New York? Go to museums? No, we shop. I shop for her. I give her money, our money. And you have Gromyko's protection, just as I have hers. No one can touch us. Not the KGB. Nobody. With the Gromykos behind you, you can have a fantastic career. You could replace Malik in New York or Dobrynin as Ambassador in Washington. Remember, Dobrynin once had your job. And then, who knows?"

I didn't dare tell her I had no desire to pursue such goals. I tried a softer approach.

"Lina, we can't count on Washington. Anatoly Fyodorovich is going to be there a long time. Gromyko is very wary of him. I'm sure it's a constant irritation to Andrei Andreyevich the way they gossip in Moscow about Dobrynin possibly replacing him as Minister of Foreign Affairs. Gromyko will keep him as far away from Moscow as possible, as long as possible."

"Probably," Lina agreed. From her friendship with Gromyko's wife she knew at least as much about his likes and dislikes as I did. Suddenly she returned to my other, purposefully vague hint.

"What did you mean about going somewhere else, about not returning to Moscow? You've gotten more and more hostile in your talk about things at home, the KGB, the Party. You're full of praise for the Americans and depressed about everything else. What's the matter with you?"

"You know how bad things are," I replied. "They aren't getting better, not going anywhere. What is there to hope for?" I was thinking of my own words to Johnson. "No one can change things. No one even will try."

"What does that mean?" Lina was tense. "Let the others look out for themselves. Are you saying you don't want to go back home? Do you want to stay here forever? If you do, you'll stay by yourself. I want a lot of things here, but I could

46

never live in this country for good. Besides, think about your future: it's not here, but at home.''

I had no answer. I had no way to reach her, to confide in her. I shrugged and changed the subject, hoping that Lina would forget our talk, dismiss my words as the expression of a passing mood.

For the next few days and on the plane back to New York, I weighed my alternatives. Obviously, Lina would not come with me willingly. But what would her reaction be if I were to defect suddenly, presenting her with a *fait accompli* and asking her to join me before the Soviets knew I had disappeared? Then she might very well see that she could not return to Moscow alone, that she could not live there by herself as we had lived together. She would be an outcast with no privileges and no access to the elite society she loved. If she made a rational choice, she would prefer her chances with me. Deep inside, however, I was afraid of her choice. I decided to force the issue while Anna was still in New York. If I waited too long, my daughter would have to return to Moscow.

THE DAY AFTER I RETURNED TO MY OFFICE, TO THE GRAY January chill of New York, the treadmill of the Mission and the UN, I called the CIA number and set up a meeting in the town house. My intention was to make it our last secret encounter.

Johnson had other ideas. I wanted to come out of hiding; he was prepared only to change the locale.

Before I could spell out my New Year's resolve to make my defection public as soon as possible, he told me we would no longer be meeting in the town house. The CIA had finally done what I had asked them: they changed the meeting place. Johnson had found an apartment within walking distance of the UN Plaza. I would have convincing cover for my visits to the building, for it housed a number of doctors and dentists, several of them on the list recommended to Secretariat employees in need of medical care. I could, and eventually did, become a normal patient of one of the dentists without arousing KGB curiosity.

By complying with my wishes, Johnson had put me under

a certain obligation to him. I had been prepared to insist on a prompt termination of my double life, but I left that evening agreeing instead to let it continue.

I had not given up at once or completely. I told Johnson that Lina had turned down my cautious attempt to enlist her in my plans. I also pointed out that I absolutely had to make my break before Anna left New York for good.

"What you have to realize," I said, "is that I will not go on forever. The Soviets use me, and now you're using me, and I don't like it. It's enough. I want to make a new start."

"And that's just what we're doing," Johnson replied. "We've got a perfect setup now. It's right on your way to the office and you won't have to do any more sneaking around at night. You'll have a perfectly legitimate reason to be there if anybody asks."

My determination waned as he rattled on, but my dissatisfaction did not diminish. The Americans were hemming me in, seeming to take me for granted. I would go along with the new arrangements, but not cheerfully. And despite Johnson's "perfect setup," I knew the risks were still great.

Risk took on reality just a few weeks later on an unusually bright day in early February. I walked from my office to the apartment building, enjoying the exercise and the sight of the animated lunch-hour crowds. I always found something invigorating in the New York street scenes. They didn't offer the beauty of the gold-starred blue dome of the Church of St. Nicholas of the Weavers, a landmark on my Moscow walk to work, or the shimmering repose of the Moscow River as it flowed past the gentle green slopes of Gorky Park—but they were so alive.

I felt buoyed, almost carefree, when I entered the lobby off First Avenue. I paused to let my eyes adjust to the change from the sunlit street to the gloomy interior and, as I did so, a cheerful voice startled me.

"Mr. Secretary, what a surprise. What brings you here?"

In front of me was a Secretariat employee who had once worked in my department, whose promotion and transfer, I recalled, had been engineered with the backing of Geli Dnyeprovsky, a Soviet in the Secretariat's personnel office. I stammered a greeting.

"You have a doctor here too?"

"A dentist," I said.

"Well, mine is over there." My former staff member pointed across the lobby. "Mustn't be late for my appointment. Nice to see you."

The encounter could not have lasted more than half a minute. It was completely ordinary, but it deflated my spirits. I was suddenly back in the world of suspicion, as far from the raucous liberty of midday Manhattan as were the hushed gray pavements of Moscow.

I pretended to head for the dentist's office. When I was sure the lobby was empty, I boarded the elevator. Upstairs, Johnson did not get past a handshake and a hello before I told him what had just happened. With a lot of other UN people using the building, I said, the place was not safe. I could not come to it often.

The dentist, Johnson said, was legitimate cover, especially since the KGB knew that I, like other Soviets, avoided the inferior services provided by the Mission and had permission to go to American specialists for my teeth.

He didn't understand. What concerned me was being in a place where others from the Secretariat could recognize me and idly gossip about running into me. Enough talk might send the KGB to check the dentist's records, I said, and to discover how seldom I visited him. When Johnson replied that American doctors' records are confidential and would not be disclosed without the patient's permission, I sharply reminded him of a recent scandal on that score.

"That didn't stop those White House people who stole the psychiatrist's file on Daniel Ellsberg, who gave out the Pentagon Papers. They just broke into the office and took the file. Do you think the KGB couldn't do something like that? I tell you, it's not secure."

"Maybe you have something," Johnson said slowly. "Let me see about moving somewhere else."

I stood up. "I have to leave now. I have no more time."

Johnson didn't try to stop me. "I'm sorry," he said. "I know you're upset; I understand. But when can we meet again?"

"I don't know. I'll think about it, about the whole situation.

I'm sick of all this crap. Maybe another country can protect me. If I have anything to tell you, I'll call.''

I had not planned my words or threats. They poured out before I fully considered them, the product of frustration and exhaustion. In the weeks that followed I did what I should have done before my outburst: I analyzed my real options. I concluded that I had used a weapon against Johnson which not only would not work but might injure me.

Theoretically, I did have other choices. It was just that none of them was satisfactory. I could seek sanctuary with a European government. Although I imagined that some European countries would be reluctant to strain their relations with Moscow by granting me refuge, I assumed they would nonetheless honor their traditions and give me asylum. The British, in fact, would probably be quick to offer welcome.

Yet the truth was that I would never feel comfortable anywhere but in America. I had lived here for years, and I felt that if I did have a second home, it was in the United States.

I also understood that it would be difficult to realize my hopes without the backing of U.S. authorities, without restoring contact and working relations with Bert Johnson. I could not go around him. If I presented myself at the State Department or the U.S. Mission to the UN, for instance, and requested immediate asylum, my lack of cooperation with the CIA could well influence my reception. I might receive asylum, but I could scarcely hope for much more. American officials would consider me erratic at best, suspect at worst. As soon as I had agreed to cooperate with the CIA "for a while," I should have realized that I had indentured myself indefinitely. In search of greater freedom, I had mortgaged what little I had.

It was a bitter conclusion to reach and it took me more time to accept the truth than to see it. But toward the end of February I swallowed my pride, resigned myself to the inevitable, and made an appointment with Johnson. As I saw it, my only chance to shorten my term of service as a spy was to come up with some really important revelation and thereby earn my way to freedom.

As our meetings resumed, I sensed that I was gradually regaining Johnson's confidence in my good faith. At the same time, I could see no end to my obligation to the CIA. I alternated between moods of resignation and spasms of frustration.

As winter turned to spring, Johnson agreed to set all our meetings for evening hours to reduce the chances of my being seen again by UN staffers on their way to medical appointments. And he promised to try to find another, safer location for us.

"What about using a hotel?" I asked him. "The Waldorf-Astoria, for instance."

That hotel was one of the places I visited regularly. Because many UN delegations lack space of their own for entertainment, they use the Waldorf for national-day receptions or parties for top official visitors. I often attended gatherings there. The parties were big and noisy, so I usually made a brief appearance, took time for a drink and a little conversation, and left. No one noticed how long I stayed or when I left.

Johnson agreed to look into it. His casual but professional responses set the tone for most of our talks. But at each session he also reassured me that his agents had noticed nothing unusual in the conduct of the KGB toward me. I had to admit as well that I had observed no change in the treatment I received at the Mission. My sense of danger subsided, but it did not disappear.

Three weeks later it was back, stronger than ever. I faced a risk I had not imagined before: Secretary General Kurt Waldheim had decided that I would represent him at an international seminar on apartheid in South Africa, to be held in Havana.

I had no ready excuse to avoid this unwelcome assignment. Cuba was almost the last place I wanted to go, as potentially risky a country for me to enter as any Soviet client state in Eastern Europe. In Havana I would not be able to count on CIA protection. Although my UN colleagues at the seminar could report my disappearance, they would be powerless to prevent it. If the KGB wanted to move against me in Cuba, they could fly me straight to Moscow on any pretext, and no one would or could intervene.

Johnson was concerned when I told him about my travel orders and about the danger I might face in Cuba. But after

51

considering the issue for a while, he said quietly, "The danger of that happening seems remote. But even if you were taken to Moscow, we could help. I know you don't think so, but there are ways, things we can do."

"Like what? Sending a letter of protest to Brezhnev?"

"Calm down. Let me put together a contingency plan for Moscow so you'll see we aren't as helpless as you think. Then you can decide."

When we met three nights later, he described an arrangement for contacting Americans in the Soviet capital. The plan seemed good enough, but I still wasn't convinced. The image of a cell in Lubyanka prison swam in my mind. Johnson was droning on, describing arrangements. I was furious.

"Listen, Bert!" I shouted. "They could grab me in Cuba and ship me back whole or in pieces to Moscow and you couldn't do a damn thing. It would all be over before you even got the news."

He remained calm. "Andy, we have picked up *no* indication of unusual surveillance on you. But if the KGB suspects you, your going to Havana would reassure them."

The logic of his statement deflated my anger. Although there was a risk, it was also true that the Soviets gave no sign of distrusting me. My willingness to go to Havana could work to my benefit, dispelling any incipient doubts the KGB might have developed but did not yet regard as solid. More important, it was obvious that Johnson regarded my acquiescence as another test to pass, another proof of my good faith. I was still on probation.

Abruptly Johnson asked, "What do you shave with?"

"An ordinary razor. One of those things that hold a flat blade with two edges. It can be set to different openings. Why?"

"Because it's a way to give you some extra help. Bring it here in a day or two. We'll give it back to you before you leave for Havana."

I was scheduled to fly to Cuba the following Saturday. I would get there in time to inspect the arrangements for the seminar and work on any last-minute problems before it opened on Monday. Early in the week I dropped off my razor with Johnson, and on Friday evening, the night before my departure, I went to see him.

It was our first meeting at the Waldorf-Astoria. A large reception in a downstairs ballroom gave me my excuse to be at the hotel. At the party I chatted briefly with the host and a few other UN ambassadors, but soon was able to slip out. I took an elevator to one of the upper floors.

Johnson had sketched the location of the room for me: it was down a corridor to the right of the elevator shaft. But other people left the car with me. I walked the length and width of the hotel and came to the room from the back corridor, having reassured myself that the other elevator passengers were ordinary guests uninterested in me or my destination.

Johnson was waiting for me, obviously pleased with himself. He pointed to a low coffee table and two razors lying on it side by side. "Which one is yours?" He grinned.

I examined them, hefted them in my hands, and could find no difference between them.

"They're both yours from now on," Johnson said, "but the one on the left isn't the kind you can buy at the drugstore. I'll show you the difference."

He picked up the instrument and, as I watched, set the numbers on the metal ring below the razor head at the minimum opening and then, pushing hard against the bottom of the handle, twisted the cylinder. The handle came apart, revealing that it was hollow. Into the opening Johnson slipped a tiny roll of microfilm.

"That has everything you need on it," he said. "In case you forget the details of the contingency plan we went over the other night. It's got phone numbers, locations, people to contact in case you need them."

He made me practice opening and closing the razor until he pronounced me an expert. I didn't feel like one.

I packed both razors the next morning and went to Kennedy Airport to catch a flight for Jamaica, where, after a layover, I would take another plane to Havana.

My UN associates who met me at the Havana airport were preoccupied with last-minute problems in the organization of the apartheid seminar. There was no Soviet welcoming party for me, no KGB detail on hand.

I stayed at a former luxury hotel which had become distinctly seedy. The bathrooms were a rusty mess. Plumbing fixtures were exactly the kind of thing the Cubans hoped the Soviet Union would supply to them. But the U.S.S.R. had too little of such equipment for itself. Another item the Cubans were desirous of was Coca-Cola. They missed their Cuba Libres. The Soviets were never able to produce Coca-Cola, so they asked the Czechs, who did their best, but the result was not very good. "Checka-Cola" never worked as well as Coca-Cola. The Soviet Union found it much easier to be generous with military equipment, of which they had no shortage.

I spent the next day checking arrangements for the apartheid discussions. I met the Soviet Ambassador to Cuba only when the seminar opened and he arrived to represent the U.S.S.R. at its sessions. We were not acquaintances and, although we found time for a brief talk during a break in the speechmaking, we made no effort to go beyond superficial conversation. I did, however, accept his offer to spend the evening with two couples from the embassy who were willing to accompany me for dinner and a Cuban nightclub performance. It proved to be a pleasant evening, and as I prepared to pack and return to New York, I told myself that Johnson had been right. My worry had been for nothing. The worst was over. As so often before, the worst had been mostly in my imagination.

My mood didn't last. I noticed that two of my shirts were not where I had left them. Their disappearance was annoying, but I assumed they would turn up somewhere in the suite. My nonchalance vanished completely when I went into the bathroom. The razor I had put on a shelf above the sink was not there.

Sweat broke out all over my body. Which razor had I left in the bathroom? I had forgotten to test it when I unpacked, to distinguish the original from the hollow one. Where had I left the other one? In my suitcase. That was it. I would get it, check it, find out for certain if I was safe or self-betrayed.

Walking as though I were underwater, I went back to the bedroom and fumbled through the clothes I had already packed until my fingers grasped the razor. I brought it out and stood a moment, trying to recall the procedure for opening it.

Set the number as low as possible. Twist the bottom part of the handle.

Damn. It wouldn't move. I tried again. Nothing.

54

They had taken the hollow one. I was found out.

I collapsed into a sitting position on the edge of the bed, staring at the worn, dingy carpet, unable to organize my thoughts, to get control of myself.

I do not know how long the seizure lasted, but it seemed an eternity until I began to swim back toward reason. Finally, in a corner of my mind, I remembered that I had omitted a step in the process of opening the razor handle.

I tried a third time. Do it slowly. Do it right. Set the number. Push hard on the handle and twist. Push hard. That was the action I had forgotten on the first two attempts. Now turn it.

It turned. It unscrewed. The microfilm was still safe inside.

I gasped aloud with relief. Only a hotel maid stealing a few things from her socialist brother. But was it? Perhaps it really had been Castro's security police or the KGB. Maybe they had discovered something and were sifting all possibilities. Maybe there was a mole in the CIA who had tipped them off or even, I thought with rage, one of their moronic, careless leaks. Only time could give me the answer.

From then until I returned that night to New York, I kept the razor in my briefcase and never let the case out of my hands. Home in my apartment I waited until Lina and Anna were asleep and then went into the bathroom with scissors and a pair of heavy pliers. I extracted the microfilm, minced it into slivers, and flushed it away. Then I mangled the razor itself, twisting it into an unrecognizable lump. The remains went into the trash.

For some time after, I was on the alert and suspicious of anything even slightly unusual in anyone's behavior at the Soviet Mission. But as my routine settled back into ordinary patterns, the residue of shock from my own "Cuban crisis" receded.

Contributing to the relaxing of my tensions was my somewhat surprising discovery that there were many similarities between spying and diplomacy. Spies and diplomats live double lives: one life for outsiders and another among those whom they trust or for whom they work. Both jobs require constant vigilance, good nerves, and time to devote to collecting information and compiling it for reports to one's government.

I began to feel that I was fishing in my own pond. Johnson had proved right about my ability to make the gathering of intelligence a manageable part of my routine. It took time, but I acquired the facility. He was wrong, however, about my fears eventually dwindling away. Anxiety always remained in a back corner of my mind. I was acutely aware that while diplomats usually finished their lives with honor and died in their beds, even brilliant spies often came to an abrupt and violent end or lived out their lives in prison and disgrace.

6

At one of our meetings at the Waldorf, Johnson brought with him an FBI agent, Tom Grogan, who wanted information about KGB operations and agents. My knowledge of specific KGB operational activities was peripheral. Over the years, however, because of the posts I had occupied, I had had direct and prolonged dealings with KGB agents. Formally, I had been the titular superior of many of them during my previous job at the Mission, and I was so again as Under Secretary General. In addition, a number of my classmates at the Moscow State Institute of International Relations (MGIMO) had joined the KGB and were operating professionals. I had continued an acquaintance with some of them in one way or another.

As I looked at the files Grogan brought with him, I saw I could give him a number of answers. I balked, however, at his suggestion that I improve my ties with the KGB. Grogan was especially persistent in this recommendation. The KGB, he argued, could be valuable sources and dangerous enemies. "You'd be better off staying on their good side."

"It can't be done," I told him. "Most of them are arrogant and vicious and some are just plain stupid. I try to maintain reasonable working relations, but that's never enough for them. They want to control everyone around them, to make all of us do their work and dance to their tune."

I said to Grogan I didn't intend to make KGB friends to help him out. I would tell him what I knew; beyond that he would have to use other resources.

I began by describing the KGB chief in New York, Boris Aleksandrovich Solomatin, a short, stocky major general, the *rezident,* as Soviets called him. After my appointment as Under Secretary General, Solomatin invited me again and again to his apartment for drinking sessions and "friendly talks." He was cynical, boorish, and a drunk besides. He holed up in his smoke-filled apartment, where he summoned others to him.

He did not participate in any operations outside the walls of the Soviet Mission, but he directed the agents who did. Solomatin lived in reclusive safety, seldom venturing outside the Mission, except to Glen Cove. His safety was further enhanced by the diplomatic immunity conferred by his cover title of Deputy Permanent Representative of the U.S.S.R. to the UN, and a minister's rank.

The two-room apartment in the Mission he shared with his wife, Vera, was not quite as much of a fortress as the *referentura,* but it was secure nonetheless. To thwart American bugging of his apartment, which he was convinced was thorough, permanent, and effective, Solomatin had two television sets and a stereo system, at least one of which was always on. Since he had virtually no contact with Americans, he lived by his television sets. He particularly liked news programs and would watch the CBS and ABC news simultaneously. Another of his favorite pastimes was listening to tapes of Russian patriotic songs from World War II and recounting his wartime experiences as an infantry officer.

Now in his early fifties, he was also a graduate of MGIMO, and I had known him for years. Soon after my arrival in New York in 1973, he was openly trying to involve me in the KGB's espionage activities. On one occasion, sprawled out on the sofa, a cigarette between his teeth, he fixed me with a stare and said, "You can be one of our most important intelligence officers." He reeked of vodka as he leaned confidentially closer. "You go everywhere. You talk to everyone. All

57

you have to do is tell me what you hear. After all, we both work for the Soviet state."

He said that any interesting information I provided would be sent to KGB headquarters in Moscow, where it would undoubtedly receive attention from the Politburo.

"We know how to work," he said smugly. "We're not like your Foreign Ministry bureaucrats, forever sitting on valuable information like a brooding hen who never produces any chicks. Collaboration with us will advance your career."

Solomatin's assurances were lies. It was true that the *rezident* had an independent communications connection to KGB headquarters in Moscow and that he was absolutely free to choose whether or not to share any information with Ambassador Malik before forwarding it. But when the KGB transmits information to Moscow, it never identifies the person who procured it. Not even the *rezident* who generates a cable uses his own name. He simply signs as the *rezident*.

Solomatin merely wanted me as another foot soldier. I told him that Gromyko would judge my performance by the work I did for the ministry, not on what I did for the KGB. He rubbed his temples as if he were deep in thought. I ought to consider his proposal seriously, he said.

I had no intention of being drawn into his network, but I was compelled to make several concessions to him during his tenure as *rezident*. In the fall of 1973, Solomatin introduced me to Valdik Enger, a tall, handsome Estonian. Solomatin insisted that I arrange a job for Enger in my office, where there was a vacancy. At first I refused, saying I needed an assistant who would really assist me, not someone who would be his man. The *rezident* was persistent, and finally I agreed to take Enger on, with the condition that after a few months in my office I would transfer him to another position in the Secretariat. Solomatin did not object.

Solomatin's chief aide was Colonel Vladimir Gregorievich Krasovsky, the deputy *rezident*. He was a steady and experienced KGB professional who had served several years in New York. Solomatin's close associates also included his frequent guest Georgy Arbatov, the director of the Institute of the United States and Canada of the Soviet Academy of Sciences, who often traveled to the United States. In fact, Lina and I had seen him recently at a dinner party at Solomatin's apartment.

Johnson said, "A lot of people think he's very close to Brezhnev, practically the Kremlin's spokesman. And it seems like every time he's over here he's being interviewed in the papers or on TV. Do you know him well?"

I knew Arbatov very well; in fact, I had known him since the beginning of my career. When we met at the Solomatins' dinner party he was on one of his regular scouting missions. Then, in 1976, his purpose was to sift through the political underbrush prior to the American presidential election.

President Gerald Ford was thought to be continuing Richard Nixon's policy toward the U.S.S.R. The Soviets, therefore, preferred him to any other contender for the presidency, concerned as they were with what they perceived as a threat from the right wing of American politics. Ford's challenger for the Republican nomination was Ronald Reagan, a hardline anti-Soviet and anti-Communist. The Soviets knew, of course, that even if Reagan were to win the nomination and then the election, he would eventually have to deal with Moscow, just as Nixon had. Nevertheless, the prospect of a Reagan presidency was not one they found pleasant. As Gromyko put it, "No one knows what kind of surprise this actor might spring." There was an air of uncertainty and dissatisfaction, even confusion, that affected general trends in the superpowers' relations at the time of the Solomatins' dinner.

Lina and I were the first arrivals. Vera Solomatin, a onetime research assistant at Arbatov's institute, was celebrating her enrollment as a lieutenant in her husband's organization. There was nothing unusual in that; there were many women KGB officers. The wives of many KGB professionals also worked for it, including Irina Yakushkin, the wife of Washington's *resident*. Moreover, some of the wives of my fellow diplomats in New York were KGB officers.

As Solomatin put glasses and plates on the table in the small foyer of his apartment, which also served as a dining room, he told me to go into the living room and pour myself a drink; he would join me in a minute. As I looked around, waiting for him, I noticed four copies of John Barron's book, *KGB*, sitting on a bookcase. I asked Solomatin why he had so many. He said that people in Moscow kept requesting it.

"But it's not so hot," he said. "My name and Vladimir Krasovsky's aren't even mentioned in it."

I couldn't tell whether this was an expression of regret or pride on Solomatin's part.

Krasovsky and his wife arrived with Arbatov. After several rounds of vodka toasts had warmed the conversational chill I always sensed in Solomatin's presence, Arbatov agreed to summarize the report he would be making to Moscow.

Gerald Ford had a fairly good chance of winning the 1976 election. "Of course, right now he does the usual zigzagging, taking hard-line positions, but that doesn't worry us very much. It's just the usual campaign bluster. After it's over, he'll be good old Jerry again," he said.

Neither Solomatin nor I disputed this assessment when Arbatov asked for our opinions. We and he knew that Moscow wanted reassurance on Ford's continuing in the White House, and none of us wished to be the bearer of bad news, even if we had strong presentiments of Ford's defeat. I turned the talk to my special interest, arms control, and asked Arbatov if there was anything new in that area.

Arbatov acknowledged that the negotiations' momentum had dissipated. "It's too close to the elections for the Americans to move on something as controversial as SALT," he said with evident unhappiness. "We understand that reality. It's the way things are, but it's too bad."

Solomatin, whose interest was espionage, not disarmament, broke in. "Does it really matter that much? Why should we want to speed up the SALT business anyway?"

"I know what you mean," Arbatov said, "but things are serious." He then reiterated arguments about the connection between arms-spending and the failing health of the Soviet economy. The difference was that three years after the Nixon-Brezhnev breakthrough the domestic situation was even graver. Solomatin and I listened as Arbatov ticked off the depressing list of chronic shortcomings in management, in farming, in transport and distribution.

"Zhora-sha," Solomatin finally burst out, using a nickname for Georgy common in his native Odessa, "you're a pessimist.

We've survived worse. Don't forget the war. We came through that, after all."

It was the standard, patriotic, orthodox, unthinking rebuttal to any hint of criticism. Solomatin, like so many veterans who looked back to the war with a nostalgic glow, used this retort to effectively shut off serious talk.

Vladimir Krasovsky broke the awkward silence by reminding us that this was a celebration. He suggested that we put on some music and dance. Our wives enthusiastically agreed. Krasovsky clicked the heels of his gleaming, brand-new shoes.

"Look at my *baretki*," he exclaimed, using underworld slang for shoes. "Expensive. I paid more than seventy bucks for them," he said with pride.

Lean, tall, and good-looking, Krasovsky, unlike Solomatin, engaged daily in real espionage activity. He loved to dance and was very good at it. He clicked his heels again in front of Lina and kissed her hand in a gesture of burlesque. Watching them dance, half listening to Solomatin's heavy laugh and Arbatov's banter with the other women, I was grateful that even in the age of technological miracles no one could yet read thoughts.

SOON AFTER I DESCRIBED THAT EVENING TO JOHNSON A NEW *rezident* came to New York to replace Boris Solomatin. Muscular and bald, with the eyes of a basilisk, Colonel Yuri Ivanovich Drozdov struck me as a formidable adversary. Solomatin had been a pompous recluse who lived like a bear inside the Mission, but at least he was occasionally convivial.

Drozdov appeared to have no human failings. Moreover, he was a bolder and more intrusive presence in the Mission. Although he spoke poor English and, having specialized in China, knew little about the United States or the United Nations, he tried to take an active part in diplomatic work. His ignorance, however, only seemed to make him more demanding and cocksure than Solomatin had been. I found him not just unpleasant but menacing, and made it a point to keep a distance between us.

Shortly after he arrived, however, I got a late-night summons from him. I had been working in a *referentura* cubicle going through the code cables in hopes of finding a nugget or two to pass on to Johnson. It was after eleven o'clock. I was tired and, as always when engaged in such searches, jumpy.

"Arkady Nikolaevich"—a *referentura* clerk abruptly materialized at my elbow—"you are wanted on the telephone."

I must have shown my surprise and anxiety, for the clerk repeated himself. "It's a telephone call for you."

No one except Lina and the Mission guards downstairs were aware that I was in the building. Only the code room personnel knew which room I was in. I walked in worried confusion to the telephone. My muscles tensed at the sound of Drozdov's voice on the line asking me to report to his office.

"Upstairs?" I asked, envisioning the deserted corridors of the eighth floor, given over entirely to the KGB, hallways where the blank doors were locked even during the day, a sanctum from which there could be no escape.

"No, no." Drozdov sounded impatient. "I'm on the sixth floor. Could you come down now? There's a matter I'd like to discuss."

I consented.

All I really knew of Drozdov at this point was that he looked malevolent and appeared efficient. What if he had been culling old reports on me and noticed something which Solomatin, in his haste to depart some months before, had overlooked? I found the *rezident* hunched over a stack of papers when I entered his room. Only a single desk lamp illuminated the small chamber. It was a setting for an inquisition, but Drozdov, it turned out, had not mustered me for questioning. What he wanted was a favor.

"Thanks for coming at this hour," he began. "I need your assistance. It's about Enger. Can't you let up on him? He's doing valuable work for us. I know he's sometimes too busy for other jobs, but we have to strike a balance. I hope you'll oblige us in this business."

I was simultaneously relieved and angry: Valdik Enger again. To hear his name mentioned was, of course, far better than to be confronted with accusations about my own conduct. But it reminded me once more of the ways in which the KGB had used me, had forced my acquiescence to their wishes. I complained that each time I warned Enger to put more effort into his UN work and to be more discreet about his conspiratorial activities, he apologized and promised to mend his ways, but he never did. And when I'd returned from my New Year's vacation with Lina, I had found that he was even neglecting the less-demanding job I had provided him, that of supervising the preparation of a press digest that was circulated to fifty or sixty senior Secretariat officials four times a day.

The quality of the summary had noticeably deteriorated. Inaccuracies grew. Important news articles or commentaries were omitted. Other employees told me Enger was at fault. He paid almost no attention to the work. I called him into my office for what became an angry encounter, ending with my threat to take him off the UN payroll unless he began to earn his keep legitimately.

It was that argument which had been reported to Drozdov and had prompted his call to me. In response to his appeal that I give his agent the benefit of the doubt, I decided to take what advantage I could from a situation in which Drozdov, not I, was at a disadvantage.

"I've tried to be accommodating," I told the *rezident*, "but you may not know what sort of a man we're talking about. He hasn't lived up to his word. It wouldn't take much time to do the job he has now but he won't give it any. He's too blatant about his work for you. It's causing talk and trouble and I don't see how I can go on covering for him."

Drozdov thought for a moment before replying. "I can't see that his mistakes are so important, but"—he paused again—"I'll try to look at it from your point of view. We really want him in the UN. Do you have any ideas?"

"Well, I get nowhere with him," I answered. "Maybe you can get him to do his job. Tell him it's important. He ought to listen to you."

Drozdov seemed relieved. He accepted my idea right away and we parted amicably. He never knew the fright his call had caused me.

Perhaps that incident was what triggered that night vivid dreams of my childhood. I woke several times drenched with sweat, my heart pounding. I was reliving the beginning of war in 1941, when the heavy bombing began and my mother and I hid night after night in the potato cellar under our house by the Black Sea.

PART TWO

THE EDUCATION OF A SOVIET DIPLOMAT

7

MY EARLY LIFE WAS SPENT IN MODEST BUT SECURE COM-
fort. When I was born in 1930, my family lived in the coal-
mining town of Gorlovka, in the eastern Ukraine. With my
mother as his nurse, my father practiced medicine in a small
hospital there for railroad workers.

When I was five years old we moved to the town of
Yevpatoriya, a resort in the Crimea on the Black Sea. Not
long before the Germans attacked the Soviet Union, my
father was made the administrator of Yevpatoriya's tuber-
culosis sanatorium for children of the upper ranks of the
military and high-level bureaucrats.

Although he had tried nearly all his life to avoid politics,
he was required to wear a Red Army lieutenant colonel's
uniform and, within about a year, to join the Communist
Party. His military position and Party membership were
obligatory symbols of his status, and set us on a special
social level.

My father was a warm and generous man whom the young
found appealing. The children in his care would follow him
and hang on him during his rounds. He often worked around
the clock, and I can remember being jealous of those children with whom he spent so much time. For a long time in
the early twenties he had been the only doctor in a fifty-mile
area.

My father spoiled me and my older brother, Gennady. My
mother tried to "unspoil" me, but I was stubborn and resisted any kind of discipline. She was one of three children
of a middle-class family of Ukrainian and Polish ancestry.
Her father had been a clothing designer and had a small
tailoring shop in Kharkov. My mother was very pretty, and

barely eighteen years old when she and my father were married.

While I was still very young my mother instilled in me a love of reading. Among my earliest memories are tales of Russian folklore and Pushkin's stories, which she read to me again and again.

I was an average student at school. I enjoyed literature and history, in which I received top grades, but was not much interested in math and science, in which I just got by. In fine weather I played truant as often as I could. By that time I was an avid reader, and would take a book to the beach to spend the day reading and swimming instead of going to classes.

I learned to play chess, which I liked, and to play the piano, which I did not. One of my greatest passions was stamp collecting, and by the age of seven I knew the names of most countries and colonies. As each new stamp came into my possession I would search the map to find where the country of issue was located, increasing my interest in the world outside the Soviet Union.

I tried to paint like my brother, Gennady, but at this I was a failure. Gennady was nine years older than I, and my hero. He was athletic and artistic and he was crazy about aviation. There was a small flying club nearby which he joined as soon as my mother would let him. By the time he had finished high school, he was determined to be a pilot. As a younger brother, I was a curse to him, particularly when one of his girlfriends would come to our house for dinner or for a Sunday-afternoon visit. Those young ladies had to pass beneath our apple trees, where more than once I was waiting with a bag of water to throw on them. Gennady would haul me down and whack me, but he was never able to change my mischievous habits because very often these scenes would end with laughter and wrestling and I loved his attention.

At school, Soviet influence began to make its mark on me. I became patriotic, taking pride in my Young Pioneer duties, convinced that everything good was born with the Revolution. Since kindergarten, my schoolmates and I had been indoctrinated to that effect every day. We were constantly reminded by our teachers and Young Pioneer organizers that we lived in a society of general well-being, the best and happiest in the history of mankind. Our futures were bright, but we must be vigilant against our enemies, the capitalists, who wanted to take everything we had and enslave us. We were taught to be ready to defend our motherland with our lives, if necessary, for Communism.

My happy childhood was abruptly interrupted in June 1941. I was ten years old when Hitler attacked the Soviet Union. On the first day of the war the port of Sevastopol, about sixty miles down the coast from Yevpatoriya, was bombarded. Terrified, people stood in the streets watching the red glow in the sky from the shelling. Our town, too, received a few bombs that day.

Soon there were reports of massive defeats. It was incomprehensible. We had been taught that the Red Army was invincible; anyone who dared attack the Soviet Union would be crushed. I asked my father what was happening, but neither he nor anyone else could explain. I became openly critical of the Army to a school friend. My classmate Dima shared my feelings and repeated them to his father, who, as the sanatorium's political commissar, called *my* father in to lecture him on his son's lack of loyalty.

That evening my father took me out into the garden that led from our house down toward the beach. He asked me if what he had been told by the political commissar was true. "Did you really say those things? Did you say that our soldiers were not as good as the Germans?"

His voice was low but very stern. I admitted that I had said the Soviet Army was getting beaten. "After all," I added, "it's the truth, isn't it?"

"We are at war," my father answered. "Your brother, Gennady, is in training to fly against the Germans. He will be risking his life. How do you think he would feel if he knew you thought he was a bad fighter, that he and his comrades were too weak to win?"

I started to cry. I idolized my brother. I had not meant to hurt him. My father grabbed my arm as I tried to use my sleeve to wipe away the tears. "Arkasha," he said, "it doesn't matter what the truth is. It matters what people think. You cannot go around saying whatever comes into your smart-alecky little head. People will say you're a defeatist. They'll think you picked up your ideas from me or from your mother. Do you want us to be denounced? Do you know what happens to traitors? They get shot. Do you want us to be shot?"

I had never seen my father so angry and upset. He shook me, holding me by both arms, pushing his face into mine. "You're old enough now to start learning common sense, and you'd better learn quickly. You have to keep your mouth shut about what you see and what you think. Say what you're told to say. Do what you see others do. And keep your thoughts to yourself. That way you won't get into trouble."

He pushed me away and walked back to the house. I stayed in the dark sniveling, hurt and miserable. My father had not raised his voice, but his near-whispers had been explosive. I knew he was furious, but I also realized he was afraid. And his fear sank into me and made me frightened too.

My father had called me a smart aleck, and he had been right. I was quick to question orders I disliked, and more than a little stubborn. As I grew older, I remained puzzled and occasionally disturbed by the realities I was forbidden to discuss. I saw them but, for the most part, was silent.

By the fall of 1941, German forces were occupying the Crimea and the children in the sanatorium were evacuated. My mother and I went with them. We were sent to Torgai, a small village in the lovely Altai Mountains of Siberia, where we spent the next three years. My father was away from time to time at the front, but except for the worry that caused us and our constant concern about Gennady, our life was placid. We had our food rations, we cultivated our small garden, and were fortunate to have that luxury of luxuries, a cow.

The war overshadowed everything. Everyone listened to the radio news and followed the newspaper accounts. In my father's office there was a map where we marked the shifting front line with red pins. In our tiny community we felt the defeats keenly as we swung between hopelessness and euphoria. In 1942, when an anti-Hitler world coalition emerged, including the Soviet Union and the United States, we were greatly heartened. Our feelings toward America were very warm. We knew that the United States was giving us substantial help with food and matériel. I had seen American trucks and we even had a Willys car at my father's sanatorium—the pride of the community. Wartime movies from Hollywood were often shown, many of them depicting the friendship between Americans and Russians. I felt sure we would always be friends; it was inconceivable that anything could come between the Soviet Union and the United States.

The war was still raging when, in 1944, we were able to return to Yevpatoriya. The city had suffered greatly. Dozens of buildings lay in ruins, and the famous beach contained pillboxes, minefields, rows of barbed wire. People were homeless, ill, and many had sustained the news of death in their families. Men returned from the front with missing arms or legs; other injuries were common sights. Veterans displayed rows of decorations, wearing them as they begged at street corners. They would appear at the open market trying to sell their medals, old coats, anything they had managed to hang on to through the war.

Soon I saw, as many other Soviets already had, the first signs of something as evil as war. In the spring of 1944, there was a wholesale deportation of the Tatar people from the land they had cultivated in the Crimea for many centuries. They were forced without notice from their homes, shipped east in cattle cars without food or water, some 300,000 men, women, and children, all condemned to exile on the ground that they had collaborated with the Nazi occupation. Perhaps there was some truth in it, but the explanation wasn't good enough. I knew that the fathers of several of my Tatar schoolmates were in the Red Army fighting at the front. Why would the wives and children of loyal soldiers be made to suffer so?

In September 1944 we learned that Gennady was dead. He had been shot down near Warsaw by German antiaircraft guns. He had flown since the opening of war in 1941, at first in antiquated wooden planes, and later in modern fighters, somehow surviving the odds.

71

My father and I had always been very close and perhaps because of that he told me about my brother's death within a few days of receiving the official notification. He asked me to keep the news from my mother as long as possible. I was devastated when I realized that I would never see Gennady again, that he was never coming home. It was very difficult to hide my feelings from my mother. I would begin to cry at odd moments. I tried to stay out of the house and to be near my father. He allowed me to read in his office. He encouraged me to play with my classmates, but I didn't have the heart for it for a long time.

Eventually, of course, my mother began to worry about the lack of letters from Gennady, and after my father put her off a few times, she insisted he make inquiries in Moscow. My father then gave her the small box containing Gennady's belongings that had been sent by pilots in his unit, accompanied by a letter from one who was with him on the fatal mission. In the box there were letters, photographs of the family and his girlfriend, and a few pen-and-ink sketches, at which he was accomplished: a landscape, portraits of his friends in the unit, a few places he had been. He was twenty-three. I don't believe my mother ever got over Gennady's death, but my father managed to push his grief aside, working harder and harder. But I mark that year, when I was fourteen, as the beginning of my passage from child to adult. I became aware of the real sufferings of my countrymen, perhaps because tragedy had touched me closely for the first time in my life.

My introduction to the world and mentality of the secret police came at the end of 1944, several months after the Red Army had at last driven the Germans from the Crimea. It was Christmas Eve, and people streamed down the main street of Yevpatoriya toward the Orthodox cathedral and gathered in clusters around it.

Some of my school friends and I had gone to see a movie that evening, a German musical subtitled in Russian, brought back by Soviet troops as a war trophy. It was a comedy and it had put all of us in a happy mood. As we left the movie house, none of us was ready to go home.

My friend Igor, the oldest of our group, remarked on how

many people there were in the street. Zoya, an energetic freckle-faced girl, reminded us that it was Christmas Eve and people were waiting for the service to begin at the cathedral. She proposed that we go and watch it. It was the first time I had been inside any church, and the lighted candles, the singing, incense, and splendor of the priests' robes fascinated me until the celebration ended, long after midnight.

The next morning at school, a tall young man entered our classroom and, after a whispered word in the teacher's ear, led me out. Anxiously I wondered if there had been an accident; maybe something had happened to my parents. My escort patted my shoulder and told me not to worry. He said that they just wanted to talk to me at the NKGB office.

At the two-story brown sandstone headquarters building a gray-haired lieutenant colonel named Migulin, who seemed near exhaustion behind a paper-littered desk, told me I had made a serious mistake by attending the church service. I could rectify that, however, by identifying others I had seen there.

I stammered that I had not participated in the ceremony but only wanted to watch it and that I didn't know there was anything wrong with that.

"You didn't see anything wrong, Shevchenko, because you're still wet behind the ears," Migulin admonished me. He went on to say that the priests would exploit my presence at the ceremony to demonstrate that youth was being drawn to religion. He said I could set accounts straight by helping him. Some Party members and town officials also had made my mistake. Migulin wanted the names of those I had seen in church so he "could explain their error to them too."

The proposal, as well as the realization that I had been observed and reported on, scared me. I told him that the crowd had been too big for me to recognize any individuals in it, and to my relief I got out of the NKGB office with a disgruntled interrogator's warning to "stop loafing around churches."

I rationalized the incident away. Migulin was unworthy of his organization's high mission. If Stalin knew of such conduct, I felt sure the guilty would be punished. I believed with all my heart that Stalin was good and just, almost a god. Everyone my age had been taught that catechism since early childhood. Of course, from time to time, evil men appeared around Stalin and gave him bad advice, but he had always prevailed over such people. Unknown to me then, mine was the "good tsar–evil counselors" attitude that had kept so many Russians for so many centuries in thrall to autocracy, but at fourteen I was not equipped to question more deeply. No one among my family or their friends talked openly, at least in my presence, about what Stalin was doing at the time—the terror and the purges, the concentration camps and the execution of tens of thousands of innocent people.

But my encounter with the secret police was a minor episode in a stream of bright hope everyone felt as the end of war approached.

ONE EVENING IN EARLY FEBRUARY 1945, MY FATHER, considerably excited, told my mother and me that he had to go immediately to the airfield located between Simferopol and Saki. Some very important persons were expected to arrive there. It was all a carefully guarded secret.

When my father returned home the next day, he told us he had not only seen Stalin and even shaken hands with him, he had also met two other important Allied leaders, Roosevelt and Churchill. He said they were all on their way to a conference at Yalta.

The reason for my father's presence at the airfield was that the Soviets wanted several doctors to observe Roosevelt at close range and evaluate rumors concerning his ill health. My father said that he and the other doctors agreed that Roosevelt did indeed appear to be in poor health and that he was obviously exhausted.

Long after, when I had joined the Foreign Ministry and met people who participated in the Yalta Conference, I learned that Stalin and Molotov had tried to turn Roosevelt's physical condition to their advantage. They had pressed him hard, hoping that his illness would make him more susceptible to their influence in the difficult, heated, and tense discussions. They had never had any illusions that Churchill would agree with Soviet ideas on postwar arrangements, and neither did they believe that Roosevelt could be a true friend of the Soviets, but they thought he was at least more tractable than Churchill.

My father, of course, was not privy to the talks at Yalta, but he understood that the general idea concerned the postwar world. Among the ideas to be considered, he told us, was the establishment of a new international organization for keeping peace in the world, and I believe that my interest in the UN dates from that time.

I cannot pretend that pangs of conscience, civic or personal, disturbed my adolescence after the war in any real way. For me, those were good years, most of the time untroubled ones. I played basketball and chess, collected stamps, enjoyed theatrical performances, learned how to drive our car—profiting in a bittersweet way from the fact that the war which had killed my brother had made me a pampered only child.

I graduated from high school in 1949, full of youthful enthusiasm and interested in so many things I didn't have any clear idea of what I wanted as a career. At first, I thought I wanted to be a pilot like Gennady. But I had also developed a passion for the movies and was interested in acting and, later, directing.

My parents wanted me to continue the family tradition and enter the medical faculty in Simferopol, the capital of the Crimea, a city not far from Yevpatoriya. But I was not attracted to medicine as a career.

I was sure that I wanted to go to Moscow, the center of everything, of cultural and political life, the place where the most important and interesting things were happening and where the best education was. I was still in my "film director" stage in 1949 when I visited a cousin in Moscow. He tried to convince me that I should study languages, history, law. Since the war I had developed a growing interest in politics and history. My cousin, who was a student at the Moscow State Institute of International Relations (generally known by its acronym, MGIMO), encouraged me to try for admission to this exclusive institute for future diplomatic and political cadres. The idea of being a diplomat appealed to me, and I also liked the notion that I might get to travel abroad. I didn't want to live out my life in a small town.

Bert Johnson once asked me if it was hard to gain admission to MGIMO, and I replied that the answer was both yes and no. While some students did enter on the basis of merit, by the 1970s the institute had evolved into a school for the children of the elite, who did not have to compete for admission. In Moscow it had become a standing joke that the only competition at MGIMO was among the parents—the more important and influential in the bureaucracy were the winners. I later used my own position to ensure that my son would have a place waiting for him at the institute.

MGIMO had become popular, attracting the "golden youth," the children of the highest Party and government officials, because it opened the door to travel abroad, an alluring prospect to many for no better reason than that it facilitated the acquisition of foreign goods. With expanding diplomatic relations in the post-Stalin era, traveling had become a status symbol for the upper class, and during the late sixties and seventies the level of excellence formerly characteristic of MGIMO graduates declined.

In my day, there had been at least some degree of intellectual competition. Nevertheless, the criteria for admission consisted of more than just excellent grades. My family background was good, with no record of anti-state activities, and I had received high marks in school. But there was another consideration: I had to have a special Communist Party recommendation from the Yevpatoriya committee. Returning to the Crimea, I appeared before Party officials for a long lecture on being a good Communist. By this time, of course, I was already a member of the Komsomol, the Party's youth organization. I must be aware, they said, of what an honor it was to attend the Institute of International Relations. Those so honored must never deviate, must show constant devotion to the cause of the Party and the state. I tried to look appropriately attentive and inspired, and I got the necessary Party endorsement.

8

ON SEPTEMBER 1, 1949, I BECAME A STUDENT IN THE DINGY gray four-story building half hidden by the ramparts of Krymsky Bridge which housed MGIMO.

Originally, MGIMO had been a small, special school for training diplomatic and other political cadres, with a student body of no more than a hundred. It had been an arm of Moscow University, but by 1945 it was an independent institution controlled by the Foreign Ministry, and later by the Ministry of Foreign Trade as well. The year before I became a student, three faculties were established: international law, international relations, and international economic relations. Later on, departments of Oriental studies and journalism were added. I chose the international law faculty and decided to study French, in preparation for work as a diplomat in France after graduation.

MGIMO was a place of strict discipline and heavy indoctrination. Each class had its *nachal'nik kursa* (chief of class), usually an MGB (as the KGB was then known) or former MGB officer. These people were empowered to supervise everything, including the students' personal lives. All of us were Party or Komsomol members. Neither organization defended students' rights or served their interests, but functioned as an additional overseer for the administration, ensuring strict observance of all rules, orders, and instructions. As far as I knew, the arrangement had never been questioned.

Curious as it might seem by today's Western standards, we respected the Komsomol and, even more, the Party. Our senior fellows, Party members, had either served in the Army or had worked before entering MGIMO. Their opinions influenced us, and we took their advice seriously. Without exception these men were unreserved believers in the rightness of the Party cause. We did not know that in fact the Party was virtually moribund as a political movement, having submitted to Stalin's personal control.

The curriculum was strenuous. Besides a basic university course in law, history, economics, literature, etc., MGIMO provided specialized courses in a number of fields, as well as intensive foreign-language studies. Underlying everything was a thorough program in the fundamentals of Marxist-Leninist theory, its philosophy of dialectical and historical materialism, political economy, and scientific Communism. Our zealous study bore the expected fruit, and in the main we trusted the validity of Marxism-Leninism's basic postulates.

On the other hand, however, one could not help but see that Marxism or its Leninist version was not always consistent, that it did not explain complex and diverse realities, as it purported to do. Like many others, I was aware of the discrepancies between Marxist-Leninist theory and its practical application in the Soviet Union. Nevertheless, for most of us, belief in the system remained fundamentally intact. We trusted Marxism-Leninism, despite its contradictions, because we assumed that there was no perfect social theory and because we knew so little about the functioning of other societies.

Still, we asked our professors why certain Communist "truths," such as the gradual transformation of the state into a popular self-government, the abolition of a monetary system, the abundance of material benefits for the population, had not been implemented.

Their responses varied widely. Usually, the teachers said that since our experiment in building Communism was unprecedented, theory had to be adjusted to practical necessities. Or they would simply instruct us to apply the dialectical materialist method to specific Russian historical circumstances.

I tried to figure out the essence of Marxist dialectic; it was not easy to do. One evening in 1951, a group of us were in a classroom preparing for an examination in "diamat"—dialectical materialism. A friend who had been reviewing textbooks and abstracts offered his definition. Sighing deeply, he remarked, "The dialectic is amazing. With its help one can justify any evil."

Statements like that were dangerous. Friends of mine had been expelled for making such critical remarks. We had to pass examinations without challenging theories or pressing for answers to embarrassing questions. But even though we did not actively seek out problems in Soviet society, flaws continually revealed themselves. During my years of study, theories were revised many times. Facts and concepts were always being "corrected" in textbooks and lectures. As policy shifted at Stalin's whim, men and nations who had been in favor became pariahs overnight; established dogma turned into heresy. It could be disastrous to miss a lecture where the revised truth of the day was proclaimed for us to copy down.

Our professors tried to hammer into us the idea that Soviet society was ruled by the working class, the so-called dictatorship of the proletariat, the basic Marxist-Leninist concept for the transitional period from capitalism to socialism. But the proletariat was (and is) in fact despised by the elite, except for a few designated by the Party as "heroes of Socialist labor" and used for propaganda purposes. Like others, I was not blind to the fact that Soviet society was not at all the happy, prosperous Garden of Eden for workers and peasants described by our textbooks, newspapers, and magazines and as portrayed in movies and plays.

There were many facts about Marx and Marxism-Leninism, about the Russian Revolution and its leaders, that were hidden from us. None of Leon Trotsky's works was available. Before I went abroad, where I was able to read a more truthful history of the Russian Communist Party, the epithet "Judas Trotsky" was nearly all I knew about the man. Neither could we read the writings of Zinoviev, Kamenev, Bukharin, or other prominent leaders who had been labeled "traitors" and "capitulators." Likewise, only in the United States was I able to learn that Karl Marx had condemned censorship as a "moral evil that could have only evil consequences."

Our study of Marxism was narrow: we read Stalin's writings more than any others, but the curriculum also provided selections of Marx and Lenin. The works of Engels and Mao Tse-tung were more stringently regulated. The professors and mentors did not encourage us to think and analyze for ourselves as Western students are prodded to do. We were taught to accept what was official at the moment. With the exception of the basic sciences, this approach still prevails in the Soviet Union.

Naturally, there are large gaps in such an education. For this reason Soviets sometimes appear ignorant when discussing general matters with educated Westerners. But that does not matter; it is surely the safest, long-term method of preventing subversive thoughts from entering students' minds.

Official Soviet pedagogy prescribed that independent behavior or thinking means above all the ability to understand orders and carry them out in the best way possible. What this means in practical terms is that any initiative which might go beyond established limits should be viewed as dangerous, and suppressed. It is a philosophy that has in effect made many Soviets modern serfs. Of course, when my peers and I went through that particular washing machine we hardly realized all that. There were very few people around who could help open our eyes. Most of those who were active in the 1917 Revolution had been killed in the great purges of the thirties; those still alive had undergone enough suffering, individually or through observing others' misery, to keep their mouths shut about Stalin or the nature of the Soviet system.

My studies kept me in class or in the library from early morning until well into the evening six days a week. From the truant I had been as a boy, I had evolved into a young man who liked to study. It was lucky for me that I had. When I was nineteen my father died suddenly of a cerebral hemorrhage. News of his death was a terrible blow that temporarily sent me into a kind of catatonic state. I still cannot remember clearly how my relatives brought me to Yevpatoriya for his funeral. For many years thereafter I woke from dreams calling for him.

I soon found that my father's death had practical consequences as well. Within a few months of entering MGIMO I went from the security and comfort I had known for most of my childhood to near-poverty. My mother and I had only a tiny pension to share. She needed it more than I did, so money became a constant worry. As long as I made top grades in my courses I also qualified for a small government stipend.

My life soon changed again when I met Lina at a skating party in Gorky Park early in 1951. She was blond, pretty, and slender as a dancer, and full of gaiety and verve. For me it was love at first sight. Lina, short for Leongina, was a student at the Institute of Foreign Trade. We were married in June of that year, and our son, Gennady, was born a year later.

Lina's family was a mix of Belorussian, Polish, Lithuanian, and Latvian. She was born in the small village of Dzyubovo, near the borders of all four nations. Some of her cousins, uncles, and aunts considered themselves Polish; others, Belorussian or Lithuanian. They even spoke different languages. Some had been victims of police repression during the late forties and early fifties. One of her uncles, a Pole, was executed before the war with Germany; the family never knew why. Adam, another uncle, an excellent farmer, was exiled without explanation and his property confiscated. He told me his story later when, old and sick, he was allowed a visit to Moscow to see my mother-in-law. He bitterly related his grievances against the Soviets, told of their robbery of farmers and of the terror they imposed on the Lithuanian people. In the forests of western Belorussia and the Ukraine, as well as in Lithuania, Soviet troops were actually engaged in a kind of guerrilla warfare with the local people as late as the early fifties. At the time Adam told his story I was somewhat doubtful of it. It had been drummed into us at the institute that people who spread such tales had collaborated with the Nazis.

Meanwhile, I was becoming better acquainted with the capital. To obtain permission for permanent residence in Moscow is next to impossible. Citizens may come to the city for short visits, but to stay longer than one day requires permission from the local police station, which can grant or refuse it at will. When I moved to Moscow in 1949, I was given temporary residence status. Only after my marriage to Lina, who was already a Muscovite, did I obtain permanent residence.

Our first years of marriage were truly happy. We could even disregard the depressing reality of Moscow housing, the permanent shortage of space that forced us to live in a single room of a communal apartment occupied by two other families, one of which comprised nine people. We were fifteen in all, crammed into three rooms, sharing a kitchen and a bathroom that contained only a toilet and sink. In order to bathe we went to a nearby public bathhouse, which was segregated by sex.

We were lucky to possess even these squalid living quarters. Our room belonged to Lina's mother and stepfather. At the time they were living in Austria, where he worked as an engineer in industries the Soviets had seized as war reparations. From them we learned of the possibilities of living a better life, or at least a richer one, in the West. To me, life in the West seemed fascinating in its incredible diversity and opportunity. For Lina the attraction was primarily material, and although her mother's stories about Vienna and the clothing she brought back from Austria were what fed Lina's imagination, I was not immune to these seductions either.

Every year in early fall, there was a campaign at MGIMO called *na kartoshku* (for potatoes) and we were all required to go to a *kolkhoz** near Moscow to help harvest the potato crop. The *kolkhoz*'s manpower was always severely depleted, and the misery of the *kolkhozniki*, most of whom were women, was striking. Many of them lived in one-room hovels, some with dirt floors, without running water. Even places near Moscow commonly lacked electricity. Naturally, these people were not inspired to work hard for the *kolkhoz*, as almost everything harvested had to be given to the state. They preferred to expend their energies on their own small private plots to feed themselves and to sell their

---

* The abbreviated form of *kollektivnoye khozyaystvo* (collective farm). In theory, they are agricultural producers' cooperatives jointly operated by their memberships. In fact, they are controlled by the government and the Party.

produce in the unregulated peasants' market in town, where they could get high prices for good quality.

Most students knew very little about farming or harvesting crops and our assistance was marginal at best. Moreover, the campaigns interrupted our studies, and at the end of the stint everyone had to work doubly hard to catch up.

As with our "potato campaigns," my classmates and I were required to participate in elections for the local Moscow Soviet of People's Deputies, the Supreme Soviet, as propagandists or agitators. It was part of our Komsomol duties. People were indifferent to voting, and our job was to pressure them to cast their ballot early in the morning and, if possible, to achieve the 100 percent participation that the Party insisted upon. Some would grumble since all the designated candidates would be elected in any case. We tried to convince them that the candidates were the best representatives for the jobs and that more than one candidate was unnecessary since we should not copy the example of the "rotten bourgeois democracies."

I did not understand then that the Supreme Soviet, like other local Soviets, was merely a rubber-stamp body. My classmates and I believed that the voters' passive attitude indicated "antisocial elements" who should be sought out and taught to be good Soviet citizens. Yet I understood many of their complaints since I had some of my own, and I began to feel less and less sure of the proper answers to questions they put to me as a voting agitator.

One night in a Moscow restaurant, I began griping to the worst audience I could have chosen: a high-ranking KGB officer. His daughter had been a patient in the Yevpatoriya clinic, and, grateful for the special care my father had given her, the colonel invited my mother and me to dinner. I don't know whether it was the renewed grief for my father or the wine, but suddenly I started to list things I thought were wrong with Soviet society. I complained about the backwardness of our agriculture, the low living standards of Moscow workers, the slow pace of reconstruction in Yevpatoriya, the unjust repression of some of my father's medical colleagues who had been captured by the Germans and were still treated as quasi-traitors. I told him of my experiences with the election campaign. I warmed to my subject as I lectured him on things I had learned in my special study course on France, in which I had prepared an essay on the French constitutional system, particularly electoral practices. I pointed out that whatever it might be criticized for, the fact remained that in the pluralistic French political structure, the Communist Party had substantial representation in Parliament, and voters could choose among several candidates.

With the brash impertinence of youth I reminded the colonel that it was now 1951 and that the Party had not called a Congress since 1939. My mother fidgeted and glared angrily at me, but our host did not answer my questions or argue with me. Finally, he leaned across the table and spoke quietly and bluntly:

"Arkady, I was a great admirer of your father, so let me talk to you as a friend. You're young and you need some serious advice. You talk too much. Too much talk can get you into trouble. Think what you want, but keep your tongue behind your teeth. That may annoy you, but it won't kill you. Speaking too freely, on the other hand . . . well, the consequences of that can be unpleasant.

"Your father was a fine man. Don't do anything to harm his memory."

His words were like a shower of ice, and his warning hit home. But I came out of the meeting with a feeling of sadness and futility.

My law studies raised more questions in my mind. Soviet law as defined by Andrei Vyshinsky, who achieved international notoriety as prosecutor at the show trials of the 1930s, flouted or reversed most of the basic premises of justice accepted by a large part of civilization for hundreds of years. Vyshinsky's book *On the Theory of Judicial Evidence* was the basic text at MGIMO on Soviet criminal law. His main thesis was that an accused person could be sentenced if there was mere probability of his guilt; that the confession of an accused was considered conclusive proof; and that the burden of proof of innocence rested upon the accused.

Although this philosophy was distressing, I rationalized it to myself as I had the KGB's attempt to make me its accomplice when I was fourteen. Besides, I already realized that to criticize openly was dangerous. Knowledge of this sort acts as a powerful soporific upon one's conscience. These inner debates usually ended with my reminding myself that, after all, there had been a world war, a revolution, a civil war, and another world war in quick succession. And there had been other bloody revolutions and civil wars, not only in Russia but also in America and Europe, not to mention the rest of the world. But reading stories about the purges of the "enemies of the people," it was hard to imagine that so many of our revolutionary leaders had turned out to be imperialist spies and criminals.

Then, of course, I was unaware that the period of Stalin's rule that came to be known as the years of mass terror was still going on. None of us knew about the Gulags. The few who passed rumors about the camps were dismissed as crazy or as Nazi sympathizers. For us at MGIMO—at least for the overwhelming majority—there was no choice except that which had been chosen by Stalin, whom we idolized. It was not Stalin or the system that was responsible for wrongs or mistakes, but individuals. We were sure that mistakes would be corrected. We believed that spying "imperialist aggressors" were largely responsible for the many shortcomings. We cheerfully exonerated our leaders and our system because we accepted the official version that our country had been compelled to expend too many precious resources for defense during the war. We believed it because the mementos of wartime hardships and destruction were still very much in evidence all around us.

Adding to the strange climate within the Soviet Union was the tense international situation. My hope for postwar Soviet-American friendship evaporated as the cold war began. Like most of my classmates, I accepted the official reason for this: the Americans had tried to use "atomic blackmail" on us. Moreover, we knew that their leader was the bedrock anti-Communist, Harry Truman. Of him, we were prepared to believe anything.

The most promising development abroad was Mao's victory over the anti-Communists in China. We genuinely rejoiced as Moscow acknowledged Mao's proclamation of the

People's Republic of China in 1949. Soviet-Chinese misunderstandings were almost imperceptible from 1949 to 1956, when the two nations were united in a common front against imperialism. But although we and the Chinese exchange students proclaimed our brotherhood, even during this period of solidarity the Chinese, unlike students from Eastern European countries, stayed somewhat aloof. The long tradition of mistrust between our countries never entirely dissipated, even during those cordial days.

The cold war became glacial with the outbreak of the Korean War in June 1950. At first, it seemed as if Moscow was going to be quiet about it. Events of the first week of the war appeared only in the back pages of the newspapers and were described in a rather low key. But in July, the government was organizing mass meetings everywhere. The rector of our institute energetically condemned American aggression and demanded that the United States keep "hands off Korea."

Most of us at the institute were afraid that the war could lead to military confrontation with the United States, and that we might experience a repetition of World War II or worse. Some of us did not fully believe the official version that South Korea had attacked North Korea, but to share suspicions outside one's close circle was asking for trouble.

This was the heyday of spy mania. Whether on large matters or small, the government, our teachers, even we ourselves seemed to be constantly warning people about spies or accusing them of spying.

One morning in January 1953, *Pravda* published an article entitled "Arrest of Group of Saboteur-Doctors." This amazing story launched the infamous "Doctors' Plot," an anti-Semitic campaign concocted largely by Stalin. Moscow was full of rumors. Many were apparently ready to believe that Jewish doctors injected their patients with cancer-causing agents, or infected them with syphilis, or that Jewish pharmacists, denounced as American agents, gave people pills made of dried fleas.

It was so fantastic that neither Lina nor I could believe

our eyes when we read the article. From childhood I had known many of my father's Jewish colleagues, men and women who did their best for their patients. But my wife's aunt was married to a Jewish doctor, and I began to take the matter seriously when he fearfully recounted what was happening as a consequence of the article. At dinner at their apartment Lina and I tried to calm him, saying that the "plot" was probably an isolated event, undoubtedly the result of mistakes that would be corrected. But we all knew it was little consolation to him or to the rest of us.

In the following days, however, Lina and I began to feel apprehensive for another reason. The article, after all, had supposedly been written by Stalin himself. The Party leader was infallible; we had been conditioned to accept his position on all matters as the correct one. We began to doubt ourselves: could there possibly be a basis to the terrible charges made in *Pravda*?

As crude an indicator of the anti-Semitic climate as this article was, it was only later that I realized how deeply rooted anti-Semitism was in Soviet society. For example, MGIMO was closed to Jews when I was there. Likewise, it was MGIMO's policy to admit no females. They were considered poor potential diplomats; they would marry. Since it was assumed that their husbands in most cases would not be diplomats, they could not be posted abroad with their wives. Moreover, to send women diplomats alone to work abroad was to invite danger. They could fall victim to love affairs and become easy prey to the charms of imperialist intelligence services. The fact that males were not immune to such emotional entanglements was overlooked. Of course, there are no rules without exceptions, and when Molotov's daughter applied to MGIMO, she was granted admission. She opened the way for a few other women, though they are still not much welcomed there.

Jews and women are largely excluded from the Foreign Ministry as they are from MGIMO. I knew of only one Jew of ambassadorial rank who was brave enough not to hide his cultural heritage. Stalin's death less than two months after publication of the *Pravda* article saved the lives of the "plotting Jewish doctors" and averted large-scale pogroms. At that time, however, I did not draw this conclusion; my belief in Stalin was unshaken.

9

JOSEPH STALIN'S DEATH IN MARCH 1953 WAS A TERRIBLE blow. Over the years of his rule, we had been taught to revere him as the savior of the nation. Our semi-religious adulation of our *vozhd*, or "great chief," was practically limitless. Almost everyone at MGIMO had virtually memorized *The Short Biography of Stalin*, parts of which he had written himself and which portrayed him as a superman of goodness and strength. But we believed it and loved him. There was no comparable biography of Lenin at that time.

We failed to see in him the shortcomings pointed out by some Western scholars: his greed to claim much of Lenin's honor; his strong Georgian accent accompanying his dull style of speech. For us, Stalin was a spellbinding orator and we viewed his every utterance on paper as a great masterpiece. People crossing Red Square on dark evenings and noticing lighted windows in the Kremlin were often heard to comment in tones of love and admiration that Stalin was there working unceasingly for us, constantly thinking of our welfare.

In retrospect, this credulous and naïve adoration on the part of an entire nation seems unbelievable, particularly when set against the horrors Stalin perpetrated. But the Soviet poet Yevgeny Yevtushenko truly expressed the disorientation most people felt when he wrote: "A sort of general paralysis came over the country. Trained to believe that they were all in Stalin's care, people were lost and bewildered without him. All Russia wept. And so did I. We wept sincerely, tears of grief—and perhaps also tears of fear for the future.''

The day of Stalin's funeral was bleak and wintry. I stood with the crowd in Red Square. From a distance I saw the procession of Soviet leaders and some of Stalin's relatives, including his son Vasily, an Air Force general. They followed Stalin's casket, which had been placed on a gun carriage. Malenkov, Beria, and Molotov delivered speeches eulogizing the late dictator. Beria, with a big black hat pulled down over his eyes and his heavy, typically Russian overcoat, looked as sinister as Rasputin. While he was speaking, I noticed some confusion near Stalin's coffin. I couldn't see what was happening, but later I learned that Vasily Stalin, who was dead drunk, had shouted at Beria, calling him vile names and, worse, accusing him of murdering his father.

Vasily's disorderly behavior was often the subject of Moscow gossip while Stalin was alive. There were stories that although he was drunk constantly, he would get into his car and drive as fast as possible. He was involved in several accidents in which people were killed. He seemed to lead a charmed life in not killing himself in these crashes, and he always got off with a reprimand and light punishment from his father.

This time, however, Vasily had to pay the bill. Beria did not forgive or forget. Soon after the incident at the funeral, Vasily was involved in a barroom brawl. Beria saw to it that he was dishonorably discharged from the Air Force and sentenced to eight years in prison. After that, he was exiled to Kazan, where he died of alcoholism in 1962.

We were not surprised when Georgy M. Malenkov became both Party First Secretary and Prime Minister. His prominence in the years just before Stalin's death, as well as that of Beria and Vyacheslav M. Molotov, had raised them up as the first triumvirate of the post-Stalin leadership. There were rumors that Malenkov was Lenin's nephew. It was said that Malenkov himself had concocted this story as a means of establishing his claim to be Stalin's legitimate successor. He quickly began some reshaping of domestic

89

and foreign policy. I remember the eager response to Malenkov's pronouncements favoring higher living standards, improvement of agriculture, and alleviation of state-imposed burdens on farmers.

MGIMO students speculated endlessly about what changes might come of all this turmoil, and there was talk of a power struggle going on within the Party Presidium. Nikita Khrushchev, who was much more influential than we students suspected, continued to consolidate his forces, particularly those in the Party apparatus, and was working simultaneously against both Malenkov and Beria.

Early in June 1953, my class was sent to our military-training camp. One morning, when we mustered as usual for roll call in the yard, we noticed that Beria's portrait was missing from those of the Presidium members usually standing beside the flag. This was puzzling: he was well known, second only to Malenkov. Our training officer said nothing, but we understood that something serious had happened. On July 10, after we had returned to Moscow, the press reported that Beria had perpetrated "criminal activities against the Party and the state" and had attempted to place his Ministry of Internal Affairs above the government and the Party. He was arrested at a joint meeting of the Party Presidium and Council of Ministers and later shot.

I graduated from MGIMO in 1954. Although I had liked being at the institute, I had also looked forward to an end to the monotonous and rigorous undergraduate program. In those days, MGIMO had a prestigious reputation on account of its strong academic program and the number of outstanding professors on its staff. During the ensuing decade, it trained a large proportion of the currently emerging politicians and bureaucrats who will undoubtedly play important roles in the U.S.S.R.'s destiny beyond the end of the twentieth century. Wherever one looks now in various branches of the political structure, MGIMO graduates are found in prominent positions, many approaching top official status. This is particularly true of the Foreign Ministry, where two deputy ministers—Anatoly Kovalev and my classmate Viktor Komplektov—numerous ambassadors abroad, and chiefs of many key departments are alumni. Equally, in the Central Committee, in the Academy of Sciences, and in political journalism, MGIMO graduates are numerous, influential, and well known in the West.

My intention was to do postgraduate work. However, one day the chief of the institute's personnel office gave me a message requesting me to go to an address in Moscow. He said I would be given a pass to meet with someone to discuss my future. The address was a large building in the Sadovoe Koltso section of Moscow. Upon entering it I was struck by the tight security. My pass was inspected thoroughly at several stops in the building, and I was accompanied by a guard who led me to an office where a KGB major greeted me. I recognized him as KGB because the agency's epaulets are distinctive. He was polite and well mannered. He invited me to sit down and said, "You have good recommendations from the institute. What would you think if we asked you to work with the KGB?"

I was surprised at the offer; I had never expressed the slightest interest in such a career. I told him I wanted to continue my education as a postgraduate student. He said he understood, but he advised me to consider his proposal seriously. I agreed. After a few days, with some apprehension, I asked MGIMO's personnel office to tell the major that I had decided to go on with my studies. To my relief, the KGB did not try to stop me. Its influence had been seriously undermined by Beria's fall.

As undergraduates, my classmates and I knew little of the world beyond the U.S.S.R. It might be assumed that we had access to information published in the West since we were privileged students of the diplomatic institute, but such was not the case. I had never read any "bourgeois" newspaper like *The New York Times* or *Le Monde*. Such materials were permitted only to postgraduate students, and then with many limitations. As for listening to foreign radio broadcasts, that was a punishable offense.

As a postgraduate student, however, I soon began a double education along simultaneous if diverging tracks. My second education was conducted in the special section of the library where Western newspapers, magazines, and books were kept. The librarian took a liking to me, and in violation of the rules she let me browse in the stacks where only authorized pass-holders were permitted. What I read began to give me a better understanding of the world as it was. Problems, ideas, and even solutions unknown to me created additional confusion and doubt about the validity of many things I had been taught.

Western legal periodicals like the French *Revue Générale du Droit International Publique* and others contained annexes which chronicled international events. Moreover, they had records of various agreements and full texts of speeches by heads of nations. There were even some of Hitler's statements that the censors had evidently overlooked. My understanding of recent history took a quantum leap.

But my greatest influence was Professor Vsevolod Nikolaevich Durdenevsky. In my senior year at MGIMO, I felt incredibly lucky when he agreed to be my thesis supervisor. He approved my proposal for a study of Soviet disarmament policy, and under his forceful and sophisticated guidance I produced a paper that was original but safe.

Durdenevsky believed in free academic inquiry. Thin, somewhat stooped, formal in his manner, and stringent in the demands he made on his students, he had been raised in the pre-revolutionary tradition of scholarship, and he continued to subscribe to its values. Though he occupied a senior legal adviser's position in the Foreign Ministry, he never joined the Communist Party. His expertise shielded him from politics, but his post gave him deep insights into the making of Soviet foreign policy. He seemed to me to have the best of both worlds. He had the freedom to pursue his own research and also the authority to advise those who were responsible for actual policymaking. He stood outside the bureaucracy, but he could influence its direction. I envied him and wanted to be like him.

Since Moscow's housing shortage affected MGIMO offices as well, Durdenevsky began to invite me to his home to discuss my project. There, in a study overflowing with books, my real education began. Durdenevsky refused to let me simply parrot Soviet scholarship, such as it was, on disarmament. He insisted that I read widely and draw my own conclusions.

Durdenevsky's role as my mentor was not purely academic. We became good enough friends so that he sometimes spoke of the closed world of the Foreign Ministry. I learned from him that Malenkov had been tainted by the investigation aimed at Beria. In this messy affair, Beria countercharged that since Malenkov had been Stalin's right hand in persecuting honest Communists in the great purges, he was guiltier of wrongdoing. From Durdenevsky I also heard of Khrushchev's increasingly important role in the leadership. He finally replaced Malenkov as First Secretary in September 1953.

Durdenevsky said that Nikita Khrushchev had insisted upon a substantial revision of Stalin's foreign policy, going further than Malenkov and Molotov. Too experienced to be anything but cautious in his views, Durdenevsky nonetheless did not dampen my own rising hope that Soviet policy in this field and others, after years of numbing rigidity, was beginning to move and change.

I was not alone in my feelings of hope. The students at MGIMO felt a new dynamism in the country, and we believed that things were going to be better. Many of my classmates developed expectations built around a very old Russian idea, that of an opening of our society to the energies and resources of the West. Khrushchev encouraged this kind of thinking with his travels—to Yugoslavia, India, Britain—with the cordial, if inconclusive Geneva summit meeting in 1955, and with enthusiastic efforts to break new economic ground at home that were as stirring as they were unsuccessful.

I had become interested in disarmament from reading articles about it in Soviet publications. At the same time, I wasn't sure it was worthwhile to spend a great deal of time on the subject. The record of talks on the issue was neither fascinating nor encouraging. Moreover, it was not easy to follow the exact course of progress in the negotiations. The huge piles of documents on disarmament between the two world wars that I found in the institute's library were not even indexed properly. It was obvious that there was not much curiosity about this material. The verbatim records of the UN Atomic Energy Commission, covering the immediate period following World War II, were more coherent chronologically but many documents were missing. Andrei Vyshinsky's denunciations of Bernard Baruch's plan for international control of atomic energy sounded convincing. But many of Baruch's proposals were also reasonable. The new element that lured me to the subject was what Durdenevsky told me.

From him I got the feeling that there were new Soviet disarmament initiatives in the wind. Again, he mentioned Khrushchev as their main promoter. I agreed to write my dissertation on the subject in anticipation of that hope. Durdenevsky and I collaborated on an article, "The Illegality of the Use of Atomic Weapons and International Law," published in the spring of 1955. Later my study "Problems of Atomic Energy and Peaceful Coexistence" was published. So my involvement in disarmament was to preoccupy me professionally for a number of years.

It was my study of these issues that led to my first meeting with Andrei Gromyko. Gromyko's son and my fellow graduate student, Anatoly, proposed in 1955 that we write a joint article for the journal *International Life* on the role of parliaments in the struggle for peace and disarmament. *International Life* is the semi-official organ of the Foreign Ministry; Andrei Gromyko was (and is) its chief editor. Anatoly suggested that we first show the article to his father. I eagerly agreed. Gromyko was the First Deputy Foreign Minister, well known both in the Soviet Union and abroad as an eminent diplomat.

He received us cordially at his apartment, a spacious set of rooms in one of the central Moscow buildings reserved for high government and Party officials. Although his quarters were large, they were so impersonal as to seem modest. The furniture was heavy, dark, and highly lacquered; the plush upholstery was somber.

Gromyko, however, stood out against this nondescript

background. He looked exactly as he did in photographs, strong and well proportioned, somewhat above average height, with thin, tightly drawn lips, bushy eyebrows, and coal-black hair. His intent brown eyes, his whole appearance, reflected authority and self-confidence. He spoke in a resonant semi-bass voice, with measured inflection, articulating every word with precision and weighing every phrase. As I recall this first meeting with Gromyko, I am amazed at how little the years have changed him.

After reading our manuscript attentively, Gromyko gave it his approval, making a few brief comments, sensible and to the point. In the conversation that followed, Gromyko impressed me with the warmth of his remarks about the wartime Soviet-American alliance against Hitler's Germany. At the time Gromyko critiqued our article, the iciest days of the cold war were behind us, but his observations regarding the necessity and the possibility of restoring good, if not truly friendly relations with the United States went considerably beyond the official Soviet stand on the matter.

Finally, Gromyko asked me what I intended to do when I finished my graduate work. I told him I was attracted to research but at the same time I had great interest in foreign affairs. "It's always useful to engage in research work," he observed, "and it is completely possible to combine it with diplomatic service." Anatoly told me later that his father, despite the burden of his work at the ministry, had managed to find time to write his doctoral dissertation on the dominance of the American dollar in the capitalist world.

Anatoly resembled his father in many respects—in appearance and in character. He possessed the same tenacity, excellent memory, attention to detail, and dry manner as his father. However, neither his personal life nor his career has been gratifying. His first wife left him for Anastas Mikoyan's son, whose father was a more prominent figure than Gromyko at the time. Anatoly wanted very much to be a professional diplomat, but his father's position caused him some difficulty. He did hold several posts abroad, but never rose very high in the diplomatic service. He served for a time in Great Britain, and then as minister-counselor in the embassies in the United States and East Germany. Even given the rampant nepotism common among leading hierarchs, it was too much for the Soviet elite to place their sons or daughters under the direct supervision of their parents.

As postgraduate students in the mid-fifties, Anatoly and I shared many views regarding developments in the Soviet Union. I remember that we both awaited the Party Congress of February 1956 with great interest. So many important events had taken place since the last Congress in 1952: Stalin was dead, Beria's exposure had resulted in a less autonomous and freewheeling KGB; new trends in domestic and foreign policy were evident.

At the Congress, Khrushchev's Central Committee report and the speeches of other leaders contained a number of new conclusions and assessments. Everyone was struck by the open criticism of past policies at home and abroad and by public recognition of our shortcomings in economics, agriculture, and the ideological arena.

In his report, Khrushchev mentioned Stalin's name only once, saying that "death removed from our ranks J. V. Stalin." But he hinted at Stalin's "cult of personality" and the "mistakes" he made. These were alluded to as well in reports by other leaders at the Congress, particularly that of Mikoyan, who was much more outspoken than Khrushchev. Mikoyan's speech was especially interesting to me because it answered questions that had been glossed over by our professors at MGIMO. He frankly criticized Stalin's book *Economic Problems of Socialism in the U.S.S.R.,* every sentence of which we had been compelled to learn. He said that the book "did not explain the complicated and contradictory phenomena of modern capitalism, or the fact that capitalist production has increased in many countries since the war." He went further, stating that "we do not subject the facts and figures to a thorough examination, and we are often satisfied for purposes of propaganda to select isolated facts suggesting an impending crisis or illustrating the impoverishment of the workers [in capitalist countries], but we do not provide any many-sided and profound assessment of developments taking place in other countries."

In Mikoyan's report, the validity of all our lectures and textbooks was undermined: "The majority of our theoreticians are busy repeating and playing with old quotations, formulas, and postulates. What kind of science could there be without innovation?" he asked rhetorically. "It is rather a schoolboy's exercise, but not science, because science is a creative process, and not the repetitions of hacks."

What was said at that Party Congress confirmed my suspicions that in many cases it was impossible to find the truth in officially approved works or textbooks. But all this was trivial compared to the revelation that was to come.

After the Congress the secretary of our postgraduate Party bureau told me that a closed meeting of Party members had been scheduled. A very important document was to be read to our local Party organization. I was not in the Party yet, but I was considered a Komsomol member in good standing, so he arranged for me to be admitted to the meeting.

The secretary opened by saying that he was going to read aloud another report Khrushchev had made at the Congress, one that had not been and would not be published. He also stressed that the contents were strictly for our information and must be considered secret. There was a buzz of excitement in the room as he slowly began reading the report in his clear voice:

> "After Stalin's death the Central Committee of the Party began to implement a policy of explaining concisely and consistently that it is impermissible and foreign to the spirit of Marxism-Leninism to elevate one person, to transform him into a superman possessing supernatural characteristics akin to those of a god. . . . Such a belief about a man, and specifically about Stalin, was cultivated among us for many years." *

There was even more excitement when he said that long ago Lenin had detected Stalin's negative characteristics, which had led to grave consequences. He read:

> "In December 1922, in a letter to the Party Congress, Vladimir Ilyich [Lenin] wrote: 'After taking over the position of Secretary

* Quoted from the text released by the U.S. Department of State on June 4, 1956.

General, Comrade Stalin accumulated in his hands immeasurable power and I am not certain whether he will always be able to use this power with the required care.'

"This letter—a political document of tremendous importance, known in the Party history as Lenin's 'testament'—was distributed among the delegates to the Twentieth Party Congress. . . . Vladimir Ilyich said: 'Because of this, I propose that the comrades consider the method by which Stalin would be removed from this position. . . .' "

Of course, none of us had any idea that Lenin's testament existed. It was not included in his collected writings. It was beyond imagining that such an important document could have been omitted from his works. I wondered what else had been excluded.

We listened further:

"Stalin originated the concept 'enemy of the people' . . . This led to glaring violations of revolutionary legality, and to the fact that many entirely innocent persons . . . became victims."

There it was. But these revelations brought other confusions. Were only Stalin and Beria responsible for all these crimes? Could one believe that Stalin's collaborators—Zhdanov, Malenkov, Molotov, Kaganovich, Bulganin, and Khrushchev himself—did not know what was going on and were not accomplices?

For a long time there had been whispers about Stalin's character and his treatment of people, and as I listened to the reading I recalled a conversation with Aleksandr Piradov, one of my professors. He had introduced me to a colleague at MGIMO, Grigory Morozov. Piradov said that Morozov was Svetlana Stalin's first husband, and a Jew. Curiosity impelled me to ask Morozov his opinion of Stalin as a father-in-law. He replied that Stalin had not wanted to meet him. Stalin not only disliked him because he was a Jew, but finally compelled his daughter to divorce him, and promptly married her off to Zhdanov's son. Stalin did not send Morozov to a concentration camp, but he devised a cruel punishment for him: he decreed that Morozov was not to be given employment anywhere. The poor man earned his living through articles he wrote under assumed names, his former classmates secretly helping him get them published. After Stalin died, Morozov was able to join the MGIMO professorial staff as well as the International Economic Relations Institute of the Academy of Sciences.

There was no discussion of the report after the secretary finished. His suggestion to approve "totally and without reservation" the Leninist Party line adopted by the Congress was accepted with stunned unanimity. There was none of the lively conversation that usually followed a class or a meeting. I tried to hold on to the encouragement Khrushchev had offered in saying that all this belonged to the past and now one could expect changes in Soviet society. There would be more democracy and frankness, an end to hypocrisy, and changes in domestic and foreign policy. I tried to believe that Khrushchev personally was not associated with Stalin's enormities. After all, he had had the courage to reveal the truth.

Like many Russians, I was eagerly reading Ilya Ehrenburg's novel *Thaw*. It was an appeal for more intellectual freedom in the U.S.S.R., and its title was applied to the period in Soviet history known as "Khrushchev's thaw," when he began his limited liberalization policy after Stalin's death.

Vladimir Dudintsev's *Not by Bread Alone* also became a very popular novel after it was published in installments in the magazine *Novy Mir* in 1956. Its central thesis was a defense of the individual's right to stand against officialdom. It would have been a statement of unthinkable and fatal daring in Stalin's day.

There was also a positive change in my own life. By 1955, with the fees from the articles I was now able to get published, a larger scholarship, and the proceeds from the sale of a piano, Lina and I managed to find a less crowded though still communal apartment. Its windows looked out on factory smokestacks, but we were to have a real bathroom and only one elderly couple with whom to share it. At this turning point in my life—the end of my studies and budding career prospects—I was optimistic. Khrushchev's policy innovations and my happiness with Lina and Gennady, by now a handsome and inquisitive little boy, strengthened my belief that the future was bright.

10

I WAS NEARLY FINISHED WITH MY STUDIES AND WRITING the final parts of my dissertation when I was called to the Foreign Ministry to talk with Vladimir Suslov, assistant to Semyon Tsarapkin, head of the department in charge of United Nations and disarmament affairs (OMO). Suslov, a lean, hazel-eyed man with a balding, egg-shaped head, greeted me warmly. "We know your work at the institute on disarmament," he told me, "and I've read your articles. Disarmament is becoming an important area, and we'd like you to join us in the work."

I was interested, but I hesitated. I enjoyed scholarly life, though I knew that Soviet academics had only limited access to information and to the makers of policy. But while I wanted the inside knowledge I could obtain in the ministry, I disliked the bureaucratic system. From classmates already serving as junior diplomats, I had learned of the frustrating slowness of promotions, the rigid, almost paramilitary discipline, and the hierarchy that sent orders down but was indifferent to suggestions from below, owing to the lingering influence of Party hacks who had filled ministry jobs as fast as Stalin's purges decimated the ranks of the more professional diplomats of the old school.

Yet part of me—the part that had always yearned to see Paris, New York, the West—pushed me toward accepting Suslov's offer. Lina pushed too. She cited classmates of mine who already had foreign assignments and who had brought back Western luxuries to brighten the drabness of

Soviet life. They were happy and on their way to a wider, more inviting life. "It's a wonderful opportunity," she pleaded. "It's what you've been working for, studying for all these years. You'll do a fine job, and we'll have a chance to live decently, to have good things, to get ahead at last."

Before I could reply to Suslov, however, the Foreign Ministry called again, this time with a request that I talk with Semyon Tsarapkin. I found him posing like a tsar behind his desk, strutting amid the disorder of an office piled with heaps of papers and books, ornamented by a battery of telephones, and infused with an oppressive sense of his abrasive personality.

"We're starting a new policy that will mean serious negotiating on disarmament," he began. "It's one thing to study such matters, but it's something else to be involved in the real work. Why don't you give it a try? Come on for a time and find out for yourself how you like it and whether you want to stay."

He offered me an attaché's rank, one step up the ladder from the normal beginner's slot. With no further hesitation I accepted. I joined the ministry in October 1956.

My first problem was finding a desk where I could work. I had not realized this would be a long process. I discovered that throughout the Soviet bureaucracy there were always many more people than desks, and that they were often forced into sharing these workplaces. I was lucky to be assigned to the table of someone who was temporarily in London, but I waited more than six months for my own desk.

The twenty-three-story building on Smolensk Square which houses the Foreign Ministry also contains the Ministry of Foreign Trade. The building is a cold, rough concretion of towers and wings in the Stalinist architectural style. No expense was spared on the building's flamboyant exterior embellishments, but its designers gave little attention to practical amenities within. Cavernous, echoing, dun-colored corridors with dark parquet floors and a bank of six ancient elevators consume more than 40 percent of the inner space. Rows of offices line the corridors, large, high-ceilinged rooms into which six to ten or more people are jammed together among their desks and filing cabinets with no partitions to provide privacy or respite from the general clatter of telephones and typewriters.

There were several security checkpoints in the building. The first was at the main entrance doors and a second at the entrance to the Foreign Ministry's elevators. One of my colleagues explained to me that the system existed because otherwise officers of the Foreign Trade Ministry, which occupied the first six floors of the building, could "penetrate" our ministry, and those "tradesmen" could not be trusted. There was a third checkpoint at the elevator to the seventh floor, the location of Gromyko's offices and those of the upper echelons of the ministry hierarchy. Here, the corridors were paneled with polished wood and the noise muffled by carpeted floors.

I was assigned to a tenth-floor office occupied by three other junior-level officers. We all belonged to a special *referentura* (section) on disarmament that had been recently established in OMO. My immediate superior, Pavel Shakov, was chief of the *referentura*. He was an old-guard ministry official and a diplomat of considerable experience. He was supposed to explain my duties to me, but I received only the most cursory idea of what these would involve. My wait for an assignment took longer than anticipated because nearly everyone's attention was focused not on disarmament, but, in quick succession, on events in Poland and Hungary.

My friend and former MGIMO schoolmate Vitaly had been working at our embassy in Warsaw for several years. On one of his visits home we met for dinner in a restaurant to reminisce about our school days and talk politics, as we always had. Vitaly said that, in October, Wladislaw Gomulka had been elected First Secretary of the Polish Party's Central Committee in defiance of the Soviet leadership. It was unheard of, but Khrushchev and other Soviet leaders had felt constrained to accept Gomulka because they were loath to suppress the Poles by force. That would have been risky in Poland; it was a large country with a big population. Moreover, there was something beyond Poland's size. "You know," Vitaly added, "the Poles hate us; they would fight at the drop of a hat." I knew it was true. Nevertheless, he stressed that the Polish Communist Party was in control

102

of the situation, limiting its concessions to a few domestic matters. There was no danger that Poland could break away from us.

I had another confirmation of Polish feelings from another friend and classmate, Sasha, a nephew of the famous Soviet marshal Konstantin Rokossovsky. The marshal was a brilliant commander who had fallen victim to Stalin's prewar military purges and was sent to prison because of his Polish ancestry. When the Nazis attacked the Soviet Union, however, Stalin was forced to reinstate Rokossovsky. In 1949, Stalin made him the Polish Defense Minister. Sasha told me the Polish Army hated its "Russian marshal" and was humiliated by the appointment. The Poles made several attempts on Rokossovsky's life, and his visits to army units were rare and under heavy Soviet security guard.

More shocking to me and some of my friends at the ministry were the events in Hungary. The anti-Soviet, anti-Communist explosion in Hungary immediately following the "Polish October" was an attempt at real revolution. Hungarian rebels had moral support and sympathy from the West but no military help. The Hungarians fought bravely but the uprising was crushed, with considerable loss of life among both Hungarians and Russians.

Like many of my colleagues, I thought that Imre Nagy had gone too far in declaring Hungary's withdrawal from the Warsaw Pact and his attempt at disrupting that nation's socialist system. Nevertheless, I was shaken by the brutality of the reprisals. If Khrushchev was really in favor of some democratization and liberalization in the U.S.S.R., why had the Hungarians been dealt with so cruelly? I began to wonder whether Khrushchev was actually in full control of the Party Presidium. Perhaps there was some strong, hidden opposition to his de-Stalinization policy.

Later on, another MGIMO classmate, who had served at our embassy in Budapest, enlightened me. It was in this context that I first heard of Yuri V. Andropov, our Ambassador to Hungary. My friend, who was close to Andropov and worked directly with him, praised him unstintingly. Although my friend was often florid in his descriptions, it was obvious that he really admired his boss. I was curious about why he was able to excite my friend, and I asked him what was so impressive about Andropov. He responded that although Andropov was relatively young, only in his early forties, he had been very sure about what to do during the erupting crisis in Budapest. "He was so calm; even while bullets were flying—when everyone else at the embassy felt like we were in a besieged fortress."

My friend also told me that before and during the critical days of the uprising Moscow's instructions were sometimes confusing and occasionally betrayed a lack of understanding of what was really going on. Andropov's advice to Moscow, however, was extensive and served as a basis for decisions. For instance, he had warned the Party Presidium earlier that the Hungarian Communist Party leader, Mátyás Rákosi, should be removed from his post because he had already lost authority. According to my friend, it was also Andropov who "saw through" Imre Nagy before Moscow did.

"Do you think some of the fighting could have been prevented?" I asked. He responded with his own question: "Do you think we could have done otherwise?" I began to listen with interest each time Andropov's name came up in the years afterward.

Eventually, my harried boss, Pavel Shakov, got around to putting me to work. My first assignment was an unglamorous task of housecleaning: organizing a rat's nest of files that had been neglected literally for years. Before the new section's creation, there had been only two diplomats actually dealing with disarmament—Aleksei Popov, hard of hearing and dim-brained, and Leonid Ignatiyev, whose job was to keep the files in order. Ignatiyev was the most disorganized man I have ever met. The records in his charge looked as if a war had been fought through them. It was hard to believe that disarmament negotiations could proceed at all in the face of the archives' neglect and disarray. Actually, during the years of "ban the bomb" sloganeering, not much order was really necessary since the dry facts contained in the records were ignored in favor of simplistic propaganda appeals.

Soviet diplomats needed a readily available compilation of basic documents on disarmament, a record of proposals and negotiations over the years, material that was easy to obtain in the West but had not been collected in any systematic form in Moscow. My project to get the documents in order was approved under a condition of secrecy. The documentation could be printed only for official use. Soviet censors would permit no wider distribution.

That task stirred my interest in the general organization and functions of the ministry. It also gave me the opportunity to talk about these things with some of the old-timers.

After the October Revolution the foreign service was headed by such figures as Trotsky, Chicherin, Litvinov, Molotov, and Vyshinsky. It was known as the People's Commissariat of Foreign Affairs.

In 1939, Maksim Litvinov, an old Bolshevik intellectual whose pro-Anglo-American orientation conflicted with Stalin's and Molotov's policies concerning Nazi Germany, was removed from his post as People's Commissar of Foreign Affairs. Following Litvinov's dismissal there was a mass annihilation of the apparatus of the commissariat as part of the purges. Almost 90 percent of the diplomatic personnel of all ranks were shot, imprisoned, sent to concentration camps, or forced to find other employment. Litvinov himself was lucky: he went to Washington as ambassador.

The commissariat was filled with new people assigned on the basis of emergency Party conscription. Diplomacy was conducted by men utterly lacking in experience or competence. What was of prime concern was one's Stalinist orthodoxy: an uncompromising attitude toward "enemies of the people," and freedom from any pernicious Western influence. Rapidly run through a brief training program, many new diplomats were incapable of performing complex duties.

After Stalin died, the professional standards of Soviet diplomatic personnel improved. Most of the poorly educated, improperly prepared people recruited into the Foreign Ministry in the late thirties were gradually replaced by MGIMO graduates trained for the service or graduates of other institutions selected by local Party organizations. They were trained at the Higher Diplomatic School, later renamed the Diplomatic Academy.

Within the ministry, the Foreign Minister is absolute ruler. Most junior and mid-level officials have never had a chance to talk with him although they may have spent their entire careers at the ministry. When I joined the foreign service, Dmitri Shepilov, an economist by education and profession, was Foreign Minister. He had begun to reorganize the ministry and reorient its approach, stressing the importance of economic problems in domestic and foreign policy.

This "period of economism," as the Shepilov era was known, was within the spirit of Khrushchev's thinking. I remember the consternation it caused among the older generation of diplomats, many of whom had forgotten the details of Marxist-Leninist political economy, as they began to pore over textbooks and the classics of Marxism. This was not merely subservience or striving to conform to the new leadership; Shepilov seriously intended to educate the ministry's personnel. He issued an order requiring all employees to retake courses in political economy. Furthermore, we had to pass an examination on the subject.

At the beginning of my work in OMO, I was unaware of how lucky I was to be part of that group. The "Germanists," the "disarmament boys," the "Americanists," the "Europeans" (chiefly concerned with Soviet-French relations), and a small group of others belonged to a privileged caste. We were envied by the "provincials," who frequently spent their entire careers in Africa and Asia. Not only was this an unattractive fate because of the unpleasant climates, low salaries, and lack of consumer goods, but diplomats assigned to these areas seldom advanced to senior positions. The privileged ones, on the other hand, were almost constantly in close proximity to the leadership. Gromyko knew many of them personally, remembered their names, and fostered the careers of the most able, rapidly advancing them up the career ladder. This group formed the backbone of the younger generation in the ministry.

I had learned much about past disarmament negotiations during my postgraduate years and in working on my dissertation. It was only then that I properly grasped the new reality of the nuclear age. When Hiroshima and Nagasaki were bombed there was little about it in the Soviet media. Stalin had not wanted to frighten the people or, more particularly, admit that the United States possessed such revolutionary weapons. Furthermore, acceptance of this factual circumstance was contrary to the dogmas of Marxism-Leninism which deny that any kind of new weapons, destructive though they might be, could play a role of their own to effect a change in the historical process.

The Soviet Union exploded its first atomic bomb in 1949, ending the United States' atomic monopoly. In contrast to the muted reaction regarding the detonations over Japan, the Soviets congratulated themselves loudly this time. At the end of World War II, American experts had predicted that it would take ten or fifteen years before the Soviet Union would be able to create its own atomic weapons. After only four years the U.S.S.R. had become a nuclear power. I wondered why the American experts had been so mistaken, and concluded that, in the West, Soviet achievements in atomic physics before the war had been underestimated. Moreover, if it had not been for Stalin's lack of understanding of its importance, the Soviet Union might have produced a bomb much earlier.

Efforts by Soviet atomic spies also helped speed things up. Most significant of all, however, was that the Soviet system lent itself to complete concentration on any area the leaders wished to make a top priority. In the immediate postwar period, thousands of citizens died of starvation and millions more were deprived of even the most elementary necessities, but this did not prevent Stalin from giving first call on vital resources to the creation of an atomic bomb.

Only after the U.S.S.R. had built up its own impressive nuclear potential did the post-Stalin leadership show any readiness to talk about arms-control measures for the purpose of achieving practical results. While I was still at MGIMO, the Soviet posture on disarmament changed considerably—largely due to the efforts of Nikita Khrushchev —and a number of substantial concessions to the West were made. This brought about a rapprochement between the positions of the Western nations and the Soviet Union.

On a more subjective level, I enjoyed working at the ministry and was fortunate to receive an early promotion to the rank of third secretary. Tsarapkin now liked to joke about my previous hesitations regarding a government career, and promised further promotions if I continued to work hard.

During the spring and summer of 1957, serious and pragmatic negotiations continued in London in the UN Disarmament Commission's five-power subcommittee (the United States, the U.S.S.R., the United Kingdom, France, and Canada). Nearly all my superiors were at these sessions in a delegation headed by Deputy Foreign Minister Valerian Zorin. My job was to monitor the London negotiations. As a third secretary, I had no access to the code cables Zorin sent to the ministry, and without them it was nearly impossible to do my job. I complained to Tsarapkin, who shrugged and reminded me of the rule that only first secretaries or above were permitted access to such information. However, he did agree to show me, unofficially, the most important of Zorin's cables.

By early April, I was participating fairly regularly in Tsarapkin's meetings, which sometimes lasted late into the evening. High-ranking members of the General Staff as well as prominent scientists from the Medium Machine Building Ministry, the governmental branch responsible for the production of nuclear weapons, joined the meetings. It was the first time I had a chance to take an active part in formulating proposals officially submitted in London by our delegation.

I believed that Khrushchev was making a genuine effort to reach an accord with the United States and other Western countries on at least some measures for limiting the arms race, and that he was moving our country in the right direction. Although at that point it was not easy to evaluate what was good or bad in his policies, it was evident that Khrushchev, refreshingly, was at least trying to find new ways to circumvent those die-hard conservatives who resisted any change in the old order.

When Zorin reported from London that his American counterpart, Harold E. Stassen, had expressed a willingness to discuss new Soviet proposals with us privately, and when he presented an informal paper to Zorin indicating that the American position on several points had become close to that of the U.S.S.R., I was very pleased. My pleasure, unfortunately, turned out to be premature: soon after, Stassen withdrew his paper and the American position hardened. In his memoirs President Eisenhower says Stassen had shown Zorin the paper without prior coordination with the American allies, thus provoking an angry reaction from British Prime Minister Harold Macmillan.* In any event, I was convinced that the Soviet Union was more interested in real progress than the United States was.

Tsarapkin told me that Khrushchev was very bitter about the United States' position and that of its allies. No wonder: Khrushchev was facing opposition not only from the parties to the London negotiations but in his own ranks as well. Moscow was rife with gossip about intrigues and power plays in the closed Central Committee plenum session. I heard that Molotov, Kaganovich, Malenkov, and Foreign Minister Shepilov had broken away from Khrushchev in the Party Presidium and had formed their own clique, labeled the "anti-Party group." It looked at first as if they might be successful in their attempted palace coup, but in June 1957, after the Party Presidium's decision to dismiss him, Khrushchev retaliated. He quickly convened a plenary session of the Central Committee, his stronghold of support. The Defense Minister, Marshal Georgy Zhukov, who supported Khrushchev, rounded up members of the Central Committee from the distant provinces, flying them to Moscow on military transport planes. Khrushchev won at the meeting of the plenum. Malenkov, Molotov, Kaganovich, and the hapless Shepilov were stripped of their positions and accused of anti-Party factionalism. Andrei Gromyko became Foreign Minister.

At our Party meeting at the ministry a resolution supporting Khrushchev and condemning the anti-Party group was adopted unanimously. A vote was unnecessary; no one would have dared vote against or even abstain on a resolution based on any decision of the Central Committee.

The Stalinists who survived the purges of the thirties were

---

* Dwight D. Eisenhower, *Waging Peace, 1956–61* (Doubleday, 1965), pp. 472–74.

the sternest guardians of Communist doctrine, and they still occupied strong positions in the ministry. One of them was my superior, the deputy head of our department, Kirill Novikov. Along with Tsarapkin, he sat behind Stalin during the Potsdam Conference in 1945. Intelligent and rigid, he was careful not to advertise his convictions. However, as we got to know each other, sometimes after the working day he would reveal himself. "In Stalin's time," he would reminisce, "we had real order. There were none of these rhetorical flourishes, and vacillations from side to side were not permitted. Stalin's instructions to ambassadors abroad, many of which he prepared himself, were distinguished by maximum clarity."

On the other hand, the number of young men filling the ranks of the ministry was growing. I saw this as an indication that Khrushchev aspired to replace the Stalinist old guard with less conservative people. The expulsion from power of the "anti-Party group" only strengthened my faith in Khrushchev. The existence of such a strong group among the leaders seemed to explain a lot of things: the brutality in Hungary, the uncertainties in disarmament policy, the poor results from the new domestic managers. Furthermore, I thought that the additional steps Khrushchev took against some other prominent Soviets, such as Marshal Zhukov, were justified.

Zhukov had, it was true, helped Khrushchev in his battle with the anti-Party group, but Khrushchev's later accusations that he was a "Bonapartist" and had failed to recognize Party supremacy over the military were also true.

In my time, Marshal Zhukov was perhaps the most respected military hero in the Soviet Union. He profited from the rivalry within the political leadership and became the first career military man to be elected to the Party Presidium. When he tried to downgrade the role of the Main Political Directorate within the Ministry of Defense he made a mistake that cost him dearly. Zhukov did not attempt a military coup; nor did he seek to replace Khrushchev. Although the military was known to be ambitious, neither Zhukov's appetite nor that of other military leaders had ever gone so far. He simply wanted to assert his own authority over the Army and overestimated the military's influence.

The Soviet military can exert a mighty influence in critical periods of political turmoil, such as that surrounding Beria's arrest, by bringing pressure on the high council of the Party to support some politicians against others in power struggles. It may also veto certain proposals regarding arms control, and in most cases its demands for military programs will be accommodated. However, its political importance in the power structure is limited by the preeminence of the Politburo. It is possible that Zhukov made the same mistake as do Western analysts in evaluating the military's role in Soviet political processes. Despite his widespread popularity—and there was no one among the military who could equal Zhukov in that respect—he was officially disgraced and forced to retire. The powers of the Main Political Directorate of the Army and Navy, the organization overseeing all branches of military service, were extended. Khrushchev replaced Zhukov as Defense Minister with an obedient crony, Marshal Rodion Malinovsky, who completely understood the supremacy of the Party.

Each ministry has its own in-house Party organization, and ours, to my surprise, avoided intervention in substantive business. It neither challenged nor initiated anything in the conduct of foreign policy. Its main function was to ensure discipline and to see that we fulfilled to the best of our ability our duty according to our chief's orders. The most unpleasant aspect of Party responsibility and the Party chore I found most demeaning was the task of snooping into and supervising the personal lives of others. Communists are expected to set shining examples of behavior. When, instead, they engage in *amoralka*—misconduct, the most common forms being heavy drinking, philandering, and, among diplomats, smuggling Western consumer goods— their peers are supposed to recall them to righteousness. The Party had a series of weapons for these situations, ranging from a slap on the wrist—a *vygovor,* or reprimand—to expulsion. But it prefers to redeem rather than punish. The higher a transgressor's rank, moreover, the greater the tendency to cover up his misdeeds.

111

I joined the Party in 1958 for very practical reasons: without the right political credentials I would not get Party and KGB approval for promotions or assignments abroad. Membership, however, carried obligations—it was not enough to hold a Party card and do a job well. For a Soviet official to advance, even if his work record is excellent, he must also earn the Party's blessing, and, except where favoritism provides shortcuts, the Party requires a time-consuming and often tedious display of activism.

I cannot count the hours I spent in Party organization meetings in the ministry, listening to or delivering dull reports on doctrinal matters or on the foibles and failings of other "comrades." As a rule, the pettier the subject, the longer the discussion of it.

In the fall of 1957, the London arms-control negotiations once again claimed my attention. They had concluded with sharp disagreement and acrimony. Because the results had been so poor, I was worried that the United States and the U.S.S.R. would again engage in fruitless recriminations over who was to blame for the deadlock. It was an old and childish game played by many nations: trying to gain the advantage in arms-control negotiations rather than reach fair agreement. A striking example was the test-ban talks of the late fifties and early sixties. They were like a card game. When the Soviet Union held a trump—that is, when it had just finished its own testing series, and knew that the United States was in the midst of or was preparing its new series—the U.S.S.R. would push for an agreement to stop the tests. When the United States held the trump, it would press for an agreement to prevent a new Soviet round.

In 1958, Soviet interest in stopping the tests was so great that Khrushchev personally devoted himself to studying details of the negotiations. Modifications of Soviet proposals or tactics were said to be the work of Khrushchev. One of his ideas was unilateral cessation of nuclear weapons testing.

In early February 1958, Kirill Novikov took me to a meeting in Gromyko's office, where the matter was discussed. It was the first time I had met Gromyko since beginning my work at the ministry. He opened the discussion with a propaganda tirade. He said that Khrushchev considered it necessary to develop a campaign to stop the weapons testing and demonstrate to the world that it was the Soviet Union that insisted upon it without delay. "He has decided that we must set an example," he said, "and unilaterally discontinue the testing of nuclear weapons." Our department was charged with preparing the appropriate documents.

As the meeting broke up, I went up to Gromyko. He said he was glad to see that I had taken his advice and was making practical use of my education. I asked him how we could publicly explain our position on the testing cessation: we had recently declared that the Soviet Union could not take such a step, as it would place it at a disadvantage vis-à-vis the United States. Rather testily, he replied that he was encouraged to see that I had paid attention to our former position. Frowning, he added, "No explanation of the change is necessary. The crux of the matter is that our decision will have tremendous political effect. That's our main objective."

I felt this was a rather strange approach for us to take, but I said nothing. My overriding fascination with my work, and my feelings of heady excitement as I was included more often in meetings with some of the country's most important figures, ended any lingering doubts I had about making diplomacy my life's work.

11

By SEPTEMBER 1958, AFTER I HAD WORKED AT THE FOR-
eign Ministry for nearly two years, I got my first chance to
go abroad; and not just abroad, but to America. This had
been my dream since childhood, an image that floated in my
imagination as remote and mysterious as something out of
the *Thousand and One Nights*.

I would be in New York for three months as a disarmament specialist with the Soviet delegation to the annual session of the UN General Assembly. It was a good
opportunity. Some in our department had been waiting
years for such a prize. A *komandirovka* (business trip) to
the United States was a huge bonus. Junior and mid-level
diplomats' salaries are low even by Soviet standards. But
there are some substantial privileges, and the best reward is
a *komandirovka* to a Western country where one can buy
items—from clothing to stereos, medicines, and appliances
—usually too expensive or unavailable at any price at home.

Although I had a top security clearance, every diplomat
going abroad must fill out form after form, each with a photo
attached, and be interviewed again and again by the ministry's personnel officers and finally by an instructor from the
Central Committee. The whole procedure ends with the
signing of a list of regulations prescribing in detail appropriate behavior abroad: no attendance at anti-Soviet movies,
no purchases of anti-Soviet books and magazines, and dozens of other "nos." But none of those time-consuming and
tedious processes dampened my expectations.

With no direct service, flying from Moscow to New York
then took more than twenty-four hours. As we landed, I felt
I had entered a different world. I had seen photographs of
New York, but nothing had prepared me for the impact of
the towering city on the horizon. On our way from the air-

port to Glen Cove, Long Island, where we were staying, I saw comfortable-looking houses with neatly kept lawns, the endless stream of automobiles snaking along the wide highways, and countless abundantly stocked stores. The dozens of small food shops with all kinds of fruits and vegetables piled in boxes and baskets on the sidewalks made the strongest impression of all. I had never seen such displays in the Soviet Union, where everything was scarce or unavailable. If a store had actually dared to set a box of fruit outside its door, the box would have been snatched away instantly.

It was a while before I had a chance to tour New York. We lived a reclusive life at Glen Cove. The delegation was quartered there not only to save money but also for the convenience of the KGB, who had to maintain surveillance of us. The Glen Cove villa served this purpose admirably; everyone was constantly in view, no one could wander at large, and there was little contact with anyone else. I had to share my room at Glen Cove with three other people, but I had no complaints. Everything, no matter how trivial, seemed exotic and fascinating, from the perfumed soap in a shining clean, almost individual bathroom to the larger splendors of the Glen Cove estate.

Except for the head of the delegation, Deputy Foreign Minister Valerian A. Zorin, we all ate in the main dining room. The cook was from Russia, but the food didn't taste Russian—milk and eggs, among other foods, had different flavors. But it was the bread that gave us our biggest shock: packaged white bread from a supermarket had the flavor and texture of glue. We couldn't get over the idea that Americans really bought it and seemed to like it. If the bread was disappointing, however, there was nothing better than Coca-Cola; we drank it by the gallon during the warm autumn days.

Perhaps what struck me more than anything else was the wealth and volume of information of every imaginable kind in newspapers, magazines, books, television, and radio. I couldn't get accustomed to the incredible openness of American society. It was appealing and at the same time somehow frightening. I was like a starving man at a feast. For three months I read every American publication I could get my hands on, and gained a significant education in that short time.

I also discovered that I could buy *Pravda* and various other Soviet periodicals at newsstands that carried international publications. We had been told that the United States suppressed information about our country because it didn't want Americans to know about our better life in the Soviet Union.

We left the estate mainly to attend meetings at the UN. I was awed by the buildings, and as enthralled as any tourist by the many nationalities and languages encountered at every turn. I spent most of my time following disarmament discussions. I realize now they were dry and slow, but to me then they were fascinating, enlightening, containing so many new facts. A few strongly critical remarks about the Soviet position brought me up short occasionally and forced me to reevaluate a number of things I had taken for granted.

My basic task was to help prepare reports and assessments of these discussions and make suggestions about how to vote on various draft resolutions.

Contacts with foreign diplomats, including delegates from socialist countries, were restricted. I could meet them only with special permission from my superiors. Only experienced people could be trusted to talk with foreigners. Membership in the delegation had given me an inflated sense of self-importance, but my minor role took the wind out of my sails. Nevertheless, I was happy: to be included in the minuet danced at the UN was exciting. I learned a great deal from watching the delegates' proceedings and much more from my limited conversations with foreigners, including those exotic creatures—Americans. They had a free and open way of talking—even criticizing aspects of their own government's policies—that took my breath away.

I had never seen so many contrasts and such energy as I experienced in New York. I wondered if the rest of America bristled with the same sort of drive. It simply never came to rest and all was jumbled together: the soft, old-style buildings and the tough, brittle new ones, the bridges, the world arriving every day in the harbors, the splendor of the rich midtown streets, the range of diversions from seedy bars and strip joints to sumptuous museums and elegant restaurants. The free spirit of the people was stunning. I marveled at the way New York seemed not to care about the face it showed the world, as if it displayed its tawdry as well as its fine sides with the same shrug of its shoulders—take it or leave it.

I found it a place of constant din, traffic snarls, and tiny, dim streets like dirty black typewriter ribbons threading through the monolithic buildings. It was the opposite of Moscow in this too: there was no space, no broad boulevards or wide avenues with stately phalanxes of trees such as exist all over Moscow. It seemed odd to me that New York's space was up, not out.

On a few occasions going back and forth, we were driven through some of the worst slums of Harlem and the Bowery. These side trips were meant as object lessons about what evils were surely in store for those who lived under a dying capitalism and as a deterrent against any thoughts we might harbor about staying in the United States.

My first encounter with consumerism occurred on a visit to Woolworth's five-and-dime store. I had never seen such a plenitude of goods—and none of the long waiting lines that are a way of life in the U.S.S.R. But for me, the crown, the jewel, of the great city was its bookstores. If I had been allowed, I would have spent all my time in them. The variety of titles, including Russian-language books by Soviet émigrés and defectors, was seductive, almost overpowering.

Almost. On a per diem allowance of ten dollars I could do a lot more browsing than buying, and I wanted to get presents for Lina and Gennady. I discovered that nearly all Soviets in New York, high or low, shop whenever they have a free minute. They usually headed for Orchard Street in downtown Manhattan, where many stores are owned by Russian-speaking Jewish émigrés. There it was possible to acquire outmoded items at bargain prices. The Soviets stock up on clothes, shoes, fabrics, all kinds of goods that are rarely, if ever, accessible even to many senior officials at home. The KGB was not fond of our forays to Orchard Street, and we often detected them skulking around after us as we searched for bargains. Nonetheless, they did the same themselves.

Not only our residence at Glen Cove but also our means of transportation restricted our freedom. A group of several people was assigned to a single automobile, which made everyone in the group dependent upon everyone else. The arrangement, at the end of each daily UN meeting, was for all those assigned to a given car to assemble at the Soviet Mission to be driven out to Glen Cove. Naturally, the system never worked as it was supposed to, since not everyone finished work at the same time. The result was endless inconvenience and friction.

One evening a colleague, Misha, and I missed our car, and the officer on duty told us that the next one would not come for several hours. We decided to see a movie at a nearby cinema. This was a violation of the rules: one simply did not go to a movie on one's own, whether the subject was anti-Soviet or not. It then turned out that we also missed the last car to Glen Cove. We thought we had better take the train since we couldn't afford a taxi all the way to Long Island. We arrived around midnight and were met by Yuri Mikheyev. Mikheyev was called "little mouse" behind his back because of his uncanny resemblance to one. He was not very well liked because everyone knew him to be an informer of the pettiest type. "Valerian Aleksandrovich [Zorin] is waiting for you. You'd better not keep him waiting." He smirked. We knew at once we were in trouble.

Zorin, dressed in a bathrobe, was at his desk in his large, dimly lit office. "Where the hell have you been?" he shouted as soon as we appeared. "I've had to put out a search for you stupid bastards." We began our excuses, but he was in no mood to listen to them. He cut us off and leveled a finger like a pistol as he told us with steely fury that if it happened again we would be sent home immediately and he would see to it that we were never allowed to go abroad again. It was the ultimate threat, and one that Zorin had the power to make good on, and it kept Misha and me chastened for the rest of our stay.

Reined in as we all were, spending most of our free time at Glen Cove, we were able to save a great deal of our salaries and per diem. I bought Lina clothing and fancy shoes and as many toys as I could for Gennady. They were delighted with the things when I returned home, although Lina scolded me for not having loaded my suitcases, as many of my colleagues had done, with cheap American fabric we could resell at a high profit in Moscow. I consoled her with the idea that there might well be other trips, and that someday we could possibly go together.

Now, in fact, I became the one who dreamed of returning to the tantalizing freedom I had briefly tasted in New York. "Paris is worth a mass," Henry IV had said, converting to Catholicism to make himself King of France. Experiencing the West, to me, had become a benefit worth all the compromises that went with making a career in the Foreign Ministry.

Further positive changes toward the West occurred in our foreign policy. In 1959 Khrushchev was invited to make an official visit to the United States, the first by the leader of our country. That summer, prior to his trip, Zorin called a meeting of his subordinates who were working on disarmament. In his characteristic monotone he said that Khrushchev had decided to "undertake a major new initiative." At the UN General Assembly session in New York that September, he would propose a policy of general and complete disarmament. "From now on," Zorin declared, "the struggle for general and complete disarmament will be a principal and long-term policy of the Soviet Union." He also warned us to be silent about our preparatory work on the proposal.

I was depressed by this sudden, dramatic turn in our position, and began to have doubts about Khrushchev's wisdom and ability to deal with disarmament problems. It was exasperating to realize that the more or less serious arms-control discussions which had commenced at the end of the fifties would degenerate into another noisy propaganda battle. If up to this time no agreement had been reached on modest, partial measures for limiting the arms race, it was obvious that there would be even less chance that the world would consent to disarm as by the waving of a magic wand. I have always considered fantasy in diplomacy a waste of time, and we had the absurd task of demonstrating the un-

119

demonstrable. Only by recourse to the most duplicitous sophistry was it possible to maintain that general and complete disarmament would be easier to achieve than partial disarmament, as we were now instructed to claim. Nor did military leaders approve of reviving the notion of general and complete disarmament. I heard more than one grumble that the idea would have a bad influence on young people's morale. But they dared not challenge Khrushchev.

A veneer of propaganda obscured almost everything related to Khrushchev's visit to the United States. He was obviously delighted that President Eisenhower had invited him to pay an official visit. The mere fact of the invitation was important to him: he saw it as the United States' admission that the U.S.S.R. was an equal with whom solutions to international problems must be sought. The Soviet Union had striven persistently for such status. Khrushchev felt that his visit would bring him and the Soviet Union prestige, regardless of whether the talks with Eisenhower succeeded or failed.

Moreover, he desired American aid and wanted to develop trade between the two nations. Thus Soviet media began to "recall" Lenin's forgotten pronouncements on the importance of economic cooperation with capitalist countries and the need to study "American efficiency."

Khrushchev spent thirteen days in the United States. His visit had a considerable impact on Americans, and his style created a popularity that remains even today. Americans saw a Soviet leader in the flesh who proved to be sociable and earthy and who treated everyone he met without ceremony or affectation. He talked to journalists with a sense of humor and without using notes or prepared texts. Most of all, he bore no resemblance to the reclusive, sinister Stalin.

When he appeared before the UN General Assembly with his proposal for general and complete disarmament, Khrushchev achieved his predicted propaganda success. Western leaders recognized it as a ploy, but no one spoke out openly against it.

Khrushchev's next venture was to bring him trouble on the domestic front. Claiming that "the clouds of war have begun to disperse," as a result of his "historic" visit to the

United States, he initiated a significant reduction of Soviet armed forces. At a session of the Supreme Soviet in January 1960, a law was passed approving a decrease of 1.2 million personnel in the military.

Khrushchev justified his decision by saying that modern defense potential was determined not by the number of soldiers under arms but by nuclear firepower and the quality of delivery systems. He grossly inflated Soviet nuclear and missile capabilities, boasting that "we now possess the absolute weapon," that Soviet missiles were so accurate they could hit a "fly in outer space." As broadly theatrical as history has revealed Khrushchev's threats to be, many people in the West, including politicians and military experts, believed them. But such statements were simply a form of psychological warfare; the real situation was as different as day from night. Khrushchev, however, went even further: he asserted that "military aviation and the Navy have lost their former significance." This was not something the military leaders and the armaments industries could let pass unchallenged.

The decline in morale and fighting spirit in the armed forces reached alarming proportions. In the spring of 1960, Navy Captain Barabolya visited us, and in a passionate outburst described how naval officers had wept as they watched nearly completed cruisers and destroyers at the docks in Leningrad being cut up for scrap on Khrushchev's orders.

More significant than the Navy's chagrin, however, was the alarm felt by Central Committee ideologists. By reducing the conventional forces, especially the Navy, Khrushchev was undercutting the most efficient means of aiding pro-Moscow liberation movements and the Soviet Union's allies in the Third World. In the long run, these moves cost him heavily.

In concentrating too closely on his Western initiatives, Khrushchev made yet another mistake: turning his back on China. The strain in Soviet-Chinese relations, hardly visible on the surface, became public when the U.S.S.R. took a neutral stand during the border conflict between China and India in 1959. Khrushchev tried to placate Mao by flying to

121

Peking for the PRC's tenth anniversary celebration immediately upon returning from the United States.

The conversations with Mao, in which he tried to preserve the Communist monolith, failed. The visit took place in an atmosphere of unrelieved tension, and Khrushchev's farewell was even colder than his reception. Friends in the Central Committee told me that the Chinese had accused him of sacrificing revolutionary struggle for détente with the Americans and other "imperialists." This threatened to undermine Kremlin claims of leadership in revolutionary movements. Now the Soviets had to compete with the Chinese in leading the world revolution, and the result was a resuscitated militancy in Soviet foreign policy.

By 1960, Khrushchev was at his zenith as Kremlin leader; his struggles with his most formidable opponents were behind him. Yet his policy was frustrated by something beyond his control. Many of his programs were stalled or failing. He was stretched too thin, attempting to achieve too much in too short a time. Some of his actions ran not simply against individual rivals in the leadership or vested interests of various power groups, but counter to the basic rules by which the system functioned.

Inevitably, difficulties forced him to repudiate the "spirit of Camp David," to slow his efforts to reorganize the armed forces, and to shift his economic priorities. The policy reversals were manifested in several ways. The first public sign was the reaction to the U-2 incident. American reconnaissance aircraft had been making overflights of Soviet territory for some years, and the Soviet leadership was well aware of them. Gromyko had advised Khrushchev not to shoot down the planes so as to avoid excessive deterioration in Soviet-American relations. In Gromyko's judgment, a strong protest and warning could suffice to forestall further overflights. Khrushchev dismissed Gromyko's counsel, and when Soviet antiaircraft defenses shot down a U-2 and took the pilot, Francis Gary Powers, prisoner, Khrushchev made the most of it.

He was a volatile man who made little effort to control his emotional temperament. He decided to set a trap to disgrace Eisenhower publicly. Powers was alive and in Soviet hands, but Khrushchev, concealing this, tricked Eisenhower, successfully luring him into denials concerning the overflights.

Incidentally, Khrushchev's scheme was nearly revealed prematurely as a result of Yakov Malik's talkativeness. Malik, a Deputy Foreign Minister at the time, was one of the few who knew that Powers had survived, and in conversation with an ambassador from one of the socialist countries, he could not resist the temptation to show off. He told the envoy that the U-2 pilot was alive and would testify publicly. Fortunately for Khrushchev's hoax, the ambassador was security-conscious and immediately informed the Central Committee of this chat.

Furious, Khrushchev decided to expel Malik from the Party and to dismiss him from his post. Malik, however, succeeded in getting an audience with the Premier at which he apparently fell to his knees and wept as he begged forgiveness. By this time Khrushchev's U-2 scheme had come to successful fruition, and he contented himself with devising a humiliating punishment for Malik: to make a public confession at a Party meeting of the entire Foreign Ministry.

The ministry's oval conference hall with its marble columns and elevated rostrum was filled to overflowing. Mounting the rostrum, obviously pained and embarrassed, Malik bleated: "Comrades, I have never before revealed state secrets." Everyone howled with laughter. In another time he would have ended up in prison or worse, but now he received only a *strogach* (severe reprimand).

After the U-2 incident Khrushchev torpedoed the Big Four Conference in Paris in May 1960. That summer I joined the special ad hoc team that annually prepared instructions and other materials for the opening fall sessions of the UN General Assembly. But for me it was not routine business. One day, I was called into Pavel Shakov's office. "Arkady," he said, smiling pompously, "you've been included among the experts in the Soviet delegation to the next session of the UN General Assembly. You understand, of course, that this is a great honor and imposes great responsibility on you. Nikita Sergeyevich will personally lead the delegation." I could not believe this stroke of luck. My colleagues and I were aware that this might be a turning point in my career. I again began to prepare for a trip to New York.

12

IN EARLY SEPTEMBER 1960, WHEN I SAILED FROM KALININgrad to New York with Nikita Khrushchev, he was the unchallenged leader of the Soviet Union.

To travel with him, to have the chance to make myself useful to him and other senior figures in his entourage, was an extraordinary opportunity. Ministry officials of my age and rank normally were expected to be neither seen nor heard. Anonymous foot soldiers of Soviet diplomacy, we might have the good fortune several times a year to attend a staff meeting with a Deputy Foreign Minister or, in exceptional cases, with Gromyko. Yet at the age of twenty-nine I was making a ten-day Atlantic crossing on a small passenger liner, the *Baltika*, with the top man in the Soviet Union, assigned to work with him on what was to be a major presentation on decolonization and disarmament to the UN General Assembly.

Nikolai Molyakov, deputy chief of the Department of International Organizations, in which I worked, was appointed general secretary of the delegation. To a large extent he selected the delegation, and I was on good terms with him. By this time I was experienced in my disarmament duties, and I was familiar with the details of the Soviet proposals to be made at the General Assembly. I had been present at some discussions on disarmament in Gromyko's office, and when Molyakov recommended my inclusion in the delegation, Gromyko approved it.

Besides the many Soviet officials, leaders of the Communist parties of several other socialist countries had joined Khrushchev on the *Baltika:* János Kádár of Hungary, Gheorghe Gheorghiu-Dej of Romania, and Todor Zhivkov of Bulgaria. Since each of these luminaries had a large entourage, one can imagine how many highly placed Party and state officials and diplomats were crowded onto the little *Baltika*. The number of comfortable staterooms was limited, and there was only one restaurant for all the passengers. Consequently, the first and indeed most sensitive problem facing U.S.S.R., Ukrainian, and Belorussian delegates was which stateroom they would occupy, and whether or not they would be among those who would eat in the restaurant with Khrushchev and the other leaders. This was partly a matter of comfort and convenience, because those who were not included among the privileged were to be herded into the hold and quartered with the crew.

Soon after we boarded the *Baltika*, Molyakov approached me with a conspiratorial air and whispered triumphantly, "Arkady, you will be in a stateroom on the deck and not in the hold, and you have been assigned to the restaurant where Nikita Sergeyevich will be eating." He broke into a broad smile, slapped me on the back, and declared, "Friends have to help one another." Molyakov was certain I would not forget such an important favor.

Far from luxurious, my stateroom contained a bunk bed, a small table, two chairs, and a wardrobe. The first night out, however, I experienced a taste not only of the bounty provided for the elite—a banquet of caviar, sturgeon, and other delicacies—but also of Khrushchev's boisterous, accessible style.

The dinner had been formal and restrained, with most of the voyagers dressed as though they were on parade. But as it concluded, Khrushchev left the main table to make the rounds of the dining room. At our table he saw that the enormous meal had defeated our appetites. "What's the matter," he laughed, his finger wagging in mock reproof, "doesn't the production of the *Baltika*'s food department please you?" Before we could answer, he swooped down on his son-in-law, *Izvestia* editor Aleksei Adzhubey. Khrushchev picked up his glass of beer, sniffed it, and pronounced in a loud voice: "I know you. You are trying to camouflage it, but I caught you drinking a beer that is half vodka." Everybody roared with laughter.

This was the first time I had been so close to the Soviet leader. Short and fat, "N.S.," as he was referred to in his inner circle and among diplomats, was a plain man, almost bald, with small, piggish eyes and several large warts on his round, typically Russian face.

As we sailed through the Baltic Sea, it was relatively calm; there were few clouds. Two destroyers which had been escorting the *Baltika* made their farewell salutes and turned back. We were alone for the time being, though we encountered a number of Soviet vessels as we crossed the Atlantic. Moscow had ordered them to change their courses so they would sail near us.

I wondered what would happen to the *Baltika* if we encountered a storm. I knew the ship didn't even have an anti-pitch stabilizer. Shortly, my fears were realized. A savage gale broke out and the little ship tossed as the Atlantic heaved. The restaurant, the halls, and the deck were deserted. The majority of the passengers were lying in their staterooms suffering from seasickness. A good half of the ship's crew was sick too.

Khrushchev, however, remained hardy and undaunted, not succumbing in the slightest. As if nothing had happened, he continued to go to the restaurant in high spirits, deriding those who, in his words, had shown themselves to be weaklings.

I lay in my berth almost the entire day, getting up only to run to the bathroom. That evening, Molyakov dropped in. His breath reeking of vodka, he taunted me: "What are you doing lying down?" He claimed that the best medicine for seasickness was to toss down "two hundred grams" (of vodka), and urged me to accompany him to the bar. His suggestion made me feel even sicker, but I thought perhaps it would be more pleasant to die in the bar than on my bunk, so I went with him.

A number of Khrushchev's intimates were there, all tipsy, telling bawdy stories and evaluating the charms of the stewardesses, waitresses, and secretaries who had been included in the staff of the delegation. Those of us from the Foreign Ministry usually were careful because Gromyko did not like us drinking and talking too much. But we knew that he, unlike Khrushchev, would never appear in the bar, considering it beneath his dignity, so we were less constrained than usual.

The Bulgarians frequented the bar, and in general made no effort to avoid contact with us. The Bulgarian leader, Zhivkov, conspicuously displayed special attention toward Khrushchev, and in conversations with him constantly emphasized his assent to N.S.'s every utterance. The Bulgarians—at the slightest excuse, and even with no excuse—loved to expatiate on their similarity in spirit to the Russians and on the historic friendship of Russia and Bulgaria, hinting rather broadly that they and only they were the Soviet Union's true brothers and allies.

The Romanians, on the other hand, kept themselves aloof, and there was an obvious chill between them and the Soviet delegation. At his table in the dining room, Gheorghiu-Dej generally remained silent. Khrushchev was annoyed at this but did not display his feelings toward the Romanians publicly, except on one occasion when he lost control of himself before a small group of Soviets and declared that Gheorghiu-Dej was not a bad Communist in general, but that as a leader he had no force; he was too passive. He added that in Romania, and even in the ranks of its Communist Party, pernicious nationalistic and anti-Soviet attitudes were developing which must be cut off at the very root. "A firm hand is required for that," he declared. "The *Mamalyzhniki** are not a nation, but a whore." Khrushchev stopped short, realizing he had gone too far. "I am referring," he added lamely, trying to extricate himself, "to pre-revolutionary Romania."

The Hungarians appeared outwardly to be loyal, but they did not proclaim their "eternal friendship" in the manner of the Bulgarians, and they maintained absolute silence concerning the events of 1956. János Kádár impressed me as

* A derisive and insulting Russian nickname for Romanians, derived from the Russian word *mamalyga*, meaning a kind of thick Romanian porridge.

intelligent, shrewd, and energetic. On the *Baltika,* he had evidently decided to relax and enjoy himself, devoting himself to playing cards. Card-playing, indeed, seemed to be an obsession with the Hungarians: give them five free minutes, and they would break out a deck. On this trip, even Khrushchev got a little angry at the day-and-night card games. After playing around the clock, Kádár was frequently too tired to appear for breakfast.

There was no discussion with our socialist friends of the content of the proposals Khrushchev intended to make in New York. We had received strict instructions not to reveal anything to them; not to give them any information about our materials; and to conceal our style and methods of work. Khrushchev had informed the Bulgarian, Hungarian, and Romanian leaders only in the most general way about his proposals.

Once, Molyakov cynically observed that we should be "very careful talking to our friends," and that we "must not discuss official matters with them without special authorization. They're almost certain to blab about everything prematurely. There may even be concealed enemies among them, agents of Western intelligence services."

I asked Molyakov, "What are we supposed to do?" I told him that to avoid discussing the proposals with them was awkward, because they were constantly expressing interest in our position.

"Nothing is awkward except putting your trousers on over your head," he replied, using an old peasant saying. "Let them wait. Nikita Sergeyevich will address the General Assembly, and then they will learn about our proposals."

This represented the true attitude of the Soviet leadership toward our supposed brothers and allies. I was aware that we did not share all information with them, but I had not suspected that such an arrogant posture toward these "friends" was actually the basis of our relations with them. Assurances of fraternal friendship between the U.S.S.R. and other socialist countries, which the Soviet leaders and propagandists were constantly proclaiming to the world, and which Soviet ideologists maintain is the basis of "the indestructible law of socialism," were in fact nothing but hypocrisy.

In the mornings, Khrushchev would appear on deck, seat himself in a rocking chair, and have his assistant, Oleg Troyanovsky, read aloud to him the latest news summaries sent by radio from Moscow. Our communications with Moscow were not perfect, however. The *Baltika* was not properly equipped, and there were times when we were unable to reach Moscow immediately.

Khrushchev was unaffected in his treatment of everyone. He mixed with members of the crew and did not avoid conversations with people whom he did not know personally. He gladly let himself be photographed with members of the delegation, despite the disapproval of his KGB security guards. He greatly enjoyed deck sports. He was an ardent shuffleboard player, eagerly trying to beat his competitors by as many points as possible.

One often saw him with a book, but his knowledge of literature was unsystematic and fragmentary. He was acquainted least of all with Western literature and he said that if he ever had the time, he would like to fill that gap. Khrushchev did not know a foreign language and had no intention of studying one. "It would be better for me to master Russian properly," he acknowledged self-critically. His lack of education was apparent; he made grammatical errors in speech and often misplaced the accent on words.

Khrushchev was truly different from other Soviet leaders. Gromyko was more typical of the Soviet bureaucratic character, avoiding simple human contacts with ordinary people. Unlike most Western leaders, ranking Soviets occupy their high positions for many years, if not for their whole lives. As their feel for the people becomes ever more remote, they are slowly cut off from their countrymen's needs and thinking.

The storm, which had become stronger and laid even more of our company low, turned out to my advantage. Whether it was Molyakov's recommended vodka or the resilience of youth, I overcame my seasickness. With most of my superiors still on their backs, I was ordered to work directly with Gromyko and Khrushchev.

I had the opportunity to talk with Khrushchev alone a number of times, playing shuffleboard with him or promenading around the deck. He manifested a lively interest in everything, asked many questions, and often answered them himself, not waiting for my reply. He was a clumsy man and in this informal setting his general appearance was messy, with his baggy suit and wide, rumpled trousers. He was often mercurial, good humor changing quickly to bursts of anger at the slightest turn. Occasionally, when he was alone or with close associates, he betrayed an uncharacteristic melancholy, a kind of sad weariness. That image, however, was transient, hardly noticeable behind his usual vigorous cheer.

The preparation of the proposals, or "the new major Soviet initiatives," as they were called by the inner circle of the Central Committee and the Foreign Ministry, was in the main completed in Moscow. On the *Baltika* they were rendered into final form and polished up, primarily to give them a maximally attractive propaganda coloring. Khrushchev demanded that the texts of the proposals and the drafts of his own speeches be composed in a simple style, intelligible and accessible to the widest number of people, even to those with no connection to politics. He loved to repeat one of the sacred truisms of Marxism: "An idea becomes a material force when it takes possession of the masses."

The quest for trenchant expressions, the hunting out of vivid and compelling comparisons and arguments, the search for popular Russian sayings and proverbs, were no less important in the course of our work than the substantive formulation of the proposals. Compilations of proverbs and famous sayings were standard reference works for those who prepared materials for Khrushchev. Aleksei Adzhubey and Pavel Satyukov, chief editor of *Pravda*, who spent his entire life working in the Party apparatus, were Khrushchev's indispensable assistants with respect to literary and propaganda inventiveness. In their mastery of this skill they greatly surpassed Gromyko, who provided ideas and thoughts but did not possess eloquence or literary artistry. Gromyko did not like Adzhubey's elevation. Although Khrushchev valued Gromyko's extensive diplomatic experience, he could not resist teasing him, often calling him an arid bureaucrat. "Look at that," Khrushchev would say, nodding toward Gromyko and smiling. "How young Andrei Andreyevich looks." (He really did look very young for his years.) "He doesn't have a single gray hair. It's obvious he just sits in a cozy little place and drinks tea." These jests were not at all pleasing to Gromyko, but he always managed to force a smile.

Khrushchev himself worked assiduously on the texts of his speeches. For hours on end, in his cabin or out on deck, he dictated drafts of his ideas at such a pace that the harried stenographers barely had time to turn the pages of their shorthand pads. The drafts were often chaotic, containing numerous factual inaccuracies, and even the most experienced stenographers were sometimes unable to render in grammatical Russian many of the clumsy phrases he composed. Nevertheless, his speeches were lively and vivid, and his turns of thought, his arguments, and his reasoning were distinguished by their originality and persuasiveness, flavored with the pungent sayings and proverbs of which he was so fond.

In the evenings after dinner, we usually assembled in a small hall where films were shown or crew members presented amateur entertainment. Khrushchev always came; he did not like to be alone. He loved movies and would watch any picture that came along—Soviet and foreign films alike—but he was especially delighted when old prewar Soviet movies and newsreels were shown.

Khrushchev drank hugely—vodka, wine, and cognac— but he did not become intoxicated easily. Sometimes, in the evening, after he had been drinking hard all day he would indulge in pranks and jokes without inhibitions. His frequent companion in drinking bouts was János Kádár, himself no mean imbiber. Khrushchev would drop in on Kádár in his cabin several times a day. But it was Todor Zhivkov who was his most frequent guest and conversational partner. Although the stolid Bulgarian was not as engaging as Kádár, he and Khrushchev could converse more easily. Zhivkov understood nearly everything in Russian, unlike the Hungarians and Romanians, who frequently had to use interpreters.

One evening, as we were gathered in the hall waiting for a film to be shown, Khrushchev, who had been drinking heavily, decided to have some fun. Nikolai Podgorny, who at that time held Khrushchev's old job as Party boss of the Ukraine, was sitting next to him. Khrushchev turned to him and said, "Why don't you dance a *gopak** for us. I miss Ukrainian dances and songs." Khrushchev had obviously enjoyed his sojourn in the Ukraine and often reminisced fondly about his days in Kiev.

Podgorny looked at Khrushchev in amazement. He was in his sixties, and to dance the *gopak* was impossible at his age and inappropriate to his position. Khrushchev egged him on, repeating his request. Podgorny realized his leader was not joking. With obvious reluctance, he stood up and awkwardly bobbed up and down a few times, simulating the motions of the *gopak*. It was embarrassingly clear that he could not do it, but Khrushchev clapped loudly and praised Podgorny. "Well done!" he said. "You are in the right place there in Kiev."

In one of our conversations Khrushchev asked me if I was related to Taras Shevchenko, the well-known Ukrainian poet. I told him I was not, but that my parents and I had been born in the Ukraine, and that although I had spent most of my adult life in Russia, I considered myself a Ukrainian. My response seemed to please him, and for a moment I was afraid he was going to ask *me* to dance the *gopak*. But with a broad grin, he merely clapped me on the shoulder and said, "It's good to be proud of your nationality."

Emboldened by the gregarious informality aboard ship, I decided to risk voicing some of my concerns about our latest approach to disarmament policy. The promise of "serious negotiations" on arms reductions had drawn me to the Foreign Ministry in the first place, but now there was a shift away from realistic talks toward the propaganda program of general and complete disarmament.

Cautiously, I suggested to Khrushchev that propaganda

---

* A strenuous Ukrainian national dance for men, performed in a squatting position, rapidly kicking one leg out and then the other, all the time moving around a large circle.

could not replace the real talks needed to make progress in stopping the arms race. I was somewhat surprised that he heard me out. Then he said that there could be two levels of work in the field: his campaign for general and complete disarmament as a propaganda effort with a foundation of real negotiations on concrete, if limited, steps. "Every vegetable has its season," he said, using a hoary adage to lighten his tone. He stressed that it would not be wise to reject partial measures, but the principal matter was general and complete disarmament, and it was political art to choose when to emphasize one or the other.

"Never forget," he lectured me, "the appeal that the idea of disarmament has in the outside world. All you have to do is say, 'I'm in favor of it,' and that pays big dividends." Admitting with a grin that he neither expected the West to disarm completely nor contemplated such a course for the Soviet Union, he added, "A seductive slogan is a most powerful political instrument. The Americans don't understand that. They only hurt themselves in struggling against the idea of general and complete disarmament. What they are doing is as futile as Don Quixote's fighting the windmills."

Khrushchev said that propaganda and true negotiations should be considered not contradictory but complementary. Although his ends-justify-the-means approach was cynical, his frank justification of his policy was much more persuasive—as the truth usually is—than the hypocritical slogans of Valerian Zorin and others.

While my effect on policy was negligible, the impact of that transatlantic trip on me was enormous. The simple fact of proximity to Khrushchev and his top advisers gave me an importance in the eyes of others which led to rapid advancement. However, my direct contact with the Soviet leader, his entourage, and the pervasive cynicism of the real policymakers was disturbing as well as exhilarating. I clearly saw the Soviet leaders' appetite for ever-widening power. Peaceful coexistence was the Lenin-era maxim Khrushchev had revived and trumpeted. It provided the smokescreen behind which efforts to expand Soviet influence were planned.

One subject that was discussed candidly related to the

situation in the former Belgian Congo, then newly independent and torn by civil strife. The turmoil made the nascent nation fertile ground for Soviet manipulations, but that very distress may have also helped the country avoid the Soviet orbit. For whatever reason, events in the Congo did not go Moscow's way. Khrushchev was enraged that "the Congo," as he said, "is slipping through our fingers."

Throughout the voyage he was obsessed with the United Nations' involvement in the Congo, especially with the performance of the UN peacekeeping troops there and the activities of Secretary General Dag Hammarskjöld. "I spit on the UN," he raged after Oleg Troyanovsky read him some particularly bad piece of news from Africa. "It's not *our* organization. That good-for-nothing Ham [the Russian word for "boor" applied as a nickname to the UN chief] is sticking his nose in important affairs which are none of his business. He has seized authority that doesn't belong to him. He must pay for that. We have to get rid of him by any means. We'll really make it hot for him," he growled.

Out of his fury came the zany proposal to install a three-member executive, a troika, in place of the Secretary General. The plan was a recipe for emasculating the UN, but Khrushchev would hear no opposition to it, and offered the idea formally in his address to the General Assembly. Gromyko recognized that the project went completely counter to long-standing Soviet policy against any revision of the UN Charter, but even he could not dissuade Khrushchev.

Khrushchev's personal threat against Hammarskjöld returned to my memory in September 1961, when the Secretary General died in a mysterious plane crash in the Congo. Friends working on African affairs once told me they had seen a top-secret KGB report indicating that the aircraft had been shot down by pro-Soviet Congolese forces penetrated and guided by operatives from the U.S.S.R.

Khrushchev gave me yet another jolt one day with a rambling but coherent description of his intentions to exploit what he called "intra-imperialistic contradictions" to advance Soviet power. He was on deck holding his tattered but beloved straw hat on his head with one hand to keep it from being blown away. "I can't part with it," he said with

134

a chuckle. "It helps me think. And I don't imagine that my hat would be very much to the taste of the sharks."

That word, with no other prompting, set him off. Seeming to think aloud, he said, "In New York we will have to deal with a whole school of imperialist sharks, and of various breeds."

For the next half hour or so, he analyzed the major Western countries and Soviet strategy for pitting them against one another. The British, he conceded, were a hopeless case, fervently anti-Soviet. "The lion's mane may be mangy," he said, "but he has a powerful bite still. It's not for nothing that we have that saying: 'An Englishwoman never stops shitting.' "

France was another matter, "the link which we must seize in order to drag the entire European chain to us." Gazing at his paunch, he reminisced about his recent visit to Paris. "They feasted us and treated us to champagne in a fabulous way. And just as fabulously, we gratified de Gaulle's self-esteem. We deluged him with compliments. That's the trick with him."

There was no similarly easy maneuver for handling the Germans, he judged, but their economy and technology represented an even greater prize. West Germany had to be convinced that it could never hope for reunification. "If necessary," Khrushchev mused, nine months before the Berlin Wall became a reality, "we will make a display of force to sober up those West German politicians who don't understand the situation." Once they had acknowledged the inevitable, however, he felt it would be possible to win trading concessions from the Germans and exploit their economy to improve that of the Soviet Union. "Don't forget, it was Germany who became our first trading partner after the Revolution."

As for the United States, for the time being he saw little hope of changing its attitude, but there were many opportunities for "kindling distrust" of the Americans in Europe. "We threw a little scare into the NATO countries last year with the spirit of Camp David," he said in recalling his 1959 talks with President Eisenhower. "We must work further at turning the United States against Europe, and Europe

135

against the United States. That was the technique Vladimir Ilyich [Lenin] taught us. I have not forgotten his lesson," he said, wagging a finger at me.

While we were putting the final touches to Khrushchev's main address to the General Assembly, setting forth the "successes" of socialism in the Soviet Union, some of us began to wonder if the speech wasn't overloaded with statistical data on our achievements. When I gingerly mentioned to Khrushchev that perhaps it would be a good idea to think about shortening his speech by omitting several sections which had no direct relevance to the central themes of the Soviet proposals to the UN, he became very angry. "Those people in the UN ought to listen to us," he said. "All they do is chatter idly and spoil mountains of paper every day. We can't be worried about economizing on pages when it's political indoctrination we're undertaking in the UN." He said Lenin had taught that "socialism enjoys the power of example" and that "it is necessary to show by example the meaning of Communism." Khrushchev then launched enthusiastically into a lecture on the importance and usefulness of applying the theoretical legacy of Marxism-Leninism in practical work, saying that he himself always found the appropriate guidance in the works of Marx and Lenin.

We all knew Khrushchev had never been a theoretician. Nevertheless, he would often hold forth at length about theoretical problems. As I approached him on deck one day, he took a handkerchief out of his pocket and blew his nose loudly. During this pause, he spotted Gromyko, who was standing some distance from us, his old-fashioned Italian Borsalino pulled down over his ears and his dark blue mackintosh tightly buttoned up from top to bottom. Gromyko, looking very serious, was conversing with the Ambassador to Great Britain, Aleksandr Soldatov.

"Look there," said Khrushchev. "Andrei Andreyevich is an excellent diplomat and tactician; he knows negotiations from A to Z. But as an ideologist and theoretician he's rather poor. He has little taste for theorizing. But we're working on him. We'll make something of him yet."

I was somewhat embarrassed at such comments about the man who had influenced me to join the foreign service.

Khrushchev, however, never gave a thought to the fact that he was talking to the minister's subordinate.

After several days the *Baltika* emerged from the storm zone, having made a wide detour south of its intended course. A warm breeze and bright sunshine put the passengers into a happy mood as they thronged on deck.

Khrushchev began to spend a lot of time in the open air. On one occasion, I saw him standing alone, leaning on the ship's railing and looking through his binoculars at the bright ocean. Evidently, his conversational companions had just left him. I approached him and just at that moment his arm slipped off the rail and he lost his balance. I quickly held him up. He turned to me and said with a gay sparkle in his eyes, "I'm not a sailor, but I'm surefooted on deck. And if I were to fall overboard that wouldn't be a calamity. Right now we aren't too far from Cuba, and they'd probably receive me there better than the Americans will in New York."

I do not know why Khrushchev suddenly thought of Cuba. Perhaps the relative nearness of the island even then aroused the idea he later developed into the Cuban adventure which led to the sharpest crisis of the nuclear age.

"I hope," he mused thoughtfully, "that Cuba will become a beacon of socialism in Latin America. Castro offers that hope, and the Americans are helping us." He said that instead of establishing normal relations with Cuba the United States was doing everything it could to drive Castro to the wall by organizing a campaign against him, stirring up the Latin American countries against him, and establishing an economic blockade against Cuba.

"That's stupid," he exclaimed, "and it's a result of the howls of zealous anti-Communists in the United States who see red everywhere, though possibly something is only rose-colored, or even white."

Then, having smacked his lips with gusto as if anticipating a tasty meal, he predicted: "Castro will have to gravitate to us like an iron filing to a magnet."

I mentioned that although the Cuban leadership was moving toward socialism, I had heard that the head of the International Department of the Party Central Committee, Boris Ponomarev, was not sure about Castro's real views.

"Well, Ponomar* is a valuable Party official, but as orthodox as a Catholic priest," growled Khrushchev with some irritation, adding that he would form his own judgment during his meeting with Castro in New York.

We were excited when the *Baltika* entered New York Harbor and passed the Statue of Liberty. We were standing on the upper deck of our ship, which had been painted white a few days previously during a special stop in mid-ocean. But the splendor of our liner contrasted sharply with the dirty, half-decayed berth into which the *Baltika* began to move. Khrushchev and all of us were shocked. No one had expected anything like this. With obvious displeasure, Khrushchev growled, "So, so, another dirty trick the Americans are playing on us."

It was not the Americans who were to blame, however, but our Ambassador to Washington at that time, Mikhail Menshikov, and Valerian Zorin, who had recently become the U.S.S.R.'s representative at the United Nations. They had been too literal in carrying out instructions from Moscow that they should not spend too much money for a New York berth for the *Baltika*. No doubt they had worked very hard to find our cheap moorage, but they got no more than they paid for. The dilapidated pier near Thirty-fifth Street had actually been abandoned until Menshikov rented it.

In general, Menshikov, Anastas Mikoyan's protégé, was not particularly distinguished for his intelligence or his abilities. In Moscow, "Smiling Mike," as he was known in the United States, had the reputation of being a conceited snob. As for Zorin, he was a dogmatist to his very bones, and always followed instructions to the letter, sometimes not considering, as he should have, to what they might lead. The ancient pier was a case in point.

We quickly discovered another difficulty. The International Longshoremen's Association, in an anti-Soviet gesture, had decided to boycott Khrushchev's arrival and

---

* The name "Ponomarev" derives from the Russian word *ponomar*, a sacristan in the Orthodox Church.

refused to service the *Baltika*. Consequently, the ship had to be moored by its own crew. It was comical to see how clumsily we diplomats helped the sailors pull on the ropes.

After Khrushchev settled in at the Soviet Mission on Park Avenue, Zorin held an evening conference to review the Premier's schedule in New York. Zorin told us that "Nikita Sergeyevich attaches special importance to a meeting with Fidel Castro."

The main difficulty was that Castro had moved from midtown to the old Hotel Theresa in Harlem. The place was dilapidated, and there were winos hanging about the nearby street corners, but Castro was trying to show he was a man of the people. Khrushchev's security men objected to a visit there—as did the U.S. Secret Service. Zorin suggested inviting Castro to the Soviet Mission, but Khrushchev was adamant. He would visit Castro in Harlem to show him respect. He wanted to demonstrate that although he was the leader of a great nation, he didn't care about matters of protocol and security. He too was a man of the people.

When Khrushchev returned from Harlem, he was extremely pleased with the way things had gone. He told us he had found that Castro wanted a close friendship with the U.S.S.R. and had asked for military aid. Moreover, he got the impression that Castro would be a good Communist. While Khrushchev was enthusiastic, he also added that it would be necessary to be cautious. "Castro is like a young horse that hasn't been broken," he said. "He needs some training, but he's very spirited—so we'll have to be careful."

Khrushchev's pride was hurt when New York authorities advised the Soviet Mission that, because of security problems, he could not travel outside the limits of Manhattan. Khrushchev, who had planned to spend his free time in Glen Cove, immediately politicized the limitations on his movements. In his first speech to the General Assembly, he accused the United States and the American authorities of not having created "favorable conditions" for the representatives of the member states and of restricting and encroaching upon their rights.

He declared: "The question arises: isn't it time to think

about choosing a different location for UN headquarters, one that will more effectively promote the fruitful work of this international organization? Such a place, for example, might be Switzerland or Austria. I can declare in the most responsible way that if it were deemed desirable to locate the headquarters of the United Nations in the Soviet Union, we would guarantee the most favorable conditions for its work, and complete security for the representatives of all states.''

Of course, Khrushchev was only playing to the galleries. Moving the UN was the last thing Moscow wanted. Neither in Moscow during the preparations for the session nor on the *Baltika* had the question of moving UN headquarters been discussed. Khrushchev's ''responsible'' declaration concerning the relocation of UN headquarters to the Soviet Union was particularly irresponsible. Such a facility in Moscow could become a Trojan horse, kindling the regime's fear of any kind of UN presence in Moscow. That fear was already so great at the very time Khrushchev was making his remarks that the Soviet government was refusing to allow a single foreign employee in the modest UN information center in Moscow.

There was another factor weighing against moving the UN out of the United States. The present location enabled Moscow to dispatch practically unlimited numbers of KGB officers under cover of a UN title. Naturally, the KGB was vehemently opposed to moving the UN out of New York: it would mean liquidating one of its principal centers of espionage. In this respect, Vienna or Geneva could never take the place of New York.

When I worked in our UN Mission during the 1960s and later when I was Under Secretary General in the 1970s, I often heard KGB opinion on this subject. The slightest rumor that UN headquarters might move was cause for panic.

Khrushchev spent a great deal of time at the UN. He broke all previous records for speeches delivered there, addressing the Assembly eleven times during one session. For him, there were no rules. That became clear when he engaged in various antics, in one case going so far as to achieve international notoriety.

On October 1, 1960, I was sitting in the Assembly Hall not far from him. I wanted a cigarette, but smoking in the hall was forbidden. I got up to go out into the corridor, but Lev Mendelevich, deputy chief of the Department of International Organizations, shook his finger at me and said, "Are you out of your mind? Nikita Sergeyevich is about to speak. What will they think if you leave the hall now?"

Although Khrushchev's speech was on the restoration of the legal rights of China in the United Nations, he decided to use it to launch a personal attack on the Spanish leader, General Franco. In particular, Khrushchev declared that Franco "had established a regime of bloody dictatorship and was cutting off the heads of the finest sons of Spain."

Frederick Boland, the Irishman who was President of the Assembly at the time, was a calm and self-possessed man. But Khrushchev was going so far in his remarks that Boland interrupted him. This was a startling thing for him to do, breaking in when a head of state was speaking, but Boland requested that Khrushchev not indulge in personal attacks on the heads of other UN member states. The rebuke did not have the intended effect. Khrushchev seemed to grow more incensed, and he continued to revile Franco.

After his speech, the Spanish Minister of Foreign Affairs, Fernando Castiella, took the floor to respond. Khrushchev completely blew up, forgot all rules of diplomacy, and began to shout insulting remarks at the Spanish minister. The actor in him took over as he punctuated his insults by pounding with his fists on the desk, and then, having removed his shoe, he banged it resoundingly on the desk as well. Other members of the Soviet delegation also began to make noise and beat their desks, though they did not take off their shoes.

When he had concluded his rejoinder, Castiella returned to his seat in the hall, coincidentally situated directly in front of Khrushchev's desk. As the Spanish minister approached his seat, Khrushchev, unable to restrain himself, leaped from his chair and, brandishing his fists, lunged at the frail and undersized Castiella. The Spaniard assumed a comical defensive pose, but security guards rushed up and separated them.

We were stunned at Khrushchev's behavior. At the Mission after the close of the session, everyone was embarrassed and upset. Gromyko, noted for his strict, impeccable behavior, was white-lipped with agitation. But Khrushchev acted as if nothing at all had happened. He was laughing loudly and joking. He said that it had been necessary to "inject a little life into the stuffy atmosphere of the UN." He did not seem to realize or care what the other UN members would think about him in the wake of this escapade.

When Khrushchev left New York in mid-October, the United States was in the final weeks before its presidential election. Publicly, Khrushchev claimed to be indifferent to the outcome. He had called the two candidates, Nixon and Kennedy, "a pair of boots," explaining that "you can't say which is better, the left or the right."

But in private Khrushchev had a different attitude. At a luncheon before his departure, he became angry at the mention of Nixon's name. "He's a typical product of McCarthyism, a puppet of the most reactionary circles in the United States. We'll never be able to find a common language with him." Khrushchev was so convinced of this that he had rebuffed attempts by Nixon and Eisenhower to cool his hostility. We knew they had passed word to him that he shouldn't take at face value what Nixon was saying in the campaign. Nixon was simply talking for effect, Khrushchev was told; the truth was that Nixon desired better relations with the U.S.S.R. But Khrushchev dismissed these assurances.

Khrushchev said that "we can also influence the American presidential election." He proudly related how he "saw through" the Americans right away when the Eisenhower administration asked us to release Powers and the pilots shot down in the Arctic before the election. "We would never give Nixon such a present!" he exclaimed.

Khrushchev had expressed satisfaction with some of Kennedy's statements. He said that while Kennedy's judgments were frequently contradictory and vague, he obviously feared war and was thus making overtures for improvement of relations with the U.S.S.R.

It is easy now to accuse Khrushchev of lack of political foresight. It was Nixon, after all, who became the first President of the United States to officially visit the Soviet Union and who championed the policy of détente in Soviet-American relations. However, the most perspicacious Soviet prophet could hardly have foreseen that in 1960.

13

IT WAS NEW YEAR'S EVE WHEN I ARRIVED IN MOSCOW VIA train from Paris. Usually dark and gloomy, the city blazed with lights and decorations heralding the arrival of 1961. On my way from the railroad station I reflected on the exciting and intense year that was now ending. The fact that I had been in Khrushchev's retinue ensured me a continuing and higher role in the disarmament negotiations; Khrushchev always greeted me cordially whenever our paths crossed during the years after the voyage on the *Baltika*.

I knew Khrushchev was pleased when John Kennedy won the presidential election; he greatly preferred the young senator from Massachusetts. Although Kennedy was a little-known quantity to most of the Soviet leaders, Richard Nixon was all too well known. Khrushchev remembered a brief encounter with Kennedy during his official visit to the United States in 1959. He saw what he wanted to see in Kennedy's call for a "manifestation of wisdom and maturity, entering into a constructive exchange of views and negotiations with the Soviet Union." He appraised as sober and realistic Kennedy's criticism of the U-2 incident, and the speech in May 1960 in which Kennedy declared that if he had been President, he "would not have authorized such a flight." He also liked Kennedy's statements that the United States "did not desire a nuclear war."

But the honeymoon did not last.

Cuba sparked the first open clash between Khrushchev and Kennedy. Khrushchev knew there was a possibility that the United States would try to destroy the Castro regime, but he did not expect Kennedy to undertake such a step so soon after assuming the presidency.

When on April 15, 1961, an émigré armed force supported by the United States landed on Cuba near the Bay of Pigs, Khrushchev's plans were upset in two ways: he was compelled to speak out in defense of Cuba, exacerbating his relations with Kennedy instead of improving them as he had wanted, and the abortive invasion intensified the anti-American temper in the Politburo and the military leadership. The failure of the Cuban operation gave Khrushchev and the other leaders the impression that Kennedy was indecisive. This had far-reaching consequences and inspired future crises, not only in the Caribbean basin but in Europe as well.

It was against this background that Khrushchev and Kennedy met in Vienna in June 1961. Leonid Zamyatin, deputy chief of the Department of the United States in the Foreign Ministry, told me about it. Zamyatin always seemed to be very well informed and he was relatively young to be enjoying such a rising career. His amazing aplomb and self-assurance helped compensate for a lack of genuine talent and enabled him to promote himself. Gromyko soon appointed him chief of the ministry's press department. Zamyatin's time-serving in that post stood to his advantage later when he was designated director general of Tass, the Soviet news agency. He eventually became Brezhnev's main spokesman and chief of the Central Committee's International Information Department. Along with Georgy Arbatov and Vadim Zagladin, he was part of a troika of the most familiar Soviet faces appearing in the West whenever the Kremlin needed to influence public opinion there.

Zamyatin told me that the Vienna meeting had amounted to no more than the two heads of state taking each other's measure, and that Khrushchev had not intended to resolve any matters of substance during the encounter. The Premier, Zamyatin said, had concluded that Kennedy was a mere "boy" who would be vulnerable to pressure. "At present," he continued, "Nikita Sergeyevich is thinking about what we can do in our interest and at the same time subject Kennedy to a test of strength."

Among the people who met Khrushchev upon his arrival in Vienna was his erstwhile rival, Vyacheslav Molotov. At that time Molotov was the Soviet representative to the International Atomic Energy Agency, a relatively minor position in the Soviet foreign service.

Shortly before that I met Molotov and his wife, Polina, who had spent several years in exile on Stalin's orders. My family and I were on vacation at a *dom otdykha*, a ministry rest home, in the small village of Chkalovskaya near Moscow. The Molotovs and we shared the same villa there. Molotov no longer belonged to the top elite and had to spend his vacations in the same places as junior and mid-level diplomats.

As a result of our proximity and conversations, I had the opportunity to observe him at length. Although he had not lost his vitality or clarity of thought, I sensed in him an underlying depression and unease. He never mentioned what had happened to him, nor did he express any opinion about Khrushchev. Nevertheless, he maintained a lively curiosity about the Foreign Ministry and pressed me for details, both gossipy and substantive. Once he mentioned that in his day foreign policy had been much more solid and logical. He spent many hours of the day writing, and when I occasionally saw him in his room, I would always find him at his desk.

It gave me an odd feeling to be near a man of such savage reputation, justly infamous for his brutality during Stalin's rule. I thought it inappropriate for Molotov to hold any government position, and was glad to learn that soon after our meeting at the villa, he lost his post in Vienna and was ousted from the Party. His rehabilitation in Soviet publications during Brezhnev's time and finally, in 1984, his readmission to the Party at 94, are indications of the revival of Stalinism in the Soviet Union.

Some time after the abortive Vienna Soviet-American summit, I was assigned to a group working on German affairs. The team was swamped with demands for statements, draft messages to the heads of Western countries, and with preparing Khrushchev's voluminous speeches on the German question. The man who became my temporary superior was Anatoly Kovalev, a MGIMO graduate and Gromyko's adviser at the time. Kovalev was almost impossible to please. He frequently rejected drafts and texts presented to him, demanding they be totally reworked, usually with the comment that "every word in this is completely trite," as he tossed the paper back to its originator. Unhappy ministry personnel in turn accused Kovalev of paying more attention to phrasemongering than to substance, of preferring high-flown language to a clear exposition of the Soviet position. But since Gromyko also could not endure simple language, Kovalev's style suited his requirements well.

Kovalev was a favorite of Vladimir Semyonov, the Deputy Foreign Minister in charge of German affairs. In the mid-fifties Semyonov had been High Commissioner of Germany in the Soviet Zone, and when he talked about his days as commissioner, and later as Ambassador to East Germany, he would boastfully declare, "I was the master of nearly half of Germany."

He had done a lot of writing on theoretical subjects, quite enough, as he apparently saw it, to justify his casting himself in the role of a second Lenin. He even bore a certain physical resemblance to Lenin, with his bald spot, egg-shaped head, and bulging brow. He obviously enjoyed himself as he paced about his office, keeping his right hand in the pocket of his vest, as Lenin had done, while lecturing his subordinates. All of this provoked a good deal of laughter behind his back, as did the fact that he frequently published articles under one of Lenin's pseudonyms, K. Ivanov.

The Soviet position regarding Germany was that two sovereign states had appeared on German soil. As a result of developments in the postwar period, each was an "independent nation." It was therefore impossible to achieve "a mechanical integration of the two parts of the former Germany." I once mentioned to Semyonov that the idea of two German nations did not correspond to the characteristics of nationhood in accordance with Marxism-Leninism.

Semyonov replied disdainfully that Marxism-Leninism was an ongoing dialectical teaching, continually developing innovations. I felt as if I were before a MGIMO professor again, and I could not believe that he could delude even himself.

But the German people resisted the artificial division. East Germany had difficulties enough with West Berlin demonstrating for GDR citizens the incomparably higher living standards of the West. How could the Walter Ulbricht regime indoctrinate the East German population politically and ideologically with West Berlin undermining its efforts? Many GDR scientists, technological experts, intelligentsia, and large numbers of the most active strata of the population, especially the youth, were streaming into West Berlin and via that city to the Federal Republic. In a relatively brief period, more than three million people had fled the GDR to the West.

To stop this exodus, construction of the Berlin Wall began on the night of August 13, 1961. In many offices of the ministry a crisis atmosphere prevailed as we waited to see what kind of countermeasures Kennedy would take. But with the exception of one tense moment in November, when American tanks drove up to the line dividing Berlin in a direct confrontation with Soviet tanks, no incident occurred that threatened to develop into a military clash.

Pressure on West Berlin coincided with another Soviet move which created worldwide indignation. It was the decision to violate the informal moratorium on nuclear testing that we and the Americans had observed since 1959. The weapons planners must have strong-armed Khrushchev into resuming the tests, for we were in the midst of consultations with the Americans on ways to end them completely. I could scarcely believe it when I was instructed to help prepare our statement justifying the new round of tests. Kirill Novikov told us to draft a "convincing and solid explanation" of the decision.

"But it's idiotic," I protested. "It can't be justified. The whole world will condemn us for doing this. It'll look as if

147

we don't give a damn about the talks, as if the whole thing was just a charade on our part, and some of us *do* give a damn. I can't invent arguments for the indefensible."

"Arkady, Arkady," Novikov interrupted sharply, "no one is asking your opinion. This is an instruction. The decision has been taken, and that means it's justified. You find the justifications. Blame the French. They're America's NATO allies, and they've been testing despite the moratorium. We've been forced to this decision by the military preparations of the West. You know what to say. Just get to work and shut up."

He turned away, gulped a glass of vodka, and flicked his hand in dismissal. I could see that he shared some of my dismay, but he was too sensible, or perhaps too weary, to let his opinions show. Most of my colleagues, even my contemporaries, had constructed the same mask. Most of the time I wore it too. I had a few friends I could speak to frankly—as long as we talked in the privacy of an apartment, and after drinking had warmed our conversation—but I had almost no reliable outlet for the anger I often felt. Within, I seethed; outwardly, I conformed.

It appeared that Khrushchev's policies on Germany and the resumption of nuclear testing contradicted his course toward a businesslike dialogue with Kennedy, which was important if he was to carry out his planned economic reforms in the Soviet Union. But it was just classic Khrushchev: displaying a bold initiative and throwing his enemy into confusion. Khrushchev did not try to exacerbate the situation in Europe further. In October, he withdrew his threat to conclude a separate peace treaty with the GDR. It was no longer worth antagonizing Western Europe and promoting unity between it and the United States.

In the meantime, at the Twenty-second Party Congress in the fall of 1961, the Party's new program was adopted. For years people had wondered when we could expect to experience the perfection of a Communist society. After all, it had been decades since that idyllic life had been promised. Well, the new program purported to answer the question and give a timetable at long last. But without detailed knowledge of the economy and its development trends, most of us could not perceive how far from reality were the goals of the new program. Its pledge was to construct, in the main, Communism in the Soviet Union by 1980. It also vowed to ensure that the Soviet Union would be first in the world in per capita production by that time.

Proclamation of these goals inspired a happy optimism about our future. Enthusiasm was further bolstered by other decisions. Not only were Stalin's sins more fully aired than they had been five years before, but an energetic program of de-Stalinization was endorsed. It seemed possible at last that some of Stalin's fellow travelers might have to atone. Stalin's mummified corpse was removed from its place of honor next to Lenin's body in the Red Square mausoleum. Although his reburial was not announced, the symbolism was strong.

In 1962 the literary journal *Novy Mir* published Aleksandr Solzhenitsyn's breathtakingly frank novel about the prison camps, *One Day in the Life of Ivan Denisovich*. It was a sensation. For most of us who had not known the reality of the camps, the book gave the final lie to any notion of Stalin's good intentions. But this second false spring, a "thaw" more invigorating than the brief period after Khrushchev's secret report in 1956, soon ended with a firm reassertion of censorship and cultural orthodoxy. It left behind, however, a residue of candor in our lives. None of us was foolhardy enough to speak out, but we enjoyed an almost conspiratorial traffic in forbidden books, poems, songs, by those who were braver than we.

I SPENT NEARLY THE WHOLE OF 1962 IN GENEVA AS A MEMber of our delegation to the Committee on Disarmament. Negotiations on Khrushchev's fantasy of general and complete disarmament were among the most tedious, enervating experiences of my career. It was no less frustrating to have Valerian Zorin as head of the delegation. The worst part of it was that Zorin's faculties had begun to fail him. He would lose his memory in the middle of a conversation. Sometimes these seizures occurred during formal discussions. He would be presenting an argument and suddenly his mind

149

would take him to a completely unrelated subject. In talks with his aides the same thing happened. He would go silent and then look up at us in a daze, asking, "What year is this?"

This was bad enough, but more devastating was the inaction of my senior colleagues in the face of Zorin's obvious illness. They never told Moscow that anything was wrong. They kept pretending that all was normal until, in July, Gromyko arrived in Geneva to participate in the final stages of the conference on the neutralization of Laos. After a session in the garden of the Soviet villa when Zorin lapsed into nonsense, Gromyko drew me aside. "Has this been going on long?" he asked. I told him the truth: it had been happening for months.

Within a few days Zorin was sent home for treatment, and Vasily Kuznetsov came to replace him. Had it not been for Gromyko's visit, however, I do not know what would have happened. We had sat paralyzed while Zorin's condition deteriorated. No one had dared take the responsibility of acting. On a small, sad scale it was the pattern I was to see over and over for years to come.

Another reason I chafed under the tedium of our work in Geneva was that just before I arrived in February 1962, my daughter was born. She had been premature, but was nevertheless healthy and cheerful. I wanted to get back to Moscow, and Kuznetsov agreed to let me go when the committee recessed that fall. But negotiations among the United States, the United Kingdom, and the Soviet Union on halting nuclear weapons testing continued. Semyon Tsarapkin replaced Kuznetsov during the recess, and he insisted that I stay on.

I spent the evening of October 22, 1962, playing chess with Tsarapkin in the Soviet villa on the Chemin du Boucher, a quiet little street. Having deliberately lost several games to the capricious Tsarapkin, who bitterly resented being defeated, I went off to bed. He and I shared the villa with four other members of our delegation. The house was small and living arrangements were far from ideal. Tsarapkin, as head of the delegation, commanded a bedroom and bath for himself. The rest of us lined up mornings for the remaining bathroom. We spent much of our days stumbling over one another, since we not only lived in the tiny villa but worked there as well.

As I went to bed that October night, I had no suspicion that within a few minutes President Kennedy would announce his order to the U.S. Navy to intercept all Soviet vessels bound for Cuba, to inspect them, and to refuse to allow any ships carrying missiles of an offensive nature to proceed.

Everyone knew that the situation in that part of the Caribbean was tense. But we did not expect that Cuba would so quickly become the center of a potential cataclysm. We had been considerably more concerned about the intensifying hostility between Moscow and Peking and about strains in Europe.

On the morning of October 23, however, Cuba had our complete attention. Silently we sat in the living room reading the newspapers brought to us every morning from the Mission. The front-page headlines in the *International Herald Tribune* announced Kennedy's Cuban quarantine. No one wanted to be first to display his agitation or fear of the possible consequences. Finally, a colleague broke the silence by turning on the radio for the latest news, and we heard a torrent of commentary on the impending Soviet-American confrontation.

Tsarapkin paced the room. A big man, he seemed even bigger because of a disfiguring disease he had suffered as a young man which left parts of his body, fingers, ears, nose, grotesquely enlarged. He tried to act calm and optimistic. He told us we could be completely confident of victory in the just cause for which the Soviet Union was fighting. He declared firmly that the Americans had gone too far and that they would undoubtedly get what was coming to them. The Soviet Union would not permit the United States to get away with such a capricious act.

We murmured assent to Tsarapkin's views. Many of us, however, felt differently. Doubts about the reasonableness of Khrushchev's actions were deep among us, as I discovered as soon as we could talk out of Tsarapkin's presence.

Right after breakfast Tsarapkin and I headed for the Soviet Mission on the Avenue de la Paix, not far from our villa. Nikolai Molyakov, permanent representative of the U.S.S.R. to the UN office in Geneva, greeted us cordially, although there was no love lost between him and Tsarapkin.

A short time before the Cuban crisis, an episode occurred which greatly aggravated the natural antipathy between the two men. Tsarapkin, like all Soviet diplomats, had a very low per diem while he was assigned abroad, and tried to economize. Most of us at the villa hardly ever ate at restaurants. We often cooked for ourselves. But Tsarapkin's behavior was extreme: He went so far as to deny himself a normal diet. Huge lumps of lard were sent to him from Moscow, and in Geneva he bought eggs almost exclusively because they were cheap. One day his diet nearly cost him his life, when he consumed a large amount of lard and hard-boiled eggs and developed an intestinal blockage.

On the following day, I went to visit him at the hospital. To my surprise, the hospital staff told me that "Ambassador Tsarapkin has disappeared." I informed Molyakov immediately and he mobilized the entire Mission in a search. Soon, however, Tsarapkin turned up. As soon as he had received treatment, he slipped out of his hospital room through a window and set out on foot for our villa. He was well known in Geneva because of both his position and his appearance, and he did not want his embarrassing ailment and its cause to become known.

Molyakov, who had overall responsibility for the welfare of Soviet diplomats in Geneva, was furious that Tsarapkin had failed to call or contact him after he left the hospital. He was further upset when he found that Tsarapkin had been registered under an assumed name, leaving Molyakov to figure out how to get the Soviet government to pay hospital expenses for a nonexistent Soviet citizen. For his part, Tsarapkin was angry with Molyakov for alerting the Mission to his "disappearance" and thus to his hospitalization.

But on the morning of October 23, Tsarapkin and Molyakov were not thinking of their personal animosity. Molyakov announced that he had received absolutely no instructions from Moscow on how we were to proceed in the rapidly unfolding crisis. Tsarapkin said that he wanted to know whether he should continue negotiations with the United States and Britain on cessation of nuclear testing. Molyakov could give no help. Tsarapkin decided to query Moscow and commissioned me to prepare a cable.

There was no response from Moscow. For thirteen days we and the rest of the world held our breath. And for all that nerve-wracking time, the members of the delegation sat in ignorance of Moscow's thinking. We had known nothing of Khrushchev's plans to place missiles in Cuba, and we could not explain Soviet policy to Western negotiators or our allies in the socialist bloc. It was a surrealistic experience. We could follow the developments of the crisis in the Western press and over the air, but knew nothing of our own government's plans or position.

Why Khrushchev had risked such a venture was not clear to me until I returned to Moscow at the end of 1962. From people like Vasily Kuznetsov, who was involved in resolving the crisis in New York, friends in the Central Committee, high-ranking military men, and others, the truth emerged.

The idea to deploy nuclear missiles in Cuba was Khrushchev's own; many years later he admitted as much in his memoir.* Beyond a defense for Cuba, the more important gain would be a better balance of power between the United States and the U.S.S.R. Khrushchev's plan was to create a nuclear "fist" in close proximity to the United States, and at first glance it seemed seductive. The Soviet Union could get a "cheap" nuclear rocket deterrent, and accomplish much with very little.

With several dozen medium-range missiles installed in Cuba, the Soviets would have the capability of launching a nuclear strike against the United States that would threaten New York, Washington, and other vitally important centers along the East Coast. Moreover, Cuba's nearness to the United States would mean that the effectiveness of the American early-warning system would be impaired. In comparison with missiles based on Soviet territory, warheads from Cuba could be delivered in far fewer crucial minutes.

* *Khrushchev Remembers* (Little, Brown, 1970), p. 493.

Khrushchev's calculations were based upon the assumption that he could dupe the Americans by installing the missiles rapidly and secretly. Then he would confront the United States with a *fait accompli*. He believed that after successful implementation of the plan, the United States would not dare strike a blow, since this would threaten to unleash a nuclear world war.

To a substantial degree, such premises were based on Khrushchev's assessment of Kennedy's personal qualities as President and statesman. After the Vienna summit, Khrushchev concluded that Kennedy would accept almost anything to avoid nuclear war. The lack of confidence the President displayed during both the Bay of Pigs invasion and the Berlin crisis further confirmed this view.

I saw what Khrushchev's attitude was at the end of 1961, when I attended a meeting in the office of his personal assistants. Someone had remarked that Khrushchev, to put it mildly, didn't think very highly of Kennedy. At that moment, the Premier himself entered the room and immediately began to lecture us about Kennedy's "wishy-washy" behavior, ending with the remark: "I know for certain that Kennedy doesn't have a strong backbone, nor, generally speaking, does he have the courage to stand up to a serious challenge." Khrushchev's impression of Kennedy was a prevalent one among Soviet leaders generally.

In the West there has been a view that the Cuban operation was undertaken by Khrushchev at the instigation of the military. This is incorrect. Khrushchev imposed an arbitrary decision on the political and military leaders. Although some of them supported his idea, most were not interested in "quick fixes" and surrogate nuclear missile capability. They wanted solid, long-range programs to achieve parity with the United States both in quantity and in quality of strategic nuclear weaponry, and later to pursue superiority. That would take time and would involve astronomical expense, but there was no risk. Inevitably, these expenditures would undermine Khrushchev's plans to aid the consumer. Khrushchev had unrealistically committed himself with widely touted promises "to catch up with and surpass

America'' by 1970 in per capita production. He wanted guns *and* butter, or a modest amount of butter anyway.

The more serious among the military also foresaw that the United States might uncover the planned missile shipments to Cuba and try to stop them. They were well aware what little they could accomplish in that eventuality with their conventional forces. Khrushchev simply dismissed both possibilities and prevented comprehensive discussion of the issue by the Party Presidium (the Politburo) while severely limiting the number of top political and military officials who knew about the operation.

Once the crisis developed, Khrushchev had only two options if he decided on confrontation: a nuclear war, for which the United States was much better prepared, or a war limited to the area, also advantageous to the United States. Given the American geographical position and strength in the area, the Soviets would find it costly to penetrate the blockade or defend their ships. Moreover, Vladimir Buzykin, head of the Latin American Department in the ministry, told me that there were no contingency plans in the event the Cuban operation failed. By establishing the quarantine, Kennedy had presented Khrushchev with a *fait accompli* instead of the other way around.

In the aftermath of the crisis, it was plain that we had not been on the brink of nuclear war. At no moment did Khrushchev or anyone else in Moscow intend to use nuclear weapons against the United States. When the crisis broke, our leaders were preoccupied almost exclusively with how to extricate themselves from the situation with a minimum loss of prestige and face.

As a result of the missile crisis, military arguments prevailed: the Soviet Union should opt for numbers and quality of strategic nuclear weapons. In ensuing years, whenever opposition to the idea was voiced, someone would be sure to say, "Remember what happened with Cuba?" I recall a usually calm Kuznetsov declaring emotionally that in the future we would "never tolerate such humiliation as we suffered in the missile crisis." Khrushchev had to forget butter. He had to proclaim himself in favor of expending "enormous financial and other resources to maintain our military might at the appropriate level,'' adding that such necessity diminished the possibility of ''direct benefits to the people.''

There were other signs of Khrushchev's concessions to ideological hard-liners. He began to expound a more ''balanced'' assessment of Stalin, saying there had been two sides to his activities, the negative and the positive. He wavered on the limited liberalization he had initiated. His thaw proved neither stable nor coherent. He condemned an exhibition of abstract art in Moscow. Within a few months, he pounced on ''perversions'' in literature, declaring that the Party would fight ''decadent bourgeois tendencies'' wherever they might surface.

In the West, it is often said that Cuba was the beginning of the end for Khrushchev. This is true, but only to an extent. There were many more factors that precipitated his fall. But for me, the crisis stripped away my illusions about him. With relief I accepted the offer of an assignment in New York at our Mission to the UN, and Lina and I enthusiastically made plans to leave Moscow.

14

A YEAR BEFORE WE ARRIVED IN NEW YORK IN THE SUMMER of 1963, the Soviet Union had acquired a new building on East Sixty-seventh Street to house the Mission. Originally designed as an apartment house, it became a mix of offices and apartments for the diplomatic and clerical staffs.

Because so many people lived there, the smells of borscht and cabbage cooking hung in the air on every floor. In the elevators it was routine to meet diplomats' wives carrying bags of dirty laundry on their way to the basement washing machines. It was a poor arrangement: there was not enough office space for Mission personnel, and it was completely inappropriate for use as a residence.

Initially, Lina and I shared a room in a three-room communal apartment. The other two bedrooms were occupied by a military intelligence (GRU) general and his wife and a young couple with an infant. Although the accommodations were terrible and the lack of privacy miserable, we were all glad to be there.

In her first trip abroad, Lina was as excited and impressed with the United States as I had been five years before. And with my monthly salary of six hundred dollars we felt rich. We could buy good food—and of an astonishing variety to us—clothes, and other things we could neither afford nor find in Moscow. Like most other Soviets, our life was secluded. We spent our free time with a few friends, went to a movie occasionally, and familiarized ourselves with New York.

At first, Gennady and Anna stayed behind in Moscow. Gennady was eleven years old and could not go to school in New York. (At that time the Soviet school there went only through the fourth grade. Our son was in the fifth. Of course, no one was allowed to send children to American schools.) But we brought him to New York for every summer vacation. Anna joined us a month or two after we were settled.

I was already familiar with the UN's glass slab on the East River, but I would come to know it as well as my own room. My work put me into hundreds of discussions in the Security Council and the General Assembly and its committees, working sometimes around the clock during international crises, which stirred the UN to feverish activity. There were interminable consultations and tense days and nights studying the texts of messages to or from Moscow or drafts of speeches in the stuffy, small offices in the Mission building.

Disarmament matters continued to be my specialty, but as I went from the job of political officer to that of chief of the Mission's Security Council and Political Affairs Division, I acquired familiarity with many other issues. With the exposure went a schooling in the rigidity of Soviet policy

157

and in the futility of efforts from below to alter thinking at the top. Policy did change, often without warning, but never because a subordinate managed to make a persuasive case to his superiors, who in turn were subordinates of others.

Occasionally, however, my work was rewarding. Ambassador Nikolai Fedorenko, the head of the Mission, was an elegant man and a lenient boss whose expertise and consuming interest in foreign affairs lay in China. For other matters he relied on his staff and delegated a good deal of responsibility to junior officials.

Fedorenko was a colorful personality, but calm and gentlemanly with an aristocratic manner. In his prime he had been quite handsome, and was refined and engaging in company. I found working with him a pleasure. As a preeminent scholar of classical and modern Chinese literature, he spoke the language so fluently that he interpreted at the meetings between Stalin and Mao, including the last one in 1950. Even the Chinese were said to be impressed not only by his mastery of the modern language but also by his proficiency in ancient Mandarin.

I had been curious about China and its people since my MGIMO days, especially after the first Chinese students joined us at the institute after their revolution in 1949. Although we proclaimed our solidarity in social and academic activities, there was an uneasiness between us and the Chinese that no propaganda fanfares about eternal friendship and praise for the Chinese Revolution could obscure. One of my tutors while I was a junior diplomat, Ambassador Lev Mendelevich, once told me flatly, "You'll never be able to understand the Chinese and their logic, Arkady. None of us will."

I thought he was probably partially correct, but I had a growing conviction that we just didn't want to understand them. I believed we ought to study both East and West. After all, the threat from the Orient had been mesmerizing Russians since the invasions of Genghis Khan, feeding our uncertainty as to whether Russia would be a bridge or a battleground between East and West. Knowledge has often fostered toleration, even understanding. But should conflict develop, one is still better off with knowledge, for it is a great weapon in the arsenals of both offense and defense.

Fedorenko had spent many years in China before and after its revolution, and loved everything about it: the culture, art, history, traditions. He personally knew Mao and his main collaborators, as well as most of the prominent modern Chinese writers. This led to his major role in translating Mao's works into Russian.

Stalin's favor ensured that Fedorenko's career would prosper. Yet I do not believe he ever forgave Stalin's treatment of Mao and the Chinese. I also had the impression that the Soviet-Chinese rift became a personal tragedy for him, and was the main reason his official obligations as Ambassador to the UN were sometimes delegated to subordinates. He retreated more and more into scholarly pursuits. This attitude earned him Gromyko's distrust. In Gromyko's view, there could be no greater sin than a casual approach to one's formal duties. But there was more to it than that. Gromyko deeply and genuinely disliked Fedorenko because his personal style—long hair, flashy clothes, bow ties— clashed with the strict, official appearance Gromyko thought should be standard for all serious men.

Gromyko also envied Fedorenko's status in the Academy of Sciences and resented his appropriating furniture and knickknacks from the Glen Cove estate, which Gromyko considered his own property. Lidiya Gromyko managed to make off with two antique hall mirrors from the Long Island mansion to decorate her Vnukovo dacha, but lost a pair of bronze candelabra that the Fedorenkos spirited away before she could.

Fedorenko, like Malik, who later replaced him as Ambassador, detested Gromyko. But unlike Malik, who was a lion with his subordinates and a mouse with Gromyko, Fedorenko did not fear the minister. He was not afraid of losing his job, and in fact quit the bureaucracy long before retirement age.

He liked to spend as much time as possible in the serenity of Glen Cove, where he could think and write and forget the UN. From time to time, I joined him there for a drink and to talk. During those conversations in a relaxed atmosphere,

Fedorenko would smoke his aromatic pipe and sip a glass of the best cognac as he complained in melancholy tones that Stalin had never properly understood the Chinese character, nor the phenomenon or magnitude of their revolution. He criticized Stalin's view that Mao was a "margarine Marxist," a "peasant leader," but not a "great revolutionary."

He argued that Mao was right to not merely copy the Russian example in trying to find China's way to socialism. Fedorenko said that Stalin had always distrusted Mao, was unsure of him almost until the eve of his victory, and had courted Chiang Kai-shek as a buffer at the same time.

To Fedorenko, Mao was a great people's hero, an outstanding thinker, a man of simplicity and elusive charm. Stalin regarded Mao almost as a pupil and dealt with him as a mentor who knew when to pat him on the head or rap his knuckles with a ruler.

Normally reserved and softspoken, he grew boisterously excited as he described how, during a visit by the Chinese leader to the U.S.S.R., Stalin had wounded Mao's pride and dignity by keeping him sitting outside his office in a corridor, forcing him to wait for hours to meet with him, ignoring his presence in Moscow, thinking he was showing his superiority by doing so.

"It was so petty. Stalin's contempt was so disgusting that I didn't know how to prevent Mao from exploding," Fedorenko would sigh.

Mao had to restrain himself. He badly needed economic help from the Soviet Union. He wanted as well the Treaty of Friendship, Alliance, and Mutual Assistance as protection against Japan and a hostile America. Stalin finally gave Mao the treaty as a sop, and economic assistance initially smaller than what the U.S.S.R. had agreed to provide to some of its Eastern European satellites.

Fedorenko said that Khrushchev had repeated many of Stalin's mistakes and in addition made some of his own. One of the major ones was over the question of atomic weapons. The Soviet Union had promised to give China such weapons, but never wanted to implement its pledge and ended by reneging altogether. Again the Kremlin had insultingly treated China like a child. Naturally, this behavior exacerbated Peking's growing animosity toward Moscow. To Khrushchev, it was simply unthinkable to consider China an equal. He was unwilling to reach any kind of compromise on the matter. I once heard him declare: "The Soviet Union has been and must remain the indisputable leader of the world revolutionary movement. Mao has to know his place."

In the wake of the widening gap between China and the Soviet Union, a number of us concluded that our hardening stance toward China carried far-reaching implications for the U.S.S.R. China was our neighbor, like it or not. It was the most populous nation in the world and one with whom we shared a border more than four thousand miles long. What was Khrushchev doing? Many of us thought him reckless. But at our junior levels we could do nothing to change the policy of chauvinistic, patronizing behavior which the Chinese aptly called "hegemonic." Both Stalin and Khrushchev miscalculated that China would endure anything the Soviet Union wished to inflict and would not leave the "community" of socialist countries. It apparently did not occur to either of them that Mao might eventually pay them back in the same coin. Here lay the seeds of the split between the Soviet Union and China, planted in the soil of a historic mistrust. But our leaders, more than our history, were to blame for the Soviet Union's paranoid approach to dealings with Peking.

When Fedorenko and I spoke, Soviet-Chinese relations were at a very low point. Chinese reaction to the Cuban missile crisis had been violent. Peking charged Khrushchev with "adventurism" for having installed the missiles in Cuba and then with "capitulationism" for their withdrawal.

On the other hand, paradoxically, after the Cuban debacle Soviet-American relations improved and Kennedy's prestige in Moscow rose considerably. I arrived in New York to assume my duties on the same day President Kennedy made his speech at the American University in Washington in which he indicated his determination to improve relations with the Soviet Union. It was a welcome signal of Kennedy's good will and Khrushchev reciprocated. The two leaders began to develop a more rational approach to some important matters. Soon, the long negotiations on the test ban produced positive results. All nuclear tests in the atmosphere, underwater, and in space were to cease. On August 5, Gromyko, Secretary of State Dean Rusk, and British Foreign Secretary Lord Home put their signatures to the treaty. It was the first real breakthrough in arms control in the atomic age. A large majority of the world's nations quickly followed suit and joined the treaty.

But these signs of amelioration between Moscow and Washington were again a false spring. This time, however, Khrushchev was not to blame for the deterioration.

In November 1963, President Kennedy was assassinated in Dallas. Everyone in the Mission was stunned and confused, particularly when there were rumors that the murder had been Soviet-inspired. These accusations were based on the fact that the assassin, Lee Harvey Oswald, had lived in the Soviet Union for some time. Almost immediately, Moscow cautioned us to be vigilantly circumspect, and to report anything, no matter how small, about what was going on. We were also instructed to express sincere condolences to the American people and the United States government from the Soviet government.

In the aftermath of this awful event we were relieved to learn that Lyndon Johnson's administration did not intend to accuse the U.S.S.R. of participating in the assassination. But it was a question that lingered on. Americans would occasionally ask me whether the Kremlin had forgiven Kennedy for his humiliation of the Soviets over Cuba, or if that could have been a reason for Soviet participation in the plot. I always said I didn't believe it had anything to do with the President's death. Our leaders would not have been so upset by the assassination if they had planned it, and the KGB would not have taken it upon itself to venture such a move without Politburo approval. More important, Khrushchev's view of Kennedy had changed. After Cuba, Moscow perceived Kennedy as the one who had accelerated improvement of relations between our countries. Kennedy was seen as a man of strength and determination, the one thing the Kremlin truly understands and respects.

In addition, Moscow firmly believed that Kennedy's assassination was a scheme by "reactionary forces" within the United States seeking to damage the new trend in relations. The Kremlin ridiculed the Warren Commission's conclusion that Oswald had acted on his own as the sole assassin. There was in fact widespread speculation among Soviet diplomats that Lyndon Johnson, along with the CIA and the Mafia, had masterminded the plot.

Perhaps one of the most potent reasons why the U.S.S.R. wished Kennedy well was that Johnson was anathema to Khrushchev. Because he was a Southerner, Moscow considered him a racist (the stereotype of any American politician from below the Mason-Dixon line), an anti-Soviet, and anti-Communist to the core. Further, since Johnson was from Texas, a center of the most reactionary forces in the United States, according to the Soviets, he was associated with the big-time capitalism of the oil industry, also known to be anti-Soviet. He "smells oily" was the way he was described in Moscow.

The strange coalition had formed, the Soviets reasoned, because, for his part, Johnson strongly opposed Kennedy's desire to increase taxes on big oil; the CIA could not forgive Kennedy for his refusal to let the American Air Force aid the Bay of Pigs mercenaries in their attack, in which the Mafia was also interested, hoping to recover its lost Cuban business.

I thought that if someone outside the United States was involved in the assassination, Fidel Castro was a likely prospect. My colleagues in New York and Moscow said many times that Castro was terrified of Kennedy. Cuban leaders naturally harbored great hostility toward Kennedy, and these feelings were flagrantly displayed by one of Castro's closest associates, Che Guevara.

In December 1964, Guevara came to New York heading the Cuban delegation to the General Assembly session. Fedorenko thought they should meet, but Guevara was completely indifferent. The ambassador invited him to our Mission, assuming that a frank conversation could best be held on secure premises. Guevara refused to come to the Mission but said he would meet Fedorenko at the UN. The conversation took place in the Secretariat building in a cramped office that resembled a bomb shelter.

Guevara was wearing his usual beret, his usual green fatigues, and smoking his usual cigar. He was sullen. What was going on at the UN interested him very little. He spoke chiefly about the fact that the U.S. threat to Cuba had not been eliminated. Condemning Kennedy as a criminal, he was equally critical of President Johnson. It wasn't just the great powers, he said, who ought to benefit from peaceful coexistence. The concept should be applied to all countries without exception. He confirmed that when Khrushchev had suggested installing missiles in Cuba, the Cubans had welcomed the idea and had promptly agreed to it. Guevara said that the possibility of removing the rockets from Cuba had never crossed their minds.

He also stated bluntly that Cuba's leaders hoped Moscow understood that they could not help having a "bitter taste left in their mouths." The Cubans felt that the Soviet Union should have been tougher in defending its position. Fedorenko responded with the official explanations. The chill with which the talk began prevailed until its end.

Under Johnson's presidency Soviet-American relations steadily deteriorated, exacerbated by the escalating war in Vietnam. At the UN we were instructed to use every possible opportunity to excoriate the United States for its aggression against that country. But when the United States requested a meeting of the Security Council to consider Vietnam, we were ordered to object, and to say that the question should be settled only within the framework of the Geneva Agreements of 1954.

"This is stupid," I told Fedorenko. "Everyone can see that Soviet policy is first-class crap and what we want is propaganda points instead of a peace agreement in Vietnam." I suggested we report to Moscow that an absolute majority of UN member states favored discussion of the matter and that we should take that fact into consideration. Fedorenko refused.

"In principle, I agree with you," he said, "but it's our basic policy. If we advise the government to change it, they'll probably fire us and send people here who will do what they're told. Would that be any better?''

Although I spent time in Moscow in the summer of 1964, I got no inkling then of Khrushchev's impending ouster. Extreme secrecy and strict limits on the number of key players were the main ingredients of the successful palace coup in October 1964. Before then, the fact that Khrushchev's power was tottering was virtually invisible. Khrushchev himself was unable to detect the intentions of the powerful Kremlin group that engineered his fall.

NB Americans invariably seek the single main reason for any important action. Soviets don't approach things that way. There were many reasons—all important—why Khrushchev's opponents evicted him from power. If there was a last straw, however, it was probably his determination to order yet another shake-up of the Party apparatus at the coming November plenum of the Central Committee. This time it was to involve not only mid-level apparatchiki but higher cadre as well. Khrushchev's meddling could no longer be tolerated.

The Party bureaucrats had already been alarmed over Khrushchev's decision to divide their authority in the provinces into separate industrial and agricultural sectors. They feared a loss of personal security under the new rules governing Party organization that Khrushchev had virtually imposed at the Twenty-second Party Congress in the summer of 1961.

They were particularly angered by new provisions for systematic change in the composition of Party bodies, including limited reelection to these bodies for a specific number of successive terms. For example, members of the ruling Presidium were to have no more than three terms (fifteen years). The city and regional officials were to have even more frequent elections and a tenure of no more than six years. Nothing could have disturbed Party functionaries more. They could no longer count on a sinecure, with all its attendant privileges, as a lifelong career.

Khrushchev intended to implement these new rules and also revealed his plan for a major reshuffling of the senior

Party apparatus. Thus he encroached upon the holy of holies, the sanctum of the ruling class.

Khrushchev's style of rule and the changes he tried to set in motion finally turned all the major vested interests against him. His revelation of Stalin's crimes antagonized the KGB. The military resented his decisions to reduce excess manpower in the Army, forcing large numbers of officers into retirement. His adventure in Cuba had ended in disgrace. His economic and agricultural experiments had largely failed. His intermittent efforts to loosen, even slightly, restraints on writers and artists, to open the U.S.S.R. to more contact with the West, never consistent, had only brought trouble, especially for the orthodox ideologues and the KGB, who could tolerate no relaxation of censorship.

I think that Khrushchev realized what he was doing, but like so many of his other plans, his efforts to restructure the Party and government were poorly thought out. He had overestimated his strength and authority. Resentment of him grew to such proportions that key Presidium members agreed that he must go. That factor was decisive. Since the October Revolution, succession of power in the Soviet Union has been initiated and implemented, not by a majority of the rank-and-file Party members or apparatchiki, but from the top by a small group of the most influential politicians who make the decision in strict secrecy. The coalition that toppled Khrushchev, led by Suslov and Kosygin, used that tactic.

They understood that while Khrushchev was in Moscow he might be able to outmaneuver them as he had done before by launching a counterattack upon them, accusing them of "anti-Party activities." To the surprise of all—the Soviet people, the Party in general, the diplomats, as well as the rest of the world—Khrushchev was caught off guard.

He left Moscow to vacation in the Caucasus in the fall of 1964, and the group moved quickly, confident that the Party, the Army, and the KGB would support them. In October, Khrushchev lost his posts as First Secretary of the Central Committee and Prime Minister. He was replaced in these offices by, respectively, Leonid I. Brezhnev and Aleksei N. Kosygin. Khrushchev was allowed to keep his membership

166

in the Party and was pensioned off. Fate was much kinder to him than to many other Soviet politicians. In Stalin's day he would have been executed; Khrushchev was allowed to die in his own time.

His fall left me with mixed feelings. There is no doubt that Khrushchev was a complex and contradictory personality who left a significant imprint on Soviet and world history. I liked his energy, his earthy humor, his relative openness. I had hoped he could dispel the Stalinist legacy and set the Soviet Union on a more liberal course. Even though he had centered power in himself, he had tried to bring about reform at home, letting some air and light, for a while at least, into our stagnant society.

In Khrushchev were combined Communist orthodoxy and the deft intriguer. Realism and pragmatism cohabited in him with the adventurism and irrationality of a gambler: bluffing, bragging, and threats with a businesslike approach. He understood the danger of nuclear war, but aggressive expansionism was irresistible to him. He strove to revive the economy and raise the living standards of the people, but he did so with an experimentalism that proved ruinous. In him kindness lived side by side with cruelty.

He was at once a dreamer and a cynic, endowed with peasant wisdom and cunning, poorly educated but with an inquisitive mind, vital and inventive, impulsive and easily carried away. And he was the ultimate politician. Although at the peak of his career he individually made many crucially important decisions and held great power, he never achieved the absolute and uncontrolled despotism of Stalin. Particularly during the last years of his rule, he seemed unable to understand the inherent limitations and constraints on the ability of any single individual to determine the domestic and foreign policy of the Soviet Union.

Khrushchev's paramount fault was that he simply could not weigh the consequences of his actions thoroughly or coherently. It was the flaw which preordained his ultimate fall.

World reaction toward him was as contradictory as his own personality. Khrushchev became the most popular Soviet statesman in the West. But despite his charisma, he never succeeded in winning the affection of his own people. He desired unstinting praise. On his seventieth birthday in April, all the Party members in the Soviet Mission were obliged to assemble to endorse a formal resolution of fervid greetings. Fedorenko led the compulsory choir. His glowing rhetoric glorified Khrushchev's "wise, far-seeing leadership." The rest of us applauded and followed suit.

All those tributes came back to me in October, when Khrushchev was deposed. That occasion, too, required an act of obedience. Fedorenko stood before us again, this time to condemn Khrushchev's "adventurism." The resolution we then approved unanimously pledged our full support to the new Soviet leaders.

Both the April and October performances were meaningless except as reminders that we were puppets, expected to conform to any shift, denied any role beyond the anonymity of the easily replaced chorus member. Still, it was not a totally uncomfortable part to play. There was no risk. There were rewards, material ones for the most part, but also the satisfaction of winning approval from one's peers and superiors. There was also a bitter, perverse sort of pleasure to be savored in being a willing servant of the Soviet system: I was not the only hypocrite. The leaders had to pretend that they thought me loyal, a true believer in a tawdry philosophy. They had to lie as well—to me, to everyone, to themselves.

Most of the time I just worked. From 1964 to 1966, a kaleidoscope of events flashed and blurred at great speed. The international barometer almost always indicated storm. Soviet-American relations worsened from month to month over Vietnam. Turmoil in Cyprus, the Congo, and the Dominican Republic, as well as the conflict between India and Pakistan, kept the UN in nearly continuous session.

I looked forward to a pleasant break when I was called to Moscow to help prepare for the visit of French President Charles de Gaulle in 1966. I was eager to see what was going on in Moscow after Khrushchev, and I hoped to be able to meet our new leader, Leonid Brezhnev.

It had come as quite a surprise to all of us at the UN when Brezhnev was elected—or more precisely, selected—as

Party First Secretary. Mikhail Suslov or even Kosygin seemed to be far more prominent. Brezhnev was simply one among many ordinary faces that from time to time appeared and disappeared on the political horizon. He had begun his political career at the end of the thirties during the period of Stalin's purges. It was whispered that he had made use of that atmosphere for his own purposes and was favorably noticed by Stalin. After the dictator's death, however, Brezhnev was downgraded. But it was not long before Khrushchev again raised him from what was destined to be a routine Party career by making him a member of the Presidium and the Secretary of the Central Committee. In 1960, when Brezhnev became Chairman of the Presidium of the Supreme Soviet, I thought his political career had stalled, since that position as nominal chief of state was below that of the Party and government leaders. Traditionally, it had been given to persons who were sure to inoffensively mark time in the office until death or retirement. That had been the case with all Brezhnev's predecessors: Mikhail Kalinin, Nikolai Shvernik, and Kliment Voroshilov.

Khrushchev considered Brezhnev his man since it was he who had advanced him, but Khrushchev was mistaken. Brezhnev's ambitions were revealed at Khrushchev's removal. He had not been active in the ouster plan, and in fact had probably not been informed about it until Suslov told him at the last moment. Brezhnev did not defend his patron; on the contrary, he joined the group opposing Khrushchev.

Later on, Fedorenko told me that Brezhnev's position as First Secretary of the Central Committee came about under somewhat special circumstances. Suslov and Kosygin, the prime movers against Khrushchev, underestimated Brezhnev. Suslov seemed satisfied to be the Party patriarch and main ideologist. Kosygin was happy to be Chairman of the Council of Ministers and play the major role in both domestic economic and foreign policy. But it was difficult for them to agree on who should hold the position of First Secretary of the Central Committee. They finally settled on a dark horse—Leonid Brezhnev. They did not anticipate his further advance. Although they realized he could use his position to achieve his personal goals, they were aware of his

169

rather low intellect. They were convinced that this unprepossessing man would be unable to hold his own against them.

After becoming First Secretary, Brezhnev moved very cautiously. One could not detect who was really number one in the post-Khrushchev Kremlin. There were no drastic changes in foreign or domestic policy. The men who brought Khrushchev down were apparently unanimous in their determination to overthrow him, but otherwise they had different interests. What bothered me most was the new leadership's resurgent and visible course regarding a reassessment of Stalinism.

Since Brezhnev was a professional Party apparatchik, he began to strengthen his position among his cronies and those who had been through similar experiences and held like views in the Party. He promised to reunite the agricultural and industrial branches of the apparatus and to annul Khrushchev's reelection innovations.

By the spring of 1966, when I arrived in Moscow, Brezhnev had created a broader base of support in the Party. At the Twenty-third Congress, the Party Presidium was renamed the Politburo, as it was called when Lenin was alive. Brezhnev's post of First Secretary now became General Secretary. Behind this symbolism, Brezhnev's power was becoming entrenched. Naturally, Moscow jokesters were among the first to depict the attitude of the new leadership. Fedorenko told me a story that illustrated Brezhnev's power and the age-old Russian love of word play: A worker asked Brezhnev how to address him. He responded bashfully: "Just call me Ilyich." This was Brezhnev's patronymic name—the same as Lenin's—and indicated that Brezhnev was far from bashful. I soon saw that the egotistical image portrayed in the anecdotes around town was not far off the mark when I met Brezhnev while working on President de Gaulle's visit to Moscow.

Anatoly Kovalev, who was in charge of dealings with France, had arranged my participation in the project. In our first discussion he said candidly that because of worsening relations with the United States and China, we had to promote better rapport with Europe—and France was the number one target.

As I listened to Kovalev's exposition, memories from my youth came to mind. For a long time after World War II, Charles de Gaulle was portrayed for students at MGIMO as a chicken-brained cog in the military wheel, with pompous ambitions and fascistic dictatorial tendencies. As late as 1966, top political people regularly disparaged him, calling him a "long-nosed frog-legs."

Kremlin leaders were aware that negotiations with the French President would be difficult, but they were ready to ignore some of the interests of the French Communist Party, one of the largest in Europe and very critical of de Gaulle, to lure the general to their side against the United States.

Nevertheless, the question of how the French Communists would react was of concern to officials working on the matter in the Central Committee and in the Foreign Ministry. I was surprised to hear Kovalev state, without the usual diplomatic varnish, that "the French Communist Party is necessary to us, but it is not at all necessary to us that they achieve victory in the elections and come to power in France. That would cause more complications than benefits for us. After all, they could hardly retain power for very long, considering the French character and life-style. De Gaulle and the Gaullists—they're the real force. We've got to bet on them."

Gromyko was not present at the meeting with Brezhnev, but I knew his influence had increased enormously under the new reign. When I first entered his office on my visit home, one of Gromyko's assistants let it drop that the minister was on a casual "first-name basis with Comrade Brezhnev." From further conversations around the ministry I gathered that Gromyko was becoming Brezhnev's mentor in foreign policy matters.

The contrast between Brezhnev and Khrushchev was what struck me most. His well-tailored suit, an elegant shirt with French cuffs, and a pretentiously mannered style were very far from Khrushchev's baggy clothes and hearty, unaffected approach. Brezhnev exuded smug self-confidence, but he was also pleasant and cordial. After some small talk

171

he slowly read the material prepared by us. I sensed in his platitudinous observations about our proposals that he was not sure what he was talking about, as if he did not understand just what we sought from de Gaulle.

Unlike Khrushchev, Brezhnev seemed to have no ideas of his own to contribute. Khrushchev had always countered or embellished any suggestion with his own usually sensational, often original concepts. Brezhnev appeared to dramatize the truth of another joke making the rounds, in which a politician, asked whether the cult of personality had finally been eradicated after Khrushchev's expulsion, replied, "There can be no personality cult where there is no personality." Brezhnev was certainly no visionary, nor even an intellectual. His strength was that he was a man of unusual organizational ability. He also had a gift for compromise and was adept at maintaining a fine balance among different— even opposing—forces. He was an uninspiring leader whose illusion of strong and steady helmsmanship was mainly a scaffolding built around him by his subordinates.

De Gaulle's visit had a special significance for Brezhnev. It was at this time that he began his efforts to push Kosygin aside and to take important foreign policy matters into his own hands. Brezhnev wanted to be the one to deal with de Gaulle, but perhaps his choosing that visit to start wading into foreign policy was not the best. The general was a hard nut.

De Gaulle impressed me as a man of intellect, pride, and dignity. At the same time, he was tough and arrogant. At one meeting while we were racking our brains on ways to please him, Kovalev suggested that de Gaulle should meet our top military leaders and, as the first foreigner to be so honored, be shown the Soviet space center at Baikonur in the Kazakh steppes. The Politburo approved the idea and it was a success. De Gaulle displayed overt delight at the opportunity, the only sign of real pleasure he gave during the entire visit.

The result of the negotiations between the Soviets and de Gaulle did not fully meet Soviet expectations. He was cautious on European problems and refused to accept our formulations on the German question or on disarmament in the final Soviet-French declaration. He more or less shared Soviet criticism of American policy in Vietnam, but stopped short of declaring that it was an aggression, as Soviet leaders wanted.

IN MY NEW POST AS CHIEF OF THE SECURITY COUNCIL AND Political Affairs Division of the Mission, I had a staff of more than twenty diplomats. I soon discovered that in fact there were only seven who were real diplomats; the remainder were KGB or GRU professionals under diplomatic cover. Among them was Vladimir Kazakov, an energetic young man, definitely a rising star in the KGB, and Ivan Glazkov, a major general and chief of GRU operations in New York.

A number of Soviet nationals working in the UN Secretariat were also included in my division, in violation of the rules governing international civil servants. Their extra duties at the Mission produced little good work and they were there at the expense of their actual jobs in the Secretariat. It was common talk around the Secretariat that the Soviets were lazy drunks. In many cases it was true.

Yuri Ragulin, a Secretariat staffer and son-in-law of the Ambassador to East Germany, Petr Abrasimov, was one who exemplified the Soviets' poor image. He would often show up for work hours late, or not at all, as a result of his incessant carousing. Once, at a party at a friend's apartment on Manhattan's upper West Side, he became so drunk that he fell from a window on the fifteenth floor while vomiting out of it. He was unbelievably lucky: he landed on the roof of a church located next to the building. He was badly injured but he survived. The fire department had to rescue him from the roof. If he had been an ordinary junior diplomat, of course, he would have been dismissed and sent home immediately, but his father-in-law came to his rescue.

Another practice that caused disparaging gossip in the Secretariat was the government's insistence on kickbacks from Soviet nationals' UN salaries. At the end of each month, Soviet employees of the Secretariat lined up at the Mission bookkeeper's office to hand over the money they

173

earned at the United Nations. The Mission required all Soviet nationals employed in the Secretariat to cash their paychecks before coming to its financial office, where they were obliged to turn in all their cash. They would then be paid their "salary" according to the scale established by the Soviet government, which deducted a considerable amount of the money received from the UN. For example, in my time the monthly salary of a senior UN officer (P-5) was about $2,000 per month, more or less. The Soviet scale set the salary of such an officer at the level of that paid to the Mission's counselor (less than $800 per month). Thus, the Soviet government took more than $1,000 each month from a P-5's UN salary.

Naturally there was resentment at this extortion, but there was very little lagging in turning over the money. Every month the Mission's bookkeeping department listed the names of those who had delayed even for a few days in returning their "excess funds." They were reported to the ambassador and to the Party organization. "Malicious debtors," those who hung back for some time, were subjected to public criticism at Party meetings. Moreover, the ambassador would personally scold them for not observing "discipline."

These kickbacks provided significant benefits to the Soviet Union. The Mission managed to cover almost all its expenses from the earnings of UN employees. The United States is the big loser in this, because it bears the heaviest financial burden of contributions to the UN budget. To add insult to injury, at least half the Soviet nationals working in the international organization are not diplomats, but KGB or GRU professionals. Through the kickbacks, the United States indirectly finances the activity of Soviet intelligence services.

Secretary General U Thant, Dag Hammarskjöld's successor, most likely knew of this practice, but there was little he could do about it. If he objected, the Soviets would simply deny everything and that would be that. Soviet nationals would not dare to supply the proof.

U Thant, who was quiet to the point of torpor, was a marked contrast to the colorful Hammarskjöld. He played a useful role in allaying overheated passions during the Cuban missile crisis and in working out its settlement afterward. But his decision to recall UNEF, the UN force deployed in the Sinai Peninsula, on the eve of the Six-Day War in 1967 was considered a mistake by many UN members and earned him considerable opprobrium.

15

ON SUNDAY EVENING, JUNE 4, 1967, I WAS WITH FEDOR-enko at Glen Cove. Over a glass of cognac, we discussed the growing tensions in the Middle East. It was becoming obvious that war was in the offing and that difficult days were ahead of us in the Security Council. As usual, Fedor-enko was calm. He referred to a top-secret cable we had recently received saying that Moscow had advised Nasser against starting a war. I doubted that the Egyptian leader would listen. My previous experiences with representatives of Arab nations taught me that our government followed the Arab line, not the reverse. In the Security Council we had standing instructions to permit no decisions against Egypt, Syria, or Jordan. We were also to make every effort to obtain Council condemnation of Israel.

About 4 a.m. I was awakened by the officer on duty at Glen Cove. "Hans Tabor* is calling on an urgent matter," he said. "Should I wake Nikolai Trofimovich or not?" he asked. I replied that I would talk with Tabor first.

Tabor excitedly told me that war had erupted between Egypt and Israel and that he wanted to inform the Soviet representative of his intention to convene the Security

---

* Permanent representative of Denmark to the UN, and President of the Security Council at the time.

Council as early as possible in the morning. I woke Fedorenko, and he agreed to Tabor's proposal.

Fedorenko said we should return to the Soviet Mission immediately, where we would find instructions from Moscow. As we drove, we listened to the news on the car radio. According to press accounts, Israel had destroyed almost the entire Egyptian air force on the first day of the war.

When we arrived at the Mission there were no instructions. We waited for a while, but as there was still no word, we went to the UN. Our first meeting was with the Egyptian representative, Mohammed el-Kony, a total mediocrity. He was cheerful, insisting that reports of Egypt's loss of its air force were inaccurate. "We deceived the Israelis. They bombed some of our false airfields, where we deliberately placed fake plywood airplane models. We shall see who wins this war."

I was far from sure his evaluation was correct, and I said as much to Fedorenko, who agreed: "One can hardly trust El-Kony. Let's wait and see what Moscow says."

The morning session of the Security Council didn't last long. After that, Hans Tabor conducted private consultations among Council members and interested parties. The military situation was cloudy. Even if Israel had destroyed a major part of Egypt's air strength, Israeli tanks had not yet encountered Egyptian armor. At the same time, Syria, Jordan, and Iraq had begun operations against Israel.

Confusion prevailed among members of the Security Council. The figure who stood out in these consultations was Ambassador Arthur Goldberg, the American permanent representative to the UN. Able, intelligent, and eloquent, Goldberg was our vigorous and formidable opponent. Fedorenko and others in our delegation referred to him as a "slick Jew who could fool the devil himself." But while they disparaged him, they envied his talents. Although we were advocates of differing positions, Goldberg and I had developed a personal rapport and good working relations. I particularly valued his businesslike approach to difficult and delicate problems. He disdained the idle talk so characteristic of many UN meetings. And he was a master at devising compromise formulas. Goldberg's many years as a union lawyer, his work as Secretary of Labor in the Kennedy administration, and his service on the U.S. Supreme Court gave him exactly the right kind of experience for working among the differing positions in the UN.

During the consultations, Goldberg insisted that there be an immediate cease-fire. At the same time, he informally suggested that the cease-fire be coupled with a return of Israeli and Arab forces to their positions on May 18, before Egypt moved its troops into Sinai and Aqaba. Goldberg's proposal meant that Israeli forces should withdraw from the part of the Sinai they occupied and that Egyptian forces should likewise withdraw to their previous position behind the Suez Canal. The Egyptians categorically refused. They wanted only the removal of Israeli forces and sought to keep their troops massed on Israel's border.

The instructions that finally arrived from Moscow had a wait-and-see tone, while generally supportive of the Arab position. We were ordered to consult with the Arabs and condemn Israel in the strongest terms.

A deadlock developed in the Security Council on June 5. Later that evening, Fedorenko and I met again with El-Kony and representatives of Syria and Jordan. I advised Fedorenko to try to influence them to accept Goldberg's informal proposal. He agreed, but El-Kony was adamant. I thought the Arabs were making a terrible mistake. They seemed to be quickly losing the war, and I felt that if they did not agree to Goldberg's idea, they would regret it.

Around midmorning on June 6, we received a telephone call on an open line from Moscow—an extraordinary occurrence—from the Deputy Foreign Minister, Vladimir Semyonov. He said that there would soon be new instructions and that we should arrange a meeting with Goldberg immediately upon receiving them. Our new orders were to accept Goldberg's idea, but if it proved impossible to get a decision on that basis, we were to agree to the Security Council's proposed resolution on a cease-fire as the first step. The instructions, signed by Gromyko, stressed: "You must do that, even if the Arab countries do not agree—repeat, do not agree."

We tried to contact Goldberg, but were unable to reach

him for some time. It was plain that the tide of war had turned very much in Israel's favor. Now Moscow wanted the quickest possible action by the Security Council. When Fedorenko finally got to Goldberg, it was too late. Goldberg said that his previous plan had been informal and that the United States now insisted only upon an immediate cease-fire. He added tartly that the Soviet side, Fedorenko in particular, had made no positive response to his initial idea, and that now the most urgent consideration was to stop hostilities without further complications. We accepted his proposal.

The Security Council adopted several resolutions before the war ended with a shaky cease-fire. There then began the endless discussions regarding withdrawal of Israeli troops from occupied Arab territories and the Middle East peace settlement.

The lesson for the Arabs should have been clear. The Soviet Union was ready to supply weapons to some Arab countries, to train their armies with Soviet advisers, to give them economic aid, but it was not prepared to risk military confrontation with the United States in the region. Soviet leaders were eager to establish their influence in Arab countries, but they had never been willing to defend their clients effectively. On the contrary, the Six-Day War demonstrated the U.S.S.R.'s willingness to turn away from these countries in a critical moment after having encouraged the passions which precipitated the showdown.

I watched this process closely for more than ten years. At the United Nations and in the Foreign Ministry, the Soviet Union tied itself increasingly to the more extreme Arab positions and regimes. With quiet backing from Gromyko, I tried to moderate this, to rebuild working contacts with Israel and Egypt. But my efforts were of marginal importance. Without determined support from Moscow they meant little.

It was ambition for a foothold in the Middle East which, in 1948, had prompted the Soviet Union to be the first nation to recognize the new Jewish state. With no ties to the Arabs in the region, Moscow hoped to be able to influence the Jews, many of them Russian-born, who created Israel. Nasser's revolution in Egypt and America's refusal to aid his

178

economic projects in the mid-fifties opened another door for Soviet political and military activity. But whether the client was Egypt or Syria, South Yemen, Iraq, or the Palestinians, the Kremlin's purpose was always the same: to establish and widen Soviet power in the Middle East, to use the area and its rivalries as a means of contesting and undermining Western strength. Party policymakers regarded the Arab world as fertile ground for the furtherance of Soviet ideology. Military strategists saw its geography in terms of transit and servicing for Soviet ships in the Mediterranean and the Indian Ocean, as staging areas for troops, as proving grounds for Soviet weaponry. Against these drives diplomats could bring little moderating force to bear.

Defeated, at least by proxy, in the Sinai and on other fronts, the Soviets also lost in the Security Council their diplomatic push for immediate Israeli withdrawal; the United States vetoed Moscow's proposal. Hoping to muster a majority for the idea in the General Assembly, the Soviets called for an emergency session of that body and sent a high-powered delegation to New York headed by Premier Aleksei Kosygin and Gromyko.

Kosygin still retained his role as Kremlin spokesman on foreign affairs, although his position had been substantially weakened by Brezhnev's expanded authority in the field, guided by Gromyko. Kosygin, another of the Soviet leaders who first attained prominence in the wake of Stalin's purges, rose and survived within the Soviet hierarchy by pursuing a technocrat's career. Dry even by Soviet standards, he deviated from the standard bureaucratic model only in the notable patience he showed subordinates. Kosygin was more intelligent than many of his colleagues, and normally expressed himself clearly, logically, and directly—traits at variance with the circuitous evasiveness so characteristic of Soviet bureaucrats. Free of personal foibles or idiosyncrasies, he was so ascetic that in New York his daughter Ludmilla, armed with a long shopping list of her own, could not think of anything to buy that her father would want or need.

During the mid-sixties, Kosygin was tough and effective in promoting some needed economic reforms. His efforts to encourage less rigid economic management without interference from Party functionaries failed, but it was not really Kosygin's fault; even Khrushchev failed to alter the system.

I believed that Kosygin, out of self-preservation, deliberately chose to avoid the many intrigues and power plays in the Kremlin. Later on, Brezhnev pushed him aside still further, and several times Kosygin submitted his resignation to the Politburo. Although there was little rapport between the two men, Brezhnev turned these offers down, and continued to pretend respect for Kosygin while in fact ignoring his views more and more. Kosygin had also disliked Khrushchev, whose freewheeling style was absolutely incompatible with Kosygin's well-organized, cautious approach.

Kosygin regarded the West as a useful source of help to the Soviet Union. He favored development of trade and economic relations with the United States and Western Europe. But here too he was cautious, sometimes suspicious. He was also more orthodox than Brezhnev in his approach to the war in Vietnam. (Brezhnev had already begun to consider how best to exploit American involvement in Vietnam to benefit the U.S.S.R. without unduly irritating our "comrades" in Hanoi.) In the summer of 1967, however, Kosygin was the Soviet leader charged with opening a dialogue with a U.S. President. In addition to representing the U.S.S.R. at the emergency General Assembly session, he intended to discuss both the Middle East and Vietnam with President Johnson. But he had practically no authority to make any commitments and was given very little room for flexibility, and Kosygin correctly anticipated that his meeting with Johnson would produce no progress on either issue. The prospect of returning to Moscow completely empty-handed disturbed him. Ambassador Dobrynin and Kosygin's assistant, Boris Batzanov, another MGIMO graduate, told me that Kosygin did not want to see Johnson. Failure in the discussions would undermine his prestige as a negotiator and would bolster Brezhnev's efforts to reduce Kosygin's role in foreign affairs. Yet the conference had to take place; it was a Politburo decision. For a short while, Kosygin thought he had found a way to avoid the meeting in an apparent impasse between the Politburo's instructions that he was on no account to travel to Washington and the Americans' refusal to have the President come to New York; the two sides argued for days over the locale of the summit, neither giving ground. Finally, a suitable neutral territory was found: a university president's home in Glassboro, New Jersey. Kosygin returned from Glassboro with very meager results. "We agreed on next to nothing," he grumbled.

At this moment Soviet leaders were, as Adam Ulam has observed, "still undecided on how to exploit the attrition of U.S. power and prestige that resulted from America's disastrous policies in Southeast Asia."* And there was as well a division in top-level Soviet thinking over the approach to take toward the Middle East—whether to adopt an inflexible stand against Israel or a position that would leave room to maneuver between Arabs and Jews. Then and in later years, Gromyko leaned toward ambiguity. Kosygin, however, had come from Moscow with a draft speech that condemned Israel as an aggressor against Egypt, Syria, and Jordan, demanded complete withdrawal from all the land taken in the Six-Day War, and offered no affirmation of Israel's right to exist.

After considerable discussion, all of which Kosygin listened to with calm, unemotional interest, Gromyko and Dobrynin were able to persuade him to include a mention of the historical record of Soviet support for Israel's nationhood. Moscow approved it, but the Soviet delegation had to be content with a characteristically negative formulation: "The Soviet Union is not opposed to Israel . . . each nationality has the right to creation of its own independent state." The rest of the address, however, was violently anti-Israel, and the draft resolution, condemning Israel for aggression, called for an unconditional withdrawal of its troops from all occupied Arab territories.

The proposal was unrealistically harsh, since it was not mitigated by any recognition of Israel's concerns. It proved too strong to attract majority support at the General Assembly, but when Latin American nations drafted a compromise resolution, the Arab states rejected it as too weak. Kosygin

* Adam B. Ulam, *Expansion and Coexistence: Soviet Foreign Policy, 1917–73.* 2nd ed. (Praeger Publishers, 1974).

181

returned to Moscow, while Gromyko stayed at the UN, negotiating through Dobrynin with Goldberg a third version that called both for withdrawal of troops and for the right of all states in the Middle East to independence and to live "in peace and security." Even that formulation, however, failed to meet Arab demands. The emergency session ended in failure.

The diplomatic pace picked up again in November, when Deputy Foreign Minister Vasily Kuznetsov arrived with orders to break the stalemate. While he consulted with the Arab delegations and the major powers, I acted as an intermediary to the non-aligned nations who were trying to draft their own compromise and were keeping their maneuverings as secret as possible. The non-aligned compromise language failed to satisfy all the Security Council members, and Lord Caradon, the British Ambassador to the UN, took the lead in the effort to reach an acceptable compromise. The witty and talented Englishman found the key that finally unlocked the impasse. His formulation, calling for "withdrawal of Israeli armed forces from territories occupied in the recent conflict," was purposely ambiguous about the key issue of whether or not Israel had to give up *all* its conquests.

The negotiations that produced this intentionally imprecise wording were intensive and arduous, with genuinely skilled diplomats—Kuznetsov, Caradon, Dobrynin, and Goldberg—at work. But Resolution 242, adopted unanimously by the Security Council, did not resolve the problem. All sides—the Arabs and Israel, the Soviet Union and the United States—interpreted it in different ways, and many efforts to implement the resolution brought no result.

IN EARLY AUGUST 1968, I LEFT FOR A VACATION IN THE Soviet Union. When I arrived at the Foreign Ministry in Moscow, I found the offices of Gromyko and Kuznetsov in turmoil. Everyone had worked to exhaustion over the situation in Czechoslovakia, and when I learned of the preparations for a military invasion, I felt lucky not to be in New York trying to defend the Soviet position.

In New York I had been following developments in

Czechoslovakia for some time with Jiri Hayek, the Czech representative to the UN, who later became his country's foreign minister, and Milan Klusak, son-in-law of President Ludvik Svoboda. At the end of 1967 Antonin Novotny was dismissed as Czech Party leader, replaced by Alexander Dubcek in the period that came to be known as the "Prague spring." Brezhnev appeared to be making an effort to resolve the problem of the so-called Czech "revisionists" through dialogue, and seemed willing to accept the process of liberalization. Whether this was so or not, however, there was strong pressure from some Politburo members (particularly Mikhail Suslov and Petr Shelest) to curb this liberalization process by force. Among the leadership there were qualms about invading Czechoslovakia until virtually the last moment—memories of world reaction to Soviet treatment of Hungary in 1956 were still strong. In the end, the Politburo sanctioned invasion, inventing as its justification the "Brezhnev Doctrine," which maintains—contrary to the principles as well as the letter of the UN Charter—that the Soviet Union and other Communist countries have the right to intervene militarily if, in their view, one of them pursues policies that threaten essential common interests.

On August 21, Soviet troops with token detachments from four Eastern bloc countries invaded Czechoslovakia in a swift operation. A three-star general told me that the Army had learned its lesson well after its experience with Hungary, and because of that the operation in Czechoslovakia was a "brilliant one." That was true; the Soviet emergency mobile force—paratroopers, tank units, and other troops—accomplished all its objectives in a matter of hours with no losses.

After Khrushchev's ouster, the military was directed by the Party Presidium to create a mobile force for such emergencies, for use not only in Soviet bloc countries but in any part of the world. This program provided for construction of aircraft carriers, helicopters, and military transport planes capable of carrying light tanks, cannons, and tactical missiles and also for training a special paratrooper force headed by officers who spoke foreign languages. The mobile force is much stronger and more sophisticated today than it was in 1968.

In spite of the crises, frustrations, and upheavals during the sixties, I had moments of satisfaction in my work. Final negotiations in 1968 leading to the Non-Proliferation Treaty were not easy, but compromises were finally found. To a substantial degree their success was due to energetic efforts by the peripatetic Vasily Kuznetsov, who again had come to New York.

Unlike most others who had risen to power under Stalin, Kuznetsov was a responsive human being as well as a sophisticated politician. We had enjoyed close business associations as well as personal rapport as far back as the early sixties when I was in Geneva participating in disarmament negotiations. Kuznetsov was the highest-ranking Soviet official I ever heard express himself so bitterly about the Stalinist era. One afternoon we were walking beside Lake Geneva, admiring its beauty, when he suddenly began speaking about the hellishness of life under Stalin. "Any moment you could expect a knock at the door. You never knew if tomorrow you would go to your office or to jail." He particularly despised the *anonimki* (anonymous letters) that reached his desk describing the wrongdoings and peccadilloes of this or that diplomat. That filthy practice, usually based on nothing beyond the sender's malice or envy, has continued to flourish, but it had been an art during Stalin's days. "If someone wants to correct something he should do it openly, not cravenly send these sniveling, spiteful notes," Kuznetsov said.

Kuznetsov's openness may have reflected the fact that he had lived for several years in the United States. In the early thirties he stayed with an American family in Pittsburgh, where he took advanced training as a metallurgical engineer. Back in the Soviet Union, he later became chairman of the Soviet Trade Union Council. After Stalin's death, he was appointed Ambassador to China, and he bloomed as a diplomat. Sober-minded, reasonable, pragmatic, and cautious, Kuznetsov had unique abilities when it came to maneuvering in the intricate labyrinth of Soviet foreign policy. With endless patience, he was able gradually to persuade both adversary and Politburo to make one small and seemingly insignificant change after another until a compromise was within reach.

He had an extraordinary sense of timing: he knew exactly when there was no other choice but to be unyielding and tough and when to show flexibility. He also had a deep understanding of the flow of mood in the Kremlin, and possessed a talent for being businesslike and cordial and at the same time bluntly frank with his counterparts at the bargaining table. Invariably, Kuznetsov was assigned to critical negotiations in which he might be required to save a situation.

For Kuznetsov's efforts in achieving approval of the Non-Proliferation Treaty, Lord Caradon, the British representative to the UN, paid tribute to him in an original manner. In a speech before the Security Council in June 1968, Caradon concluded with the following:

> As I have sat here in the Council, I have occupied myself by composing these memorable lines which I dedicate to the Deputy Foreign Minister:
>
> When prospects are dark and hopes are dim,
> We know that we must send for him;
> When storms and tempests fill the sky,
> "Bring on Kuznetsov" is the cry.
>
> He comes like a dove from the Communist ark,
> And light appears where all was dark;
> His coming quickly turns the tide,
> The propaganda floods subside.
>
> And now that he has changed the weather,
> Lion and lamb can vote together.
> God bless the Russian delegation.
> I waive consecutive translation.

Despite serious tensions over Vietnam and the Middle East, there was positive cooperation between the two superpowers in achieving approval of the Non-Proliferation Treaty. We divided the UN membership into two categories: those nations that could be influenced by the Soviet Union and those that could be persuaded by the United

States. My colleague Oleg Grinevsky and I visited the U.S. Mission to discuss how to work on one or another UN representative, how to convince him to vote for the treaty, or how to continue joint efforts in various capitals of non-nuclear states to gain their support.

I discovered an interesting thing. The American delegation could contact their ambassadors to African, Asian, or Latin American countries directly and ask them to do business at the highest levels of the host governments. We, however, had no right to communicate with Soviet embassies abroad. We had to ask Moscow to issue instructions to our ambassadors to hold such discussions. Our ambassadors' replies were first given to Moscow and then to us. It was ridiculous, but even the Soviet Mission in New York was not permitted to coordinate its actions with the Soviet Embassy in Washington. If it was necessary to discuss a matter with the American government, we had to cable Moscow, and Moscow would transmit it to Dobrynin, despite the fact that the Soviet Mission and Embassy are located less than two hundred and fifty miles apart. This does not mean that the Soviet ambassadors in New York and Washington have no conversations at all, but such communications are unofficial.

Our roundabout means of communication meant that in some instances the resulting message was as garbled as the fourth telling of a story. Some Soviet ambassadors reported to Moscow their success in obtaining approval of the treaty. But this could be misleading, because neither the ambassadors nor in some cases the officials they talked to in various capitals were aware of pertinent details. Often the positions taken by some of these countries' UN ambassadors were different from what we were told by Moscow. We would then have to clarify with Moscow what was going on, requiring further talk between the Soviet ambassadors and leaders of different nations, which once more went back to Moscow, and through Moscow to us. If this process had not been so frustrating, it would have been a perfect Laurel and Hardy plot.

Joint Soviet-American efforts were decisive in ensuring the approval of the Non-Proliferation Treaty by a UN majority. A strong Albanian attack and the positions of Tanzania and Zambia were not surprising: they had acted under China's influence. Cuba's stance upset Kuznetsov very much. Despite his efforts and others', Cuban representatives strongly criticized the treaty, declaring that it would just "legalize the gap between the strong and the weak."

In general, relations between Moscow and Havana had been characterized by a certain amount of discord. In the early sixties Soviet leaders felt that conditions for socialist revolution in Latin America had not yet matured, and they did not support Castro's goal of overthrowing various governments in the area. On the contrary, Moscow was interested in developing normal relations with many of those governments. But Castro created a center of guerrilla warfare in Cuba.

It was the Cuban crisis, of course, that precipitated the worst erosion of relations between Havana and Moscow. In 1962, Castro demanded the recall of the Soviet Ambassador to Cuba, Sergei Kudryavtsev, and actually selected his replacement, Aleksandr Alekseyev, who at that time was a counselor in the Soviet Embassy in Havana. It was widely known that Alekseyev was a professional KGB officer. If Castro knew Alekseyev was KGB, and most likely he did, he didn't care. They were personal friends and drank and womanized together. Worst of all, the relationship strengthened the KGB's natural inclination to accept Castro's ideas about subversive activities. Reluctantly, Moscow agreed to Alekseyev's appointment, although it was highly irregular for a KGB officer to be appointed to an ambassadorial post.

Castro boycotted the celebration of the fiftieth anniversary of the Soviet Revolution in October 1967, although he knew the importance the Soviets attached to this event. He criticized the Soviet Union for failing to give effective assistance to Egypt during the Six-Day War; he expressed disgust with the Soviet attitude toward the Chinese.

Castro intended to be actively involved in the non-aligned nations movement, often disregarding coordination and guidance from the U.S.S.R. While Moscow did not object to Cuba's promoting its ideas among the non-aligned nations, it was not much pleased by Castro's growing influence in the Third World.

At the UN the Cubans tended to ignore unofficial gatherings of the socialist countries. Before any major vote in the General Assembly, the Soviet Mission would convene a meeting of its allies and let their representatives know what the Soviet position was on the particular issue. These meetings might take place at the Mission, or in the Indonesian Lounge at the UN, or even in the corridors there. Sometimes there was discussion about the Soviet stand—Romania and other allies would occasionally express reservations. The Soviet delegate would also ask the allied representatives to solicit votes from countries outside the bloc. The Cuban Ambassador to the UN, Ricardo Alarcón, would often not show up at all at these meetings, and not bother to call. This infuriated Ambassador Malik, who had replaced Fedorenko in 1968. "Where is Alarcón?" he would demand. "Call the Cuban Mission." When Alarcón did come, he said very little. He would not share information fully with the Soviet Ambassador about what was going on at meetings of the non-aligned countries. If he was asked directly, he would smile knowingly and remain silent.

Castro got away with tantrums and insults because Cuba was important to the Soviets' future plans. Although Castro had asked China for support, Peking couldn't afford to give Cuba much economic aid. So Castro had no choice but to return to Moscow's embrace. Gradually, however, the Kremlin became more sympathetic to Cuba's contention that socialist revolution in Latin America should be accomplished by military rather than peaceful means.

By 1970, I HAD REACHED THE LIMIT OF UNINTERRUPTED time diplomats were allowed to work abroad. Normally, extended duty lasts four or five years up to two terms in the same country. (A notable exception to the rule is Ambassador Dobrynin in Washington.) If one should be selected for a third tour of duty, however, the assignment is carefully scrutinized by the Foreign Cadres Department of the Central Committee.

Soviet diplomats generally are kept in the dark about their future jobs at the conclusion of extended duty abroad. A new posting often depends upon accidental circumstances —such as a vacancy in the central apparatus of the ministry —and, mainly, on personal connections and friendships in the ministry and the Central Committee. Therefore, nearly all Soviet diplomats anticipating new assignments experience a period of nervous strain and active lobbying in order to obtain an appointment in a location they desire. I was lucky, insofar as I knew in advance about my future job.

I had arrived in New York as a first secretary and left with the rank of envoy extraordinary and minister plenipotentiary, a quick career jump by Soviet standards. My material dreams had also been realized. While living in New York, Lina and I had acquired a large apartment in Moscow and had furnished it in style. In 1968, we bought a dacha, the ultimate symbol of privilege in Soviet society.

When Gromyko, on a visit to New York in 1969, offered me a post as his adviser, I accepted with alacrity and anticipation. It was not just the promotion in status I welcomed. I hoped that at Gromyko's side I might be able to play an active part in shaping Soviet policy toward the goals in which I believed.

In April 1970, Anna, Lina, and I left New York on the Soviet ship *Aleksandr Pushkin.* We docked in Leningrad and caught a train for Moscow. My mother-in-law met us at the station.

"Arkady, you had several phone calls from the Central Committee. They wanted to know when you were arriving and asked you to ring back," she said.

"Who phoned?"

"I don't know, but they left a number."

A few hours later, I called the Central Committee. An unfamiliar voice replied, "Ah, Arkady Nikolaevich. You're in Moscow already. I am the assistant of Boris Nikolaevich [Ponomarev]. He wants to talk to you as soon as possible."

"But I just got home," I protested. "I should go to the ministry to see Gromyko first."

"I urge you," he pressed, "to drop by here first thing

tomorrow morning—if only for a few minutes—before you go to the ministry."

I hurried to the Central Committee offices the next day, but there was no cause for alarm. Ponomarev only wanted to offer me a job in his department. He described the attractive prospects of a career in the Central Committee and told me I could expect rapid advancement with him. I did not answer him directly and said I would have to discuss it with Gromyko. I could see he wasn't used to such evasions, but he made no objection.

A few hours later, I told Gromyko of Ponomarev's offer. He did not conceal his irritation at the attempt to pirate his employee.

"Shevchenko, what do you want? Do you want to work for the Central Committee or to be my adviser?" he asked bluntly.

I told him I hoped to stay with the ministry and was grateful for his offer. He seemed pleased and promised to sign the order for my new appointment the same day. Later he called Ponomarev and told him in no uncertain terms to stop trying to raid the ministry.

16

WHEN I ARRIVED AT THE SEVENTH FLOOR OF THE FOREIGN Ministry to take up my new duties, I was ushered into the study of Vasily Makarov, Gromyko's senior assistant. Makarov was a surly, pompous, sarcastic contrast to Gromyko's cool but generally courteous personality. He had worked with Gromyko for many years and had become a powerful figure as the guardian of his doorway. After watching Makarov work—brusquely rejecting the pleas of many senior diplomats for "a few minutes" with the minister, coldly ordering department heads to rewrite and scale down papers they had to submit for Gromyko's attention—I understood why Gromyko had chosen and kept him. Makarov was the perfect watchdog. He scared off intruders. He sheltered his master from unnecessary contacts with lesser humans. He helped deflect the pressure of the real world so that Gromyko could maintain the reserve which helped him to seem a superior being. High-ranking diplomats made a practice of giving him expensive presents to grease the way for their reports to Gromyko or their appointments to coveted jobs. Makarov accepted such bribes as his due; he would even commission purchases for himself, telling me pointedly on one occasion how much he needed a rug of a certain size and color for his apartment.

We had known each other for years and had maintained correct relations. He asked me to sit down next to his desk, but it was some time before we were able to talk. His telephones rang constantly and every few minutes subordinates appeared requesting instructions and advice. The atmosphere was harried and tense.

This wasn't surprising. Egyptian President Nasser was expected to visit Moscow soon, and the situation in the Middle East remained explosive. Finalization of the Soviet–West German treaty was under way. Willy Brandt was expected in Moscow in August, negotiations on the Conference on Security and Cooperation in Europe and on SALT were in progress, there were preparations for the visit of French President Pompidou, plus the ever-present turmoil of Soviet-Chinese relations and those related to the war in Vietnam. Finally, I was able to tell Makarov that I wanted to see Gromyko as soon as possible to discuss my exact functions and other matters concerning my future work.

Makarov grimaced. "Are you blind? Can't you see what's going on, how busy Andrei Andreyevich is? If you think his main idea is to meet with you, you're crazy!" Then he recovered himself. "Arkady, relax. Familiarize yourself with your new environment."

I told him I couldn't wander around looking at the ceiling. I had to know what I was going to do, and only Gromyko could tell me that. I said further that I needed a study on the

191

seventh floor close to Gromyko so I could come quickly if he should summon me. I also had been led to understand that I would read all political documents directed to Gromyko's attention or for his decision, and all code cables received in the ministry.

"You want too much, Arkady," he rumbled. "I doubt if you'll get it."

When I finally saw Gromyko, he told me that my range of duties and responsibilities would be very broad. I was to be prepared to deal with any problem. He adjured me to forget about *Fedorenkovschina,* alluding to Ambassador Fedorenko's light approach to business. Gromyko also told Makarov that I was to have access to all secret information; that he expected me to review and comment on sensitive proposals and issues and to report personally to him.

I had met Gromyko so many times in so many different circumstances that I thought I knew him rather well. But only after I had worked under him for some time did I fully realize what a complex and difficult man he is. Andrei Gromyko appears to be an efficient machine, constructed to perform and to endure, serviceable, impressive, and almost completely devoid of human warmth. He can joke and he can rage, but underlying any such expression is a cold logic and discipline that make him formidable as a superior or as an adversary.

Gromyko's devotion to the Soviet system is complete and unreserved. He is now himself a fundamental element of the system—one of its most powerful driving forces, at once its product and one of its supreme masters. On one occasion, when a journalist asked him for biographical information, he remarked that "my personality does not interest me." This was not a pose but the plain truth, although he is in fact a quite extraordinary personality. Khrushchev once said that if he were to order Gromyko to "drop his trousers and sit on a block of ice for a month, he would do it"—the Premier's way of paying homage to the near-legendary tenacity and persistence of his Foreign Minister.

Gromyko's rise as a major political figure on the world stage as well as within the Soviet Union is remarkable, the more so because he actually began his governmental service in the Foreign Ministry—whereas high-level Soviet politicians nearly always emerge from the ranks of the Party bureaucracy. Andrei Andreyevich Gromyko was born in 1909 into the family of a semi-peasant/semi-worker (Gromyko's own description) in the Belorussian village of Starye Gromyki. His family name derives from that settlement. After graduating from the Minsk Agricultural Institute, Gromyko moved to Moscow, where he worked as a senior scientific associate in the Institute of Economics of the U.S.S.R. Academy of Sciences from 1936 to 1939. He joined the Communist Party in 1931 and entered the foreign service in 1939.

Gromyko owes his early prominence to Stalin's wholesale purges of the first generation of revolutionary civil servants. He stepped into jobs whose previous occupants had been condemned to summary execution or slow death in the prison camps. Often their replacements were time-serving mediocrities, in whose company Gromyko stood out. He was not only loyal and disciplined; he was also intelligent, well educated, hard-working, and quick. True, he had no experience in diplomacy. Nonetheless, he began his diplomatic career as head of the American Department of the People's Commissariat for Foreign Affairs, and by 1943 he was the Soviet Ambassador in Washington—the survivor of a personal interview with Stalin which had begun, I was told, with Stalin's assistants making grisly wagers about whether Gromyko would go west (to the United States) or east (to Siberia).

Fedor Tarasovich Gusev, Party Secretary of the People's Commissariat in 1939, later a prominent diplomat and adviser to Gromyko at the same time as I, described the atmosphere in which Gromyko began his career. Vyacheslav Molotov replaced Maksim Litvinov as Commissar for Foreign Affairs in May 1939, signaling both a political turning away from the Western democracies and an internal upheaval that ultimately decimated the Soviet diplomatic corps. The day after Molotov took office, he summoned Gusev and the chief of the personnel department to a lecture, delivered in a steady shout, about the need to reverse an era of political shortsightedness by cleansing the staff of class enemies. Referring to his Jewish predecessor, Molotov roared, "Enough of Litvinov liberalism. I am going to tear out that kike's wasp's nest by the roots."

Gromyko does not talk much about those years. I never heard him utter any critical remark about Stalin or Molotov. I believe he had great respect for both of them. Once he told me amusedly how Stalin had advised him, while he was preparing for his Washington assignment, to go to American churches and listen to sermons in order to improve his English. Stalin's education, of course, had been provided by the Orthodox Church when he was a seminarian, and he reasoned that since priests' language and diction must necessarily be good, that was the best place to study a language. Gromyko admitted he was confused by Stalin's admonition, and could not imagine how an atheist Soviet ambassador might appear in churches without a very strange reaction from the public and the press. It was the only order Stalin gave him that he ever disobeyed.

The impact of Gromyko's youthful schooling under Stalin and Molotov was obviously profound; there are manifestations of it even now. But to my surprise, after working with him for a while, I discovered he was not the sort of diehard Stalinist that so many of his colleagues from that period became. Gromyko's political outlook took shape at a time when the Soviet Union and the United States were wartime allies working to defeat Fascism. He cherishes the memory of Franklin Roosevelt, whom he considers a great man, "a wise statesman with a wide range of interests." The deep influence of these formative beginnings can be seen in Gromyko even in times when hostility prevails in Soviet-American relations. Thus, in his address to the United Nations General Assembly in 1984, while castigating U.S. policies, he once again reiterated that "today, more than ever before, our country believes in the maintenance of normal relations with the United States," and he made reference to the years of the World War II alliance.

Gromyko took part in the Yalta and Potsdam conferences in 1945. He led the Soviet delegation at the Dumbarton Oaks meetings and later, after Molotov's departure, also headed the delegation to the conference that drew up the United Nations Charter. As one of the UN's founding fathers he

194

became, in 1946, the first Kremlin representative to the UN Security Council, where he earned his reputation as "Mr. Nyet" by casting more than twenty vetoes in two years. Since that time Gromyko has been personally involved in every important aspect of East-West relations, particularly Soviet-American relations, and has dealt with all American Presidents from Franklin Roosevelt to Ronald Reagan, along with their secretaries of state from Cordell Hull to George Shultz. Among present members of the Politburo, he and Defense Minister Dmitri Ustinov share the distinction of being the only ones to have served prominently under all Kremlin leaders from Stalin to Chernenko.

A special piece of good fortune cemented Gromyko's position at one point when his career seemed blighted. He had returned to Moscow in 1948 to become first among Molotov's deputies, but in 1952, a new Foreign Minister, Andrei Vyshinsky, contrived to disgrace him. Vyshinsky, the bloodthirsty prosecutor of Stalin's purges, was an equally ardent dogmatist in behalf of Stalin's foreign policy. Gromyko's enthusiasm for the cold war approach, by contrast, was restrained. The two men fell out. Vyshinsky, the experienced inquisitor, uncovered a flaw in Gromyko's seeming respectability and exploited the opening to banish his senior aide.

The key Vyshinsky turned was one Gromyko himself had forged. Relatively modest in his personal habits and style of life, Gromyko had committed one uncharacteristic act of abuse of authority. Egged on by his wife, Lidiya Dmitriyevna, he had used Foreign Ministry workmen and special access to materials to build a handsome brick villa, a dacha, in the Moscow suburb of Vnukovo. Among the elite such violations of the law were and are common practice, commonly disregarded. Anyone who could manipulate power for private ends did the same sort of thing—and still does. (I used ministry employees to redo my own Moscow apartment in the late sixties.) Few are ever punished. Status protects them from scandal.

Vyshinsky, however, learned of the construction project and used it to engineer a formal Party reprimand for Gromyko and his reassignment as Ambassador to Great Britain.

To replace him, Vyshinsky promoted Yakov Malik, who had distinguished himself as a secret-police informer during the thirties and as Gromyko's vitriolically anti-American successor as Ambassador to the United Nations. Malik must have delighted in supplanting Gromyko, who probably thought of himself as an exile, impotent in London.

Stalin's death in March 1953 brought a sudden reversal of fortune. Vyshinsky was removed and most of his cronies were ousted with him. Malik went to London, and Gromyko returned to reclaim his position in Moscow.

Since that time Gromyko's path has been steadily upward, his authority ever more secure. Although it was Khrushchev who made him Foreign Minister in 1957, Gromyko survived his patron's fall; it was known that Khrushchev, at Gromyko's expense, had given extensive foreign policy responsibility to his son-in-law, Aleksei Adzhubey.

In Khrushchev's time, moreover, Gromyko had made one decision which proved to be inspired. He cultivated Leonid Brezhnev, then the figurehead Chairman of the Presidium of the Supreme Soviet, the rubber-stamp parliament. To others, Brezhnev seemed a colorless, unimaginative Party careerist without distinction. Luck and instinct made Gromyko see something more.

When Brezhnev needed help in preparing himself for meetings with foreign leaders, Gromyko gave it. He took Brezhnev's responsibilities as nominal head of state seriously. Occasionally he would give the policy briefings himself. And when he found out that Brezhnev needed a speechwriter, he assigned his own, Andrei Aleksandrov-Agentov, to do the job. Aleksandrov-Agentov and another ministry official, Anatoly Blatov, became in time Brezhnev's intimate and powerful staff advisers on foreign policy. They reached that eminence, however, as Gromyko's protégés.

Gromyko also strengthened his ties to Brezhnev at the personal level, taking up hunting so that he could join the Party leader at his favorite sport. Until then, Gromyko had limited his exercise to morning workouts with barbells and occasional walks. If his hunting started as a political avocation, however, it became in time a real delight to him. I have never seen him as cheerful as he was one Sunday in 1972 when he entered his Vnukovo dacha a little before lunchtime proudly bearing a mangled duck he had brought down that morning, smiling with a sincere pleasure he rarely, if ever, shows the world.

Through Brezhnev, whom he called by a nickname, Lyonya, Gromyko achieved not just security but genuine authority over Soviet foreign policy. Once Brezhnev took command of foreign affairs, edging aside Prime Minister Aleksei Kosygin in the late sixties, he moved Gromyko from the role of mentor and confidant to that of co-architect. The transition was formalized in 1973 when Gromyko became a Politburo member, one of the few without the usual Party background to reach such eminence in the Soviet system.

Most Western observers failed to notice Gromyko's changed status in the Kremlin upon Brezhnev's ascension. Henry Kissinger was incorrect when he referred to Gromyko as being "an implementor, not the maker, of policy"* before he was elevated to the Politburo in 1973. In fact, Gromyko had been shaping policy for some time. His status was almost imperceptible because Gromyko is not someone who would reveal publicly—particularly to foreigners—his real power and influence. Always aloof and reserved, Gromyko preferred the shadows.

Elected along with Gromyko to full Politburo membership was Yuri Andropov, chairman of the KGB. These two emerging political figures were not personal friends, but their relations were nevertheless very cordial. Gromyko never liked KGB types. He and, especially, his wife were always suspicious of the secret police and remained alert when KGB officers were present. Gromyko, however, did not look upon Andropov simply as the chief of the KGB, and Andropov accorded Gromyko similar special respect. Andropov's recognition of Gromyko's personal seniority was unusual in dealings between two more-or-less equals among Soviet politicians. It undoubtedly stemmed from the fact that Gromyko had been Andropov's superior when the latter was a diplomat. It was manifested in Andropov's reg-

---

* Henry Kissinger, *White House Years* (Little, Brown, 1979), p. 789.

ular visits to the Foreign Ministry, where the two met privately and at length. Gromyko did not reciprocate; he never went to KGB headquarters, unlike many other members of the Kremlin group. The rapport between Gromyko and Andropov was further cemented by Gromyko's enthusiastic willingness to groom Andropov's son Igor, who became a diplomat.

Gromyko's personal relations with Chernenko before the latter became General Secretary were rather restrained. He preferred to deal directly with Brezhnev and Andropov. Like others in the Politburo, he considered Chernenko a second-rate opportunist. But also like the other old-guard members of the Politburo, he thought Chernenko the best choice available after Andropov's death. Moreover, because of the situation at the time of Chernenko's succession, Gromyko himself has become one of the most influential figures in the Politburo, exercising a more prominent policymaking role than he has ever done before. Because of his extraordinary experience and political skills as well as his mastery of foreign affairs, other major Politburo figures are undoubtedly strongly influenced by his recommendations and opinions. His voice in any possible redirection of Soviet foreign policy may well be weightier than that of any of his colleagues. When I observed his performance at Politburo meetings in the early 1970s, it was even then difficult, if not impossible, for others to argue with him or challenge his views. Today, I doubt that anyone except Defense Minister Ustinov would risk confronting him.

Some Western analysts, nonetheless, have questioned Gromyko's power, arguing, rightly, that he has no political base among key Soviet institutions—the Communist Party, the military, or the KGB. But these analysts miss the point: Gromyko himself has become a Soviet institution —a symbol of the regime's continuity and stability, and its formidable defender, respected not only within the Soviet Union but also by his adversaries and enemies abroad.

Gromyko's experience has made him probably the best-informed Foreign Minister in the world. To a certain degree, his political longevity is also due to the fact that, though an economist by training, he has astutely avoided dealing with domestic problems. He knows that the Soviet Union's economic morass is nearly unresolvable, and that more than one politician's career has foundered in its quicksand.

He has also displayed political acumen by staying clear of intra-Party and bureaucratic feuds and rivalries. He has tried as far as possible to remain neutral, keeping out of behind-the-scenes conflicts and intrigues in the Kremlin. That and his knack for accurately assessing the balance of power in the Politburo have saved him from the struggles among the leadership that have destroyed, professionally and physically, so many capable politicians.

Throughout his career, whether as simply an implementor or a full-fledged maker of policy, Gromyko has always understood perfectly his place and possibilities and he is intolerant of those who, in his view, do not understand theirs. Caution has always been second nature to him. What began as a natural reticence eventually developed into reclusiveness. Diligence, obedience, and persistence were the keys to promotion, and the best protection against the danger of being caught on the wrong side of a policy debate, especially in the years under Stalin.

Gromyko remains in many ways an orthodox Communist. Nonetheless, he takes a longer view of the importance of Soviet-American relations for the future than many people in either the Soviet Union or the West perceive. During the years I worked with him, I knew that Soviet-American relations were his central, special field of interest and activity. I never noticed in Gromyko that kind of hatred toward the United States or its people that many other Soviet politicians of his generation—as well as some younger men—display reflexively. He assesses the United States in terms of its might and its potential as a Soviet rival in world affairs. Like many of his colleagues, Gromyko respects American power. It is not that he is pro-American but that, unlike some other Soviet leaders, Gromyko believes the United States to be not only the Soviet Union's main adversary but also its partner as long as the interests of both nations—whether temporary or more long-term—are parallel or coincide. I do not think that his basic approach in this respect has changed.

In Gromyko's approach to world affairs there exists a good deal of classic balance-of-power politics. He is a dogged and crafty practitioner, constantly seeking advantage for the Soviet Union, but also willing to accommodate Western interests in whatever measure the tactical situation dictates. Gromyko's views on Soviet-American relations, on European affairs, particularly regarding Germany and France, on arms control and SALT, substantially affect the main trends of Soviet foreign policy.

One should remember that he was a major architect of détente with the United States, and is associated with it more intimately than any other present Politburo member. He clashed with the late, staunchly anti-American Defense Minister Andrei Grechko over détente, as well as over the SALT I negotiations, to such an extent that the two men were sometimes not on speaking terms for weeks. In the end, however, Gromyko's views prevailed on both these issues. It was in fact Gromyko—not Ambassador Anatoly Dobrynin—who was at the Soviet end of the Kissinger-Dobrynin diplomatic channel during the Nixon administration. When Dobrynin's reports arrived in Moscow, Gromyko was the first to receive them, he decided to whom they should be shown, and his proposals served as the basis for decisions on Soviet-American affairs. Gromyko also tried to restrain—often in vain—the anti-American zeal of that quintessential cold warrior at the United Nations, Yakov Malik.

His closest subordinates have also concentrated on the United States or Western Europe. Gromyko made Georgy Kornienko, his associate of many years whose special area is the United States, First Deputy Minister. His confidant in his inner circle is Deputy Minister Anatoly Kovalev, whose career has been devoted to European affairs. More recently, another former head of the ministry's American Department, Viktor Komplektov, has joined this group as Gromyko's deputy. They all enjoy easy access to the minister. In contrast, the head of an African desk may go for many months without seeing Gromyko except at a meeting of the ministry's Collegium, and he would be right to suspect that Gromyko rarely gives reports from his region more than a quick glance. Despite countless invitations, Gromyko has never visited any black African nation. With the exception of Cuba, he has never been to a Latin American country. China interests him primarily through the prism of Moscow-Washington-Peking relations. In conversations with us on his staff his usual reason for turning such invitations down invariably ran: "Why do I need to go? And what am I going to discuss? Nigeria [or some other country] is not a great nation like the United States."

If I understand correctly how Gromyko's mind works, my impression also is that he was simply bored with persistent challenges to Soviet domination in Eastern Europe and viewed these countries as a burden to us. He never said so openly, but my feeling was that it was always a nuisance to him to deal with the leaders of Soviet-bloc countries or to visit them. Among the hawks of the Central Committee, he even earned a reputation for being ideologically soft. Until his admission to the Politburo, I heard open criticism from some of these orthodox hard-liners that Gromyko was becoming too keen on *Realpolitik* in dealing with the Americans.

Once, in 1972, I saw him uncomfortably reminded of the need to prove his doctrinal commitment. We had arrived in New York for the UN General Assembly session, leaving behind in Moscow a copy of Gromyko's draft address. The speech had been prepared within the ministry and sent to the Politburo at the last minute for what should have been routine approval. Instead, the ministry forwarded a message from a Brezhnev assistant—not directly to Gromyko, but to Makarov—that some Politburo members thought the opening portion of the text lacked the requisite ideological flavor. He suggested that further citations from Brezhnev—only one had been included in the draft—could strengthen the presentation of the Soviet Union's peace-loving foreign policy.

When Gromyko saw that the message had been signed by Aleksandrov-Agentov, his former speechwriter, he grew angry. "What's gotten into Aleksandrov?" he spluttered. "Who does he think he is?" Gromyko understood, of course, that Aleksandrov was merely conveying Brezhnev's or some other Politburo member's idea. Gromyko handed the message to me. "Here, Shevchenko, you take it. Put in one more quotation from Brezhnev, but otherwise don't change anything else." He felt that his position under Brezhnev's leadership was strong enough to allow him to be completely himself.

Aleksandrov, it would seem from this incident, had quickly forgotten that he had been Gromyko's protégé, and had dissociated himself from his former Foreign Ministry background. He had, by that time, joined the ranks of Central Committee apparatchiks and his influence in the entourage of his new boss, Brezhnev, was considerable. The incident was typical of the many minor personal betrayals among the elite. And I must acknowledge that I also betrayed Gromyko in some measure, by failing to tell him of Aleksandrov's attitude toward him behind his back. Nor did I inform Gromyko that the Secretary of the Central Committee, Boris Ponomarev, and his men often denigrated him, referring to him as "only a Foreign Ministry bureaucrat." After Gromyko rose to the Politburo, however, no one, at least in my presence, made such remarks.

Under Gromyko the Foreign Ministry's role and influence generally in the decision-making process has been restored and increased since its decline under Molotov's successors —Vyshinsky and Shepilov—after the Second World War. Gromyko is not simply as cunning as Machiavelli and not merely a remarkable diplomat. *Time* Magazine once suggested that he might be legitimately compared with Prince Talleyrand, who not only was an original thinker but also survived both the French Revolution and Napoleon, and restored the Bourbon monarchy. Although Gromyko would certainly disclaim such a similarity—on the basis of Talleyrand's princely heritage, if for no other reason—the comparison is in my own view not too farfetched.

It would be an oversimplification to describe Gromyko merely as a "diplomat for all seasons," as he has sometimes been called in the West. He is a man of strongly held ideas and convictions which he has in many cases put into operation brilliantly and with great sophistication. He might veil his intentions from others for years, but he never abandons them, stubbornly continuing to build, "brick by brick," as he is fond of saying, the foundation for their realization.

Perhaps the ultimate secret of Gromyko's strength as a politician is his adeptness at finding solutions and compromises that prove finally acceptable to diverse components of the Soviet upper stratum. Nikita Khrushchev, in contrast to Gromyko, offers an example of what can happen to a Kremlin leader who is unable to grasp this basic principle of political wisdom in the U.S.S.R.

As a diplomat, Gromyko has few equals. Always meticulously prepared, he easily and aggressively dominates most of his opponents, putting the other side on the defensive even if the Soviet Union's position is wrong. He can be just as forceful if the situation requires him to be a gracious, agreeable partner. He is a master of detail, smoothly collecting something for nothing from his counterpart who may not even notice what is happening until it is too late. He is a good actor who can easily conceal his real mood and intentions. His usual demeanor is serious and sober, but he can and does occasionally throw tantrums, either real or fake. He can be stolid and sphinxlike or banter and joke, although most of his attempts at wit are rather heavy-handed.

Gromyko excels in knowing when and how to compromise and when to bully. I have been amazed to see him suddenly and at the outset of a negotiation give up something that was supposed to be our reserve position, and have been equally bewildered when, with incredible persistence, he defended what he could have yielded with no difficulty, something that had already been approved as a point of concession by the Politburo.

Gromyko has been around for so long he takes it for granted that everyone else in diplomacy may fade into oblivion but he will go on forever. The Marxist axiom that objective future historical development is on the side of Communism—synonymous in Gromyko's mind with the Soviet Union—is his practical guide. Since time is already on the Soviet side, he reasons, he can afford to stick to the same view for weeks, months, years. Even when it is obvious that Soviet objectives are unrealizable at some given time, he is undaunted and stubbornly pursues his goal. It is astonishing how many times he has gotten his way in the end. Henry Kissinger, who sat across the table from Gromyko so often, knows this well: he has summed up Gromyko's approach as "patiently accumulated marginal gains until they amount to a major difference," and "[a reliance] on the restlessness of his opposite number to extract otherwise unachievable advantages."*

At his present level of power, Gromyko is far removed from the old familiar "Grim Grom" or "Mr. No" for the West and "Mr. Yes" to his master in Moscow. He would no longer sit on a block of ice at anyone's behest. He is not the same man who denied to John Kennedy in 1962 that nuclear missiles had been deployed in Cuba while Kennedy possessed photos of those missiles. I do not believe Gromyko really knew at the time exactly what was going on in Cuba—Khrushchev was more than capable of leaving him in the dark on this or that point, as indeed he did on this occasion with Ambassador Dobrynin as well. Now, however, there are no Kremlin secrets to which Gromyko is not privy.

To work with Gromyko is to visit Hell; he is extremely difficult to please and his moods can be as mercurial as were Khrushchev's. One never knows exactly what Gromyko wants because he always wants more than he is precise about. He cannot tolerate indecision or persons who do not respond clearly and immediately to his questions. He simply ignores the fact that it is sometimes next to impossible to produce answers to complex matters on the spot. At times he can be rude and crude with subordinates, loudly and arrogantly promoting the idea of his own omniscience and others' stupidity. Later, in another situation, particularly a social one, where he is always ill at ease, he may speak pleasantly, almost diffidently, as if nothing has happened.

Gromyko rarely praises anyone, even if he is satisfied with his performance. Yet it isn't only foreigners who respect him. I would not say, as Henry Kissinger did, that I like him, but in many ways I too respect him. Beyond his abilities as a statesman, Gromyko is not as personally venal

---

* Henry Kissinger, *White House Years* (Little, Brown, 1979), pp. 789–90.

as most Soviet leaders, and I do not believe, knowing his character as I do, that he has ever sent anyone to the Gulags.

The shelter Gromyko has built around himself over the years is formidable. It gives him that isolation from normal human problems that most Soviet political leaders seem to crave and that the rulers since Khrushchev have made intrinsic to their style. Gromyko inhabits this cocoon as though born to it. As his daughter Emilia once said to me: "My father lives in the skies. For twenty-five years he has not set foot on the streets of Moscow. All he sees is the view from his car window."

At the time I became his adviser, that car would bring him to the ministry at about ten o'clock in the morning six days a week and usually take him home again by seven or eight o'clock at night, unless there was an especially demanding matter to deal with. Once inside the Stalin-era skyscraper that houses both the Ministry of Foreign Affairs and the Ministry of Foreign Trade, Gromyko took a special elevator, reserved for his use and that of a few very senior officials, straight to his seventh-floor office. There, except for a meal in a private dining room, he stayed the entire day, reading those documents his personal staff felt it was essential to show him, seeing a carefully screened group of senior ministry officials or top foreign visitors, talking on the special Kremlin telephone system (the *Vertushka*) to those of his rank outside the ministry, or sometimes with his deputies, but rarely with many heads of departments even within his own ministry.

Gromyko is an excellent family man; he has been married only once and has a well-deserved reputation for being faithful and solicitous to his wife, Lidiya Dmitriyevna. Her influence upon him is considerable; he listens to her attentively. Her advice extends beyond their personal life to government affairs, particularly in the selection of people for top posts at the ministry. A ministry wag once dubbed her "the real chief of the personnel department."

Gromyko's son, Anatoly, who now heads the African Institute of the U.S.S.R. Academy of Sciences and is a corresponding member of this prestigious Soviet institution, is close to his father. Like his mother and a very few others, Anatoly can speak truthfully to his father and give him the unvarnished facts about Soviet existence outside the rarefied atmosphere of the Kremlin.

Gromyko is also close to Emilia, an accomplished, well-educated woman who holds the Soviet equivalent of a Ph.D. in the history of science. She was indulged by her father and could be as headstrong as he in getting what she wanted. A case in point was her choice of a husband: she married Aleksandr Piradov, a professor of international law at MGIMO. Piradov was much older than Emilia, and it was his third marriage. His first wife had been the daughter of one of the old Soviet political leaders, Grigory Ordzhonikidze, who committed suicide in the thirties; his second, the editor-in-chief of one of the most popular Soviet monthly magazines, *Health*. Intellectual and witty but a lazy man who talked too much, Piradov was a Georgian with a taste for empty promises and good wine. Emilia's parents were not in favor of the marriage, but she was determined to have him and the Gromykos bowed to her wishes. After they became grandparents, however, they reconciled themselves to reality, and their grandson, Andrei, has become their favorite.

Gromyko, who has a doctorate in economics, has never given up his scholarly interests. His books, *Export of U.S. Capital* (1957) and *U.S. Dollar Expansion* (1961), were initially published under the pseudonym "G. Andreyev," which he has also used for a number of articles. The two books have since been revised and combined into a single volume entitled *External Expansion of Capital*, published in 1982 under Gromyko's real name. He continues as nominal editor-in-chief of the monthly political magazine *International Life* and many articles in it, including some of my own, were screened by Gromyko.

Although a refined man with a taste for art, Gromyko does not attend a cultural or sporting event if it is not required of him. He is an avid reader, not only of political subjects but of history and fiction as well. His taste runs from Tolstoy to Shakespeare to Mark Twain. His English is fluent and nearly every day *The New York Times, Time* Magazine, and/or other Western periodicals are brought to his home. Occasionally he even savors American comic strips and political cartoons. He is also fond of reading historical archives and is known to be an admirer of Prince Alexander Gorchakov, an outstanding Russian military commander and diplomat of the last century.

He enjoys films and sees them at his home in Moscow or at the Soviet Mission in New York. At Glen Cove the staff always keeps on hand a print of the prewar Soviet movie *The Queen of Spades,* based on Pushkin's tragic novel. It is one of Gromyko's favorites; he has seen it at least a dozen times and the staff knows he might request them to run it again at any time. He liked Hollywood's *Gone With the Wind,* but was indifferent to *The Godfather.* His favorite foreign films are those made in the United States during the war and postwar years when he lived in Washington and New York. In private showings held for him in the Mission, he remembers the actors' names and gives running commentaries on their performances and backgrounds. It is almost as though that brief period of the Soviet-American alliance against Hitler was the high point of his life, the idyll he seeks to recapture through his dealings with Americans.

Nevertheless, his understanding of America (and of the Soviet Union, for that matter) is incomplete. There are no ordinary people in his political landscape. In New York, Gromyko sees nothing but the inside of official buildings where he works or sleeps. His only walks take place on the one-kilometer circuit inside the walled grounds at Glen Cove. He is a rather ascetic man who neither smokes nor drinks and has always enjoyed excellent health. In the early seventies, however, his health began to deteriorate. He developed trouble with his blood circulation and had several fainting spells, one of them during a Politburo meeting. He was ordered to maintain an easier work schedule and get more rest. He has subsequently devoted more time to bear and duck hunting, as well as to playing chess with his wife, Lidiya, and his deputy, Anatoly Kovalev.

Gromyko is attentive to his wardrobe. He wears well-tailored suits of expensive foreign material made up for him in the Foreign Ministry tailor shop. His taste, however, might be described as fossilized conservative, not having changed a jot in the years since I first knew him. His personal preference for an old-fashioned Borsalino hat once cost me a lot of time, trouble, and aggravation. This particular hat, which he had bought decades before, was finally worn beyond repair. On one of his annual visits to New York, his assistants were dispatched all over the city in search of another, but came up empty-handed. Gromyko insisted upon an absolutely identical hat—a style one haberdasher described as not having been in demand in fifty years. Lidiya Dmitriyevna put the dilemma into my hands: "Arkady Nikolaevich, you know New York better than anyone else among us. Will you use your connections to try to get the same Borsalino for Andrei Andreyevich?" Tracking down a rare stamp or a unique curiosity might have been easier, but after scouring, with the help of an American friend, dozens of shops from Orchard Street to uptown, the hat was found in a dusty storeroom.

Gromyko, who turned seventy-five on July 18, 1984, is still better preserved than his colleagues of similar age. Far from seeking retirement, he attracted more attention than ever before as a formulator of Soviet foreign policy. Western speculation, indeed, has given him the dubious honor of being the single most influential initiator of the Kremlin's 1984 ultra-hard line toward the United States. But this assumption seems to me wide of the mark. It is, to the contrary, more likely that Gromyko was a moderating factor within the Politburo, acting to counter the chill and sometimes unprecedented hostility dominating relations between Moscow and Washington at the end of the Carter administration and during the first years of the Reagan administration. It is quite possible, indeed, that Gromyko was even more distressed than his colleagues, as he views the best achievements of his life's work crumbling. One might well expect him to react harshly as he did when he was cornered in Madrid in 1983 to answer for Soviet actions in the Korean Air Lines incident. Gromyko could have had very little to do with the decision to shoot down the plane and I am sure he would have had little patience with such a plan. He is much too shrewd and experienced to make his country the butt of the world's opprobrium by encouraging bully tactics.

In 1960 he advised Nikita Khrushchev not to shoot down the American U-2 spy plane, but was overruled.

Nor should one be surprised at Gromyko's anger whenever the question of Soviet violations of human rights is raised with him. Emigration and the handling of Soviet dissidents are practically the exclusive domain of the Central Committee and the KGB. Gromyko simply does not—and does not want to—deal with these matters. He is interested in ideas, not individuals, in political concepts, not personal tragedies.

During this period of time, the collective Soviet leadership has, in general, been more belligerent and hypersensitive than usual. Not only has the Kremlin suffered serious setbacks, both internationally and internally, in recent years, but it was also beleaguered by a transition in leadership which has extended beyond Chernenko's selection. A hard, aggressive response and tight cohesion among themselves are together the traditional Soviet defensive reflex whenever the leaders feel that the West might think them vulnerable, or when they have been found out in some misdeed. This is Gromyko's attitude as well. As superpower relations went from bad to worse, the Kremlin lost more than it anticipated or could afford. Soviet leaders want to avoid the risk of nuclear catastrophe. They are concerned about American military programs, particularly the "Star Wars" initiative. Their greatest fear is that they will be left behind in an uncontrollable competition for more and more technologically sophisticated strategic or space-based weaponry. They have also had to adjust to the reality of the deployment of American Pershing II and cruise missiles in Western Europe. They understand that poor relations with Washington have backfired in Western Europe, created strains among the Warsaw Pact countries, and given Peking a trump card to play against Moscow.

Gromyko undoubtedly recognized the significance of all this better than anyone else in the Politburo. He understands that it is in Moscow's interest to establish normal relations, no matter who is President and whether Moscow likes him or not.

Barring unforeseen illness or accident, Gromyko will

probably be around for some time to come. And I would not be surprised to see him, like the persistent political bulldog he is and at the proper time, again try to restore Soviet-American relations to a normal level, even if he must do it "brick by brick."

It was not surprising that Gromyko relinquished his post as Foreign Minister in 1985. He actually had not run the Foreign Ministry on a day-to-day basis for quite some time. Although Gromyko was in better shape physically and mentally than a number of his old Politburo colleagues, he too has had health problems and is, after all, 76 years old. His selection as Chairman of the Presidium of the Supreme Soviet, the titular head of state of the Soviet Union, has not removed him from the center of power in the Kremlin. He remains one of the most influential figures in the Politburo and I am sure that Mikhail Gorbachev as well as the new Foreign Minister, Eduard Shevardnadze, will listen carefully to his views and will continue to follow his advice regarding foreign policy.

17

SUMMER IS THE TIME GROMYKO BEGINS TO CONSIDER HIS annual foreign policy address at the September opening of the UN General Assembly. He often reminisced about his work at the UN as the first Soviet representative to the Security Council, frequently citing the United Nations Charter, a document he knows almost by heart. Although unsentimental, he has a warm feeling about the birth of the organization. Over the years, however, his attitude toward the UN changed. His concept of the institution's future and role in international affairs has yielded to a hardening criticism. Nevertheless, Gromyko believes that the UN is an excellent training ground for young diplomats.

Since I was fresh from my UN experience, Gromyko put me to work supervising preparation of his address that fall. He made it clear that he didn't want to dwell on the matter and left preliminary thinking about major points to me. He told me casually to find the right people to work on the project.

I was shortly educated about the importance of following precisely Gromyko's every utterance. I had not rushed to pick a team to work on the speech since I wanted to find out who would be best and there was plenty of time. Early in the following week, while I was in Gromyko's office on other business, he asked me whom I had chosen. I said I would soon have a roster for him.

His head snapped toward me, and he fixed me with a finger stabbing the air as he raved for a good half-hour about my being a stupid, irresponsible ass who did not have the ears to hear his instructions. I was so taken aback by the violence of his outburst that I was sure I would never be able to regain his confidence. But the next day he greeted me in the usual manner. To my consolation, I discovered that an order to report to his office inevitably strikes dread into the heart of the recipient, even a Deputy Foreign Minister. Not only does Gromyko expect anyone he calls to appear instantly, but his most desultory suggestion is to be observed as a crisis order. His summons can mean anything. Visitors never know whether they are to suffer through a coarse assault on their integrity and intelligence or a tedious, meticulous examination of some trivial problem that has caught the ministerial fancy. His occasional fits of good humor, marked by awkward jokes, are not enough to dispel his dour reputation, which long ago earned him the nickname "Grom," the Russian word for thunder.

One victim of his thunderbolts was Rolland Timerbaev, a senior political officer in the UN Mission in 1962, who was assigned the thankless task of supervising the Mission's move from an old building on Park Avenue to the new quarters on East Sixty-seventh Street. When Gromyko was shown the completed work that autumn, he spent more than a half-hour of his tour stuck between floors in a faulty elevator. Finally freed, he decided that Timerbaev should have a new career. "Let him sit at the reception desk," was his order, "and keep an eye on the elevator to make sure it's working." The poor man occupied his new post for the rest of Gromyko's stay in New York.

Impatience rather than vindictiveness is Gromyko's hallmark in dealing with those who rank beneath him. In that sense his managerial style is typical of top Soviet bureaucrats. They are rude to their underlings to demonstrate their own importance. Gromyko will often call a meeting of his three or four ranking assistants and, if he is in a bad mood, vilify them as "dolts" or "schoolboys" who are "not fit to work in the Foreign Ministry." A report with a few minor errors or a document submitted late can touch off one of these explosions, though it usually passes quickly.

Gromyko cannot tolerate anyone whom he considers "not serious." We learned to be completely "serious."

The staff of Gromyko's personal office is called the Secretariat and is rather small (eight to ten people). However, when Gromyko became a member of the Politburo, his office was expanded to include a military adjutant, KGB guards, a personal physician, and a few other personnel. Several ambassadors-at-large who are entrusted with various special assignments are also under his direct supervision. Similar functions are performed by a few independent advisers who do not belong to the minister's Secretariat but report directly to him. These advisers are also high-level diplomats, usually with the rank of ambassador. There is practically no difference between the ambassadors-at-large and the independent advisers, and the existence of these two categories represents one of the vagaries of the bureaucratic machinery.

A separate small group of advisers reporting to the minister compiles information on many issues based on code cables from Soviet ambassadors abroad, KGB and GRU *rezidenti,* radio interceptions, and materials from the world media. This group also serves as liaison between the Foreign Ministry and the KGB.

Although global political goals are obvious to the top echelon of the Foreign Ministry, long-term policy planning is almost nonexistent. During the sixties, the ministry attempted to rectify this by creating a special Directorate for Foreign Policy Planning. Gromyko initially displayed interest in the work of the Directorate, but he soon lost it. At its inception, the Directorate looked as if it would be an important project. The Politburo authorized its creation with an unprecedented number of personnel (it was much larger than any operational department), with a special ranking system and higher salaries than other departments of the ministry. Several prominent scholars were invited to become employees along with the bureaucrats. Within a few years, however, the Directorate had failed utterly. Its lengthy assessment papers with different options for policy proved to be a "scholastic and unrealistic academic exercise," as Gromyko and other ministry officials described it. Gromyko put the Directorate's products on the shelf and reverted to running his ministry on the basis of day-to-day priorities, along with a few short-term goals.

The Directorate gradually evolved into a way-station for ambassadors or other senior diplomats awaiting new assignments and a haven for diplomats approaching retirement who still had good connections but who were no longer considered fit to perform well in the operational departments. People in the ministry began calling it the garbage can.

There were, however, some able people in the Directorate, and I asked several of them to work on Gromyko's address to the General Assembly. Tradition and propaganda imperatives dictated that the chief Soviet spokesman use the occasion to present some awe-inspiring proposal to demonstrate the U.S.S.R.'s commitment to world peace. The project was a thoroughly cynical one, but it demanded enormous effort from all sections of the ministry. The pressure was heavy, especially since the speech had to contain a novel idea at its center.

Yet when the working group finally produced and Gromyko approved a draft declaration on international security, there was nothing but a rearrangement of the shopworn ideas the Soviets had been promoting for years. It amounted to glossy propaganda with little genuine, workable substance. The central thrust was directed against the United States and China. For me, the only difference was that I had assumed a major role in a charade where earlier I had been just a minor player.

Working with Gromyko in the course of this exercise was enlightening. Certainly I knew that our leadership made every effort to utilize the United Nations in the interests of the Soviet Union and did not often act in consonance with the provisions of the UN Charter; other UN members conducted themselves in a similar way. But now it was also clear that Gromyko, one of the UN's founding fathers, held a nihilistic, cynical, hypocritical view of the organization's activities and goals. He had come to regard it as no more than a forum for disseminating propaganda and abuse, ignoring it if the UN did anything out of line with Soviet policy and using it in situations where it profited Moscow or its clients. What could one expect from other Politburo members if even Gromyko displayed interest in the UN only when it was time for his annual visit to New York? Unless other, special considerations arose, Gromyko practically never gave it a thought.

It was discomfiting to realize that my seven years of service in our mission to the UN was very nearly a waste. I knew the UN's flaws and failings, but I had not shed all my illusions; it was hard for me to reconcile myself to the truth. My doubts regarding our policy toward the UN grew accordingly.

SINCE MY STUDENT YEARS I HAD HAD A REAL DESIRE TO BE useful in arms control talks. I know it was somewhat romantic, but I saw myself as a champion of peace. I was proud of the fact that I had participated in test ban and nuclear nonproliferation negotiations—negotiations that resulted in treaties of significant importance. I was contemptuous (privately, of course) of Khrushchev's silly proposal of general and complete disarmament, and concerned that such ideas would replace realism in arms control and disarmament. At the same time, I believed that my country was serious about real measures regarding disarmament, especially the reduction of nuclear arsenals. This belief, however, grew more and more shaky during the late sixties. I realized the importance of SALT, but it represented a search for an appropriate strategic balance between the Soviet Union and the United States rather than a genuine attempt to achieve nuclear disarmament. In fact, we reversed our former position over the strongly expressed wishes of the majority of UN members.

We should have tried to progress both in SALT and in other, more substantial measures on arms control and disarmament. Initially my memoranda to Gromyko on this subject were disregarded. Lev Mendelevich, who had returned from his post in New York and been appointed Ambassador at Large, joined me in an effort to modify our line in disarmament negotiations. We prepared a revised draft treaty on general and complete disarmament and submitted it to Gromyko. His reaction was negative. He did sound out Brezhnev and some others on the issue, but found the prevailing opinion to be, as he explained to us, that we could not seriously talk about nuclear disarmament without Chinese participation in the negotiations. This made sense, of course, but only up to a point, as the Chinese nuclear potential did not pose a real threat. China was only an excuse.

In May 1971, I suggested to Gromyko that we propose a conference, to be called as soon as possible, of the five nuclear powers (China, U.S., U.K., France, U.S.S.R.) to consider nuclear disarmament. Gromyko hesitated but did not reject the idea; I persisted. I drafted a text of the statement on this subject and Gromyko liked it. He put the proposal before the Politburo.

The Politburo debate was not lengthy, but it provided me with a short, sharp lesson. Defense Minister Grechko (not yet a member of the Politburo, but present at the meeting) made no direct objections, but noted that one could hardly expect a positive response from either the Chinese or Americans. In any discussion on disarmament, he added, we should not permit our people to be deluded about the aggressive nature of imperialism and the danger of war. Grechko went on to make his usual speech about the lack of any real guarantee for peace other than our military might—particularly in nuclear and strategic arms.

Brezhnev countered with the observation that we were doing everything necessary to keep our nuclear strategic forces strong and that there was, therefore, no need at this point to go into a deep discussion of this matter. Gromyko followed up on Brezhnev's remarks by underlining that what was under consideration was simply a procedural proposal about the framework for negotiations on nuclear disarmament, and that it would be politically advantageous for us to propose a conference of the five powers.

In mid-June 1971, the proposal was transmitted by our ambassadors in Washington, Peking, Paris, and London to those governments. Only France, however, expressed a clear willingness to participate in the conference. China flatly refused to attend, and the United States and Great Britain were evasive.

The outcome was not surprising, but the conversations with Gromyko, Brezhnev's aides, and a number of top military and Central Committee people revealed that not only the Defense Ministry but the political leadership had not intended conducting serious negotiations on nuclear disarmament and did not envisage any eventuality of taking real measures of disarmament. To the contrary, we were building up further nuclear strategic potential. Many high-level officials smiled at some of my questions about disarmament and undoubtedly thought me ingenuous. Several of the more forthright said frankly that in the event of true nuclear disarmament we would cease to be a superpower and lose our capacity to exert an effective influence in world affairs beyond our border neighbors. The Politburo discussion on the conference only confirmed—albeit indirectly—that this was the position of our leadership as a whole.

The upshot, then, was the end of my hopes for a significant move in the direction of disarmament. It also gave me a needed lesson in *Realpolitik*. It wasn't so much that I had earlier been naïvely credulous regarding our propaganda or our position vis-à-vis the rest of the world, the United States in particular; it was simply that there comes a moment in the lives of most Soviet bureaucrats—perhaps more shocking for Soviets than for many others, jollied along as we are by our government's misrepresentations—when true intentions are seen squarely, revealed in a way so painful to your ideals that it changes you forever.

OUR RELATIONS WITH CHINA CONTINUED COLD. PEKING, as noted, had refused outright to participate in the proposed five-power conference. In the Chinese capital as in Moscow, memories were still fresh regarding the military border clashes between them, the most serious of which had occurred in 1969.

One evening in early March of that year, Yakov Malik and I were in his office when the code cable operator brought in the latest dispatches from Moscow and gave Malik one marked "very urgent." The cable said that a Chinese Army unit had invaded Damansky Island in the Ussuri River on the Soviet-Chinese border. A group of Soviet frontier guards approached the Chinese intending to tell them to withdraw from the island. The Chinese opened fire, killing and wounding several dozen Soviet soldiers. This was the latest—and worst—of a series of border incidents that had occurred over several years.

As he read the cable, Malik turned pale. I had seen him angry many times, but this was a level of fury beyond anything I had ever witnessed in him before.

"Now those squint-eyed bastards will get a lesson they'll never forget," he screamed. "Who do they think they are! We'll kill those yellow sons of bitches!" He raved on, calling the Chinese all the names he could think of, names in which the Russian language is rich.

My first opportunity to talk with someone knowledgeable about China came in a conversation with Mikhail Kapitsa, a preeminent Soviet expert on Asia, and China in particular, who had just become chief of the First Far Eastern Department at the ministry. Erudite and capable, gregarious and jovial, Kapitsa was a man of controversial behavior. His career would undoubtedly have moved ahead faster if he had not received a black mark in his dossier and a deep scar on his head when, as ambassador to Pakistan in 1961, he took up with his driver's wife. The chauffeur discovered the liaison. Rushing into the ambassador's office, where Kapitsa was using his couch as a bed, the infuriated husband clouted the diplomat on the head with a crowbar. He might have killed Kapitsa if aides had not come to his rescue. But the incident was forgiven because Kapitsa's expertise was needed. He was promoted to Deputy Foreign Minister in 1983 after Andropov became General Secretary of the Party, reflecting Andropov's interest in improving Sino-Soviet relations.

I asked Kapitsa how it could have happened that more than thirty of our frontier guards had been killed on Damansky Island in 1969, and why they had been so obviously unprepared to respond effectively.

"The Chinese completely surprised us," he answered. "The Politburo, despite all the tensions in our relations with Peking, had no idea they would do anything like that." The events on Damansky had the effect of an electric shock on Moscow. The Politburo was terrified that the Chinese might make a large-scale intrusion into Soviet territory which China claimed. A nightmare vision of invasion by millions of Chinese made the Soviet leaders almost frantic. Despite our overwhelming superiority in weaponry, it would not be easy for the U.S.S.R. to cope with an assault of such magnitude. From others I heard that the Soviet leadership had come close to using nuclear arms on China. I could not find words to express my consternation. There could scarcely be anything that so dramatically illustrated the gulf between our solemn promises regarding nuclear weapons and our willingness to consider employing such arms.

A ministry colleague who had been present at the Politburo discussion told me that Marshal Andrei Grechko, the Defense Minister, actively advocated a plan to "once and for all get rid of the Chinese threat." He called for unrestricted use of the multimegaton bomb known in the West as the "blockbuster." That bomb would release enormous amounts of radioactive fallout, not only killing millions of Chinese but threatening Soviet citizens in the Far East as well as people in other countries bordering China.

Fortunately, not many military men shared Grechko's

mad, bellicose stance. In 1970 I talked with one of Grechko's colleagues, Nikolai Ogarkov, a well-educated, sophisticated, and tough officer. That year he was made a marshal, and later became First Deputy Defense Minister and Chief of the General Staff. Ogarkov took a more realistic view of the prospect of war with China. He felt that the Soviet Union could not attack China with a nuclear barrage because it would inevitably mean world war. The alternative was to use a limited number of nuclear weapons in a kind of "surgical operation" to intimidate the Chinese and destroy their nuclear facilities. But, according to Ogarkov, that too was risky. A bomb or two would hardly annihilate a country like China, and the Chinese, with their vast population and deep knowledge and experience of guerrilla warfare, would fight unrelentingly. The Soviet Union could be mired in an endless war, with consequences similar to those suffered by America in Vietnam, if not much worse. (But one should not mistake Ogarkov's rational position on this matter as indicating any dovishness in the man. His devotion to Soviet supremacy was complete. He did not question the necessity of doing everything possible to increase Soviet might. Moreover, his sudden dismissal in September 1984, and replacement by Marshal Sergei F. Akhromeyev, was attributed to Ogarkov's insistence on military appropriations which the Politburo considered excessive.)

Disagreements about bombing China stalemated the Politburo. They were unable to reach a decision on the issue for several months. Grechko based his warlike position upon the assumption that America, then openly hostile to China, would not actively resist Soviet punitive action and would "swallow it." It was decided to put out feelers through various channels to test this notion. The Foreign Ministry, the KGB, and military intelligence took soundings of Washington's possible reaction to a nuclear strike. The Soviet Embassy in Washington was instructed to pursue this inquiry casually and at the middle level of bureaucracy. However, Ambassador Dobrynin's report contained a sober assessment that the United States would not be passive regarding such a blow at China. He concluded that there would be a risk of serious Soviet-American confrontation.

Moscow dropped the plan. Of the factors that dissuaded the Politburo from approving an attack upon China, the important one was undoubtedly the warning that the United States would rebuff it vigorously. It was one of the first indications that America might be looking to improve relations with China. This knowledge cooled passions in the Politburo and strengthened Brezhnev's middle-of-the-road position: not to attack China, but instead show Soviet power by stationing large contingents of troops armed with nuclear weapons along the entire length of the border. At the same time, attempts would be made via diplomatic negotiations to find solutions to territorial and other disputes with Peking.

But ideological combat and hostility between Soviets and Chinese always kept tensions high. The danger of explosion was always present. To accompany the gloomy atmosphere hovering about this subject, there was the usual circulation of jokes. A typical one ran:

Brezhnev calls President Nixon on the hot line and says, "I've heard you have a new super-computer that can predict events in the year 2000."

"Yes, Mr. General Secretary," Nixon replies proudly, "we have such a computer."

"Well, Mr. President, could you tell me what the names of the Politburo members will be then?"

A long silence.

"Aha!" Brezhnev exclaims. "Your computer isn't so sophisticated after all."

"No, Mr. General Secretary," Nixon replies, "it answered your question. But I can't read it. It's in Chinese."

But it was no joke to the Soviet leadership. The Chinese nuclear arsenal was growing, and the specter of military cooperation between China and the United States intensified the Kremlin's distress.

IN JULY 1972, GROMYKO ASKED ME WHAT NEW INITIATIVE the Soviet Union should submit at the next session of the General Assembly. At first, I thought he meant the ritual propaganda proposal he included every year in his speech at the UN. But in an unusually direct manner, he instructed me to concoct a proposition that would permit us to use nuclear weapons against China and at the same time would not make it look as if we were abandoning our position on the prohibition of these arms.

And so I assisted at the birth of a Soviet initiative which proposed the "renunciation of the use of force or the threat of it in international affairs and the *eternal* ban on the use of nuclear weapons." The word "eternal" was inserted by Gromyko to reinforce the impression that the U.S.S.R. did not intend to use nuclear weapons. It was a carefully worded piece of deception. On first reading, the Soviet initiative seemed to be a broad statement of Moscow's commitment to peace. Between the lines, however, was the implied threat—aimed at China—that the U.S.S.R. might react against breaches of the peace with nuclear force. On the surface, it appeared that the Soviet Union had not abandoned its support of the prohibition of the use of nuclear weapons. Actually, there was a loophole: those who disobeyed the ban on using any kind of force might be punished by nuclear reprisals.

When he returned to Moscow that fall, Gromyko left me behind in the Soviet delegation with special responsibility to see through a draft resolution on the proposal. He was worried that Yakov Malik, who was in charge of the delegation, was not flexible enough, especially about anything that "smelled Chinese," and might fail in this task. When Gromyko told Malik that I was to be responsible for the proposal, the ambassador accepted the news calmly enough. After Gromyko was out of earshot, he said to me with a smirk, "Well, Arkady, you'll have a tough time. If we don't succeed in getting the General Assembly to adopt our proposal, you'll get it in the neck before anyone else." Malik was right. I was not only not enthusiastic about my assignment, I found it thoroughly distasteful. Gromyko called us both in for a final session on strategy to achieve a UN majority for this piece of sophistry. He stressed to Malik that he must restrain his usual, freely expressed hatred of China. To get the resolution through the UN would require prudence and self-control.

"First of all, we have to avoid pointing a finger at China,"

Gromyko droned in his lecturing voice. To cover its real purpose, there was not one word about China in his formal statement.

"Besides," he continued, "we should maintain our dignity. We don't want to bark like mad dogs at every word they say. That just aggravates the polemics and makes us look like fools."

Malik looked as if he had swallowed a lemon. His face contorted as he tried to control himself. He did not dare contradict Gromyko, but his restraint didn't last long. Shortly after Gromyko returned to Moscow, Malik took on the Chinese in a vituperative harangue at a General Assembly session and again in the Security Council. The Chinese Ambassador gave a quiet rejoinder, but that only provoked Malik to new waves of invective. He could never let another speaker have the last word.

Malik's tirades made headlines and resulted in an urgent request from Moscow for a full text of the ambassador's remarks. Hours after the speech had reached the Foreign Ministry, Gromyko sent Malik a short, blunt cable: You have specific instructions about exacerbating polemical exchanges with the Chinese, the message said in so many words. You are to obey those instructions.

Forgetting that I was Gromyko's adviser—or so enraged that he was unable to take account of his audience—Malik erupted in a fury. "He's a fool, a marshmallow. He has no idea how to handle the Chinese. You have to be tough with those yellow bastards. You can't ever let up."

But Gromyko knew better than Malik what the leadership wanted. When the General Assembly approved the Soviet proposal with only minor modifications, he expressed his satisfaction and congratulated us, saying, "We have achieved our aim and are morally free to use nuclear arms against China if the Maoists try to invade the Soviet Union."

The UN resolution, however, was by no means enough. Moscow was vitally interested in securing American non-interference in the event of war between the U.S.S.R. and China, as well as in preventing American military aid to China. These twin problems had been debated several times by the Politburo, but there was no consensus about how to handle them. The Soviets thought it unwise to reveal their disquiet over these issues too directly and too formally to the Americans. At the same time, it was thought imprudent to avoid discussing these matters altogether. A middle course had to be found. That was why Brezhnev raised the problems with Henry Kissinger in an odd fashion and in peculiar circumstances.* While hunting at Zavidovo, his country retreat near Moscow, in May 1973, Brezhnev told Kissinger that something must be done about China's growing nuclear arsenal, but he didn't say what. He warned—if not threatened—the Secretary of State that any U.S. military assistance to the Chinese would lead to war, but he was vague about what kind of war and with whom.

Beyond the care needed in approaching this subject with the Americans, Brezhnev had another reason for caution in discussing Soviet-Chinese relations. The Politburo had always cherished the hope that one day relations between the two Communist countries could be normal, even friendly, but this would not happen while Mao was alive. The Kremlin's fondest wish was to see him dead.

The widening rift between the Soviet Union and China made it increasingly important for Moscow to secure the Western front in Europe. One afternoon in late summer 1970, Gromyko asked me to attend a meeting with Kovalev and Valentin Falin to discuss a general review of Soviet plans for Europe—it was on the eve of Willy Brandt's visit to Moscow. At that point, Falin was riding high on his successful efforts at promoting German-Soviet relations, and those efforts were paying off with Brandt's visit.

Falin was an intelligent man with a reasonable, logical approach to problems. Calm and reflective, he was interested in substance and possessed tremendous capacity for work. As a teen-ager, he had been a lathe operator in a large Moscow factory, finishing his high school education at night after work. By the time I met him in the late fifties, he was one of Gromyko's advisers and had become a broadly educated man with an almost aristocratic fineness in his man-

---

* Henry Kissinger, *Years of Upheaval* (Little, Brown, 1982), p. 233.

ner. Gromyko greatly valued Falin's knowledge of German affairs and had made him head of the ministry's department dealing with the FRG and the GDR.

Normalization and development of relations with Bonn were a delicate issue in view of the Kremlin's mistrust of the FRG and its persistent fear of neo-Nazi revanchism there. Gromyko wanted to make sure that the position he would take with the Politburo on the Soviet-German treaty reflected his advisers' best knowledge and recommendations in some ticklish areas. Moreover, Brandt's forthcoming visit was importantly connected with sensitive aspects of Soviet relations with East Germany's Party boss, Walter Ulbricht.

Although usually not inclined to express his assessments regarding political assignments given to his subordinates, Gromyko at this meeting was less circumspect and generalized rather freely. The gravity of the subjects under discussion was further underscored by his manner. Whenever he was concerned or under stress, his face would contort with grimaces almost as if he had a tic. His nose would twitch and his thick black eyebrows would fly nervously up and down like Groucho Marx's.

"We've lost our last hope with the Chinese, and we must finalize the treaty with the FRG without delay," he said. "Brandt is smart, and I think he'll work with us on this. It's the lever to draw Europe away from American influence."

He went on to say that we could not yet trust Nixon, and that although negotiations on SALT had begun, it was still an open question as to whether we could find a common language. All of us at the meeting knew that the Politburo was divided over SALT, and any dealings with Americans were viewed with suspicion.

Nevertheless, it appeared that something was afoot. I read several cables from Dobrynin in Washington containing faint hints that Nixon might be contemplating a change in policy, and might attempt to make a breakthrough in Soviet-American relations. However, during the summer of 1970, these intimations were greeted with skepticism. At this point Brezhnev and most members of the Politburo were more interested in European possibilities.

The Soviet-German treaty had been negotiated personally by Gromyko earlier in the year with FRG State Secretary Egon Bahr and later with Foreign Minister Walter Scheel. It had not been easy, but Gromyko had shrewdly devised some ambiguous formulations on a few key points, and Brandt had accepted them.

I was impressed with how well informed our ministry personnel were about what was going on in Bonn, including background details on the negotiations, details which could have their origin only within the office of the German Chancellor. I also saw several cables from the KGB *resident* in Bonn which were surprising in the quality and quantity of their information. Naturally, no names were mentioned in the cables, just the indication that the news was from a "most reliable source." I asked Falin how we could obtain such inside intelligence. He smiled mysteriously and would say only, "We have quite a net in West Germany, you know."

Later, from Vladimir Kazakov, head of the American desk at the First Political Directorate of the KGB, I learned the special importance of West Germany for Soviet spy operations. From him and Dmitri Yakushkin, who became the KGB *resident* in Washington, I was informed that West Germany, as Kazakov said, was "our door to the West." He meant that through Berlin it was easy for the KGB to plant agents in the West. Most of these operatives were ethnically German Soviets or natives of the Baltic republics who could enter West Germany in a straightforward manner without diplomatic cover. Arrangements for visits between the populations of East and West Germany facilitated spy transfers.

As the waltz with Brandt continued, Walter Ulbricht began to feel uneasy. Despite the general belief that the East Germans were simple, obedient allies, Ulbricht was demanding and tough. He nagged us constantly not to make too many concessions to the West Germans. He made an emergency visit to Moscow in May 1970, after which GDR Foreign Minister Otto Winzer and Deputy Foreign Minister Peter Florin phoned Gromyko's office regularly regarding Brandt's visit and the impending treaty. Gromyko became increasingly annoyed with their persistent calling and finally ordered Makarov to put them off. Makarov often told the East Germans that Gromyko was out of town. He would wear an expression of advanced boredom and frustration as he held the receiver away from his ear to escape the chatter coming over the wire, and then would hang up with a scowl and grate: "Those goddamn German bulldogs never give up. They're as thick-headed as mules." Makarov was also vexed that he could not afford to be abrasive with them.

Following the conclusion of the treaty between the Soviet Union and the Federal Republic, the Four Powers Agreement concerning Berlin was signed. Brandt had insisted upon this, but it was one of the most ambiguous agreements between nations concluded in this century. The Western powers and the Soviet Union were unable to agree even upon its title.

Negotiations were complex and painful for both sides, aggravated by the fact that the U.S.S.R.'s delegation was headed by its Ambassador to East Germany, Petr Abrasimov. An officiously self-confident man, Abrasimov often would not listen to his aides' advice and repeatedly ignored instructions, thus confusing further the already difficult issues, making mistakes in the negotiations, and going off the track time and again. Finally, however, to everyone's relief, a few sharp words from Moscow tamed him, and the agreement was concluded in 1971.

Gromyko and others often remarked that although the Federal Republic belonged to the West, its geopolitical interests would gradually push it toward neutrality and eventually perhaps closer to the Soviet Union than to the United States. This view was based on the assumption that our propaganda and blackmail would influence pacifist sentiments in the FRG to such an extent that fear of nuclear war would prevail over any other possibilities. Soviet policy was to encourage Bonn to think that only the U.S.S.R.—not the United States—could alleviate this terror. We intended to support the theme with a refrain that Moscow was Germany's natural and historic economic partner. Finally, on a firmer note, the case would be made that it was Moscow—not Washington—that held the key to German aspirations for reunification or, at least for the time being, to widening contacts with East Germany.

BECAUSE OF MY WORK AT THE UN, GROMYKO REGARDED me as something of a Middle East expert. He ordered me to follow both events in the area and the work of others in the ministry. Most revealing were the opinions of one senior official of the Middle East Department and a longtime observer of the region. Especially in the months following Nasser's death in September 1970, he divulged to me many details of the makeshift and sinister nature of Moscow's courtship of the Arab world.

Although Nasser had been a frequent visitor to the Soviet Union, often for medical treatment, his fatal heart attack surprised Moscow nearly as much as it did millions of Egyptians and their neighbors. Serious trouble was ahead for Soviet-Egyptian relations, because so much had been based on personal ties to Nasser. We had not acquired the foundation of influence we needed in political, military, or broader circles in the country. The KGB and the Communist Party had both failed to build a strong base outside Nasser's immediate entourage.

My source of information was correct about his long-range prediction, but wrong in forecasting that Anwar el-Sadat, whom he termed "an American stooge," would prove to be merely a transitional leader. Aside from thinking Sadat pro-Western, Soviet analysts regarded him as a weak, indecisive figure, rumored to be a drug addict, and due to make way sooner or later for Ali Sabry, another Nasser aide still in the leadership. Sabry was clearly Moscow's candidate to take Nasser's place, but as 1970 ended, Sadat appeared to be holding his own, and analysts in the Middle East Department were worried.

"Things are bad," one of them told me early in 1971. "Sadat is a scoundrel." What angered Moscow was the Egyptian postponement of agreement on a long-sought treaty of friendship, a document the Soviets hoped would bind Egypt firmly into an alliance. Late in the winter, a senior man in the Middle East Department spoke even more forcefully. "We're just about at the end of our patience," he said as we lunched at the nearby Prague Restaurant. It was a convenient and comfortable place to eat, but ministry employees usually went somewhere else if they wanted to hold a relaxed talk. We all knew that a good portion of the Prague's waiters were semi-professional eavesdroppers on the KGB payroll.

My friend was too wound up to be discreet. "Opinion is beginning to solidify in the leadership," he confided, "that we have to be rid of Sadat. The only problem is that we don't have a really strong figure to take over from him. But there are some possibilities."

I must have showed my surprise. "Are people really planning something?" I asked. "How do you know about this?"

"I don't know all the details myself," he admitted. "But I have my own contacts with the KGB. They've gone far enough in thinking this out so that they have a general plan to take care of Sadat—to liquidate him. Of course, not by their own hands. They have people, though, who are getting ready to act."

"Have they gone crazy?" I did not conceal my shock.

"We've got to do something," he insisted. "It's one alternative, but obviously it would have to be very carefully done."

I decided not to tell Gromyko what I had learned. Perhaps my colleague was wrong. The plan to kill Sadat, in any case, did not seem fully developed. Conceivably, my friend's KGB associates were only boasting of what they could do, not of what they were authorized to set in motion. To protest to the Foreign Minister about a policy decision that had already been taken would have been futile; to alert him to something that might turn out to be merely rumor would only make me (and him) look foolish.

And so I kept my counsel, although a friend on the Central Committee staff also remarked to me that Sadat should go, "one way or another." Within a short time, the option vanished: Sadat moved against his domestic opposition. On May Day 1971, he dismissed Ali Sabry as Vice-President and then arrested him and six other cabinet members, whom he eventually charged with high treason.

* * *

GROMYKO SENT ME ABROAD SEVERAL TIMES AS HIS REPRE-
sentative. My diplomatic mission to Africa in 1971 was de-
pressingly instructive. I had been charged with looking into
a number of complaints from African countries as well as
from Soviet representatives. The Nigerian Foreign Minister
was irate over Soviet failure to deliver a large shipment of
cement on time. In Guinea, where I stayed for several days
of delicate negotiations, there was a similar picture of frustration. Soviet planes stood idle for lack of maintenance and
replacement parts. Ambitious construction projects, fi-
nanced by Soviet credits, were half finished because promised materials had not been shipped. One large yard just off
the capital's main thoroughfare had become a ceramic cemetery, full of toilets and urinals sent by the Soviet Union for
installation in a planned but uncompleted building. Soviet
diplomats stationed in Conakry complained that their shipments of food arrived late or not at all. They were forced to
do their basic grocery shopping at the Yugoslav commis-
sary.

My experiences on the trip left me with serious misgivings
about the nature of our approach to Africa. Because of economic deficiencies and bureaucratic inertia at home we
would be hard put to meet the expectations our expansionist
diplomacy aroused. Instead of gaining friends, we would, in
many instances, lose credibility.

The United States, on the other hand, had substantial
resources to counteract Soviet expansion in the Third
World. It too, however, was plagued with inertia and uncertainty in its policies. America tended to see things in terms
of black and white, evidencing a lack of understanding of
basic Third World problems. It seemed difficult for Americans to realize that a number of these initially Moscow-
oriented countries did not want to emulate the Soviet model.
Its weak economic position deprives the Soviet Union of
certain options in the conduct of its foreign policy—options
which are available to the economically stronger West. The
economic tidbits the U.S.S.R. can afford in trying to attract
other nations to its side will not produce significant results.

While shifting allegiances in countries like Egypt and a few others may be viewed as cynical and opportunistic, there is an inescapable realism in such countries' acceptance of Soviet aid in the form of weapons and later turning to the West for economic aid. The West's great advantage is that, except in a state of war, in the long run economic assistance will always pay bigger dividends than will military aid. The free world's collective gross national product greatly exceeds that of the socialist nations. That effective weapon should be used to undermine Soviet influence.

In 1971 I was also sent to sound out the Foreign Ministers of Bulgaria, Hungary, and Romania on how to coordinate joint actions of the socialist countries to conclude the treaty on the liquidation of chemical and biological weapons. The Soviet Union has consistently depicted itself as a leader in the effort to destroy these ghastly weapons. In fact, the U.S.S.R. has always continued to increase and expand its sophisticated chemical and biological weapons production programs.

The military branch responsible for this sickening business has a huge department in the Defense Ministry. It has rejected any kind of international control or oversight. Several times I asked officials there why they were so adamant. The response was always the same: control was out of the question because it could reveal the extent of the development of these weapons and would show Soviet readiness for their eventual use. There is no question that the U.S.S.R. is much better prepared than the United States for this type of warfare.

While the military strongly opposed any agreement on chemical or biological weapons, the political leadership, Gromyko in particular, felt it necessary for propaganda purposes to respond to a proposal by Great Britain to conclude a special separate convention to prohibit biological warfare as a first step. The military's reaction was to say go ahead and sign the convention; without international controls, who would know anyway? They refused to consider eliminating their stockpiles and insisted upon further development of these weapons. The Politburo approved this approach. The toothless convention regarding biological weapons was signed in 1972, but there are no international controls over the Soviet program, which continues apace.

MY PERSONAL REWARD FOR BEING GROMYKO'S ADVISER was that I became a member of the *nomenklatura* hierarchy. This is a list of the most important posts in all branches of the Party, government administration, and other institutions. These positions are filled either by direct Party appointment—Politburo or Central Committee Secretariat —or with Party approval. *Nomenklatura* is a caste system which applies only to the elite class. Its many different levels enjoy varying degrees of privilege according to rank. For Politburo members there is no limit or restriction on privileges. Below this level the grading structure begins. The Central Committee establishes and defines the place of anyone who is eligible for inclusion in the various categories: high Party apparatchiki, cabinet ministers, and other persons in various important positions. Factory workers, farmers, engineers, lawyers, doctors, store managers, secretaries, and other private citizens are excluded from the system and its special advantages.

Unlike ordinary mortals, members of the elite have exclusive and extensive privileges: high salaries, good apartments, dachas, government cars with chauffeurs, special railway cars and accommodations, VIP treatment at airports, resorts and hospitals off limits to outsiders, special schools for their children, access to stores where consumer goods and food are available at reduced prices and in plentiful quantities. They live a rarefied existence far removed from the common man, and, indeed, have to go out of their way if they wish to rub elbows with the less exalted. The highest group in the *nomenklatura* is in fact separated from most citizens by a barrier as psychologically imposing as the Great Wall of China. This class constitutes virtually a state within a state. In fact, any information about this social stratum is actually a state secret. Neither the Soviet people nor the rest of the world is supposed to know anything at all about them.

The total number of those designated under the system, however, is not small. It includes many thousands, all ranked from highest to lowest throughout the Soviet Union. They form the backbone of the status quo in the governmental and societal structure. They will permit no one to transform that society or alter its foreign or domestic policy in any way that may affect their perquisites. It is no small irony to know that this fossilized elite controls the nation which calls on other countries to renounce stability for revolution, to give up privilege for the blessings of proletarianism.

I had heard about much of this before my family and I joined the anointed. When we became part of this class, we regarded the luxuries and special courtesies accorded us with delighted wonder. All too soon the garnering of more and the deference of others became something that we treated as if it were a birthright.

18

MY WORK AS GROMYKO'S ADVISER BROUGHT ME INTO DIrect contact with the Politburo and a number of key Central Committee members. Like the Tsar's two-headed eagle, these entities spring from one body, the Communist Party apparatus, and form the real power mechanism of the Soviet Union, with the Politburo having the final word.

For a long time the Kremlin has symbolized Soviet Communist power. Pictures of the walled palace complex are familiar even to schoolchildren in many countries of the world. The red brick walls protecting the heart of Soviet strength are also symbolic of the governing attitude of those who make policy within them. The most knowledgeable Western politicians and intelligence organizations can only speculate about what goes on inside.

Soviet leaders are able to conceal their policymaking processes primarily because of an extraordinary concentration of power in the hands of about two dozen men at the apex, supported by the most influential regional Party bosses. They are not controlled by any democratic institutions in the Western sense, and do not tolerate any opposition. They have never forgotten Lenin's lesson that any organized opposition to the regime may pose a mortal threat. His small party (less than 240,000) was able to seize power with popular slogans, tight organization, and strict discipline within its ranks. In Russia's only free election, within a month of the October Revolution of 1917, 75 percent voted against Lenin's Bolsheviks, whereupon, early in 1918, he dissolved the democratically elected Constituent Assembly.

Another essential element on which policymaking in the Kremlin is based is complete secrecy. A familiar joke claims that Lenin's Bolsheviks went underground at the end of the last century and have never come out—even after they seized power. There is a lot of truth in this old chestnut.

It may be difficult for people used to pluralistic systems to grasp that the Supreme Soviet (the parliament), "the highest body of state authority" according to the Constitution of the U.S.S.R., and the Council of Ministers, supposedly "the highest executive and administrative body," are absolutely and permanently controlled by the Politburo. No candidate put forth by the Party has ever failed to be elected to the Soviet parliament, and in its entire existence no deputy in that body has ever voted against or abstained on any measure presented for ratification by the government, or, to be exact, by the Politburo.

Within the Politburo there is a core that can be called the "Politburo" of the Politburo. Fundamentally, this group consists of Moscow-based members. Those from the various republics and districts of the Soviet Union play a less important role and often are not privy to precisely how certain decisions on domestic or foreign policy are arrived at. There are several reasons for this.

Non-Moscow members do not attend all the regular Thursday Politburo meetings. In addition to these sessions, moreover, there are also non-scheduled ones. Once, I asked

Vasily Makarov where I could get the record of Politburo discussions. He told me there were no verbatim records. Occasionally, however, segments of Politburo discussions have been recorded, and, of course, full texts of all decisions are kept in the Central Committee archives. The decisions are forwarded to those responsible for their implementation.

Those who must carry out the Politburo's orders are allowed to keep the decisions for reference no more than thirty days, when it is required that they be returned to the Central Committee. No one may photocopy a copy of any decision for himself, but one can request the Central Committee to send it over again for a few days' review, if needed.

Because of this cumbersome practice and absence of verbatim records, non-attending members are often unaware of nuances or conditions related to many of the decisions made. Moreover, the Politburo has no established rules of procedure. The conduct of its work is left primarily to the leader of the Party and otherwise determined by tradition.

Non-Moscow members do not receive (or receive only after a substantial delay) all the information available to those in the capital. Important code cables from ambassadors in major foreign countries, for example, are not usually available to them. Perhaps one of their most serious disadvantages is that they rarely participate in the important informal talks on crucial and delicate questions. These backstage maneuverings and confidential tête-à-têtes, so intrinsic to the Soviet character in the conduct of business, go on almost all the time in Moscow. Thus, the absentees' knowledge about what was really discussed or whose position is strongest is generally secondhand. When they take their seats at the long table in the Kremlin or Central Committee building where the Politburo meets, they usually consider proposals in a form already representing a consensus of the most powerful members.

No Politburo member who is based outside Moscow has a chance to be elected General Secretary of the Party. More than once I heard regional members—particularly Vladimir Shcherbitsky, a Ukrainian Party chief—complain about such unfavorable status.

The Party chief—the General Secretary of the Central Committee—is the supreme leader of the country. He is selected in secret within the Politburo and his appointment is confirmed at a formal session of the Central Committee. The absence of any kind of normal democratic procedure regarding succession in the Party leadership has led to an absurd situation where for twenty-two years out of the Soviet Union's sixty-seven years of existence, its top leaders have been fatally sick, incapacitated, or partially paralyzed, and yet remained at their posts.

Since Khrushchev's time the Politburo has met unfailingly every week throughout the year. If the General Secretary is absent from Moscow on holiday or on an overseas visit, a senior secretary of the Party will chair the group. When he was in charge, Yuri Andropov moved the meeting date to Friday, but the traditional Thursday session was restored by Konstantin Chernenko.

The agenda for an average Politburo meeting is extremely heavy. It normally includes thirty to forty or more items ranging from questions of the most pressing import down to very minor matters. When I asked our senior technical secretary to show me the file containing the proposals our ministry sent to the Politburo for approval, I discovered that there were several forwarded in one day. If other ministries, and the KGB and other branches of government as well, submitted a like number of proposals, I wondered how many of them the Politburo could consider seriously. But the growing burden has not led to delegation of lesser matters to a lower authority. Andropov and Chernenko did not change this style.

The pettiness of some of the questions dealt with at this highest level is hard to believe. Among the matters that regularly occupy Politburo time are lists of Soviet citizens and institutions proposed for various awards and decorations, from small distinctions to the prestigious Lenin Prizes. As another example, the construction of an apartment building for Soviets in New York was the subject of several Politburo discussions.

Behind this unwillingness to relinquish oversight of insignificant items is not fear of error, but a more profound anxiety that any one politician or economic manager might become autonomous, the master of his own house, a separate power center beyond the control of the Party leadership. The leaders understand that the economy has become so complex that to command it from a single center is no longer practical or efficient. But a vast range of social, political, and economic constraints prevents any radical change designed to replace the outmoded model. At best, only a few limited changes could be made. However, in the senescence of its system no one should expect the Soviet Union to cross a decentralized, free-market Rubicon. That would amount to the destruction of the foundations of its power, something that cannot be accepted by the Party and the state oligarchy. A free-market system would mean not only that those at the top would lose control over development but— worst of all—much of the bureaucracy's functions would cease to be necessary.

The overburdening of the Politburo's agenda also flows from a traditional rule of the decision-making system known as *perestrakhovka,* meaning something like "playing safe" and "mutual protection" or, in a purely political sense, "collective responsibility." It connotes the opposite of individual authority. The primary rule for safe behavior in any bureaucratic setting, it has become as well the Party's and the bureaucracy's guiding management precept on every level of the Soviet Union.

Uppermost in the minds of minor and major officials alike is the need for a shield against blame. Blame is the means by which powerful men have been swept from their posts; thus it is the thing most feared by the prominent. Approval or disapproval by the Politburo absolves all, for the Politburo is considered mistake-proof.

The present Soviet leadership is still grappling with the ghosts of Stalin and Khrushchev. To preserve power, the leaders feel they must share it; to protect their authority as a group, they dilute that of each member.

When one of their number tries (and fails) to hasten the pace of change, as did the ambitious Aleksandr Shelepin in early 1975, he is dismissed to the outer bureaucratic darkness—some minor administrative post. And if a policy must be disowned, sometimes a senior scapegoat will be found. In the wake of the agricultural disasters of the mid-seventies, Dmitri Polyansky went from a seat on the Politburo and Party responsibility for Soviet farming to ceremonious exile as ambassador to Japan.

Such upheavals, however, run contrary to the style and substance of contemporary Soviet rule, that of an entrenched hierarchy intent on perpetuating itself. Since October 1964, when Khrushchev was cashiered, there have been individual ousters but no mass dismissals like that of the "anti-Party group" (Molotov, Malenkov, and Kaganovich) who failed in their 1957 putsch against Khrushchev. The casualties have been men like Shelepin, Polyansky, and the Ukrainian leader Petr Shelest, who doubted the wisdom of Brezhnev's decision to receive President Nixon in 1972, and who tolerated the expression of more Ukrainian national feeling than Moscow thought safe.

The removal in 1977 of Nikolai Podgorny, whose protocol role as head of state Brezhnev wished to claim for himself, reflected the slowness with which the rulers act. Podgorny's unpopularity in the Party had been clear since 1971, when, out of some 14,000 ballots cast to approve the official leadership slate proposed to the Twenty-fourth Party Congress, about 270—a high number by Soviet standards—were marked against him. In any event, these departures occurred singly and without incident. In collective leadership the loss of any one member leaves the organism unimpaired. To avoid convulsions in their midst the Soviet leaders put maximum effort into working out likely subjects of disagreement before a potentially prickly issue must be formally addressed within the Politburo.

Even so, it often happens that a Politburo session concludes with several agenda items left untouched. The leftovers—or emergency issues which come up between the weekly meetings and require quick action—are then handled by *oprosniy poryadok*, a poll of the resident Moscow leadership, often excluding the out-of-town members. Central Committee couriers bring the papers to the Politburo members and wait while they write out their approval or comments in the margin. For these polled questions a majority of the Moscow members is enough to ensure collective responsibility. The regional leaders are informed later.

Politburo meetings sometimes include prolonged examination of major questions. During my time as Gromyko's adviser those discussions led to decisions that remained closely guarded secrets. For instance, while Willy Brandt was in Moscow in August 1970 in connection with the conclusion of the Soviet-FRG treaty, after lengthy debate the Politburo decided that any negotiations about the reunification of Germany might take place only if West Germany withdrew from NATO and became "a socialist state" in the sense of the term understood by the Soviet Union.

In important foreign policy matters the Kremlin leadership's typical double-handed approach was expressed in the approval of a plan to send submarines to probe Swedish and Norwegian coastal areas soon after Swedish Prime Minister Olof Palme visited Moscow in 1970 and received assurances that the Soviet Union intended to widen the friendly cooperation with his country. At a meeting in the spring of 1972, it was decided to sign the convention on the liquidation of biological weapons. But General Aleksei A. Gryzlov told me that Defense Minister Andrei Grechko had instructed the military not to abandon its program to produce these weapons. It is not possible that the Politburo was unaware of this order.

While outsiders, Western and Soviet, often imagine the Politburo as a scene of constant intrigue and periodic, dramatic conflict, what I have observed is more placid. There are intrigues, of course, but these are mostly bids for increased personal power and do not concern the basic political line or ultimate objectives. It is occasionally true, as jockeying for position takes place within the Politburo, that contending members will adopt positions on issues to serve as rallying points for their supporters. Once power is achieved and new political alignments are reached, however, these policy positions can be quickly dropped and business proceeds as usual.

The Politburo agrees on two fundamental propositions: the necessity of consolidating the power of the Party and

238

the elite class, and the need to maintain themselves as the directors—infallible and indispensable—of a closed regime.

In the West, Kremlinologists, politicians, and statesmen often speculate on which members of the Soviet leadership are doves and which are hawks. The implication is that there is within the top level of the Soviet hierarchy a group of peace-loving men who have no extraterritorial ambitions for the U.S.S.R., or are ready to curtail subversive activities by various pro-Moscow Communist movements in different parts of the world. If the West behaves in ways which are helpful to this group, so the argument goes, their views can prevail in Politburo debates, and the Soviet Union will steer a less aggressive course.

But the differences and contests among the Soviet leaders cannot be understood by using simplistic labels such as "hawks" and "doves," "hard-liners" and "moderates." Men do not reach the pinnacle of Communist power without a strong grasp of political reality. Nor do they achieve their positions without an abiding commitment to the rightness of the Soviet system. Once they must work with one another —even while seeking to bolster their own authority or diminish the standing of other contenders for power—they base their conduct on a blend of ideological and pragmatic motives. The fable of doves and hawks contesting in the Kremlin has been encouraged for Western consumption by Soviet propaganda and disinformation outlets.

It is true that the top leadership contains elements which are more prone to advocate the use of direct force (some of the orthodox in the Central Committee of the Party and in the military) while others favor the use of political measures (some in the Foreign Ministry and in the economic sector). But these are merely differences with respect to means. Soviet leaders are *all aggressive*, all hawks with respect to the final goals of their policy. Those who have held power from Lenin through Chernenko, and whoever may succeed him, are all cut from the same cloth.

For its defense of the system inside and outside the Soviet Union the Party employs a spectrum of elaborate propaganda methods. The efficacy of sloganeering as a mobilizer of Lenin's activist workers and soldiers was not lost on

239

those who inherited power in the U.S.S.R. A huge propaganda machine became a cornerstone of the regime, and every Soviet citizen gets a daily dose of hypnotism from infancy until death. However, sooner or later many recognize propaganda for what it is. There is resentment at the government's constant lies and the discrepancy between slogans and reality.

Yet the indoctrination is sophisticated, and millions would uphold a great deal of what they have been taught, especially regarding foreign policy and conditions in capitalist countries, because they have been so well conditioned. More than 90 percent of the Soviet population has never been out of the country and has little or no access to factual information. The state propagandists' usual method is a practical application of Pavlov's theory of conditioned reflex. An unrelenting massage by songs, speeches, newspapers, books, television, films, theater, art, poetry, and so forth, combined with the pleasant stimuli of material rewards for chosen segments of the populace, evokes the desired response of submission to the system. And for the gripers and troublemakers there are less pleasant stimuli: intimidation, harassment, imprisonment, or worse.

BY THE EARLY SEVENTIES, LEONID BREZHNEV HAD FIRMLY established his dominance in the Politburo and as leader of the Soviet Union. But unlike Stalin or Khrushchev, Brezhnev had to grant the Politburo a substantially bigger role in the decision-making process. In that respect, he was weaker than either of these two predecessors. Nevertheless, as General Secretary of the Party he exercised great influence on both the composition and the functioning of the Politburo. Moving with his customary caution, he gradually managed to remove those Politburo members who might try to resist or oppose him in internal or foreign matters. He replaced them with Andrei Gromyko; Andrei Grechko, the late Defense Minister; Konstantin Chernenko, Secretary of the Party; Yuri Andropov, KGB chairman; Dmitri Ustinov, the Defense Minister; and Nikolai Tikhonov, who succeeded Kosygin as Prime Minister. These men supported

Brezhnev's domestic and foreign policies. Furthermore, through his own office staff, Brezhnev created the means by which his closest assistants could directly influence the operation of the Central Committee as well as various ministries. His personal secretariat was headed by his old comrade Georgy Tsukanov, aided by Andrei Aleksandrov-Agentov, Anatoly Blatov, and others.

Aleksandrov-Agentov and Blatov told me quite openly that they often suggested ideas to Brezhnev without asking the advice of the Foreign Ministry—although Brezhnev usually consulted Gromyko on a personal basis—or the Central Committee departments, and that in a number of instances he had accepted their proposals. His office staff was invaluable in Brezhnev's efforts to increase his own authority and it enabled him to act without informing the Politburo about some issues of significant importance, such as his trips abroad or preparation of his major political speeches.

During my three years as Gromyko's adviser, Andrei Kirilenko was considered Brezhnev's heir apparent. Ill health as well as the rise of Chernenko and Andropov, however, removed him from the competition. In this connection, I should note that the prolonged absence from public view of various Politburo members is not necessarily a sign of disgrace or a prelude to removal, as has often been suggested in the West. These enigmatic disappearances are mostly the result of bureaucratic requirements. After Gromyko fainted at a meeting in the early 1970s, the Politburo decreed mandatory month-long vacations twice a year for its members.

Politburo paperwork must pass through the apparatus of the Central Committee. Brezhnev put one of his most reliable cronies in a key position there: Konstantin Ustinovich Chernenko, who headed the Central Committee's General Department and the Politburo's Secretariat for a number of years before his promotion to the Politburo itself. The son of a Siberian peasant, a Party member since he was twenty, he steadily made his way from the provinces to the top in Moscow, first as Brezhnev's aide and then almost as his alter ego. I met him after Brezhnev became Party leader in 1964 and had occasion to talk with him both in Moscow and in New York.

He was stocky and stoop-shouldered and for some time has had emphysema, which has evidently become more serious recently. He did not have a first-rate intellect, but he was a pragmatic, businesslike man who knows what he wants. He is demanding, rude, authoritarian, arrogant, and possesses immense self-confidence. He was also so dull a public figure that, in my time, there were not even the usual anecdotes or jokes about him among the Soviet population. As younger men, he and Brezhnev used to get together for heavy drinking sessions while they socialized. Non-drinking Soviet leaders like Suslov, Kosygin, and Gromyko despised this practice.

Generally taciturn, Chernenko tended to speak in sharp, abrupt sentences, frequently interrupting others, inspiring timidity in his subordinates whether they were affected by his strong physical presence or connected to it only by telephone. On a visit to New York in the mid-seventies, for instance, he had Ambassador Malik, notorious for his own imperious behavior, quaking like a mouse. In Moscow, I saw Vasily Makarov, Gromyko's assistant, nervously answering Chernenko, on the other end of the line, with a stream of rapid yeses.

While I was UN Under Secretary General, Chernenko came to New York to examine the procedural work of the body and its meetings. He showed some interest in the UN's technical facilities, but none in political discussions there or in the city of New York or the people at the UN. He was all business and practically humorless.

Chernenko's rise to full Politburo membership was so rapid that he aroused the resentment of others. Some key Politburo members, particularly the late Mikhail Suslov and Aleksei Kosygin, considered Chernenko a parvenu, a man lacking the proper qualifications for becoming their colleague, much less those fitting him to become their leader. Their judgment was essentially correct. For a long time, one of Chernenko's chief Party responsibilities was that of "agitprop" (agitation and propaganda), a crude and strident form of political indoctrination. He was never a First Party Secretary in any region, nor did he see military service in World War II. He was the first Soviet leader since Lenin without real military experience. As the Politburo's technical secretary, a post he held for some years, he was seen by its old members as merely a senior clerk, and by no means their equal.

In the last period of his rule, the slowly dying Brezhnev depended more and more upon Chernenko. As usual, a joke summed up the situation: "Brezhnev has been dead for quite some time now, but Chernenko hasn't told him about it yet." Brezhnev's blind, trusting reliance on Chernenko was an opportunity the latter did not waste. He went all out to promote himself and build enough power to compete for the succession. His maneuverings, however, came to nothing after Brezhnev's death. Chernenko lost his bid for the General Secretaryship.

His defeat at the hands of Yuri Andropov probably further undermined his health, and was no doubt a serious blow to him, bolstered as he had been for so long by Brezhnev's prestige. Although the truth will likely never be known, I feel reasonably sure that this was why he disappeared from public view for a while during Andropov's rule.

Yuri Andropov stood somewhere between a Party functionary and a bureaucrat. Intelligent and very shrewd, he managed to push himself to the top using his loyal KGB supporters and by projecting himself as the man who could resolve the nation's problems. As KGB chief for many years and responsible for the suppression of dissent, Andropov was in no way a progressive liberal. I was amazed, therefore, at how quickly and easily so many in the West, especially students of Soviet affairs, appeared to fall under the spell of the KGB's disinformation campaign representing Andropov as a "closet liberal" and as an "open-minded reformer." When selected as Party leader, he was the oldest man ever to have gained that position, and he was ill for most of his short tenure. Konstantin Chernenko was even older than Andropov when he succeeded him in February 1984, at the age of 72.

Chernenko's main strength rests on his lifelong career as a professional Party apparatchik. He was a firm advocate of strict party control over all aspects of life in the Soviet Union. He belonged to the Party elite, the true ruling class of the U.S.S.R. Because he was one of their blood brothers, they will trust him above anyone who has not made his life's work in the Party. Chernenko was a master of wheeling and dealing in the Central Committee, an ideologue and propagandist. While he was intimately acquainted with the intricacies of Party work, however, before he became General Secretary he had little experience or expertise either in domestic economic management or in substantive foreign policymaking. At Politburo meetings he rarely expressed his own views on such matters, invariably supporting those of Brezhnev.

Some Western analysts thought that Andropov was overestimated and that the danger was in underestimating Chernenko. But most of these speculations were built on sand. The real potential of any Soviet leader is an equation with so many unknowns that highest-ranking Kremlin officials themselves, not only outsiders, have a longer record of miscalculating the prospects of their own colleagues than of reading them accurately. Initially the future roles of Stalin, Khrushchev, and Brezhnev were all underestimated; Malenkov's was overestimated.

In Chernenko's case, of course, there were factors that made prediction easier. As with Andropov, the tenure of the septuagenarian Chernenko was of a transitional character. Even in the first months of his rule he was already displaying obvious physical infirmity. What was certain, however, was that, unlike Brezhnev, and unlike Khrushchev and Stalin, he will never become the sole repository of Kremlin authority. He had no choice but to abide by the collective will of the tiny inner circle in the Politburo that has actually run the Soviet Union ever since Brezhnev became incapacitated at the end of the 1970s.

Chernenko was chosen by this group because even though they may personally despise him, he also suits them. The gerontocrats of the Politburo and in the Party apparatus have accepted him as their chance to retain power a while longer before the younger generation replaces them. This may seem a trivial reason, but one must remember that the affairs of great nations are not always conducted by great men.

Chernenko was the oldest man in Soviet history to become General Secretary of the Party, and was the weakest, least able leader the Kremlin has had. Others have waited too long for their turn at leadership to be ignored for much longer. Before I broke with the Soviets I learned, through friends and associates in the Central Committee and the Foreign Ministry, that influential elements of the Party and the government elite were increasingly concerned about the need to infuse fresh blood into the ruling gerontocracy, which has now reached unprecedented antiquity.

At the Party Congress held in February–March 1981, it was decided to begin calling on younger men, and Mikhail S. Gorbachev, fifty years old, a Secretary of the Central Committee for some time, was elected a full member of the Politburo. Before 1978, he was First Secretary of the Territorial Party Committee in Stavropol in Caucasia. The resort city of Kislovodsk is located in that area, and I first heard of him from the local people while Lina and I were vacationing there in 1977. During our stay, I met and talked with him.

Gorbachev is intelligent, well educated, and well mannered. He is a graduate of the Moscow University law faculty, and also studied agriculture at an institute in Stavropol. At his post in Caucasia he earned a reputation as an energetic regional Party leader and manager and as a competent agricultural specialist. He was also known as a reasonable man, with less arrogance than most professional Party apparatchiki. Apparently he was also clever enough to listen to the people he served. Beyond his personal attributes, Gorbachev was fortunate to hold office in an area of productive land and kind climate, which made his job that much easier.

More important, however, was the fact that his territory enjoyed special care and generous funding from Moscow because of the famous Caucasian mineral springs, around which developed resort towns favored by the elite. The mineral waters became not only an aid to the health of many high-ranking Party and government members but also a foundation of Gorbachev's rising career. Kosygin, Andropov, and other Soviet leaders were there periodically for medical treatments and rest. As the local party boss, Gorbachev had the opportunity to meet them many times and, as the Russians say, *pokazat tovar litsom*—to show himself at his best.

I found him to be open-minded, and to understand the real necessity of moving agriculture and the economy forward. According to Robert Kaiser of the Washington *Post*, who was in the U.S.S.R. in the summer of 1984, there were reports in Moscow that Gorbachev was seeking a sharp turn in economic policy and asking economists for briefings on the reforms designed by Pyotr Stolypin, Tsar Nicholas II's enlightened prime minister, who encouraged entrepreneurship among the peasants. He was also reportedly calling for information on Lenin's New Economic Policy (NEP) of the twenties, which revived some limited forms of free enterprise in the difficult years following the devastation of the Revolution and Civil War.

Gorbachev had a powerful position: he became both a full member of the Politburo and a Secretary of the Central Committee, responsible for the day-to-day conduct of Party business. These posts clearly made him a claimant on the crown of General Secretary, although he was the youngest man in the Politburo. Some in the Central Committee referred to him as "a young boy."

Two other men from the regions, both about seven years older than Gorbachev, rose to prominence in the last years of Brezhnev's rule and were elevated further by Andropov. These were Grigory V. Romanov, former Leningrad Party chief, who was moved to Moscow to become a Party Secretary, and Geidar A. Aliyev, once Azerbaijan KGB boss and later Party chief, who has also become a full member of the Politburo and First Deputy Prime Minister.

Aliyev is known for his zeal in the latest anti-corruption drive and for his efforts in behalf of good economic management.

Romanov was a more dogmatic and arrogant man than Gorbachev, but he has been effective in dealing with both Party and economic affairs in Leningrad, his political base, which he ruled firmly. A naval architect by education, he worked for a while as a design engineer, but has spent most of his life as a Party apparatchik.

There have been a good many rumors about him over the years, mainly caused by his family name, which is the same as that of the Russian imperial dynasty. Not only his name has been compared with that of the tsar, but also his behavior. There is a story that Romanov, on the occasion of his daughter's marriage, requisitioned from the Hermitage museum a unique Sèvres dinner service designed for Catherine the Great. During the festivities, several pieces of the priceless set were said to have been broken by drunken guests. Supposedly, this anecdote was later widely circulated by Andropov while he was KGB chief to disparage Romanov, whom he viewed as a potential rival in the Kremlin power struggle.

Romanov's ignorance of Western systems was also made public in an anecdote: In 1978, in a talk with Senator Abraham Ribicoff, the American expressed doubt about whether other Democratic Senators would vote for ratification of the SALT II treaty. Romanov interrupted with the question: "Can't you discipline them?"

After Gorbachev was selected as new Kremlin leader he soon was able to dismiss Romanov.

Another relatively young man on Moscow's political scene is the 58-year-old Vitaly Vorotnikov, also recently seated on the Politburo. He is a blend of Party apparatchik and government bureaucrat, with some diplomatic experience thrown in (he is a former ambassador to Cuba). He may well play a more important role in the future than in his present post as Prime Minister of the RSFSR (the Russian Soviet Federated Socialist Republic, the largest and most important of the constituent republics of the U.S.S.R.). Vorotnikov, like Gorbachev, Romanov, and Aliyev, has also served as a regional First Party Secretary.

The job of first secretary of the Party of a territory, district, or region in the U.S.S.R. could be compared to that of an administrator of a colony. His ability to govern the territory is important, but even more so is his talent for personally serving and entertaining visiting officials from Moscow. Gorbachev's was a very characteristic Soviet (and perhaps not only Soviet) pattern of finding a way to the top. Men like him constitute the backbone of power in the Soviet Union and form the majority in the Central Committee of the Party.

Traditionally, candidates for Politburo membership come mainly from among secretaries of the Party committees of the territories and regions of the U.S.S.R. They are usually middle-aged, fairly knowledgeable about economic and agricultural matters, competent organizers by Soviet standards, and deft manipulators of propaganda and ideological indoctrination. What they lack, as a rule, is an objective understanding of international problems, world history, and foreign policy. Here they are in fact prisoners of Soviet propaganda and do not know much more than what is published in *Pravda* or in the magazine *Kommunist*. Those who do become Politburo members, therefore, invariably start out with a great deal to learn about foreign policy.

In the Soviet power structure the Foreign Ministry holds special status. In the West, there is an assumption that the ministry reports to departments of the Central Committee and to the Council of Ministers. That is incorrect. On most questions, the Foreign Ministry, unlike other ministries, is directly responsible only to the Politburo. Of course, in different periods the ministry's role in shaping and implementing foreign policy has varied. From 1939 to 1949 and again from 1953 to 1956 under Vyacheslav M. Molotov, its profile was higher than under Vyshinsky in the last years of Stalin's rule, or under Shepilov. Although Khrushchev valued Gromyko's experience and the expertise of his personnel, he often disregarded or bypassed the diplomats and delegated authority to members of his inner circle. Occasionally Khrushchev would brag that he himself was his own Foreign Minister. But under Brezhnev, the ministry's role again increased substantially.

Ministry proposals on matters of foreign policy are submitted to the Politburo in the form of a *zapiska*, a memorandum to the Central Committee (actually to the Politburo). These proposals are usually initiated by the ministry, except for the infrequent occasions when the Politburo instructs the ministry. A number of them are offered to the Politburo after preliminary consultation with other ministries in cases

248

where responsibilities or interests overlap. During my work with Gromyko, I cannot remember any case when the Politburo failed to adopt a ministry proposal.

The Foreign Ministry accumulates and controls all correspondence and communications between Soviet embassies abroad and Moscow, effected via its secret code service. Not even the Central Committee possesses a code service for communications to foreign Communist parties. It uses the ministry's or the KGB's service. The ministry makes the decisions concerning distribution of code cables from the various ambassadors. Moreover, important information is not always circulated to all members of the Politburo, not even all those based in Moscow. For instance, only Brezhnev and Gromyko saw some of Ambassador Dobrynin's cables from Washington.

In the last analysis, it was Gromyko and the now new Soviet Foreign Minister Eduard Shevardnadze who decide whether to circulate a cable to the general distribution list (all members of the Politburo and the secretaries of the Central Committee) or only to the General Secretary. In addition, a large number of dispatches are for internal distribution only and do not leave the Foreign Ministry.

Thus the ministry has a strong hand in deciding what matters should be reported to the Politburo for its consideration and is in a position to exert considerable influence upon the decision-making process. Furthermore, it is entitled to direct ambassadors without Politburo approval if its instructions fall within the general guidelines of Soviet foreign policy.

The Foreign Ministry prepares the draft texts of most government statements, Tass statements, and many major pronouncements by the leadership on foreign policy. These are, of course, subject to final approval by the Politburo.

In the early seventies, Brezhnev toyed with the idea of making Gromyko a Party secretary in charge of coordinating foreign policy. However, Gromyko declined the post because he realized that he might become a general without an army; the Foreign Ministry is an important instrument which he preferred at that time to retain under his direct control. Gromyko's appointment as First Deputy Prime

Minister after Brezhnev's death added little to his established authority. It is not the Council of Ministers that makes crucial foreign and domestic policy decisions, but the Politburo.

The division of responsibility between Party and diplomatic service, of course, is rarely neat. Political geography ensures overlapping jurisdictions. Several Central Committee departments have responsibilities that intrude on those of the Foreign Ministry. For instance, liaison with Eastern European socialist countries, Vietnam, Mongolia, Cuba, and some others is more a Party function than a diplomatic one. Charged with these relations is the Central Committee Department for Liaison with Communist and Workers Parties of Socialist Countries, headed for many years by Konstantin V. Rusakov.

The International Department, one of the Central Committee's most important, is run by Boris Ponomarev, a Party secretary and a candidate member of the Politburo since 1972. The department guides and instructs Communist parties abroad, and front organizations like the World Peace Council, and exercises the same functions with leaders of various pro-Moscow liberation movements and other Third World political groups whose activities are also of concern to the Foreign Ministry.

The Department of Foreign Cadres screens Foreign Ministry nominees for diplomatic posts, comparing its dossiers with those of the KGB. Without approval from this department, the ministry cannot send diplomatic or technical personnel out of the country. Since 1978, moreover, the activities of a newly created Department of International Information have gone well beyond those of the Foreign Ministry in expressing Moscow's views to the world. The veteran diplomat and former director general of Tass, Leonid M. Zamyatin, is its chief. In this area also, Gromyko's increasing power has led to a change. The Foreign Ministry started to hold more or less regular briefings for foreign reporters in Moscow, thus counterbalancing the International Information Department's activities in this field.

Despite tensions that sometimes arise from overlapping each other's turf, diplomats and ideologues in the Central

Committee more often than not try to compromise their differences rather than let them break into open conflict that must be arbitrated by the Politburo.

Ponomarev, a vigorous and determined disciple of Mikhail Suslov and his doctrinal rigidity, was Gromyko's rival in a sense, but with much less authority. Short and unprepossessing, he has a quick intelligence but a dry-as-dust manner. His toothbrush mustache and bright round eyes give him the look of a surprised terrier, an animal he also resembles in tenacity. I knew Ponomarev as a scholar of Marxist-Leninist ideology who had risen to a Party secretaryship in 1961 at the age of fifty-six. His reputation was that of a true believer, not only able to recite page after page of Marx and Lenin, his idols, but energetic in extolling Communist dogma to Party audiences at home and to conclaves of Communist, "progressive," or "workers' movement" forces abroad.

In one respect he is a contradiction. He is well educated, well read, and keenly interested in world affairs, but he nevertheless writes the dullest of official prose. To his subordinates' dismay, moreover, he enjoys writing for himself and does so with an ease and speed most other Soviet leaders lack. "Whenever we submit a draft to him, we cross our fingers," one of his assistants told me, "for fear that he will 'improve' it by adding a couple of pages of his own."

He has not realized all of his high ambitions. Although supported by Suslov and respected by Brezhnev, he has not been able to advance to full membership in the Politburo. Gromyko's hand may be visible here; he dislikes Ponomarev intensely. Once when we were talking about him and his department, Gromyko said with considerable heat that there should not be two centers for handling foreign policy. It is likely that he used this argument with Brezhnev to oppose Ponomarev's ascension to full Politburo membership. His candidate status leaves him a rung lower than Gromyko, although Gromyko has never held a Party secretaryship.

Ponomarev's ambition has been demonstrated, however, in his steady accumulation of personnel and responsibilities for his department. Attentive to detail and keenly aware of the value of expertise, he has been energetic in recruiting able associates. He has tried again and again to lure people away from the Foreign Ministry. Although I refused such an offer of his, we remained on cordial terms, and I became useful to him in a minor way as a source of supply of vitamin E pills from New York. Ponomarev, who took scrupulous care of his health, apparently thought the American brand more efficacious than whatever was dispensed through the elite medical section of the Health Ministry.

One of the International Department's main weaknesses was the limited extent of its independent information-gathering system abroad, although some from the department were sent to work in several embassies. Nevertheless, by building an alternate set of contacts through Communist parties and leaders of various political forces in the Third World, Ponomarev has continually worked to enlarge the information he receives and the policy areas in which he tries to apply it.

As the upholder of a militant internationalist faith, committed to the eventual triumph of Communism in the world, the department is the justifier of Soviet expansionism. In its role as liaison with extremist movements and an instrument to influence public opinion in the West, it is also the inspirer of much of the disorder which threatens Western stability and Western interests in the Third World.

One of Ponomarev's most able lieutenants is Vadim Zagladin, a relatively young man for the post he holds. Zagladin chose the Party as his avenue to power some three decades ago. He has risen far, riding not just on the authority Ponomarev has delegated to him but on his own considerable ability as well.

I met Zagladin during our days at MGIMO and watched his rise with a mixture of admiration and distaste. After Khrushchev's denunciation of Stalin in 1956, he, like many of us, became genuinely enthusiastic about possibilities for changing what was obsolete in Soviet life and government. That surge of idealism, a common phenomenon among young intellectuals in those early post-Stalin years, carried Zagladin and others into Party work. What began as something of a crusade, however, turned into a career. The impulse for change and renewal became an appetite for power.

Gradually even Zagladin's sophisticated irreverence gave way to a pompous, insensitive self-importance. It was a disillusioning deformation to observe.

By the late fifties Zagladin had become head of a small group of consultants in the International Department, an office he turned into a substantial power base. The seven or eight consultants were speechwriters and analysts for the Central Committee. Drafting addresses and articles for Party bosses, including Leonid Brezhnev, providing background papers on current international events, assessing situations and personalities in foreign Communist parties, the consultants expanded their role to that of policy advisers.

Once while I was working as Gromyko's adviser, Zagladin and I had a talk that became fairly heated. Speaking of the situation in Africa, I remarked on the futility of "playing with some pissant little 'liberation' committees that come into being overnight and disappear after a few months." Zagladin's response was revealing. "You sound just like your boss," he said. "Gromyko has no smell for the ideological side of things. He's just too pragmatic, and so are you. You Foreign Ministry people don't understand the power of Communist ideas in the world and the way to exploit them." In his view the International Department was not only better attuned to reality and opportunity but in some aspects of Soviet foreign policy also better equipped to exercise management authority. From a Marxist perspective it could achieve more satisfying results than professional diplomats. I pointed out that there were in fact only a few people in the International Department who were specialists on foreign policy matters such as intergovernment relations or on problems of general international interest like disarmament or Germany.

Working in the ministry, I had at least the personal satisfaction of participating in specific negotiations, and I thought it was a poor thing to make one's living by serving the notion that the Party represented the best interests of the people. Although a handful of factory workers and farmers are members of the higher Party bodies, they are so overwhelmingly outnumbered by Party, government, military, and intellectual figures that they play no role in these

253

bodies whatsoever. The elite class and its bastions of power are very far from ordinary people and oblivious to their vital needs. Compared to other major world societies, in fact, it fits Marx's definition of a ruling class more closely than any social or economic stratum or any surviving remnant of monarchy.

19

RICHARD NIXON ARRIVED IN MOSCOW ON THE WET, gloomy afternoon of Monday, May 22, 1972. Although I had been extensively involved in preparing for his visit, I was not among the small group of official welcomers who greeted the President at Moscow's Vnukovo Airport. Like others at the Foreign Ministry who worked on Soviet-American affairs, I had been discouraged from going to the airport. Because of the war in Vietnam the Politburo had decided to accord Nixon a reserved public welcome, and only a small number of people saluted him at Vnukovo and on Moscow's streets.

Despite Politburo restrictions, there was high excitement among ministry officials, whether or not they were directly involved in Soviet-American relations and irrespective of whether they approved of the visit. Soviet interest in improving relations with the United States had been foreshadowed by Khrushchev and fixed by Brezhnev, especially after the latter took hold of foreign policy at the end of the sixties. Behind them was the historic shift in Soviet priorities that followed Stalin's death.

The transformation was not easy. Hostility toward the West remained strong. Russians had not forgotten their history, the centuries of invasions by Teutonic Knights, Poles, Swedes, French, and Germans. They had not forgiven the

British and American interventions in 1919. But in the latter half of the twentieth century, a growing awareness of the meaning of nuclear war smoothed the way for beneficial economic cooperation with America and Western Europe.

For me and many of my colleagues the new opening to America, although not universally welcomed in the Kremlin, represented hopes for a realistic foreign policy and not one governed by the subjective intentions of one statesman or another. We understood that improving relations with America would not be easy, but felt that it was worthwhile to make a serious attempt.

Those who disagreed were mostly concerned about the timing of Nixon's trip. New U.S. actions in Vietnam—the recent mining of ports—were loudly condemned. Soviets also remembered Nixon's personality from the famous "kitchen debate" with Nikita Khrushchev at the American Exhibition in Moscow in 1959. His strong anti-Communist philosophy provoked bad feeling about him among orthodox anti-Americans at the ministry and in the Soviet Union generally.

I had an encounter with one anti-Nixonite the morning after the President arrived. Fedor Tarasovich Gusev, a veteran diplomat, former Ambassador to Great Britain and Deputy Foreign Minister, was a colleague in Gromyko's office. For Gusev, who was old and sick, the post of adviser to Gromyko was a kind of honorary retirement. He was an honest and decent man, which in no way altered his Stalinist view of the world.

He shook a copy of *Pravda* in front of him, and with great animosity shouted, "Arkady Nikolaevich! This is really too much. I can't believe my eyes. You people have even distorted history to please that son of a bitch!" Gusev was referring to the opening sentence of Nikolai Podgorny's toast at a dinner given in Nixon's honor the previous night. I had written Podgorny's speech. I drew Gusev's indignation because Podgorny had said, "This is the first official visit by a President of the United States of America in the history of relations between our countries."

"Roosevelt was the first American President to visit the Soviet Union," raged Gusev. "We should remember that.

And that was a time of real cooperation, not like all these stinking dealings with Nixon."

I tried to calm him down by saying that no one had rewritten history: Roosevelt went to the Yalta Conference, but it was not an official visit. Gusev was not to be placated. "Bah! I know all these twists and turns. You're making Nixon's visit too important. And just remember, you'll be sorry for it."

In hindsight, Gusev was probably right about inflating the trip's importance, but I disagreed with his approach to relations between the superpowers and I still do. There must continue to be a Soviet-American dialogue irrespective of whether the leaders of the two nations like each other or not.

My interest in the United States had continued to grow from the time of my first trip to New York in 1958. But my direct work in the complex and fascinating relations between the Soviet Union and the United States began in Gromyko's office at the turning point in their improvement, characterized by President Nixon as "entering an era of negotiation" after "a period of confrontation."

While I was in New York, just before I joined Gromyko's staff in Moscow, Ambassador Anatoly Dobrynin told Yakov Malik and me about his series of confidential exchanges with Henry Kissinger. This arrangement became known as the "back channel." I was glad to learn of this evidence of mutual confidence, but Malik was unimpressed. "You can beat the air with him as long as you please," he said sourly, "but I don't trust Nixon or his little professor."

Whatever Malik's opinion, at the close of the Johnson presidency a change for the better in Soviet-American relations was obvious. Not only had there been close cooperation between Moscow and Washington in concluding the protracted negotiations on the Treaty on Non-Proliferation of Nuclear Weapons, but in connection with the signing of that treaty on July 1, 1968, the superpowers had announced their agreement to begin discussing the Strategic Arms Limitation Talks (SALT). If it had not been for the Soviet invasion of Czechoslovakia, the SALT deliberations could have begun much sooner than they did. Moreover, the Soviet-

American summit meeting might well have taken place in October 1968.

Officially, neither Malik nor any of us at the Mission was supposed to know about the back channel: this was the prerogative of Politburo members and secretaries of the Party, along with a few trusted bureaucrats. Secrecy was further maintained to the extent that only Brezhnev, Gromyko, and some of their closest aides knew the contents of certain important messages received via the channel. Direct, secret discussions between Dobrynin and Kissinger fit Soviet instincts and diplomatic traditions as conveniently as they did the political style of Richard Nixon and his top foreign affairs adviser.

It is an old Russian (and Soviet) characteristic to love secrets. Throughout history there have occasionally appeared men of different cultures and nations who seem to be able to work through and with each other to achieve complementary and positive goals for their countries, though they be adversaries. I believe that the personalities and abilities of Dobrynin and Kissinger resulted in such a combination.

As Gromyko's adviser, I learned the real significance of the Dobrynin-Kissinger channel, as a means of handling ultrasensitive business between Moscow and Washington. Not since the days of World War II had such a range of matters been as earnestly reviewed, more or less free of polemics and ideological propaganda. In spite of entrenched suspicions and rivalries on both sides, there was real progress made through this means of exchange.

From 1969, Anatoly Dobrynin had been the crucial point of contact. Few Soviet envoys could have been so well prepared for the role. Fewer still could have carried it off with such finesse. Dobrynin is an exceptional Soviet diplomat, not just because of his unusually long service in Washington or his access to and influence in Moscow's highest political circles. His personality also sets him apart from most Soviet diplomats, who dogmatically follow instructions, concerned above all with securing their careers. Though he has a historian's academic training and an aviation engineer's degree he put to use in a wartime factory, Dobrynin has been a professional diplomat nearly all his life. As a young man, he became one of Moscow's best American specialists.

He was minister-counselor in Washington from 1952 to 1955. Later, he was head of the ministry's American Department until he returned to the United States as ambassador in 1962. I met him in New York in 1958, when he was UN Under Secretary General. From that time on, ours was a friendly relationship. Tall and imposing, he impressed me at our first meeting as an affable man. I was a little uncertain as he scrutinized me, his bespectacled eyes lit by a kind of foxy, mocking look. In fact, he is not tricky or wily. He is naturally lively and curious with a penetrating intelligence. Generous and cordial with subordinates or equals, he can also be refreshingly candid with officials of higher rank, especially with Gromyko, whom he once served as an assistant.

Dobrynin's large reservoir of self-confidence has not made him arrogant. Imaginative and suave, he has an intuitive gift of understanding what makes people tick, and easily makes himself quite at home nearly everywhere, an indispensable quality in sophisticated diplomacy. Later, advising me how best to succeed at the UN, Dobrynin recommended that I do my part steadily, quietly, and with a smile. He abhorred temperamental pyrotechnics and said that flying off the handle rarely achieved desirable results. He himself has employed this philosophy skillfully and has won the confidence of many American officials and private citizens.

Henry Kissinger was charmed by him. He described with admiration how Dobrynin "moved through the upper echelons of Washington with consummate skill," and asserted that "his personal role . . . was almost certainly beneficial to U.S.-Soviet relations."* But despite Kissinger's assessment of Dobrynin's "central contribution" to the improvement of relations between Moscow and Washington, I believe this to be an overstatement. There is no doubt that Dobrynin played an important and positive role in this respect. But, while he is not hostile to America, neither is he an ardent admirer of the United States or an untiring advo-

* Henry Kissinger, *White House Years* (Little, Brown, 1979), p. 140.

cate of friendship with it. For all his ability, efficiency, and goodwill, Dobrynin remained the instrument of Brezhnev, Gromyko, and other Soviet policymakers.

As a realistic promoter of rapprochement with the United States, Dobrynin was useful to Gromyko in two capacities: his trusted intermediary with Washington and his articulate supporter in the Politburo. Especially in the period leading up to the first Nixon-Brezhnev summit in May 1972, Dobrynin went to Moscow frequently, not just to consult with the Foreign Minister, but, with Gromyko's blessing, to lobby skeptics in the leadership. While careful to stay within the bounds of Communist orthodoxy, he spoke privately and at Politburo sessions with the same convincing charm as he did with Americans.

The real Dobrynin is a sincere and staunch supporter of the Soviet system and its regime. He has no hesitations about the rightness of Soviet policy even when it is aggressive or mendacious. Not only are political dissidents traitors in his eyes, but defecting dancers and artists as well. Dobrynin enjoys dealing with Americans as much as he delights in being the Soviet Union's knight in the international chess game. But America is his opponent, and he is determined to win. Many times in private I saw his amiable blue eyes flash with hatred when he was enraged over some American action or position.

U.S. negotiators who have dealt with him know his mastery at exploiting American weakness, playing artfully on American masochistic tendencies, the curious sense of guilt they often display, while in a semi-joking way blaming them for any diplomatic deadlock or prodding them to writhe for the sins of the world. He is so skillful with this technique that many times the Americans end up pointing their fingers, not at the real culprits, but back at themselves. It is no wonder that American journalists have remarked that after having known Dobrynin for years, drinking with him, discussing everything from bird migrations to current films or arms control with him, they still found it hard to say whether, deep down, he is a hard-liner or a liberal.

The fact that he functions smoothly in the international arena makes him a formidable weapon. His expertise at homing in on whom to see and to cultivate in Washington, his sense of what button to push to influence the decision-making process, his easy access to almost everyone, make him not an American but a Soviet ace.

It should not be forgotten that such ambassadors as W. Averell Harriman, Charles E. Bohlen, and Llewellyn E. Thompson were the men through whom much of America's important business with the Soviets was conducted. They were respected in Moscow. The locus of dealing with the Soviets was largely shifted to Washington as a result of the Dobrynin-Kissinger channel.

The amazing thing is that the White House itself contributed to this change perhaps more than the Kremlin did. The result was an obvious Soviet advantage. There are far fewer doors open to American ambassadors in the U.S.S.R. than there are to Dobrynin in the United States. Shifting so much serious diplomatic business to the orbit between Sixteenth Street and Pennsylvania Avenue further contracted access to Soviet government departments for American diplomats in Moscow.

"We have Dobrynin in Washington," Gromyko once remarked with a shrug. "What else can the Americans want?" Hence his reluctance to deal with American ambassadors in Moscow, who now see Gromyko rarely, and other Soviet leaders even less. Ambassador Malcolm Toon's complaints that the United States had relied too much on Dobrynin to make its views known to the Kremlin and not enough on its professional staff in Moscow were understandable. The plight of Ambassador Jacob D. Beam, who was not even informed about Kissinger's secret visit to Moscow in April 1972, is a case in point.

The practical advantages for the Soviets in this arrangement are considerable. If the Kremlin has second thoughts as a negotiation proceeds or an action unfolds, there is no official commitment to the U.S. representative in Moscow. The Kremlin can always "correct" Dobrynin, saying that he expressed the Soviet position improperly. And Dobrynin can always delay the answers, claiming he is waiting for instructions from the Politburo. His frequent trips to Moscow for consultations facilitate slowdowns in any negotiations. Kissinger recognized that he used this tactic successfully. At the same time, the importance of a direct, confidential channel between the Politburo and the White House is considerable. It would be as wrong to underestimate such an arrangement as to undermine the position of the American ambassador in Moscow. The question is to find the appropriate balance and proportion.

Dobrynin has the reputation of being easy to work with because he has an excellent sense of what is acceptable to the Soviet leadership. His reporting to Moscow is unaffected by the urge of most Soviet ambassadors to tell their superiors what will agree with their preconceptions. Dobrynin's cables invariably attracted attention; Gromyko routinely began his working day with them. Dobrynin is a hard worker, more often than not writing out his own cables in a style distinctive not only for precision and clarity but also for the colorful detail he provides in describing the setting of a conversation or the mood of those with whom he talks. He has a remarkable memory. He often provides verbatim records of conversations he has had, and through these reports he is able to make the Soviet leadership listen to real and occasionally sharp criticism of its conduct and beliefs. As a diplomatic reporter, Dobrynin gives the Kremlin leaders an instructive counterweight to the propagandistic rote reporting of Tass and other Soviet correspondents and diplomats. His discipline and energy have held him to a rigorous schedule, notwithstanding a battle with cancer, from which he has allegedly suffered a long time.

Dobrynin deserves particular credit for marked improvement in the quality of information from Washington since the fifties and early sixties. His predecessor, Mikhail Menshikov, was as poor at attempting to enhance the Soviet image as he was good at distorting the facts in his messages to Moscow. To please Khrushchev, "Smiling Mike" broke all records for disingenuousness. For example, Menshikov reported that President Eisenhower was almost unanimously condemned by the American public for the U-2 spy missions over Soviet territory and the consequent failure of the four-power Paris summit in May 1960. Dobrynin would never descend to such nonsense.

At the same time, Dobrynin has always been cautious about giving Moscow his personal analysis of American politics, which, according to Kissinger, was without exception "acute and even wise." Kissinger felt confident that, as a result, "the Kremlin would have at its disposal a sophisticated assessment of conditions here," which would reduce "the prospects of gross miscalculation." In many instances he was yielding to wishful thinking. Unlike his reporting on specific negotiations, Dobrynin's general analysis of U.S. politics often contained a flavoring of propaganda. I cannot blame him for it; it was the price of continually proving his loyalty to the Soviet system and a way of avoiding accusations of becoming "Americanized," an epithet occasionally attached to him by the envious in both the Central Committee and the Foreign Ministry. Although he understands the U.S. governmental system, even Dobrynin dared not produce an accurate analysis of the division of power in America between the executive and legislative branches, a matter of confusion to the Soviets during the Watergate debacle. Most of that kind of reporting he lets his aides prepare.

Dobrynin is far and away the best informed of the Soviet ambassadors. He receives a volume of highly classified information from Moscow that is immeasurably larger than any sent to other Soviet missions abroad. An exception is made for Dobrynin regarding the Soviet mania for secrecy. Even Kremlin bureaucrats understand that he should be properly prepared for any eventuality. Regardless of snide remarks and jealous gossip about him, he is highly respected in Moscow and has always maintained close, if sometimes informal touch with influential people dealing with U.S. affairs.

Dobrynin's wife, Irina, is a sprightly and valuable asset to her husband, a perceptive observer and a skilled hostess. Although she urged that her husband be allowed to give up his "killing job" and retire to Moscow to teach history, I found it hard to imagine Dobrynin's returning to the Soviet Union in such a capacity. Aside from the question of finding a replacement for him, Gromyko would be hard-pressed to fit Dobrynin into any top-level post at the ministry without pushing aside some other senior figure and seeming to pave the way for his own replacement.

Aside from his diplomatic expertise, Dobrynin possesses Party credentials unusual for a Soviet official who has spent so much of his time out of Moscow. After five years as a candidate member he received full status in the Central Committee in 1971. Not only does he frequently appear at Politburo meetings but, unlike other officials who merely accompany their ministers there, he speaks alone and sometimes at length to the Party's ruling body. It is therefore safer, as well as more convenient, for Gromyko to keep him in Washington. They are personally close. The minister, who calls most of his subordinates by their last names, always addresses the ambassador as Anatoly Fyodorovich.

The irony of Dobrynin's career in Washington, where he has become an institution—esteemed, formidable, and the dean of the diplomatic corps—is that at the outset of his success, he risked being branded a liar. In October 1962, on the eve of the Cuban missile crisis, Dobrynin assured the Americans repeatedly that the Soviet Union had not and would not install offensive nuclear missiles in Cuba. I doubt very much that he knew the real situation. Khrushchev was using his young ambassador to buy time without telling him the truth. Dobrynin worked to restore his credibility and succeeded, perhaps most spectacularly in Kissinger's eyes.

The main differences in their positions were that Kissinger had greater latitude in maneuvering as well as more authority in his position. Likewise, Kissinger's influence on the White House was stronger than Dobrynin's on the Kremlin.

Nixon's victory in the 1968 presidential election and his choice of Kissinger as his Assistant for National Security Affairs disturbed Moscow at first. Both men were avowed and open anti-Communists. After publication of his *Nuclear Weapons and Foreign Policy* (1957), Kissinger was labeled by the Soviet Union as its "bitter enemy and an imperialist lackey." Nevertheless, Soviet dislike of him was mixed with a grudging respect for his intellect and his position at the center of American political power, especially in his connection to Nelson Rockefeller. The Soviets saw Rockefeller as a pillar of American capitalist society, something they both hated and admired. But as Kissinger's thinking evolved, the Soviets began to reevaluate their impressions of him, and their attitude toward him began to change. By the time he joined the Nixon administration, Kissinger had ceased to be a "warmonger." Moscow then perceived him as a leading scholar of the "realist" school.

When Nixon spoke of entering an era of negotiations in his inaugural address, he sounded the right note to Kremlin ears. Moscow looked forward to a welcome change in its dealings with the United States. But in his assessment that negotiations with the Soviets would not go easily, Kissinger was right.

All Soviet negotiators are agents of limited authority who may not express opinions differing from the Politburo's position. An American is likely to be more open and flexible, but a Soviet's first instinct is to be suspicious of goodwill and to doubt his counterpart's objectivity. Part of this intractable attitude can be blamed upon instructions. In order to make them tougher bargainers, Kremlin leaders usually do not include in their representatives' directives any fallback position, thus leaving them singing one stubborn note at the bargaining table until a compromise is worked out back in Moscow.

There is also another Soviet approach to negotiating tactics. Any means, fair or foul, is sanctioned by the Politburo to get what it wants. Soviet negotiators have sometimes departed from the stubborn phase suddenly and altered their positions in wild swings. But while they seem to twist and turn, they remain adamant until they must compromise. When that moment arrives, the Soviets are masters at selling their concessions for the highest price.

Whenever the U.S.S.R. has felt it convenient, all these levers have been pulled, as they were in the course of U.S.-Soviet negotiations leading to Nixon's Moscow visit and the SALT agreements.

Under Gromyko's close supervision, a special team was established at the ministry to prepare for the Nixon visit, headed by Vasily Kuznetsov and including Georgy Kornienko and me. Kornienko had made American affairs his career specialty. He had been minister-counselor at the embassy in Washington, and in 1966 was appointed chief of the ministry's American Department. He had risen to First Deputy Foreign Minister, reflecting Gromyko's reliance on his expertise.

Kornienko's promotion was due to his intelligence and hard work, but it had taken its toll in a history of heart trouble and high blood pressure. His professionalism and discretion had made him a Gromyko favorite, and the two men shared the conviction that U.S.-Soviet relations demanded priority consideration in Moscow's diplomacy. Kornienko's commitment, however, stopped there. While he felt that dealings with the United States were crucial, he never expected them to be easy and was always conservatively skeptical of whether they would turn out well.

Many in the Foreign Ministry were incensed at the linkage concept promulgated by Nixon and Kissinger, making progress in relations conditional upon Kremlin cooperation in resolving problems like Vietnam, the Middle East, and European security. Part of their anger stemmed from their impotence. Soviet leverage in dealings with the North Vietnamese or the Arabs was not as great as the United States believed. The Americans consistently exaggerated the degree of Soviet influence on the Vietnamese and on Soviet Arab clients; these countries were by no means obedient marionettes. And Moscow, proclaiming that its help to the North Vietnamese and others represented its "internationalist duty" and solidarity with "fraternal, progressive allies," also limited its own ability to employ its aid as a device for pressuring its comrades in behalf of its own interests.

A major irritant in Soviet-Vietnamese relations sprang from Hanoi's tendency to play off the Soviets against the Chinese, extracting aid from both but siding with neither. Moscow wanted Hanoi to declare itself in the quarrel with Peking. Ho Chi Minh and his successors preferred cautious neutrality. In the same fashion, they managed to keep the Soviets at arm's length in the conduct of the fighting. Sometimes the North Vietnamese complained that deliveries of weapons and matériel were slow. Occasionally they concealed their strategic planning—as well as their dealings with the Chinese—from Soviet advisers. The latter, along with their superiors in Moscow, viewed the Vietnamese as stubbornly independent and secretive. Ilya Shcherbakov, the Soviet Ambassador to Hanoi, complained bitterly about this to Moscow. If the Americans knew the contents of his cables, I thought, how much they would relish the Soviet dilemma. Later, Moscow sometimes received better information about the talks with Le Duc Tho in Paris from Henry Kissinger than from our Vietnamese "brother."

The Soviet Union had also worked itself into a position in the Middle East that left it few options. After Nasser's death, there was little to do but support Arab extremists. With President Sadat consolidating his authority, to the Soviets' horror, Moscow believed that any deviation from the hardest possible line would complicate further Kremlin efforts to save what remained of their tattered influence in Egypt.

No wonder Gromyko grumbled that we wouldn't pay in advance, not knowing what we might gain in improving relations with the Americans via the linkage concept. "A bird in the hand is worth two in the bush," he would say whenever linkage was mentioned. It was not just that policy, however, that delayed the Brezhnev-Nixon meeting—there were other factors as well prompting the Kremlin and the White House to wait and see. But the Soviets were taken by surprise.

When Kissinger began his triangular diplomacy by secretly visiting Peking in July 1971, it was a shock to the Soviet leadership. Gromyko went about for weeks with a black expression.

After Nixon's trip to China in February 1972, and the announcement of the Shanghai communiqué, there was a heated meeting of the Politburo. Just a few months before, China was admitted to the United Nations. As a formal matter, the Soviet Union had been China's supporter for many years, but the final victory was a Pyrrhic one. At the same time Yakov Malik welcomed the PRC delegation, he received word from Moscow of Peking's "complicity with imperialism."

The statement in the Shanghai communiqué that both sides should not "seek hegemony in the Asia-Pacific region and each is opposed to efforts by any other country . . . to establish such hegemony" made the Soviets furious since the direction of the warning was obvious. Henry Kissinger confirmed that the Kremlin was correct in its assessment of the communiqué. "The two sides," he wrote, "kept their eyes on the common objective of resisting what the communiqué came to describe as 'hegemony.' Simply put, this meant resistance to Soviet attempts to overturn the global balance of power."*

Publicly, Soviet leaders said merely that it was "only natural" the two nations should restore relations. But they were experiencing acute distress. Gromyko told us that sooner or later Nixon and the Americans would be burned in their dealings with Peking as "we were burned." Vasily Makarov said that Brezhnev had given Gromyko a thorough dressing-down for not anticipating the American-Chinese rapprochement.

Despite everything, I felt a clearcut revival of self-assurance in our leadership. After the many troubles of the 1960s, beginning with Berlin on through Czechoslovakia and our attempts to catch up with the United States in the arms race, the Soviet Union had recovered and was emerging as an even stronger U.S. rival. Our leaders were reassessing the international situation and had begun to redirect the course of our foreign policy. My hopes for a change increased, although I realized they were somewhat contradicted by what I had come to understand about our policy toward the UN, disarmament, and other matters.

I was glad to take part in the preparations for the summit and to work to make it a real success. The key was to undo the knots in SALT. I had followed my country's acrobatics at the initial discussions of the problems surrounding strategic arms control while in New York. In Moscow, I became directly involved in SALT.

In the sixties, the Soviet Union had deployed the Galosh antiballistic system around Moscow to defend against offen-

* Washington *Post*, January 30, 1983.

sive missiles, claiming that its purpose was to save lives. During his meeting with President Johnson at Glassboro in 1967, Kosygin had implied that the United States only wanted to talk about limiting ABMs, whereas the Soviet Union believed that offensive strategic nuclear missiles should be dealt with first. By the time I became Gromyko's adviser, Moscow had reversed its position 180 degrees, and wanted first of all to limit the ABMs. That somersault was proof of the Soviets' desire to halt implementation of the American ABM system, Safeguard, a countermeasure to Galosh, which had proved less effective than anticipated.

There was, however, serious interest in getting an agreement on SALT. The Soviet leadership craved parity with the United States. Additionally, the Politburo's anxiety about the uncertain outcome of a spiraling competition for strategic advantage was paralleled by increasing concern about the costs entailed in its military program. There were strong warnings from Soviet economists that if armaments spending continued at the same pace, production of consumer goods and agricultural products would be in serious jeopardy. Moreover, America's unquestionable lead in vital computer technology had aroused Soviet fears that the United States might emerge the winner in the arms rivalry.

Brezhnev felt that even without a treaty the mere fact that the SALT negotiations were proceeding was beneficial. They could help create pressure on the U.S. Congress to cut some military programs. They could be exploited to create the appearance of Soviet-American collusion against China and evoke suspicions among the NATO allies. That was one of the main reasons the Soviets favored strictly confidential negotiations without reporting to the United Nations, a drastic departure from their traditional preference for open negotiations on disarmament.

SALT was as painful as childbirth to the Soviets, particularly the military services. After decades of complete secrecy regarding military developments, it seemed inconceivable to disclose to the enemy even the names of Soviet weapons systems. Ridiculous as it appeared, the Soviets simply could not bring themselves to use their own terminology and decided to adopt NATO designations for their weaponry. Defense Minister Grechko remained permanently apoplectic during SALT. His incurable distrust of, and violent opposition to, the talks, so well known to all of us involved in the negotiations, affected even the more realistic and sophisticated generals and politicians in a negative way. Grechko would repeatedly and irrelevantly launch into admonitory lectures on the aggressive nature of imperialism, which, he assured us, had not changed. There was no guarantee against a new world war except a continued buildup of Soviet armed might.

Grechko, regarded by many in Moscow as a blockhead, not only had the support of the old-guard military but also owed a good deal of his rise to his World War II friendship with the young Leonid Brezhnev. Personal ties between the two men remained strong, and Grechko used his free access to the Party leader to try to convince him to continue the U.S.S.R.'s military buildup. Obedient to higher orders, Grechko reluctantly accepted the opening of SALT, but almost immediately began a guerrilla campaign that helped to stall the process. He imposed tight control on his subordinates, inhibiting their collaboration with the Foreign Ministry. Where Nikolai Ogarkov and his colleagues had initially been able to speak relatively freely, Grechko now required that all military presentations be based on formal briefing papers submitted to him for advance approval.

The gag order was a real impediment to internal negotiation of the SALT issues. Relations between Grechko and Gromyko, never good, worsened to the point that for some time the two ministers had no personal communications at all. This rivalry of silence also extended to various officials in both ministries. Grechko's attitude, moreover, conflicted in some degree with that of his senior experts. Ogarkov, for example, once said, "We have some people who are very old-fashioned in their thinking. They are still learning the lessons of World Wars I and II. They don't always understand modern military problems." Ogarkov named no one in particular, but his cryptic reference was understood to include Grechko.

It was thus during SALT that Dobrynin's role as the direct contact with the White House became so important, because Brezhnev and Gromyko, not unlike Nixon and Kissinger, distrusted the ability of the Soviet bureaucracy to work for and produce an agreement. At the inception of the talks, Gromyko had tried to engage the military actively in the negotiations. He wanted to ensure that he and the Foreign Ministry would not appear to be the only advocates of arms control. He hoped to bring the Soviet armed forces command around to thinking in terms of limiting weaponry, not just acquiring more. "It's hard to discuss the subject with the military," Gromyko told me. "But the more they know, the more contact they have with the Americans, the easier it will be to turn our soldiers into something more than just martinets."

By the time Gromyko made these observations, he had already lost in his attempt to put men in uniform at the head of the SALT team; Grechko categorically objected to it. The task was therefore assigned to Deputy Foreign Minister Vladimir Semyonov, who, as the chief Soviet representative, began SALT discussions in November 1969 with the American delegation headed by Gerard Smith.

Smith was also unhappy that some key matters were taken out of his and Semyonov's negotiations and discussed via the back channel. "Doubletalk" became Smith's epithet for SALT.* To an extent he was right. But while the negotiations were important in many respects, it would have been impossible to make crucial breakthroughs without the secret direct communications between the leaders of the U.S.S.R. and the United States.

The military men on the Soviet delegation included several officers with real expertise in the field of strategic weaponry and, just as important, with promising career prospects. In the past the soldier participants on the Soviet side at disarmament talks had more often than not been both uninformed and near retirement. Including younger, more adept men in the SALT group was an important step toward committing the armed forces to the arms-control process. At Gromyko's suggestion, the Politburo required all seven delegates to sign every report or recommendation the Soviet

* Gerard Smith, *Doubletalk: The Story of SALT I* (Doubleday, 1980).

team cabled home. With military signatures linked to diplomatic ones, Gromyko was working to blunt opposition to SALT from Moscow's defense establishment. But it was very odd to see the cables signed by seven people; I believe it was a unique occurrence in Soviet diplomacy.

Gromyko did not undervalue the generational change that had brought a new and more imaginative breed of soldier to the top of the military structure at the end of the sixties. Instead of the tired and often narrow men whose thinking derived from their experience as field commanders before or during World War II—such as Marshal Matvei Zakharov, Chief of the General Staff, who literally slept at his Moscow desk—there were among the new senior officers some with broadened views and inquiring minds.

Ogarkov, whom I met when he was the ranking Defense Ministry representative on the SALT delegation in 1970, was an example of this changing outlook and temperament. He impressed me with a direct answer to the kind of question most of his colleagues would have evaded. He was a tough, strong defender of military programs, but when I asked him whether he thought we needed SALT, he replied that he did, as long as certain conditions could be met.

When the SALT delegation met, from time to time I heard Ogarkov go beyond this curt but direct judgment. When the discussions wandered into complicated side issues, he would often bring them back into focus with a sharp presentation of the central questions. It became clear that he saw SALT in a sophisticated political framework and believed it was possible to obtain an agreement that would enhance Soviet security.

General Nikolai Alekseyev, Ogarkov, and other sophisticated military officers approached SALT as a means to achieve by negotiation what the Soviets feared they could not attain through competition: a restraint on America's ability to translate its economic and technological strength into military advantage and a breathing space during which the U.S.S.R. would work to narrow the gap. Vladimir Semyonov was a skilled diplomat, but a man who rarely let principle stand in the way of ambition. He was slippery and flexible enough to escape any dangerous or demanding situation. His colleagues saw Semyonov as an opportunist, always ready to shift his position to fit prevailing policy winds in Moscow.

Semyonov's laziness and his habit of hospitalizing himself for rest cures irritated the workaholic Gromyko. But Semyonov's undeniable skills as a negotiator qualified him to head the SALT delegation. Gromyko had no qualms about leaving his deputy "all knotted up" in the technical aspects of arms control because the minister regarded those talks as largely a sideshow. "The best way" to reach agreement, he told me emphatically, "is the direct way." For Gromyko that path led through Dobrynin to Kissinger and Nixon.

Gromyko's approach stemmed from his view of SALT as the vehicle for a much more important political process. His goal, endorsed by Brezhnev and encouraged by Dobrynin, was to win a broad set of understandings with the United States with arms control as the centerpiece but not the only aspect of the arrangement.

Since Semyonov's role was to a degree a subsidiary one, he was held under a tight rein. Moscow's instructions to him were slow to change, and information was restricted. Whether in Helsinki or Vienna, Semyonov was cut off from a great deal of the flow of Foreign Ministry cables.

Although he had formal responsibility as a deputy minister for supervising a number of sensitive policy areas, including relations with Germany, Semyonov regularly returned to Moscow to try to get me and Gromyko's other assistants to bring him up to date on a wide range of policy matters. Often Gromyko kept him in the dark about the progress of SALT. While Semyonov was aware of the existence of the Dobrynin-Kissinger channel, he did not know —often until long after the fact—what had been discussed or accomplished in Gromyko's "direct way."

Kissinger, who had his own reasons for treating the American negotiators in a similar fashion, has recorded two occasions when the dual system went awry. In both instances, one in May 1971 and the other in April 1972, Kissinger did not exclude the possibility that Semyonov's actions were attempts "to play our two channels against each other." *

That was not so, however. In May, the Soviets ceased their filibustering tactics, in the hope that domestic American anti-ABM campaigns would force the Administration to agree only on limiting the ABM systems. Dobrynin agreed in principle to link defensive and offensive weapons. But at a private dinner with Gerard Smith, Semyonov offered to discuss the ICBM freeze *after* the ABM agreement was concluded—the old Soviet position already rejected by Kissinger. This did not mean, however, that Semyonov was trying to retreat from progress made in the secret Kissinger-Dobrynin dealings, but simply that he was operating on outdated instructions from Moscow, knowing no better.

The second incident occurred in Helsinki when Semyonov indicated that Moscow was reconsidering the last major SALT issue—establishing ceilings on land-based and submarine-launched ballistic missiles—about which Kissinger and Brezhnev had actually reached agreement during the American's clandestine trip to Moscow. Although Semyonov only hinted at this, Kissinger and Nixon apparently saw it as an effort to deprive the President of credit for concluding a SALT deal at the summit itself. They were wrong. Semyonov had not really received any new instructions from Moscow other than a few tentative and imprecise words from his own informants within the ministry.

The changing Soviet position on submarine-launched missiles, clearing the way to an agreement, was a major Gromyko victory over Marshal Grechko, who obstinately resisted it to the very end. Several times I witnessed heated debates on this issue at the Military Industrial Commission (VPK), where Dmitri Ustinov, then Party Secretary, played a crucial role. While Gromyko, with Brezhnev's backing, clashed with Grechko, Ustinov tried to find a middle way out, driving Grechko to greater anger.

By that time our working group in the ministry had finalized other draft documents for the summit. Among them was the Declaration on the Basic Principles of Relations

---

* Kissinger, *White House Years*, pp. 817 and 1155.

between the Soviet Union and the United States. Brezhnev and Gromyko attached great significance to this. Apparently, the Americans did not realize at first the special meaning of this document for the Soviet side. Kissinger seemed puzzled by Brezhnev's observation that it was even more important than the projected SALT agreement.

To the Americans, the declaration was no more than a set of generalities flavored with propagandistic rhetoric. To the Soviets, it was a device to silence those in the leadership who had doubts about the Moscow summit, particularly since it was taking place during the resumed American bombing of Hanoi and other Vietnamese territory.

The provisions of the declaration that U.S.-Soviet relations would be conducted "on the basis of peaceful coexistence" and based on principles of "sovereignty, equality, non-interference in internal affairs, and mutual advantage" were not just words to the Soviet leadership. They represented a fundamental change in Washington's policy toward the Soviet Union. The declaration was considered juridical recognition by the United States of the Leninist idea of peaceful coexistence, a great triumph for Soviet foreign policy.

The most powerful boost to Soviet egos was U.S. acceptance of the principle of equality. Nothing would sound better to the Soviet leadership, suffering for years under an inferiority complex vis-à-vis the United States. Moscow would have been happy even if the summit's only product had been the declaration of principles.

Unlike the declaration, an easily formulated sop to the more distrustful elements in the Politburo, the joint Soviet-U.S. communiqué was a delicate matter. It touched upon concrete problems on which U.S. and Soviet positions were drastically different. When the papers on the Basic Principles of Relations between the Soviet Union and the United States and the joint communiqué were distributed to Politburo members and candidate members, Boris Ponomarev tried to get some changes in the wording. He communicated his desires through a phone call I received from his deputy, Vadim Zagladin.

"It won't do, Arkady." His voice purred with an edge of

274

menace over the telephone line. "The joint communiqué's language does not properly emphasize our support for the struggle of national liberation movements in the developing world. It doesn't show the right degree of ideological strength. The foreign [Communist] parties won't understand our putting out a statement with the Americans as empty as this."

I knew precisely what Zagladin was worried about. Gromyko had ordered us to produce a draft that played down the standard rhetoric about Western imperialism and Soviet vigor in international ideological combat. "Don't wave a red flag in front of the bull," Gromyko had commanded.

From Zagladin's point of view, we had done the job too well. Neither in the statement on Basic Principles nor in the draft joint communiqué did the Soviet Union affirm its long-standing demand for the complete withdrawal of Israeli troops from the territories occupied in 1967. Nor was there a word about racism or decolonization or the Soviet commitment to social justice for the oppressed in Asia and Africa. On Vietnam the two sides simply registered their flat disagreement.

As Zagladin said, the documents were politically hollow except for the statement in the Basic Principles that U.S. and Soviet "differences in ideology and . . . social systems . . . are not obstacles" to developing "normal relations." To the guardians of Communist doctrine, that formulation constituted a retreat from ideological militancy.

I knew, however, that Gromyko's position had Brezhnev's endorsement, and that Brezhnev's stance, thanks to skillful pre-summit maneuvering, was one his colleagues could not reverse. "We have absolutely clear instructions on this from Andrei Andreyevich," I told Zagladin. "If you have objections, why not have them raised at the Politburo?"

Zagladin tried again. "Gromyko, of course, understands these questions," he conceded, "but we have our opinion too."

"Of course you do. Still, the point is that your opinion doesn't fit with our instructions. Since it differs, report it to the Politburo. Let them decide. But at this point, your views can't change our orders.''

"You know, Arkady, we have power too.''

"Yes, but in foreign affairs your power is limited.''

When the draft was sent in advance to the Politburo members, only Premier Aleksei Kosygin raised questions about the wording. His assistant asked me to come to the Premier's office, but the interrogation turned out to be brief and mild. At the Politburo session the Foreign Ministry version was approved as a negotiating instrument without real debate.

While the Politburo considered the item for which I was responsible, I sat with Kuznetsov, Kornienko, and Makarov, behind Gromyko at the long table in the Kremlin. Brezhnev asked whether all members of the Politburo had received the draft U.S.-Soviet documents in time and if they had studied them. Most of the members nodded silent assent. "Can I assume that the draft is approved?" Brezhnev asked. No one spoke. "The draft is approved," said Brezhnev after a few more moments of silence. Makarov put his hand on my shoulder, whispering, "Okay, Arkady, that's it. You can go.''

From that and other experiences, from preparing Gromyko for many sessions and from talking with those who participated in Politburo meetings more often, I feel certain that this procedure was routine rather than unusual. As I waited in an anteroom for my turn, other advisers were called in to the Politburo chamber for a short time and then sent back to their jobs. Over bottles of mineral water and dry biscuits the Soviet leaders plowed through their formal exercises as rapidly as they could. The session I attended, which ran from about 10:30 a.m. to about 5 p.m., with a break for lunch, was quiet, orderly, and methodical. Although an agenda is prepared, there is no quorum call or other form of parliamentary procedure.

Politburo sessions may take place either in the Kremlin office of the General Secretary or in the Central Committee building in Staraya Square. Urgent meetings, or meetings connected with the arrival of a foreign dignitary, have occurred at Vnukovo Airport. In the Kremlin, members sit around a long table with the General Secretary at its head. The second-floor room has a high ceiling and is paneled in wood. A portrait of Lenin stares down at those assembled. Windows look out on a backyard of the Kremlin. Security men guard the door to the room, although they certainly know all who enter.

The draft joint Soviet-U.S. communiqué was approved without difficulties during the Moscow summit of 1972. Gromyko asked me to accompany him and Dobrynin to his meeting in the Kremlin with Henry Kissinger to discuss the communiqué. It was the first time I had met a U.S. Secretary of State at the negotiating table.

Kissinger's easy demeanor during the talk appealed to me very much. He wanted a few minor changes in the text, but seeing that Gromyko was unwilling to agree to them, he did not insist.

On our way back to the ministry in Gromyko's car, I teased Dobrynin about his having an easy time of it in Washington with Kissinger since it was so little trouble to reach an agreement with him. Dobrynin took my remark seriously and blurted out that Kissinger was not at all as nice in most negotiations and that you had to be constantly alert with him. "Before you can even open your mouth, he'll find out things he can use against you later," he said. Whereupon Gromyko interjected, "And he's as slippery as a snake— doesn't let anyone see what's on his mind." Gromyko made this observation without hostility. Even if he was referring to an adversary, what counted with Gromyko was the seriousness of the person. He found Kissinger serious.

Gromyko was initially taken aback by the American's joking manner but soon was favorably impressed by his personality, his sophistication as a negotiator, and his deep knowledge of issues. Gromyko took enormous pains to prepare himself for each meeting with Kissinger, approaching the sessions with the eagerness of a bridegroom on his wedding night.

In fact, Kissinger's visits to Moscow prior to the May 1972 summit and his talks with Gromyko were essential to the summit's success. Here again the Foreign Ministry's importance should be stressed and Western misperceptions

277

clarified concerning the role of other institutions or individuals in the framework of Soviet-American relations. Georgy Arbatov's name is often mentioned in this connection. In the West, he was considered one of Brezhnev's most important assistants for American affairs. But I never saw him in Gromyko's office.

I first met Arbatov when I was an undergraduate student. He and my cousin, then recently finished with their studies, were starting their working lives as journalists, a field in which Arbatov excelled. He also worked in Yuri Andropov's department in the Central Committee, where he made good connections. My professional ties with him began when he and I contributed articles to the popular weekly *New Times*. They resumed after Arbatov became director of the Institute of the United States and Canada, which he helped to bring into being. He was able to recruit not only academic specialists on the United States but also diplomats and others. In a smart move, he made Gromyko's son Anatoly head of one section on American foreign policy. In addition, he brought experts from the military and the KGB to the staff or into advisory positions.

When I returned to Moscow as Gromyko's adviser in 1970 Arbatov asked me to become a part-time senior research fellow at the institute, a well-paid but not taxing responsibility which only obliged me to advise him and a few of his permanent staff, particularly the young Gromyko, on studies they were preparing. Normally, the Foreign Minister was reluctant to allow his people to work outside the ministry, but he willingly consented to my working in Anatoly's section of the institute.

Arbatov had made American affairs his specialty at the beginning of the hopeful period, a choice which brought him a number of rewards. Among them were extensive travel and a meteoric academic and Party career. He rose to prominence with the institute as his vehicle, his writing talent as fuel, and a keen political sense, a gift for intrigue, to direct him. In 1970, when he was forty-seven, he became a corresponding member of the Academy of Sciences, a position of high social and scholarly prestige. Four years later he was a full member of the Academy. Soon after that he was elected a member of the Central Committee and joined the ruling elite.

Arbatov and I collaborated on several occasions on ad hoc teams set up to draft Brezhnev's major reports. Pleasant and easygoing with superiors and friends, and more so with Americans and foreigners generally, Arbatov was arrogant and often rude with his subordinates. I have rarely known a more vigorous drummer for the Soviet system. He is a man I would not trust. Intelligent, ambitious, and unencumbered by principle or scruple, Arbatov was ready as well to serve anyone without the slightest hesitation if it served his own interests.

Arbatov achieved his greatest success as an unofficial ambassador to unofficial America. Quick and engaging in conversation, he was among the few prominent Soviets who were welcomed into corporate boardrooms, academic seminars, and Washington salons. There he could gauge influential American opinion and propound what he represented to be Moscow's thinking. Although he is a member of the Central Committee and as such a part of the ruling elite, formally he does not occupy any official position in the government. As director of an academic institution, he could pretend to be an independent spokesman as those of the Western academic world often are. Arbatov could be more forthright than Dobrynin simply because his views could always be disavowed.

Moscow permits, indeed encourages, Arbatov to forsake orthodox rigidity when he interprets Soviet philosophy or policy for the West. He can thus foster the belief in the United States and the West that his institute is as independent as American academic institutions and think tanks.

Arbatov's institute is in fact a front used by the Central Committee and the KGB for many purposes: collecting valuable information, promoting the Soviet position, recruiting Soviet sympathizers in the United States, and disseminating disinformation. On the last point, they have been particularly successful since the West sees Arbatov and his institute as the Soviets wish them to be seen.

However, the institute is essentially excluded from participation in the making of Soviet policy toward the United

279

States. No one in the institute is really consulted by the Foreign Ministry or given access to its proposals to the Politburo on Soviet-American relations.

While the Soviet Union and the United States were formulating their positions on the SALT treaty, many Americans assumed that Arbatov was a major figure in behind-the-scenes maneuvering. But all key decisions were made by the Politburo on the basis of recommendations by Gromyko, Ustinov, and Grechko, with the aid of their top professional assistants. Arbatov was not even informed about many crucial factors which determined the Kremlin's attitude. He was less influential than Dobrynin or even Semyonov. The confidentiality surrounding the negotiations was extraordinary even for the secrecy-obsessed Soviets. There were only a handful of men in Moscow who really knew everything. Arbatov had no access to Dobrynin's or Semyonov's cabled reports except when he was shown a few of them while he worked on Brezhnev's speeches. A number of times I briefed him about the contents of Dobrynin's and Semyonov's messages and regarding Gromyko's proposals to the Politburo on SALT.

Many of Arbatov's major articles dealing with SALT were not written by him: people in the Foreign Ministry actually prepared several of them. Whenever it is expedient, however, his byline is used to give an unofficial status to opinions which are in fact officially approved. I do not mean to suggest that Arbatov was kept entirely in the dark. He wouldn't have been able to do his job if he had not been brought into at least the general picture.

His primary function was to seek out trends and moods among influential Americans whose views carried weight with the Administration. He was also to promote and defend the Soviet position. In this capacity he was a definite asset for Brezhnev and others in the Kremlin. Arbatov was a master at pumping secrets out of many people who were taken in by his seeming objectivity and independence, his calculated liberalism, and his purported influence with the Soviet leadership.

Arbatov was engaged more with the negative aspects of détente than the positive ones: ideological warfare with the

United States, propaganda, disinformation, and collecting data for the KGB. The United States should have long ago pressured the Soviets for more reciprocity. Arbatov has nearly unlimited access to American media, but it doesn't work the other way around. U.S. and other Western diplomats in Moscow are often not permitted to make public the mildest statements even on their national days.

IN THE SPRING OF 1972 I WAS INVOLVED IN PREPARATIONS for the Central Committee meeting. The essence of this task was to justify to the Party at large the Kremlin's turn toward détente with the United States. It had been decided to convene a special Central Committee plenary session to guarantee advance endorsement of the new policy line.

I was the only representative from the Foreign Ministry in the working group charged with drafting Brezhnev's report. The others were Central Committee personnel, since the plenary meeting was basically their responsibility. We gathered at a Central Committee dacha about forty-five minutes outside Moscow. The setting for our work was comfortable. The two-story white brick dacha where we wrote, slept, and ate had been a gift to the writer Maxim Gorky from one of the wealthy Morozov brothers, pre-revolutionary industrialists who sponsored avant-garde culture and helped fund the Bolsheviks before 1917.

After writing separately in our second-floor rooms we would meet in the large salon downstairs to compare ideas and test our phraseology out on one another.

My job was to prove that Nixon's visit would be in the interest of the Soviet Union and that any agreements with the United States would not signal cessation of the ideological struggle with "imperialism," affect continuing support to "liberation movements," or undermine our efforts to reach real military parity with the United States.

I wrote that the Nixon visit was important not only because it was the first by an American President to the Soviet Union since World War II but also because it represented "a great victory" for the peace-loving policies of the

U.S.S.R. It was "convincing proof" of the "powerful rise of Soviet influence throughout the world."

My argumentation was unoriginal. Nor, because of the generalities in which it was stated, was it controversial. Most of the phrasing survived into the final report Brezhnev delivered to the closed plenary session, and his themes became the standard public and private defense of the Soviet push for détente.

But I knew the report had not so much ended internal Soviet debate over détente policy as sidestepped it. Brezhnev got the Central Committee's endorsement for the summit after perfunctory discussion at the plenum, but he achieved this mandate by outmaneuvering some of his skeptical Politburo colleagues, not by confronting them or their abiding reservations. He forestalled debate by taking the matter to the Central Committee, where he could count on the fact that most of the members—local and regional Party officials—were resoundingly ignorant of foreign policy and respected his authority. And he kept the discussion on such a general plane that there was no occasion to air such troubling, specific questions as Vietnam or East-West trade.

The question of how to reconcile Nixon's reception with Soviet support for Hanoi did arise in the drafting process. Central Committee staffers at the Gorky dacha urged me, for instance, to strengthen the passages I had written on Southeast Asia with thundering condemnations of American imperialism. When I brought the completed first draft back to Moscow and reported their pressure to Gromyko, however, he instructed me to stick to the mild formulations I had used. "We have to state the principle [of opposition to U.S. intervention], but calmly, without special shrillness," he said. "We don't need hysterics. This is not propaganda for the hack writers who always go overboard in the press." In the final stages of rewriting by Brezhnev himself, it was Gromyko's line which prevailed.

Nixon and Kissinger need not have worried as much as they evidently did that the Soviets might withdraw their invitation when American forces mined the principal harbors of North Vietnam two weeks before the scheduled summit. By then Gromyko and Brezhnev were irrevocably committed to receiving the President in Moscow and to making that visit the ceremonial and substantive turning point toward better superpower relations. They had already cast their lot with Washington in April when Moscow had, in effect, made only a *pro forma* protest over the renewed bombing of North Vietnam. The mining added insult to that injury, but despite the bitterness felt by the Soviets' Vietnamese allies, the Kremlin did not reconsider its drive for accommodation with the United States. Hanoi's request to cancel Nixon's visit was ignored.

On the contrary, preparations for the summit were barely affected by the mining. On May 9, a holiday celebrating the German surrender in 1945, I was at home, expecting to spend the day with my family and a few friends. But that morning my telephone rang and I was ordered to report immediately to Vasily Kuznetsov at the ministry. There, I learned that Haiphong harbor, through which Soviet weapons deliveries were made to North Vietnam, had been mined by the Americans.

The question put to me and two other senior ministry officials in Kuznetsov's office required a basic and profound policy choice. Where did Soviet priorities lie? With the Vietnamese, whose cause we had long championed? Or with the prospects that the already announced U.S.-Soviet summit would bring an agreement on SALT and a breakthrough toward better political relations with Washington?

The others were as unsure as I was of what course to advocate. Georgy Kornienko wondered if Washington might be trying to provoke a cancellation of the Nixon visit. Anatoly Kovalev speculated on whether and how we might be able to speed up arms deliveries to the Vietnamese through China. The talk wandered from the real issue until Kuznetsov cut in. "This is no time to philosophize," he said. "We have to make a statement, and someone has to draft it."

He assigned Kovalev and me to that task, ordering us to prepare a short but sharp condemnation of the American course, at least as a preliminary indication of a policy line that might not be made completely clear until it had been further considered. While we wrote, he said, he would try to reach Gromyko, the Soviet military leadership, and, if possible, Brezhnev, to get their guidance.

Perhaps half an hour later, he was on the telephone to us in Kovalev's office. He did not specify whom he had reached but said, "Things are a lot clearer. You should not go to extremes in the statement. Keep it calm, firm, a strong condemnation. The mining has to stop." I was surprised. He made no mention of possible retaliation. "And just so you understand," Kuznetsov finished, "at the top they regard the Nixon visit as the most important consideration. It will go ahead as scheduled. No matter what."

I felt dazed. The decision itself was not what dismayed me. I had worked hard with some optimism on the preparations for the Nixon visit. What made me reel was the speed with which American actions against Vietnam had been dismissed, the instant calculation that the U.S.S.R. had to turn its back, shedding a crocodile tear or two, on its Asian ally.

The more profound issue involved in the promises Brezhnev held out of a liberalized U.S.-Soviet trade relationship was, on the contrary, muffled. On this question Kosygin and Podgorny had doubts about Brezhnev's position, but they lacked the power to thwart him. Kosygin recognized the importance of Soviet-American economic relations and even favored their development, but only on the condition that the Soviet Union remain as self-sufficient as possible. According to his aides, he repeatedly disparaged proposals that the U.S.S.R. should "squander" its natural resources in trade arrangements that he feared would make it too dependent on Western markets. Where Brezhnev saw in multibillion-dollar deals an opportunity to import efficiency, Kosygin perceived the danger of exporting irreplaceable oil, gas, and minerals to strengthen the capitalist world at the long-term expense of Soviet development.

In the course of the summit meeting Kosygin registered a measure of his skepticism about the reception accorded Nixon. In delivering an address of welcome to the American President, he omitted a number of the more optimistic or flattering phrases from the text which the Foreign Ministry had prepared for him. Even so, the effect of the speech was not hostile. It conformed to the Politburo line, and only a few insiders knew how much cooler he had made its language.

It is likely that Kosygin sought to use the issue as a way to challenge the preeminence Brezhnev had earned at his expense. In any case, certain concerns he voiced in grumbling to his intimates are as old and enduring as Russian history. In the eighteenth century, the landed nobility, the boyars, vainly resisted Peter the Great's reforms as alien European transplants. In culture and in politics the conservative Slavophiles sought in the nineteenth century to make a virtue of Russia's backwardness, to retain its isolation as its strength. After World War II, Stalin linked ideas of nationalism to policies of economic independence.

Kosygin stood in this tradition, whether from principle or from ambition. But Brezhnev invoked the contrary view—also a recurrent one in the nation's past—and carried a majority of his colleagues with him. For his address to the Central Committee I found citations from Lenin endorsing expanded economic ties with capitalist countries and corporations. The fact that Lenin had adopted such policies to deal with post-revolutionary economic chaos did not diminish Brezhnev's willingness to apply his scriptural maxims, out of context, some fifty years later.

The central characteristic of this pre-summit debate, however, was its whispered, inconclusive nature. Typical of the style of Brezhnev-era politics, the arguments were not permitted any full consideration. Differences were muted by pretending they did not exist, or did not matter much.

In any case, I thought the results of the Moscow summit were basically positive. I hoped that it would foster cooperation with the United States and ultimately aid our leadership's understanding of real American intentions. Above all, I was glad the SALT agreements were concluded. They limited development of antiballistic missile systems and strategic offensive arms, and marked a significant step in arms control. Of course, the agreement on strategic offensive missiles established quantitative ceilings but not really qualitative limitations. Thus, the SALT I accords should not be faulted for what happened later. The United States nearly froze its strategic arsenal of its own free will during the seventies while the Soviet Union continued to increase its military potential within the limits defined by SALT. In 1972, there was no real parity in the strategic nuclear balance; the Soviets were behind the United States in the efficiency and effectiveness of their missile systems, although they were ahead in conventional forces. The SALT agreements permitted both sides to proceed with modernization of their strategic offensive arms. Moscow did so in full; Washington did so on a much smaller scale.

The summit also provided an opportunity for the leaders of both countries to know each other better, an element whose importance is often overlooked in our age of growing impersonality. Brezhnev and other Soviet leaders, however, never really felt at ease with Richard Nixon, and they did not understand him well. As a result, and because of their own suspicious natures, they distrusted him. Whatever he did regarding Soviet-American relations, including steps of which the Soviets approved, the fact that he remained their ideological enemy overrode any sincere rapport that might have developed between the leaders. The enigma of Nixon is perhaps not so surprising when even Henry Kissinger, a man who knew him well, noted of his character that "several warring personalities struggled for preeminence in the same individual."

In one of our pre-summit meetings in Gromyko's office, as we were unsuccessfully trying to think of a suitable gift to present to Nixon, Gromyko remarked, "Almost all Americans have some kind of hobby. Does anyone know what Nixon's is?" he asked, looking around at us. After a moment of silent headshaking from the assembled group, Gromyko said dryly, "I think what he'd really like is a guarantee to stay in the White House forever." All of us perceived Nixon's personality as so impenetrable that we had no idea what would please him. Ministry experts finally decided to give him a hydrofoil, for no other reason than that Brezhnev had one and liked it.

Soviet leaders did, however, find in Nixon's behavior definite similarities to their own, and concluded that it might be possible to deal with him in the world of realpolitik. His pragmatism, his dry manner, his natural inclination toward secret arrangements, and the way in which he exercised his presidential power appealed to the Soviets and were characteristics they understood and were comfortable with.

The Kremlin also had the impression that Nixon was more powerful than he really was, a factor that eventually led them into serious misconceptions about American policy. Brezhnev labored under an inferiority complex in talking with Nixon, which, of course, he did his best to keep from showing when he was in the presence of the Americans. But during private discussions with Gromyko and a few others involved in negotiations at the Moscow summit, he occasionally betrayed his true feelings. Many times he read and reread the talking points the ministry had prepared for his discussions with Nixon. He once remarked that he did not feel sure Nixon would understand what he was trying to say. Gromyko was much more confident, and by the end of the summit his respect for Nixon was evident. In an expansive moment after it was over, Gromyko joked that if Nixon should ever apply to join the Communist Party, the matter "could be studied."

However, both Brezhnev and Gromyko believed that to reach agreement with Kissinger was perhaps even more important. The Soviets enjoyed working with him so much that in Gromyko's inner cabinet after the Moscow summit he was referred to by a Russian nickname, Kisa (pussycat). In no way did this mean that the Soviets viewed him as easy to deal with or as being in their corner, but it has always been the Russian custom to devise fond nicknames for people they like and respect. Gromyko saw him as a formidable opponent who could "read character like a book." The fact that Kissinger represented United States power and possessed intelligence along with exceptional negotiating skill added strength to his charm—irresistible to the Soviets.

One unfortunate result of the Moscow summit was that it promoted the illusion that the Kremlin might be willing to modify its Marxist-Leninist ideological schemes. Brezhnev won approval of his policy by stressing short-term benefits and by blurring the underlying issues. When the high hopes of 1972 wore thin and the inherent contradictions and rivalries between Soviet and American policies grew sharp, the consensus he had manufactured also began to erode. But if the Soviet leadership misperceived the neo-isolationist mood in the United States brought about by Vietnam, there were also groundless American expectations that the Kremlin would be content with the role of junior superpower.

My last work in Gromyko's office was to help draw up the Soviet position for the coming Paris Conference on Vietnam scheduled for February 1973. Gromyko assigned me to the rewriting of the statement prepared for him by the ministry's Southeast Asian Department. It was so overloaded with stereotypical accusations of American imperialism that Gromyko complained he could not work with the draft. "I give up," he stormed. "Those guys have no idea what to say or how to say it. Here, you do it."

While Gromyko was ready to go forward with the practical business of ending the Vietnam War, in fact accepting division of that country, other Soviet leaders held far different opinions. Yuri Andropov was among those who opposed the agreement on ending the war because he believed that pressure from the American public and the Congress would eventually force the President to withdraw from Vietnam. Brezhnev overruled the dissenters, but something a KGB officer said stuck in my mind—he told me that Andropov, with unusual bluntness, had remarked, "We'll win the Vietnam War not in Paris but in the streets of America."

I was unable to follow the final debate very closely. Although I was to have been a member of the Soviet delegation to the Paris Conference, before it began I was appointed UN Under Secretary General.

20

In December 1972, Gromyko called me into his office, where he received me with unusual cordiality. As I walked down the length of the wood-paneled room, edging by his huge conference table, he invited me to sit down at a small table adjoining his desk. He sucked on his lips, and then said with his customary formality, "It has been suggested to me that your name be proposed as a candidate for the post of Under Secretary General of the United Nations. Kutakov* is incapable of coping with his duties, and the situation has to be remedied. How do you feel about it, Shevchenko? If you wish, you can think it over and give me your answer tomorrow."

Gromyko was talking about a promotion to one of our most important diplomatic posts abroad. He was making me the kind of offer one simply does not refuse in the Soviet Union, and his commanding tone made that clear.

But I knew it was not merely Kutakov's failure in the Secretariat that prompted Gromyko to want me as his replacement. He needed someone in New York who belonged to his inner circle as he had in Washington in the person of Anatoly Dobrynin. And no doubt Lidiya Dmitriyevna Gromyko would welcome the idea. She and Lina had become increasingly friendly while I was Gromyko's adviser.

The minister's offer was not a complete surprise. On several occasions colleagues had mentioned that I was being considered for promotion—either in the ministry or abroad. I was inclined to go abroad. I do not know whether this preference already reflected a latent drive toward breaking with the Soviet system; if the germ of that idea was in my subconscious, an overseas posting would certainly facilitate matters. Or it may have been only the result of growing frustration with my job, with the regime and the leadership. Of no small importance was Lina's desire for another foreign posting. One matter of concern was our daughter, Anna. She was ten years old. If we stayed in Moscow for several more years it would become impossible to take her with us. There were no Soviet high schools abroad, and the rules prohibited children over fifteen or sixteen from attend-

---

* Leonid N. Kutakov, former rector of MGIMO, was my predecessor at the UN.

ing foreign schools where they could be "negatively affected by bourgeois ideology."

Like Lina, I was fond of New York, where I felt so much freer than in Moscow. On the other hand, for career advancement the ministry was the place to be. The UN Secretariat was, in comparison, second-rate. Besides, the UN was becoming known more and more as a sinecure for the budding careers of the children of the elite, and it was the fulcrum of KGB operations. Still, the post of Under Secretary General was an exception. Anatoly Dobrynin and other prominent diplomats had filled it in the past and had gone on to higher levels.

There was really nothing to think over, and I accepted Gromyko's offer at once. He looked at me intently and an unusual expression flickered across his face. I realized it had been a smile. "All right," he said, "we'll submit the proposal to the Central Committee."

On the morning of February 23, 1973, Vasily Makarov telephoned me soon after I arrived at work. "Arkady," he growled, "drop by my office and be prepared to do a dance." In Russian this means one can look forward to a pleasant surprise. When I entered his office, Makarov had on his desk the official decision of the Central Committee, signed by Leonid Brezhnev.

I had expected the Central Committee's action to be positive. It was unlikely to respond negatively to a Gromyko proposal, and indeed it had acted quickly. All that remained now was for Kurt Waldheim, the UN Secretary General, formally to appoint me, but I foresaw no difficulties there, since this position is traditionally held by a Soviet. By gentlemen's agreement, the Secretary General always accepts the candidate nominated by the Soviet government.

After Waldheim's acceptance and shortly before I departed for New York, Gromyko and I had a talk about my new duties. He discussed at length the necessity of the UN's functioning strictly in accordance with its charter. I must see to it that no deviations were permitted. He said that the United Nations should refrain from discussing matters which the Soviet government found unpleasant.

At one point, I suggested that it might be a good idea for

me to develop good working relations with the new Secretary General, Kurt Waldheim.

Gromyko frowned. "In principle, that is correct, but you can't expect to derive great benefits from it. What important questions can you talk about with Waldheim? Neither he nor the UN as a whole is a great power. Never forget, Shevchenko, you're a Soviet ambassador first, not an international bureaucrat." He instructed me on my role. "For example," he pointed out, "we have little information about what's going on in China. What are the intentions of the Chinese? Develop close relations with them and their friends and find out as much as you can. Don't hesitate to meet with anybody, even with representatives of those countries with whom we do not maintain diplomatic relations and whom we publicly attack. I give you authority to see the ambassadors from the Republic of South Africa and South Korea, anyone from whom you can elicit information."

I added Israel to the list and mentioned that in the past I had good relations with the Egyptians, particularly with Ismail Fahmi, then Minister of Foreign Affairs.

The next day I was summoned to the office of Mikhail Suslov, one of the last major figures from Stalin's time to survive in authority under Brezhnev. He was cold, rigid, brusque, and I knew that Gromyko had a distant and strained relationship with him. The two were not so much antagonists as ill-matched colleagues. Suslov, who died in January 1982 at the age of seventy-nine, gave first priority to Communist doctrine and its purity in practice. Gromyko, more flexible but no less an exponent of Soviet power, dealt with the world as it was, not necessarily as Marxism-Leninism decreed it should be.

Even though repeated illness in his later years limited Suslov's day-to-day role in Party business and bureaucratic infighting, he enjoyed immense prestige. And he was capable of using it, if not to further his dogmatic views, then at least to slow or block deviations from what he conceived to be the proper course of Soviet policy. A gaunt figure, well over six feet tall, he joined the Central Committee in 1941, became a Party secretary in 1947 and a member of the Presidium (as Stalin called his last Politburo) in 1952. Seniority alone would have made him powerful, but his political stature was also based on his many years of advancing the careers of younger men who were obligated and faithful to him.

When Khrushchev was ousted in 1964, Suslov could have succeeded him as General Secretary, but he preferred to concentrate on ideological matters. But neither Suslov nor his colleagues wanted someone in the top Party post who might possibly dominate them.

Suslov, however, only appeared to be satisfied with the role of Party patriarch and guardian of ideological purity. Cloaked in the robe of doctrinal infallibility, he regularly issued reminders of what he saw as the correct Marxist-Leninist policy. He also oversaw the work of the Central Committee commissions on ideology and foreign affairs. These commissions, made up of the appropriate secretaries and department heads, have significant roles as advisers to the Politburo. Suslov's rank assured that his views, through his subordinates, would be given weight.

Suslov himself took on a number of foreign duties, traveling to Communist Party congresses abroad to admonish and instruct his "fraternal comrades" in a high-pitched, monotonous voice that often seemed at odds with his calm, deliberate manner. Having headed the Communist Information Bureau (Cominform) when it expelled Marshal Tito's Yugoslav Communist Party in 1948, he took a special interest in the international Communist movement throughout his career, always retaining the strictness of his early days even as diversity became the rule among non-Soviet Communist parties.

He was, as some of my ministry colleagues bitterly joked, Stalin's "anachronism," a Stalinist who had survived his mentor and outlived his era. My conversation with him confirmed for me the accuracy of this sarcastic tag.

In Suslov's office, I found an imperious man whose gray-blue eyes peered through thick-lensed glasses under a shock of graying blond hair that seemed in permanent disarray. Skin taut over sharp, high cheekbones, he looked tired. He went quickly from a handshake and congratulations to the business of indoctrinating me in his views of the UN.

Slowly drumming his long, bony fingers on his desk, he declared that in assuming my new post I should look upon the United Nations as he did, as a setting to be used to the maximum extent for propagating progressive ideas. To make sure I understood him, he expressed this thought three times. Since the majority of UN members were new, developing countries, he said, there was the danger that they might fall victim to neocolonialist and bourgeois ideology. The Soviet Union's task, the responsibility of all dedicated Communists, was to prevent such an occurrence.

He added that he knew Gromyko regarded the UN, first of all, as an international organization where caution should be the rule in introducing ideological considerations into debate. "I disagree with that approach," he said flatly.

Suslov's view that ideology should be paramount in every aspect of government went hand in hand with a Stalinist style of instruction. His method was to deliver at every opportunity a barrage of repetitious slogans and vilifications against all who were suspected of the slightest deviation from orthodoxy. His meticulousness in doctrinal matters matched an ascetic personality. His habits were so precise that it was a standing joke that you could set your watch by the appearance of his homeward-bound automobile every day at precisely 6 p.m. at the intersection of Arbat Street and the Smolenskoye Koltso adjacent to the Foreign Ministry.

I listened to Suslov attentively during our interview and offered no dissent. But Gromyko's orders were my real orders.

My family and I arrived in New York in April 1973. The work in the Secretariat was demanding, and on top of the UN job came my responsibilities to the Soviet community in New York, no less real for being unofficial duties. I was well aware that our government paid little attention to the special status of Soviet nationals working in the Secretariat. But when I became one of them, I began to comprehend what that meant.

As defined in the UN Charter and in the staff regulations,

the duties and obligations of members of the UN Secretariat are "not national but exclusively international." All of them should live up to the oath or declaration they swear:

> I solemnly swear . . . to exercise in all loyalty, discretion, and conscience the functions entrusted to me as an international civil servant of the United Nations, to discharge these functions and regulate my conduct with the interests of the United Nations only in view, and not to seek or accept instructions in regard to the performance of my duties from any Government or other authority external to the Organization.

I knew many people who fulfilled these obligations with integrity and diligence. But of course the UN is filled with vested interests, private and national. The U.S.S.R. and the Soviet bloc are not unique in their disregard of its international purpose. But in the UN the Soviet Union is alone in one respect among the other nations on earth: its mendacity and cynicism are fully institutionalized. Every Soviet national who takes the organization's oath must commit perjury. Before an individual's candidature is submitted by the Soviet Union to the Secretariat's Office of Personnel Services, that individual undertakes an obligation to do his or her best in the interests of the Soviet Union and to use his or her prospective job to achieve this purpose.

Duties and rules governing Soviet nationals in the Secretariat are defined in detail in a special document titled *Polozheniye o sovsotrudnikakh mezhdunarodnykh organizatsy* (Statute on Soviet Employees of International Organizations). Even the term *sovsotrudnik* (a contraction/combination of *sovietsky sotrudnik* meaning "Soviet employee"), commonly used internally by the Soviets in referring to their UN Secretariat staff members, is suggestive. Through an elaborate organizational structure, the Soviet Mission maintains full control over the daily work of Soviet nationals in the Secretariat. All these staff members are part of the *Ob'yedinenniye referentury* (United Sections) of the Mission, where they receive direct instructions about how they should do their jobs in the Secretariat and what their specific contributions should be to the work of the Mission itself. These employees in fact prepare draft speeches for the Soviet representatives as well as background notes on UN business for the Mission. At the same time they are obliged under UN regulations not to engage in activities incompatible with the proper discharge of their duties for the UN, and not to communicate to any person information known to them by reason of their official position.

Secretariat staff members should not be involved in any political activity inconsistent with or reflecting upon their independence and impartiality. But almost all Soviets in the Secretariat are members of the local Communist Party unit actively functioning in New York in the guise of a trade union organization. Not only must these Secretariat employees attend regular Party meetings along with all other Soviets, but Party resolutions and decisions are mandatory instructions for them whether they are consonant with their duties in the Secretariat or not.

Moscow takes particular care to prevent the development of any kind of international loyalty in their people in the Secretariat. Again, unlike any other nation (excluding some of the Soviet bloc countries), the U.S.S.R. precludes its citizens from permanent or career appointments at the UN. They customarily serve a single, short-term tour. However, after many long debates, the Central Committee decided to allow certain exceptions to this rule and now permits some officials to stay at their posts up to seven or eight years. Finally, upon completion of their tours, Soviet performances are not evaluated under Secretariat criteria but in summaries prepared by supervisors in the Soviet Mission and the Communist Party organization.

Of course, international civil servants are not expected to give up all ties with their countries or beliefs. But in good faith they cannot and should not act exclusively as national representatives, as the Soviet Union demands. Thus, no Soviet national can meet the primary requirements of the international civil service. I was in no way an exception to the Soviet rules. I knew it; the Secretary General knew it. But neither Waldheim nor any other Secretary General has complained about this, as far as I know. There was in fact no choice; any Soviet replacement for me could act no differently than I did.

Disregard of their obligations within the Secretariat, however, has produced great disadvantages for the Soviet Union and its bloc compatriots. Secretariat officials and Under Secretaries General from other nations often shun discussions when Soviets are present, or they pursue such talks in the most formal and wary manner. Frequently I was not given information on important matters. Everyone knew that the Soviets and their fellow travelers would not maintain confidentiality or, worse, would use advance information to further the interests of the Soviet Union at the expense of the UN or other nations. It was frustrating and degrading to have to perform under such circumstances, knowing that I was a distrusted pariah among my colleagues.

In any event, Kurt Waldheim received me cordially. Mine was one of the largest departments in the Secretariat with diverse responsibilities. The situation was complicated by the fact that my government forced me to be responsible for the work of all Soviets at the UN. Moreover, I had to set an example of dutiful inspiration that over the years I found harder and harder to fake.

Nonetheless, I was glad to return to New York and looked forward to my new job "on the other side of the river," as the Soviets described it. In a sense, I felt about the UN the way one does about his first love. The UN was and is a place where representatives of the world can informally discuss a spectrum of serious and interesting problems. Often it is not the public deliberations that lead to better understanding and tolerance but off-the-record talks. Occasionally these pave the way for agreements that are impossible to achieve through bilateral diplomacy alone. Even archenemies frequently speak sensibly at the UN behind the scenes.

I do not want to idealize the UN. From its inception it has been used by many different factions for shallow or destructive purposes. Its ideals have never been implemented, and, human nature being what it is, perhaps never can be. Sometimes the UN disserves rather than serves the cause of peace; inflates polemics instead of fostering reasonable solutions. The Security Council is more often than not paralyzed by disagreement among its permanent members. And yet, all this granted, there have been circumstances where the UN proved to be irreplaceable in defusing potential explosions and contributing to practical arrangements to bring hostilities to an end. Among the many sources and kinds of power and influence on the planet, the UN is one of the humblest, and perhaps should be. Its strength, such as it is, is more moral than military. Men and nations will always be diverse, differing in needs and desires. The UN will ever fight a sorry battle on the fringes of interstate passions, chipping away at overheated elements, sometimes succeeding, more often not. Perhaps its best role is merely to draw off poisons from the international community, to take the world's opprobrium without making overt gestures of its own. But civilization has not advanced by force alone. The most significant advancements have come through intellect and the willingness of men and women to try to go forward in cooperation—a revolutionary attitude in any age.

My job in the Secretariat brought me new experiences and challenging tasks. I was middle-aged and set in many of my concepts and methods. To work under rules of conduct and intent so different from those to which I was accustomed was sometimes difficult for me to accept.

I set about establishing in my department order and discipline according to the inflexible Soviet model I was accustomed to. I insisted that all documents, even insignificant ones, be submitted for my clearance and approval, creating bottlenecks at every turn. I demanded that all contacts of my senior staff with other departments of the Secretariat be approved by me. Nothing was too minuscule for my attention. I even attempted to encroach upon the responsibilities and functions of other departments.

In an abuse of power, I helped the North Koreans pursue one of their interests by manipulating procedures in the First Committee of the General Assembly. This provoked an angry protest to the Secretary General about my behavior from representatives of the United Kingdom, the United States, and France.

I was the focal point of another protest to the Secretary General because of my treatment of a French official who

297

worked in my department. I had blocked his promotion in response to the Soviet Mission's allegations that he had collaborated with the Western powers in stalling the work of the Security Council committee on sanctions against Rhodesia. If personal antipathy to such actions rose to haunt or embarrass me when I was alone with my thoughts, I was able to justify them with the argument that I had no other choice but to be an active defender and promoter of Soviet interests.

Before I began working at the Secretariat, I had tended to think that its functions were primarily administrative: to circulate documents of the Security Council, General Assembly, and other principal and subsidiary organs of the UN; to provide services for meetings or to assist in planning and organizing the proper conduct of proceedings. In following up on implementation of Security Council and General Assembly decisions and resolutions, preparing reports and studies, participating in various investigations, maintaining liaison with outside organizations around the world, and advising various UN policymaking bodies, I discovered my department could influence—sometimes substantially—the course of deliberations and their final outcome. Sydney D. Bailey expressed it correctly in his book *The Secretariat of the United Nations* when he said that it is only in books that a neat distinction can be made between policy and administration. The primary tasks of the Secretariat are administrative, but there is at all levels room for intelligent exercise of initiative and influence.

The Secretariat not only has problems common to any large bureaucracy but suffers from some special headaches all its own. The big ones are conflicting loyalties, different administrative traditions, and lack of a cohesive executive comparable to that of national governmental institutions. For instance, just making yourself understood in the context of UN procedure was not always easy: in my department there were about 150 officers of nearly fifty different nationalities.

The ways our various responsibilities and interests filtered through our individual natures as well as our many nationalities affected how we worked together, and thus how we worked with the larger UN to which we were responsible. It was not simple.

Nor was it easy to establish normal personal and working relationships with all the members of my staff. They resented some of my decisions and didn't often hide their feelings. I was used to subordinates who did not openly display disapproval. It caused me considerable astonishment and anger at first, but I came to respect the resolve with which they defended their opinions and suggestions. Unlike the majority of my compatriots, who viewed any problem through the prism of Soviet self-interest, many of my subordinates in the Secretariat were not parochial nationalists. These people approached matters with open minds and did not fear contradicting me. Nor did they avoid criticizing their own governments' policies. No one who has not lived under complete totalitarianism can appreciate the shock such behavior gave me. For a Soviet, open disagreement with one's superior ceases with his instructions. Anyone rash enough to continue to argue would probably be in professional or personal jeopardy. In contrast, my freethinking colleagues in the Secretariat would follow orders but would not hesitate to reveal their disapproval of them.

Among the best examples I knew of loyalty to the international character of the UN were two political officers in my Security Council Affairs Division—an American, Elizabeth Jelstrup, and Barbara Blenman of Trinidad. Both of these women had served in the UN for a long time and had high standards of efficiency and competence. Either one could be relied upon to provide absolutely objective information regarding their special area of work for the Security Council.

I was jealous of my subordinates' independence; it seemed to me a natural dignity and an essential right. I particularly envied the liberty of the other Under Secretaries General. Unlike me, they were not dictated to by their governments. Moreover, they had the freedom to ignore their countries' ambassadors to the UN, if they felt it appropriate, without fear of removal or accusations of treason for their differences of opinion.

Like all other Soviets in the Secretariat who had orders to

"use or manipulate" it, I was required to exercise every effort to prevent inclusion of anything detrimental to Soviet interests in Secretariat reports or studies, whether true or not. On the other hand, I was to see that materials or conclusions favorable to the Soviet Union were included, also irrespective of the truth. The Soviets found the Secretariat useful for collecting political and technical information. We were also required to "work" among other staff members to indoctrinate them in ways Moscow considered desirable.

Every Soviet national also had a duty to help recruit his countrymen to fill posts in the Secretariat, often regardless of qualifications. The operative rule was: the more, the better. I was constantly pressured by the Mission to use my position and influence to expand the Soviet presence. There was similarly persistent wheedling from representatives of Soviet bloc countries for expansion of their footholds in the Secretariat. It was next to impossible to refuse to accept their candidates, and when I put them off, some of their ambassadors hinted about complaining to Moscow if their demands were not met. Overall Secretariat performance obviously suffered from succumbing to this sort of harassment, but very little could be done about it.

Particularly annoying were the ceaseless requests from Moscow to assist the Soviet-controlled World Peace Council. That organization, which was headed by an Indian, Romesh Chandra, swarmed with KGB officers. Every year I was expected to help organize Chandra's speeches to UN bodies, arrange his meetings with UN officials, distribute Council propaganda, and persuade Waldheim to send Secretariat representatives to attend various Council-sponsored conferences. Moscow wanted to boost the Council's prestige by creating high visibility via UN recognition of the Council's "great role in the world movement for peace." I never developed a skin thick enough not to cringe inwardly with embarrassment when I approached Waldheim's deputies with my next recommendation for UN participation in another World Peace Council activity. I never became immune to their patient, knowing smiles when I insistently proposed that the Secretary General's upcoming statement praise whatever latest peace initiative the U.S.S.R. wanted to push no matter how transparent the initiative might be. Moscow even demanded that I try to get Waldheim to praise Soviet Communist Party gatherings.

Although my job was to use the Secretariat to widen the scope of Soviet ideological and propaganda warfare, at the same time I was instructed to curtail as much as possible the flow of information from the West to the Soviet Union. Employing the Outer Space Division of my department as a vehicle, I promoted the Soviet proposal to prevent direct television broadcasting (DTB) to foreign states without their express consent. At the time of my appointment, development of communications satellites capable of beaming signals directly to specially equipped domestic TV receivers was predicted for the 1980s. Eventually, such broadcasts could be transmitted to ordinary domestic sets in any country, irrespective of the national network. One can imagine Moscow's consternation at this prospect. "It is easy to see," cried the Kremlin propagandists, "that the imperialists will do their utmost to exploit the potential of DTB in their crusade against Marxist-Leninist ideology, against the ideas of peace and social progress."

The Kremlin is right to be afraid. The Soviet people are hungry for news of the outside world. If such a flood of information and entertainment were unleashed, there is no telling what the consequences might be, but it is certain that they would be profound.

My work also included participating in numerous formal meetings and unofficial consultations, receiving ambassadors and representatives of many public organizations. Protocol functions, luncheons, dinners, receptions, and the like were requisite as well, often several on the same day. These latter are the real scourge of the working UN. But they must be attended, even though it means a tremendous loss of time and great expense to the member states to stage them.

At one luncheon given by the West German representative, Baron Rudiger von Wechmar, instead of giving the customary toast, he recommended a special code of conduct for us to follow. Among other things, the code, which was called "the nine (plus one) commandments," urged delegates to "arrive no less than 30 minutes after the scheduled time'' of any meeting to avoid loneliness. It was a joke, of course, but it turned out that there was considerable sympathy for the good sense and practical truth contained in his "commandments." Unfortunately, the number of protocol functions continued to increase.

Another routine UN quagmire was the number of speeches and statements in which representatives would repeat themselves almost verbatim from year to year. Nearly every veteran of the UN could predict almost exactly what some delegates would say. Here again, Wechmar's "commandments" contained a nugget of wisdom in its satire: "The value of a United Nations speech is measured above all by its length rather than by its precision."

The winner, champion, and recognized king of the orators at the UN was the late representative of Saudi Arabia, Jamil Baroody. A colorful personality, a superb speaker, and without doubt an original and talented man, Baroody could talk eloquently on totally different matters to different committees on the same day without any prepared texts to aid him. But his mere appearance before the Security Council or other UN bodies dismayed the gathered representatives. They knew only too well that Baroody could and would tell the plainest truth to anyone, minus any diplomatic nicety. He made no distinction or deference, whether to a superpower or a small nation. His power lay in his great intellect and encyclopedic knowledge, abetted by the fact that he had practically carte blanche to speak for Saudi Arabia without any instructions. And he usually spoke at length. Woe to any who tried to curtail his delivery. He would turn to the seeker of brevity and examine him and his nation's shortcomings in the most searing terms. Old UN hands knew enough never to try to interrupt him.

My disagreements with Yakov Malik were often over matters of form. He preferred polemics to discussion, and loved to excoriate Americans, Chinese, and Israelis. I believed we had to be at least civil to our opponents, particularly at the UN, where we often needed their tacit cooperation just to get routine business done. Malik burned bridges and seemed to revel in his ability to give offense. We were constantly at odds over dealings with the United

States. Once as we were strolling through the walled garden at Glen Cove, he inveighed against SALT. "You can't trust these Americans," he muttered angrily. "Nothing good can come of this détente business." I reminded him that he contradicted himself by opposing the arms race while at the same time throwing rocks in the path of SALT.

"There is no contradiction," he said coldly, ending our conversation.

The source of our most bitter arguments, however, was his insistence that I make the UN Secretariat take positions conforming absolutely to the Soviet view.

"You have to conduct yourself as a Soviet ambassador," he stormed at me. "I'll complain about you to Gromyko if you don't," he threatened. "As Under Secretary General you have to convince Waldheim to do what we want, not kowtow to him."

There was no way I could fulfill such a demand without a revolt among my staff and without causing the non-aligned states to openly label me a partisan. My usual response was that Waldheim was still my superior, and that I had to obey him as a Secretariat official. He would pretend incredulity when I explained this, and would simply restate his views, declaring that we had only one superior: the Party.

In many cases, I had to follow his wishes, but just as often I ignored them, knowing that Gromyko would back me up. Moreover, I had my own independent communications link with Moscow. Malik knew I could complain about him to Gromyko without his being able to screen my cables.

There were only two Soviets in New York authorized to send code cables to the Foreign Ministry: Malik and myself. In the ambassador's absence, the chargé d'affaires replacing him was permitted to do so. In the summer of 1974, Malik went to Moscow on vacation. His deputy, Vasily Stepanovich Safronchuk, a stout, good-natured, middle-aged man, became acting ambassador. Safronchuk had the ability to listen with serene tranquillity to Malik's most insulting castigations, driving the ambassador almost to hysteria. Malik was somewhat concerned about leaving Safronchuk in charge, and this time his foreboding proved correct.

Safronchuk was conducting a flamboyant affair with a

Mission bookkeeper, and one of their trysts on a deserted Long Island beach resulted in his being incommunicado during an emergency arising from the fighting on Cyprus.

In July 1974 the Soviet Mission received instructions to request an urgent meeting of the Security Council to deal with this tense situation. The Foreign Ministry also demanded an immediate report confirming execution of its order. But Safronchuk had vanished, and there was no one to sign the cable reporting to Moscow. In a panic, Richard Ovinnikov, a senior diplomat in charge of Security Council affairs at the Mission, called me to say that they couldn't find Safronchuk and that Moscow was waiting. He asked me to transmit the cable.

I told him it would look very odd to Moscow if my signature appeared on the cable, since I was not the Ambassador to the UN. I said that I would send the cable if he insisted, but advised him to wait a little longer for Safronchuk to show up.

Safronchuk soon appeared, and the ridiculous episode was settled. He was reprimanded for his breach, but the bookkeeper was sent home. Eventually, however, he was recalled; he wanted to divorce his wife and marry the bookkeeper. As a punishment—common in such cases—Safronchuk was demoted and sent to Afghanistan to serve as minister-counselor at the Soviet Embassy. Later he was rehabilitated and appointed chief of the ministry's Middle Eastern Countries Department.

The cumbersome rules that had caused Ovinnikov and others at the Mission such distress were burdensome and inefficient, but for every rule there is an exception, even for the rule of secrecy. Ours was made for the convenience of Andrei Gromyko. Whenever he came to New York, which he did at least once a year for the opening session of the UN General Assembly, all of the most sensitive diplomatic messages followed him. Just when security should have been tightest, it was systematically violated. Communications were brought to Gromyko not only in the ambassador's office, which he preempted for his stay, but also in the special four-room residential apartment at the Mission reserved for his use. Moreover, he had the cables typed out. When security men protested to Vasily Makarov, he suggested they raise the matter with Gromyko himself. No one would dare, of course. Obviously, a minister, a Politburo member, could not be expected to read some clerk's handwriting.

Another exception was made for Malik. Whereas the rest of us made it a point not to use the precise wording of any cable that set out the policy we were to present, Malik tried to stick to the verbatim text. And since his memory might fail him, he would copy complicated instructions almost word for word into a notebook he always kept in his coat pocket.

While the Soviet obsession with secrecy often irritated me, the Western—particularly American—indifference to elementary security rules struck me as dangerously careless. Some Western diplomats often brought classified cables into Security Council and other UN meetings and read them while other delegates talked. Not only could I glance at the documents my neighbors held in front of them, but, more important, the KGB could photograph them from the interpreters' booths high up in the Council chamber. When security officers from the Soviet Mission warned me not to take any secret material into the UN conference rooms because it could easily be copied from above, I knew instinctively that they were talking about a standard KGB practice, which, they assumed, the West also used. Whenever I saw an American, British, or other diplomat take a stack of papers out of his briefcase during a Council session, I was appalled at his lack of caution.

Another aspect of the preoccupation with secrecy was that it produced poorly briefed diplomats. Soviet ambassadors were not generally knowledgeable beyond matters of their direct responsibility. As far as I knew, Dobrynin was the only exception. Malik envied him tremendously.

Equally, Soviet diplomats were not officially informed as to how their proposals or reports were received in Moscow. There was no praise or encouragement, only occasional reprimands. One could likewise expect no in-depth explanation of why a suggestion had been rejected. There was either silence or a peremptory "Not acceptable. You should do . . ."

An ambassadorial rank meant a great deal in the Soviet system. I was Under Secretary General and also an ambassador of the U.S.S.R. The Mission provided me a car and a permanent chauffeur, a maid, and in addition to my New York apartment, my family and I had another at Glen Cove —all paid for by the Soviet government. Anna was chauffeured to school in my car, as was Lina on her shopping expeditions.

Anna both enjoyed and disliked living in New York. She was an avid reader and quickly went through many of the Russian-language books available in the Mission library. She soon began to read in English as well. She liked going to movies and to the Metropolitan and Natural History museums. She also loved to play on the beach at Bayville, close to Glen Cove, and became a determined if not always successful fisherman. Yet the Soviet colony's isolated pattern of existence in New York often caused her loneliness. She watched much more television in New York for entertainment than she did in Moscow. For our curious, intelligent, and lively daughter, her parents' attention was not enough. But the circle of friends permitted Anna, like all Soviet children, was very limited.

At this time, Gennady was in Moscow studying at MGIMO. He visited us during his summer vacations, but although he and Anna were good friends, Gennady was ten years older and their interests differed. Before he graduated from the institute in 1975, I arranged for him to take a few months' practical diplomatic training at the Secretariat. He enjoyed his stint at the UN, and all of us were happy to be together in New York.

Gennady was a good student with an inquiring mind. He had become interested in disarmament. His plans were to obtain an advanced degree and then become a diplomat. Lina and I were proud that he seemed to be developing solidly. He was already becoming independent from the family unit, as was right for a young man his age. He made new acquaintances and renewed old ones while he was with us in New York, and was accepted into the adult society of the Soviet community.

But Anna, coming into her teens, needed friends her own

age. She also wanted freedom to explore things beyond the limits of our apartments and her school. There was a vexing lack of opportunity for that in New York. Soviet adults could at least go out in groups on their own—to work, to shop, or just to walk. Soviet children were much more constrained. They were never allowed to go on the shortest errand unchaperoned.

Soviet youngsters were not permitted to establish close contacts with American children, of course. But neither were relationships encouraged with children of diplomats from other socialist countries. Furthermore, if Soviet girls and boys of her age whom Anna wanted to befriend were children of lower-ranking diplomats, she was not allowed to invite them to the Glen Cove estate for the weekend. Only the *nachalstvo* (bosses) and their families lived there, and there were not many children of Anna's age among them. Cooped up in our apartment in New York, Anna looked forward to her weekends at Glen Cove, where there was at least the entertainment of the beach. The *nachalstvo* likewise did not mix with the families of the staff at Glen Cove. The superintendent, cooks, gardeners, maids, drivers, and their families were *dvornya* (domestics) for the diplomatic elite, and lived in much the same relationship with them as they had with the nobles of tsarist Russia.

Suspicion, customary in society in the U.S.S.R., loomed larger among the Soviet community in New York. It consisted of more than seven hundred people who worked at the Mission, the UN Secretariat, the Consulate General, the Amtorg Trading Corporation, Intourist, Tass, etc. The reason for the heightened distrust was that nearly everyone wanted to stay in New York as long as possible, and a misstep could mean recall. At all costs they strove to avoid any criticism. Practically any fellow Soviet—not just the KGB —was a potential *stukach* (informer). In addition, the fear of being demoted (with a smaller salary) for something, no matter how trivial, was real. An anti-Soviet anecdote, "bourgeois consumerism," lack of zeal in one's work, admiring "decadent" American art or films too overtly, or the crime of crimes: seeing an X-rated movie—these potential charges drove Soviets to elaborate caution. Most of us spent time only with a few close, trusted friends, if one had them at all. Compartmentalized through distrust, but nevertheless existing in a goldfish bowl, life for the Soviet colony was dull, monotonous, stewed in its own juice.

While retribution could be swift, Soviets were still human beings. Mission personnel were admonished to avoid various discount clothing and appliance stores on the lower East Side, but since that was where the bargains were, it was also where the Soviets went. Although it was strictly forbidden, diplomats browsed in bookstores where "seditious" Russian literature was sold, furtively but daily read the New York émigré paper, *Novoye Russkoye Slovo* (New Russian Word), and patronized pornography shops, X-rated movies, and the Times Square nude shows. But these were the daring ones. The majority preferred to adjust to their bleak existence.

Adding to the tedium were endless meetings and all sorts of gatherings at the Mission. We had regular Party meetings to attend, several each month, indoctrination sessions in the "system of Party studies," joint celebrations of Soviet holidays. Seeing the latest Soviet movies in the Mission's overcrowded cinema hall, or at Glen Cove, with the same familiar faces in the audience, provided little recreation. I had never realized that someone might be interested in whether or not one attended these films until our Party secretary pointed out that people didn't see me there very much. Our claustrophobic existence, breeding gossip, suspicion, frustration, and boredom, easily led to mountains being made of molehills and promoted malice among people who, if let alone, would not have stooped to such craven witch-hunting.

Someone once theorized that it was not man's discovery of fire that enabled him to advance beyond primitivism but the invention of the fireplace. This allowed an individual to leave the common fire and retire to a separate room which had its own source of heat. Thus privacy was born. The theory was that privacy made an important contribution to the advance of civilization, permitting quiet thought and the intellectual children of that process, and also providing a healing atmosphere of peaceful solitude and allowing for expression of individuality. I do not recall the further development of the idea, but having experienced the institutionalized togetherness of a society which in fact abhors privacy as a detestable promoter of variation, I champion the notion.

Sometimes there were "evenings of friendship" with mission staffs of other socialist countries. But we never really became intimate; relations were not frank; distance was the rule. Diplomats from these countries were also excluded from our Party meetings. So much for the unity of socialist proletarian parties.

Yet, the United States was a candy store for our diplomats. During their short tours of duty they amassed an unbelievable amount of goods unavailable or too expensive in the U.S.S.R. In the late seventies, the average wage of mid-level diplomats in Moscow was 200–250 rubles ($270–$280) per month. But with a $700–$800 monthly salary in New York it was possible to purchase many things far beyond their reach at home. One could buy a Soviet car for about $2,000 equivalent if it was paid for in U.S. dollars and receive it upon returning to Moscow. In the Soviet Union, the time spent on a waiting list for an automobile is three to ten years and it costs more than 10,000 rubles ($13,000–$14,000). Automatic washing machines (still almost nonexistent and only semiautomatic), dishwashers, cameras, stereo systems, records, cassettes, crates of baby food and disposable diapers, irons, china, tissues and toilet paper, clothes, shoes, fabrics to be stored and made up in future years, were transported to the U.S.S.R. And everyone bought extra items that could be resold on Moscow's black market for large sums. From ambassadors to the lowliest clerks at the Mission, all regularly sent thousands of pounds of goods home.

In order to do that, of course, those paid at low rates severely economized on everything from their daily diets to entertainment. The problem of saving money was almost always on their minds, their permanent and often obsessive preoccupation.

Diplomatic personnel could make their money go further than Americans because they paid no taxes and because they were skillful, relentless bargain hunters. Their housing and medical care were inexpensive or free. But the medical care was often woefully inadequate. The Mission maintained a general internist in residence. There were also some medical people recruited from the Soviet community to aid him. Diplomats' wives with medical or nursing training were employed as the doctor's assistants. However, this did not really constitute effective medical care. To add to the difficulties, in case of real need it was not that easy to obtain authorization to see an American specialist. An entire bureaucratic and administrative ritual had to be gone through to get permission. In any sudden emergency, of course, a Soviet would be sent to an American specialist, but if someone became seriously ill and there was no immediate danger, the Soviets preferred to return him to Moscow so that dollars were not spent on medical treatment in New York.

The Soviet government likewise covered the housing expenses of diplomats and Secretariat staff members. But the fixed limits for renting apartments ($350–$400 average) were so low that it was hard to find a decent one. They were forced to lease apartments in areas of New York inconvenient to transportation and in locations they did not desire. Moreover, these apartments generally did not meet their needs. Frequently, a family with children rented a two-room or even a one-room apartment.

In the early seventies, the Soviets built a residential apartment house in Riverdale. But they cut so many corners to save money during construction that the building was not suited to the climate. In winter, the apartments were so cold that many residents bought electric space heaters. These wasted so much electricity and were so expensive to operate that often people bundled up in layers of sweaters or coats.

Soviet authorities tried to cram into the Riverdale building as many of their diplomats and UN staff members as possible. It was much easier to observe and control them than if they were on their own in the city. But there were so many Soviets in New York that neither the Riverdale building nor the Mission could house them all.

Such hardships did not much affect KGB officers. It was easier to hide their real identities if they rented apartments in other parts of the city. Since they received special subsidies, they did not suffer the financial strictures of most other Soviets. If a Soviet invited a non-Soviet to his apartment, it could be assumed that the host or hostess was an intelligence officer. With few exceptions, they were the only Soviets permitted such latitude in their activities and the only ones who could afford it. As Under Secretary General, I became acquainted with many more of these officers and had the opportunity to follow KGB operations in the United States more closely than at any previous time in my career.

21

IT IS NORMAL FOR A NATION TO HAVE AN INTELLIGENCE service or secret police. But the Soviet KGB is different from such institutions in other countries. Its scope is enormous. It is one of the most experienced and certainly one of the most ruthless organizations on earth. Its functions are comparable to most of those belonging to the CIA, the FBI, the Secret Service, and parts of the Department of Justice and Department of Defense combined.

The initials "KGB" stand for the Russian words for "Committee of State Security," a title the secret police have used since 1954. With the exception of its decline in status and influence in the first years after Stalin's death and Beria's execution, the KGB has been indispensable to the regime. The policies and failures of Soviet leadership after Stalin made restoration of the KGB necessary; the logic of Communist rule made it inevitable. To control a population it could no longer inspire, the Kremlin relied upon security police and informers. To obtain military secrets and advanced technology it could not develop efficiently at home, it employed espionage abroad. To subvert governments it did not persuade through normal interaction, the U.S.S.R.

fielded a secret force—of mercenaries as well as Soviets—
to advance its international goals. The global scale of KGB
operations is larger than the intelligence activities of all the
Western nations combined. Besides more than 100,000
professionals, the KGB has a specially trained elite army of
roughly 500,000. They are equipped with the latest weapons,
tanks, and artillery. They guard frontiers, the Kremlin, and
other major government offices and installations throughout
the U.S.S.R.

To protect and expand its power, the Soviet leadership
abdicated a considerable portion of it. The security police
does not run the state, but it has gained considerable leverage over the visible rulers. This is not the macabre alliance
of Stalin and Beria; the new men are more sophisticated,
less thuggish. But their power is no less great or menacing.
Secret emperors, they have not yet overcome the Politburo's power, but their ambition is strong. It was no accident
that in the maneuvering to succeed Leonid Brezhnev, Yuri
Andropov became the General Secretary.

The key to the KGB's resuscitation is in its function as a
domestic watchdog. Georgy Vladimov, once an officially
acclaimed Soviet writer, wrote a searing novella, *Faithful
Ruslan*, circulated secretly in typescript in the mid-sixties,
which told the KGB's story in allegory. Vladimov created a
guard dog, the Ruslan of the title, who had spent years shep-
herding prisoners in a Stalin-era concentration camp only to
lose his trade and *raison d'être* when the camps were dis-
banded by Khrushchev. Ruslan, however, knows only one
relationship to human beings and reassumes it even without
the barbed wire and stockades of the Gulag system. He
becomes a snarling, implacable watchdog of supposedly free
men.

So, too, the secret police exercise preventive supervision
of the population and its loyalty. The KGB could not halt
the alienation that grew among the Soviet people as Khrushchev's and Brezhnev's expansive promises of well-being
went unfulfilled. The "GehBeh," as the organization is
nicknamed after its initials, has been powerless to choke off
the grumbling of consumers who stand in long lines for
goods that are not being produced in sufficient quantity or

312

decent quality. Nor has it been able to arrest the spreading loss of faith in the regime's slogans and doctrines.

But it can report what is happening to the leadership, arrest or intimidate the few vocal malcontents who surface openly, and try to cut down the spread of an underground literature which, in the rulers' eyes, carries the seed of disobedience. The more disquieting evidence it produces, of course, the more the KGB justifies its own existence and its insistence on larger budgets, greater manpower. Since there really has been trouble—a food riot in Novocherkassk in 1962 being one violent manifestation of the people's sour mood—the leadership has acquiesced to the KGB's demands. It was easy, as well as consistent with tradition, to put resources into police work rather than work out and implement the fundamental social and political reforms which might have restored dwindling enthusiasm and economic hopes.

Distrust comes naturally to the Soviet leaders as a by-product of the general distrust pervading Soviet society from the lowest to the highest echelons, from childhood through old age. Moreover, as the leaders ascend in rank and importance, their suspicions and wariness increase at every step; the more privileged they are, the more they have to lose. They fear on every side that someone, even their closest friends, will betray them.

As guardians and enforcers of security, the KGB has veto power over hiring for sensitive posts. Without a security clearance, no student can enter MGIMO, no official can assume management responsibilities in a defense-related industry, no diplomat can gain a foreign assignment, no ordinary citizen can obtain a passport for travel abroad. A taint of suspicion can block the most promising career.

Even the top men in Moscow are constrained by the role the KGB plays in their daily lives. The *Vertushka*, the Kremlin telephone system, is installed, maintained, and, inevitably, monitored by the secret police. Their agents serve as bodyguards, chauffeurs, cooks, valets, and maids to Politburo members, guaranteeing not only security but surveillance.

The elite and the top leadership at once need the KGB

and fear it. They need it for the preservation of the system and the suppression of any opposition. They fear it because the KGB is omniscient and omnipresent. In its secret archives, the KGB preserves each tidbit it obtains about all of the more or less important persons in the Party and state. It has the power to compel anything it seriously wishes from almost anyone, using compromising facts from one's personal life or details of various "dirty deeds," in which almost all Soviet leaders—from local ones to those in the Kremlin—are implicated in one way or another.

After Stalin's death, Aleksandr M. Shelepin and later Vladimir Y. Semichastny tried to improve the organization's image. But the crucial role in the new revival of state security and intelligence operations was played by Yuri Andropov, who was the first KGB head since Beria to gain full membership in the Politburo in 1973.

When Andropov became KGB chairman in 1967, I was working at the Soviet Mission to the UN in New York. KGB officers were openly joyful upon hearing about Andropov's appointment as their chief. "At last we've got a strong man as our leader again," one of them said to me. At first, I was surprised that so many KGB officers had immediately accepted Andropov as one of them. He had no background either in the agency or in the military. I finally realized that his previous position in the Central Committee as supervisor of the Soviet bloc empire was closely linked with KGB functions. They knew their man.

As one of his first steps, Andropov restored discipline within KGB ranks, which had become somewhat loose after Beria's fall. He forbade drinking on duty, and I noticed that KGB officers stopped coming to the Mission drunk.

Andropov had a general reputation as one of the most intellectual of Politburo members. People who worked with him agreed that he was intelligent, inventive, and well educated. Observing him at various functions, I could not help but admire how masterfully he created a presence both elusive and good-natured. Andropov's style was different from that of the men who had previously run the KGB. He did not "order" but "suggested," avoiding a peremptory tone. That softness, however, was misleading. According to some

314

of his personal assistants I knew well, he was a man of strong will, self-confident and decisive. An aide summed up his character by comparing it to a fine feather bed you jump into only to find that the mattress is filled with bricks.

To all appearances he and his wife and son (who graduated from MGIMO in the late sixties) were quiet, unassuming people. But coexisting with his cultivated exterior was something cold and implacable.

I never heard from anyone that Andropov favored liberalization of any policy, even of the limited type experimented with by Khrushchev, or advocated any substantial economic reform. In fact, his merciless suppression of dissent and his strong opposition to political pluralism in the U.S.S.R. belie the image of the art-loving sophisticate softened by a civilized intellect. The actions of the KGB, none of which would have been taken without Andropov's approval, were old, unsophisticated cruelties, and they continued unabated during his tenure as KGB chief.

Moreover, Andropov was harder than Brezhnev in certain respects. One of Brezhnev's assistants told me his boss had not quite realized how widespread the practice was of incarcerating political dissidents in mental institutions. This was an area directly under Andropov's control. While I was Gromyko's adviser, I was involved in the work of the commission charged with revising the Soviet constitution. Andropov categorically objected to even studying the possibility of a change in the Soviet electoral system which would permit, in some cases, nomination of two candidates for one post in various Soviet bodies instead of the traditional single-candidate procedure. Brezhnev had been willing to consider it.

Andropov largely succeeded in restoring the KGB's power. He also increased its foreign agent machinery two or three times over. Previously KGB *rezidenti* abroad were content with a junior or mid-level diplomat's rank as cover, but Andropov elevated them to more important administrative positions with a corresponding increase in power.

At the New York Mission in the mid-sixties, the KGB *rezident,* Boris Ivanov, was disguised as a "counselor." His replacement in 1967, Nikolai Kulebiakin, was "U.S.S.R. Deputy Permanent Representative to the United Nations."

I remember many KGB expressions of satisfaction over Andropov's performance. I also recall being alarmed by the agents' growing numbers and influence. They were the most reactionary, conformist guardians of the existing "socialist order" in the Soviet Union. I had known all the top KGB in New York and Washington and most of its senior officials ever since I joined the diplomatic service. It was obvious, whether in private or in public, how cynical, power-hungry, and anti-liberal they were. And they had been unquestionably selected or approved by Andropov personally.

Under Andropov, the KGB expanded its methods for getting people "on the hook." This meant blackmailing them to force their cooperation, using compromising materials, a great many of which were inflated petty infractions or just plain manufactured stories. I knew about such KGB activities, but I never anticipated being involved in one of them.

In the spring of 1973, however, a month or so before I was due to leave Moscow for my new job, the KGB made a determined and disturbing effort to bring me under its control. I received a summons to report to General Boris Semyonovich Ivanov, the former New York *rezident*. He was then deputy head of the KGB's First Chief Directorate, the foreign operations arm. It was the first time I had seen the inside of the Lubyanka headquarters. That fortresslike edifice, an insurance company before 1917, continues to be, in a sense, a supplier of political insurance.

From the time when the Foreign Ministry was located near Lubyanka, diplomats had spoken of the KGB as "near neighbors" and the GRU, the military intelligence operation, as "far neighbors." By 1973 the ministry had moved to the other side of downtown Moscow and the distances between it and the KGB and the GRU were reversed. Nevertheless, the term "neighbors" survived, for the security police remained very much part of the geography of Soviet foreign policy.

On the morning of my appointment with Ivanov a black Volga sedan from the ministry car pool took me to the rear entrance of the KGB complex. A polite young man in civilian clothes but of obvious military bearing led me up a broad staircase through dimly lit, labyrinthine corridors to the general's second-floor office. The atmosphere was oppressive. The dark paneling seemed a continuation of the camouflage green of the bleak hallways. An oriental carpet, sofa, armchairs, and tea table were unable to impart much cheer to the cavernous room.

Ivanov, however, exuded hospitality when he emerged from an inner study to greet me like an old friend. (In fact, we had known each other only slightly in New York.) After a waitress served us brandy and mineral water, lemons, and pastries, he raised his glass in a toast. "Congratulations on your new assignment." He smiled. "We're counting on your help."

Ivanov made no bones about his interest in the UN and in me. "I don't have to tell you, Arkady Nikolaevich, that the United Nations is our best watchtower in the West," he said. "Our people there collect valuable information about the United States and other countries. You'll have a special opportunity to get to know Americans and other Westerners in your job. And you can help promote our officers in the Secretariat and protect them in case the CIA or FBI tries to make trouble for them."

He had my role all worked out. I knew, of course, that there were benefits to cooperating with the KGB. The organization helps its "friends," with good recommendations, promotions, extra money. But I wanted no part of Ivanov's proposal. Ever since Khrushchev had exposed Stalin's crimes and Beria's role in them, I had associated the KGB with murder at home and terrorism abroad. From my experiences overseas I had learned to loathe the KGB's mistrust and disdain of their fellow citizens. And its political reporting—both what I had seen in New York in the sixties and what I had read as Gromyko's adviser—had earned my contempt.

I knew better, of course, than to be so blunt with Ivanov and his associate, Vladimir Kazakov, who joined our talk. He was an American specialist who had been my theoretical subordinate at the Mission in the mid-sixties but had worked full time on KGB assignments. (He returned to the Mission

317

in 1980 as *resident*.) "My first priority in New York," I said carefully, "has to be the work of the Secretariat. My department is in poor shape. Its quality has to be upgraded if I'm going to have any influence on Waldheim."

Ivanov's round face wrinkled into a derisive grin. "That's something to aim for," he replied, "but it's hardly worth too much trouble on your part. After all, that's just work for a 'foreign uncle.' The West is always going to dominate the Secretariat, and we'll never succeed in reeducating Waldheim. He's no ally of ours. He never will be."

I was silent as he poured another round of brandy for us. Then he reached into his pocket and pulled out two letters. "These will interest you," he said, handing them to me. "We don't take them seriously, of course, but we thought you should know about them."

I read the letters in silence. One, in Russian and addressed to the Party Central Committee, denounced me for a life-style that could not be maintained, the anonymous author claimed, on my official income. Moreover, the accusation continued, my apartment was full of old religious pictures—"How can a Communist decorate his home with icons?"—and both my wife and daughter had been heard to express anti-Communist attitudes, praising life in the United States and criticizing the Soviet system. Along with these "signs of a bad family atmosphere" went my own conduct in New York; allegedly my contacts with Americans were too cordial.

The second letter, typewritten in English and addressed to me, was meant as a clever complement to the first. Purporting to be from an American, but unsigned, it "reminded" me of a promise I had supposedly given the writer at the previous session of the UN General Assembly to help a Russian Jew identified only as "Tamara" to emigrate. The letter mentioned both the sum of $1,000 it said I had already received for my services and the role of go-between played by a U.S. government official.

Together the two letters were damning—if true. Thanks to Lina's business acumen and taste, our apartment was ornamented with icons and we did live conspicuously well. She and Anna probably had made unflattering comparisons between the United States and the U.S.S.R., and I did have a number of acquaintances among the Americans at the UN. But there was no Tamara, no $1,000 bribe, and no promise of mine to help anyone leave the Soviet Union. The U.S. official did exist, however, and thus the implied accusation was that I was enriching myself counter to the laws of my country in collaboration with the representative of an enemy power.

The letters, in short, had to be the work of someone who knew me in New York and in Moscow and who wanted to ruin me. Leonid Kutakov, the luxury-loving incompetent who had held and wanted to keep the UN job I was to take, was the logical suspect. His Moscow apartment was in the same building as ours. His wife, Aza, had visited Lina on occasion. And he would know that by addressing the letter in English to Apartment 32 in our building, it would be sure to reach the KGB. Our apartment number was 52. The tenant of number 32 was a KGB officer.

My first reaction to the letters was fury. "What is this shit?" I demanded. "And how did you get a letter addressed to me? Is someone stealing my mail?"

Ivanov was instantly soothing. "Now, now, Arkady Nikolaevich," he intoned, "there's no problem. You have nothing to worry about. We wouldn't have shown you the letters if we didn't have complete faith in you. We just thought you might have some idea of who wrote them. And the one addressed to you, look," he said, pointing to the address, "it gave the wrong apartment number. The person who received it is a vigilant sort, and since it was from abroad, he turned it over to us."

Although I suspected Kutakov, I said nothing. Anonymous denunciations had sent thousands to their death in Stalin's time.

"I don't know who in hell did it," I told Ivanov, "but it has to be someone who knows me and my family, and the United Nations and the Americans there."

"Couldn't it be an effort by the FBI to compromise you?" he asked.

I shook my head. That theory made little sense.

"All right," Ivanov said, his lips set in a line, "we'll make

319

a full investigation of this affair. We'll instruct New York to check the typing against the machines which Soviets at the Mission and at the UN can use. If we find out who wrote these, we'll punish them."

The conversation was over, but as I got up to leave, Ivanov remarked casually, "You know, Arkady Nikolaevich, you shouldn't be so keen on collecting icons. And it might be a good idea, too, if you spoke to your womenfolk. They have to watch their tongues. You're going to be in a prominent position there in New York. You have to set an example for others."

His words carried an obvious threat. I was to be under close scrutiny. I had to conform to the KGB's standards of behavior. And if I failed to cooperate with General Ivanov and his organization, the false accusations from the KGB file could easily be revived. The whole point of letting me see the letters was to show me the hook on which I was meant to wriggle. To enlist me in their service, they displayed the power they held over me.

The KGB would have no real interest in uncovering the author of the letters. But to remove the hook, I had to find and discredit my accuser. Initially Boris Solomatin, the *rezident* when I arrived in New York, had seemed cooperative. He knew about the letters and promised me action to identify their source. As months passed without further word, however, I became angrier and more worried. Finally, I confronted him with my opinion of the ineptitude of his detective work. He revealed that his agents had long before discovered that the letter written in English had been typed on the office machine of Kutakov's UN secretary. She had even admitted to her part in the scheme.

But she was still on the Secretariat staff, I pointed out, and Kutakov, as far as I knew, had never been punished except by the failure of his effort to prevent my replacing him. I wanted justice, I insisted to Solomatin. What I really wanted was a written KGB report on the matter, one which would exonerate me and neutralize the letters as a KGB hold over me.

That final release, of course, Solomatin would not grant. Not only would he not pursue the matter further, he advised me strongly to leave the subject alone. "The Center knows all about it," he said. "That's enough. It's taken care of."

I persisted. "It's not enough for me. I was the one slandered. I have my name to protect. The investigation should be formally ended with a finding of my innocence."

"We all know you're innocent," Solomatin replied. "There are no charges against you and no need to go through a lot of paperwork to erase something that doesn't exist. Take my advice, Arkady." His voice was firm. "Just let it drop. It's over and done with, and no one's been hurt."

I had to let it drop. Solomatin had voiced a standard and compelling bureaucratic justification for covering up a minor mess that was neither his doing nor his to undo. For me to have pushed further would only have earned me a reputation in Moscow as a nuisance. No one wanted to be bothered; no one wanted any fuss. I would only be making trouble for myself.

TOP ESPIONAGE AGENTS MAINTAINED A LARGE PRESENCE IN New York, particularly in the UN Secretariat. Yakov Malik once told me of having informed Vyacheslav Molotov in 1946 that the Secretary General, Trygve Lie, had invited the Soviet Union to fill its quota of Soviet citizens to work in the newly established Secretariat. Molotov, Malik claimed, responded disparagingly that the U.S.S.R. should not waste valuable diplomatic talent in the Secretariat's bureaucracy. Molotov's decision was a mistake soon rectified. Moscow eventually realized that the UN apparatus was a unique spot for locating an intelligence network. Unlike Molotov, the KGB was eager to furnish unlimited personnel to the Secretariat.

A job in the Secretariat had a special advantage. Unlike officials at the Mission, the embassy in Washington, or the consulate in San Francisco, Soviet nationals connected to the UN could travel freely in the United States without having to notify U.S. authorities of their schedules or itineraries.

It was easy to distinguish KGB professionals from diplomats and others. The first giveaway was money. The KGB had it and spent it much more generously than real diplomats. A Foreign Ministry employee would need to hoard the dollar portion of his salary for as much as a year or more before he could afford to buy a used American car. KGB agents had the cash to get one as soon as they arrived in New York. They also had money to entertain lavishly. A mid-level Mission or Secretariat staffer who is regularly seen treating non-Soviets to round after round of drinks is almost certainly using KGB funds. And if the generous host or hostess is well dressed, there can be little doubt. Only the KGB pays its people well enough for them to afford the best in Western clothing.

The clothes they wear and the drinks they buy are legitimate expenses, because the second thing that gives away an intelligence operative is the effort he makes to cultivate foreigners. The recruiting specialists and the regular intelligence gatherers are supposed to meet as many people as they can outside the UN—scholars, businessmen, journalists, scientists, all kinds of experts, military men, and so on. To do their job, they have to be able to fit into an American setting. If their language is good enough, and it usually is, they'll try to pass themselves off as Westerners. Soviets who take a lot of trips are almost certainly sending their reports and expense accounts to the Lubyanka headquarters or the General Staff of the Defense Ministry.

Moreover, full-time intelligence men were easily recognizable in casual conversation. If a Soviet official didn't know the details and the jargon of the field in which he was supposedly working, or if he showed he wasn't really up on events of general interest around the UN, it was safe to assume his real work was spying. I was often surprised at how badly briefed KGB agents were. It was almost as if they didn't care about keeping their cover believable.

Ironically, I had complained to senior KGB and Mission officials. The nonchalance with which agents approached their supposed jobs on East Sixty-seventh Street or at UN headquarters angered me. Their lack of briefing was their own fault. They always said they had too little time to learn about current issues.

When I was their theoretical supervisor as chief of the

political section at the Mission in the sixties, I regularly protested the heavy workload that fell on my real staff because the KGB agents assigned to political work so rarely performed it.

Out of twenty-eight men in the section in 1968, twenty-one were KGB or GRU agents. Vladimir Kazakov, General Ivanov's future aide, was among the most forthright of them. When I insisted that he owed me some of his time, he simply said, "Don't give me any specific assignments. I can't be obligated that way. I'll probably miss most of your staff meetings. I'm sorry about it, but maybe some of the others can help you more."

As Under Secretary General, I found the situation unchanged, except that I had become the target of others' complaints. A Soviet official who failed to carry out his routine assignments for the Secretariat made his foreign colleagues angry. They had to pick up his share of the work, but unlike the compliant Soviet personnel at the Mission, they griped loudly, and to me.

There were some UN departments that didn't really mind when Soviets didn't show up for work. The work might actually flow more easily if it could be done without having to check it with a Soviet staff man. Sometimes these KGB agents would call in sick and stay out of the office for days at a time or just walk away from their desks in the middle of the day and disappear.

I had raised the issue with KGB *rezidenti* and Soviet ambassadors in a variety of ways. With Fedorenko and Malik, both powerless to change secret police practices, I had argued my case as a professional. "Damn it," I had once burst out to Malik, "these guys act as if they don't care. They don't even try to keep a fig leaf of cover over who they really are. They're so sloppy people just laugh at them around the UN." For once, Malik didn't get irritated, but shrugged helplessly.

With Boris Solomatin, when he was *rezident*, I took a different but equally unsuccessful tack. It was not my job to tell KGB men how to protect themselves, but I did have a formal rule to invoke. "You know," I pressed Solomatin once, "there's a regulation approved by the Central Committee stipulating that your people serving as Foreign Ministry staff are to give at least one-third of their time to their formal diplomatic jobs. It's a good rule but it's not being followed. And it's creating bad feelings in a lot of places. We're all supposed to be working together, but your people don't cooperate, and mine have to pick up the pieces.''

Solomatin's response was typical. ''Our work comes first, Arkady Nikolaevich. It's the most important job around here. We try to help you out, but you have to understand what's going on. Intelligence is top priority for all of us in New York. The UN doesn't matter; it's how we can use it to find out what we want. That's why we're here.''

Such disdain was common among top KGB officers as their organization gained more autonomy and bureaucratic weight in Moscow over the years. Once, however, it had brought one New York *rezident* to ruin. Nikolai Kulebiakin, a trim, cultivated man in his mid-fifties when he served in New York, decided to speak for the Soviet Union at a meeting of a UN General Assembly special committee on Palestinian refugees in the autumn of 1968. As it happened, his address was reported in the home press and he was mentioned as a Soviet spokesman at the UN.

The publicity, however, brought his downfall. A school friend from his native Odessa wrote authorities in Moscow to ask if the N. P. Kulebiakin representing the U.S.S.R. in New York was the same one who had obtained a false certificate of medical disability to exempt him from service in World War II and who had also forged his university diploma. An investigation disclosed that Kulebiakin was, in fact, a draft evader and an academic fraud. Recalled to Moscow, he was expelled by both the Party and his embarrassed employers, stripped of his medals, and denied a pension. After an appeal and a plea for forgiveness, he got his decorations back and part of his pension restored and was given a part-time job in KGB training programs. But the episode, as far as I could tell, did nothing to teach humility to any of his KGB associates.

On the contrary, the KGB respected no one else. They thought of me and other diplomats as tools for them to use. I couldn't prove it, but I suspected that they took my car

324

occasionally to use as cover in their work. It was true that my driver would only infrequently appear in a car other than my official one, but he would make these changes without notice, offering a hollow-sounding excuse that my automobile needed repair. I knew the KGB regularly "borrowed" diplomats' cars for their agents. Once in 1968 I made such a furious scene, accusing them of compromising my legitimate status, that I think they left my car alone afterwards. But I was never sure.

Soviet spies also made it a practice to ask UN diplomats, including non-Soviets, to give them lifts from the United Nations garage to other parts of the city. Riding in someone else's car, they could shake Americans from their trail and disappear unobserved into Manhattan's busy streets. I always resented it when one of the KGB agents would disingenuously ask me for a ride—"if you're going uptown toward the Mission, Arkady Nikolaevich"—but I could not very well refuse the request or protest when my passenger asked to be dropped off before we got to Sixty-seventh Street.

I had a pretty fair sense of the focus of KGB political reporting and a sideline view of the extensive efforts to recruit or co-opt non-Soviets as informants or eventual agents. Although I had to provide posts in my own UN department for a number of KGB and GRU men—nine out of twelve Soviets as well as a Czech, a Hungarian, an East German, and a Bulgarian under my supervision were intelligence professionals or co-opted by the KGB and GRU—I was not certain as to the exact nature of their espionage duties.

Their routine political intelligence gathering was orchestrated by a set of questions cabled daily from Moscow to the *rezident* and relayed by him to his subordinates at a morning staff meeting. The bogus diplomats could later be seen buttonholing people in the UN corridors, going through their shopping list item by item. It was transparent, and it rarely seemed to elicit information, from UN sources at least, that the Mission regulars were not obtaining as well.

The point of all this effort, I eventually recognized, was to score points with the leadership by producing information (and lots of gossip) in bulk. It enabled the KGB to overwhelm the relatively smaller amount of data supplied by the Foreign Ministry and by military intelligence operations, thereby justifying the expense of maintaining a huge spy network overseas. It was bureaucratic gamesmanship which may well have impressed some of the less sophisticated men at the top. It did not have that effect on Andrei Gromyko.

Not long after I started working as Gromyko's adviser, I began studying KGB political-reporting cables from New York to get some idea of their quality.* It was frequently poor. Names and ranks of UN diplomats and officials were sometimes given incorrectly. A lack of understanding of political problems was obvious. U.S. Communist Party sources were quoted as authoritative analysts of American political developments. The KGB contingent in Washington, working closely with Ambassador Dobrynin, did a markedly better job. When I mentioned my observations to another Gromyko aide, I learned that KGB output was less than universally respected in Moscow policymaking circles. "Don't worry about it, Arkady," my associate told me. "Andrei Andreyevich doesn't pay much attention to most of that crap."

Solomatin maintained close ties with the *rezident* in Washington, Colonel Dmitri Yakushkin, who was later promoted to major general. Technically, neither one was senior, and to a certain extent they competed with each other. But they tried to coordinate their operations as much as possible. However, it seemed to me that the *rezident* in New York was more independent and in a sense more prominent in the KGB hierarchy; he had many more personnel in New York than his counterpart did in Washington. Further, the anonymity offered by the size of New York City made it a better base for espionage operations than Washington. An additional factor was that Dobrynin, unlike the Soviet representative to the UN, was a ranking politician and a member of the Central Committee, not simply an ambassador. As such, he exercised a certain degree of control over the

---

* These cables, a single copy of each, were delivered to Gromyko's office only. Access to them was restricted to Gromyko's advisers and deputies and chiefs of departments.

KGB in Washington that the New York ambassador could not.

Political reporting, in any event, was not the KGB's primary mission in New York. Espionage, either traditional efforts to acquire military secrets or the newer and increasingly important task of collecting scientific-industrial know-how, was its vital job. Several times a year Moscow would send its American outposts a list of equipment to obtain or areas of scientific research to investigate. The document, usually so technical and complicated in its descriptions of oil drills and compressors, computer parts and micro-electronic gadgetry, that it baffled me and most of the other diplomats, often ran as much as a hundred pages in length and sometimes longer.

KGB agents received more frequent and more specific directives. One veteran spy in the Mission was Aleksei Kulak, whose diplomatic cover had long since been pierced by the FBI. He was also one of the few KGB people whose company I enjoyed—witty, genuinely expert in science and technology, which were his espionage specialty, and unusually frank in conversation about a wide range of subjects.

Kulak hunted for America's advanced knowledge in electronics, biochemistry, physics, and other industrial and defense secrets. Between my move to Moscow in 1970 and my return to New York three years later, I had observed the growth in this kind of activity. Technological espionage had mushroomed, and so had the personnel committed to it.

At Glen Cove alone, the escalation was striking. When I first came to the United States in 1958, there were three or four KGB communications technicians and their gear sharing the former servants' quarters in the attic. By 1973, the specialists in intercepting radio signals numbered at least a dozen, and they had taken over the whole floor. Their equipment occupied so much space, in fact, that one of the two large unused greenhouses had been commandeered to store it. These quarters were off limits to other personnel.

The rooftops at Glen Cove, the apartment building in Riverdale, and the Mission all bristled with antennas for listening to American conversations as well as for transmitting

327

Soviet messages. And the electronic explosion was only a part of the KGB's growth.

The GRU had also expanded its operations. The GRU (*Glavnoye Razvedyvatelnoye Upravleniye*)—the main intelligence directorate of the Ministry of Defense—is not a subsidiary branch of the KGB. It is a separate and powerful organization possessing its own special forces of many thousands for intelligence gathering, sabotage, and terrorist activity. GRU officers boasted of legendary agents like Richard Sorge, who warned Stalin in advance of the imminent German invasion in 1941, and postwar atomic spies in the United States. The GRU network's main interest in the United States and Western Europe is, of course, weapons and the military industry. Here the GRU and KGB often get in each other's way; they are rivals as well as partners.

When I returned to New York in 1973, the local GRU chief was Colonel Viktor Osipov, who used the cover of senior counselor of the Mission. An avid competitor of Solomatin's, he tried to impress Mission officials with his competence in military affairs. For a time, Osipov made periodic reports at staff meetings about the latest U.S. weapons systems. His zeal for the subject angered Solomatin. After one such gathering, Solomatin muttered to me, "Let this colonel bray like the jackass he is. We know a lot more than his guys." Osipov was long on self-importance and short on intellect, and Solomatin soon managed to put a stop to his briefings.

Osipov's successor, Vladimir Moltchanov, was of much higher caliber, but relations between the spy chiefs were always somewhat strained. At the Mission's New Year's Eve party in 1974, I was sitting next to Solomatin at the ambassador's table when a young KGB officer, Vladimir Khrenov, came to shake the *rezident*'s hand and wish him good fortune in the new year. After his aide left, Solomatin, in a drunken, confidence-sharing mood, pointed after him.

"See that guy," he whispered noisily. "I'm really proud of him. He's gotten two decorations in one year." Solomatin did not reveal the nature of Khrenov's feats. A bit later, as Moltchanov and I exchanged toasts, he also said he had heard that Khrenov had collected some information on

America's military space programs. "We sent most of that information home before *them*," he added smugly. The KGB and GRU were not only competitors, they spied on each other.

My relations were generally better with the GRU, whose officers were franker and less sinister. We were on a more equal footing too, because, like the diplomats, they were under KGB surveillance. Major General Ivan Glazkov, a GRU *rezident* in New York in the sixties and my neighbor in the Mission building, complained about it many times. I believe that Glazkov and other GRU officers also envied the KGB because their personnel held higher cover positions at the Mission. At the time Glazkov was only First Secretary.

One GRU agent, Kyrill Chekotillo, was uncovered by the Americans but allowed to stay on the UN payroll as chief of Sea and Ocean Affairs in my department. I suspected he was not just a specialist in these affairs, but I didn't learn his true occupation until the U.S. Mission lodged a formal protest about his conduct.

According to the Americans, Chekotillo had appeared at a marine research institute in New Jersey, claiming to be a West German. He presented a UN identity card that did not reveal his nationality. His purpose was to ingratiate himself with scientists there in order to obtain information on work they were doing under contract to the U.S. Navy.

When I confronted him with the accusation, Chekotillo only went through the motions of denying it. I warned him against compromising his status and mine, but I doubt that he paid much attention. As one of his colleagues told me, "It's not as if we have to do anything illegal most of the time. The Americans are so open, their information is just lying around on the floor all over the place. All you have to do is pick it up."

Besides picking up information themselves, the KGB tried to recruit other UN officials in the Secretariat to do its work. Recruitment was conducted through bribery and blackmail, mostly the former. For a UN Secretariat employee it could begin before he or she even came on the payroll. Since it had its own people in the personnel office of the Department of Administrative Affairs, the KGB could review the files of those seeking a UN job or a promotion. They were looking for exploitable weakness. Viable candidates were referred to a veteran KGB recruiter, Geli Dnyeprovsky, who became the mastermind of UN operations during three New York tours from 1965 to 1978. In 1978, despite energetic, open Western protests, he transferred directly to an equally strategic personnel post in Geneva, overseeing hiring and promotion in the UN's European headquarters.

Dapper, slim, unfailingly courteous, Dnyeprovsky visited me frequently. At least once a month he would begin a circuitous but persistent effort to plant one of his people on my professional staff. He always knew what positions were due to become vacant and always had a reasonable candidate to put forward. But whether he was pushing a Soviet or someone else, I suspected that Dnyeprovsky's applicant was probably co-opted by the KGB.

In most cases I had no solid grounds on which to oppose him. Indeed, some of the people he recommended proved to be good workers. But when Dnyeprovsky argued one day that I should not extend the appointment of my able, experienced administrative assistant, Helen Carlson, I resisted strongly. Although the UN mandates retirement at sixty, it is a fairly common practice to keep on valuable staffers beyond that age. Carlson was more than valuable. She handled a wide range of financial and personnel matters for me with great skill and experience.

Typically, Dnyeprovsky approached the issue indirectly. "We have a real problem, Arkady Nikolaevich," he began. "It's a matter the Secretary General treats very seriously. We just have to cut back on all these extensions people have been getting. We have to make room for others to move up. There are too many complaints. It's bad for morale in the Secretariat."

I kept a straight face. Geli Dnyeprovsky cared as much for morale at the UN as he did for whooping cranes. I knew what he was really after but I did not interrupt his polished flow.

"Now you have this American woman running administrative matters for you. I really think you'd be better off with a Soviet in that job. It's an important post. You ought to have someone you can trust."

"I do trust her, Geli," I replied. "I certainly trust her to do a first-class job. She's been working in this department since Dobrynin was Under Secretary, and no one has ever complained. But if someone new came from Moscow and had to learn the ropes, the place would be a mess in no time."

We sparred for a while longer, neither of us touching the real issue—Dnyeprovsky's determination to have a KGB colleague in the position, someone to work for his organization, not for me. Finally, he left with an appeal to "think it over carefully." He was back a few weeks later, within days after my request to extend Helen Carlson's appointment reached his desk. Again we argued, again I refused, and Dnyeprovsky, always polite, dropped the matter. It was a rare success for me but one which, in time, I had to pay for by accepting another aspirant under his sponsorship.

Most of Dnyeprovsky's and the KGB's acquisitions responded to the offer of a job or extra money for any valuable information they provided. Some of the agents were incredibly sloppy. One Soviet in the Outer Space Division, Oleg Pershikov, even left large amounts of cash lying on his desk to give to those on his payroll.

As far as I could tell, there were only two UN operations in New York where KGB penetration efforts were frustrated. One was the organization's secret archives. Soviet spymasters waged a steady campaign to place their agents in positions which would give them access to the minutes of confidential meetings and to copies of classified cables. Repeatedly the KGB sought my help in this activity, but the decision was never mine to influence.

The Secretary General's office, at least under Kurt Waldheim, also succeeded in resisting Moscow's attempts to extract sensitive information. Even though a KGB colonel, Viktor Lessiovsky, was a special assistant to the UN chief from 1961 to 1973 and again from 1976 onward, Waldheim's intimates froze him out of the office's most sensitive activities.

Waldheim gave Lessiovsky largely nominal responsibilities, busying him with supervising the order of speakers in the General Assembly, checking the minutes of staff conferences, or standing in for him at various ceremonies. At one point, Moscow decided Lessiovsky's usefulness had been impaired and recalled him, replacing him with Valery Krepkogorsky, another KGB man. Krepkogorsky, however, gained no more access than Lessiovsky, who meanwhile spent most of his time at home scheming for reassignment to New York. Once he did return, he got the same treatment in Waldheim's office. Whenever he came to me for information about the Secretary General's thinking and plans, I recalled how hard he had worked to resume the job he still could not do to the KGB's satisfaction. His superiors must have kept him on in New York because of his extensive contacts with politically and socially prominent Americans. A gregarious man, Lessiovsky really did know many people in the United States. His access to them—not to Waldheim's secrets—was what made him a valuable agent.

Lessiovsky saw himself in glamorous terms. If he was maltreated, as he continually claimed to me, by those he called Waldheim's "Austrian Mafia," he was nonetheless active in pursuit of other UN luminaries. A fixture of the midday social scene in the Delegates' Lounge, he would usually be buying drinks for an ambassador, telling amusing stories, procuring hard-to-get theater or opera tickets, name dropping, ingratiating himself.

Lessiovsky and others like him had carte blanche to develop their associations with Americans. Everyone else in the Soviet community, however, was constrained not only to limit such contacts but to report them. For years the KGB maintained a ledger book at the Mission in which all professional staff members and Secretariat personnel were to record and briefly explain their encounters with non-Soviets in New York. The entries were supposed to be made almost daily. Aside from being a nuisance, the ledger was a ridiculous security device since it clearly gave away the identity of KGB men. Their names were in the book along with ours, but they were never required to fill in any information. Their contacts with Americans and others, of course, were too secret to be openly listed.

The attempt to make Soviet diplomats detail their encounters with outsiders was typical of the mentality and the mission of the KGB overseas. It was simply an extension abroad of the obsession with security at home. But while a Soviet citizen can remain inconspicuous without much risk of attracting the attention of the secret police, it was precisely the normal behavior of a diplomat which aroused the watchdogs' suspicion.

Once the KGB identified anyone as a security risk, moreover, there was no appeal. Valery Skachkov, a young and able Soviet specialist on outer space, became a casualty of its paranoia simply because he worked with so many Americans in his field. Sent by the UN to a conference in Vienna, he was intercepted there by the KGB and flown directly to Moscow, leaving his bewildered wife in New York to pack their belongings.

A number of Soviet interpreters at the UN disappeared as abruptly as Skachkov had. Only after they were on a plane to the Soviet Union would the KGB inform the Mission's Party committee of their alleged deviations, sometimes alcoholism, but often just a natural tendency, related to their work, to fraternize with foreigners. Obediently, without discussion, the committee accepted the KGB's action in each case—verdict and sentence without trial.

When I became Under Secretary General, Aleksei Y. Skotnikov was the security officer of the Mission. He represented Special Service II of the KGB's counterintelligence arm. As a rule, this officer is the most despised man in any Soviet mission abroad. His specific task is to watch and control everyone, from ambassador to clerk, and report on their behavior and attitudes to the KGB. Skotnikov, however, was not as bad as most for his job. Sometimes he even closed his eyes to the pettier infractions of the rules, as when people ignored the ledger book. Everything changed when he was replaced by Yuri Ivanovich Shcherbakov a year later. Behind a quiet manner was a wooden-headed tyrant of the Beria school. In meetings he regularly lambasted us for our laxity in reporting encounters with foreigners. He would conclude his talks with his favorite motif: Contacts with Americans most especially should be reported because "we are surrounded by FBI and CIA agents. Vigilance will be observed!" Shcherbakov warned me many times about American spy penetration of my department.

I knew, of course, that the UN was the preserve of spies from many nations. Occasionally I ran into people from other countries who just didn't appear to be genuine diplomats. KGB operatives would often point to individuals as being an agent of this or that country. I was never sure of the truth. I seldom knew those identified except by sight, and the KGB saw real or imagined enemy agents in every corner. But during my years at the UN, the Soviet Union had the largest contingent and the most thorough penetration of the organization. Moreover, KGB and GRU agents (and those from the Soviet bloc) were caught and expelled from the United States much more often than intelligence officers of other nations.

It gave me perverse pleasure to bait Yuri Shcherbakov's spy mania. I used to egg him on, suggesting that he be tougher about screening people invited to receptions and parties at the Mission. "There are so many spies around," I told him. "Why should we invite them to our Mission?" He would nod enthusiastically and rush to Ambassador Malik to advise him to cut the guest list of foreigners for the next occasion.

Far more sinister than Shcherbakov and his ilk were the shadowy KGB assassins and terrorists, whose specialty was *mokrie dela* (wet affairs), from the so-called Department V, the KGB's Executive Action Department. While I was a postgraduate student, I had naïvely assumed that political murders, kidnappings, sabotage targeted against Western civilian sectors, had been pretty much abandoned by the U.S.S.R. after the Stalin-Beria era. I was wrong. I met some of those operatives when I first lived in New York as a junior diplomat.

One such man I knew was finally expelled from the United States after serving two tours at the Mission. Stocky, muscular, and blond, he looked like the incarnation of a Gestapo stereotype. He liked to brag suggestively about the little matters he had "cleared up." He made no effort to veil his interests. One Sunday at lunch on the New Jersey Palisades in the fall of 1965, he could not stop talking about New York's great blackout. "All those shining towers," he said, gesturing at the Manhattan skyline, "they look so strong, so tall, but they're just a house of cards. A few explosions in the right places and *do svidaniya* [goodbye]. We're only beginning to realize how vulnerable this country really is." He smacked his lips as he swallowed a piece of lobster and grinned around the table. No one commented. Most of us knew that even other KGB personnel feared this man. Some of them warned me to stay as far away from him as possible.

Another agent who arrived in New York in the 1960s to work at the Mission was the first man's antithesis in style, though not in operation. He was self-effacing, friendly, calm, and considerate. And he was good company. It was some time later that I learned from friends that he was KGB from the "wet affairs" department. Still later I found out that he had supervised the training of many "sleeping" or potential assassins and saboteurs, including Anton Sabotka* in Canada.

Sabotka had been trained over a period of years in Czechoslovakia and Moscow to carry out sabotage of vital Canadian industry, and possibly to murder when called upon to do so by the KGB. The effort failed in this case, because of Sabotka's own distaste for KGB philosophy and methods and because of Canadian awareness of his activities.

I was curious about why such KGB agents were often seen with "medical advisers" at the Mission. Unlike the Mission's doctor, who practiced medicine, these officials did not. Their jobs were to acquire as much information as possible about American medical services and advances in medicine. Some of them were epidemiologists. One agent had spoken with relish about the possibility of demolishing New York's electric power systems. Perhaps he was working out plans of an even more sinister nature with the poison and plague specialists.

A policy of violence, intimidation, and death has been a

---

* Not his real name.

historic Kremlin method of quieting opposition, from the assassination of Leon Trotsky and the Ukrainian leader Stefan Bandera to attempts on the lives of foreign political figures like Dag Hammarskjöld and Anwar Sadat. Soviet ties to guerrilla groups are so well known that the Kalashnikov submachine gun has become the symbol for international terrorism. The U.S.S.R. continues training terrorists both within and beyond its borders in order to subvert stable nations and particularly to feed upon the unrest so unfortunately common in the Third World.

In the Third World, as well as at the UN, the KGB cooperates with intelligence services of the Soviet bloc countries. Closest to the Soviets are the Bulgarians, Cubans, and East Germans. Bulgarian intelligence was the most obedient Soviet servant in terrorist operations and had widely penetrated Southern Europe and the Middle East. The Bulgarians worked on the Arabs and Turks. I saw an example of this when KGB recruitment of a Turkish diplomat in New York was accomplished with Bulgarian help.

I also heard from KGB officers in New York that they were outraged when Ludmila, the Oxford-educated daughter of the Bulgarian Party chief and President, Todor Zhivkov, tried to reawaken a sense of Bulgarian cultural identity in the late seventies. They considered her activity an "undue liberty." Ludmila became a political figure and a member of the Bulgarian Politburo. She died suddenly at the age of thirty-eight. I always wondered whether this had been another "wet affair" carried out by the KGB's Bulgarian agents.

The Sabotka case is also illustrative of another continuous and menacing KGB operation abroad. The Soviet Union sends illegals, or clandestine intelligence agents, to many countries. Sometimes their missions are carried out quickly and sometimes they remain underground for years, as in the case of Colonel Rudolf Abel, who was finally exchanged for Francis Gary Powers in the aftermath of the U-2 incident.

My former assistant Valdik Enger also had been an illegal operative at one time. I never found out where it was that he had masqueraded as a non-Soviet, but I knew who he was and what he had been when I agreed to give him a post and protection within the UN Secretariat. Although I complained about his lack of attention to his nominal Secretariat duties, I had not really expected him to conform, and I knew I was actually powerless to rid myself of him.

Enger's KGB work totally consumed him. He blatantly attempted to convert my office into a KGB nest. There were daily conferences with Soviet intelligence agents; he reproduced all kinds of documents and kept constant watch on everything going on in my department. In the end I managed to shift Enger out of my office and into a less conspicuous post where, I hoped, his indifference to his UN responsibilities would be less troublesome.

Some months before, I had written a critical efficiency report on another KGB man in the Secretariat, Yuri Titov, only to discover that most of my remarks had been expunged or completely revised by the KGB to give him a favorable rating. I managed after considerable argument to restore a few negative notes, but as an outsider my voice meant less than nothing.

Enger finally got the punishment he deserved. In May 1978 he and another Soviet employee of the UN, Rudolf Chernyayev, were arrested in New Jersey attempting to steal U.S. military secrets. They were tried, convicted, and held in prison in the United States until the following May, when they were exchanged for five Soviet dissidents who were brought to the United States. There was also a third arrest in this case, Vladimir Petrovich Zinyakin, an attaché at the Mission, but he was released under diplomatic immunity and soon returned to the Soviet Union.

That incident, I feel sure, only gave the KGB pause for a short time. The loss of two agents and exposure of a third means little to the organization. It is probably no exaggeration to count over half of the more than seven hundred Soviets in New York City as either full-time spies or co-opts under KGB and GRU orders or influence. The KGB has cemented its place in the U.S.S.R. to a point where its power is unshakable. Although I escaped from it once, I never underestimate its reach or its savagery.

22

ON SATURDAY MORNING, OCTOBER 6, 1973, MY DEPART-
ment's officer on duty called me at Glen Cove. Excitedly,
he told me that Ensio Siilasvuo, a Finnish general and Chief
of Staff of the UN Truce Supervision Organization in the
Middle East,* had reported ground and air fighting between
the Egyptian and Syrian forces and Israel. The Egyptian
Army had crossed the Suez Canal and was advancing in the
Sinai. I asked if there had been any request to convene the
Security Council. My office rarely disturbed me over
the weekend unless a UN member wanted a meeting of the
Council. He said no, but I expected someone would soon do
so.

Siilasvuo's report was clear evidence of the gravity of the
situation. Here we go again, I thought. I went immediately
to inform Ambassador Malik, but the news was already
coming over the air: Malik had been listening to the radio in
his suite. The war, begun on Yom Kippur, the Jews' holiest
day, had taken us by surprise. It should not have, perhaps.
We knew the area was volatile, that something could trigger
an explosion at any moment.

On the other hand, Malik and I had heard Sadat and other
Egyptian officials, including Foreign Minister Mohammed
el-Zayyat, who was then attending the General Assembly
session, threaten war so many times that their warnings
were no longer taken seriously. In fact, Sadat had skillfully
deceived everyone: Moscow, Washington, and even the Israelis with their well-known efficient intelligence.

Malik was elated, eager to do combat in the Security

---

* Established by the UN in 1949, composed of unarmed international military
observers to assist supervision of armistice agreements between Israel and Egypt,
Syria, Jordan, and Lebanon.

Council, and he insisted we return to New York. But unlike the opening day of war in 1967, this day produced no request for a meeting of the Security Council. Also unlike the urgency of 1967, instructions arriving that afternoon did not suggest great alarm. Moscow's orders to us were to wait and see and to consult with the Egyptian and Syrian representatives. We were also informed that the situation was being handled through Dobrynin and Kissinger in Washington. Malik saw his opportunity slipping away. "Again we're going to try to make a deal with the Americans," he cried. "Those fucking bastards are behind this Israeli aggression!"

At the United States' request, the Security Council's deliberations began on October 8. But all parties directly concerned, including the Soviet Union, disdained UN involvement. In private, el-Zayyat always spoke ambiguously and never told us anything we didn't already know from other sources. Egypt's Ambassador to the UN, Ahmed Abdul Meguid, was more candid. Knowledgeable and calm, Meguid was widely respected at the UN. He stated his country's feeling that it had to try to destroy Israel's image of military invincibility, irrespective of whether Egypt finally won or lost. At this point, Egypt was taking the position that there would be no cease-fire until Israeli troops had been driven from Egyptian soil.

Malik was in such turmoil over the situation that I believe he was actually glad to hear Jamil Baroody of Saudi Arabia castigate both the United States and the Soviet Union for transforming the Middle East into "the chessboard on which these two superpowers were playing their political game with the destiny of the peoples of that area." Perhaps he was right.

Several questions have lingered concerning Moscow's activities during the Yom Kippur War. Did the Soviets encourage Egypt and Syria to start it, and did they know in advance the exact timing of the Arab attack? If so, didn't this violate the rules of détente, the letter and spirit of the Basic Principles of Relations signed at the Moscow summit in 1972?

The visible evidence suggested that Moscow had connived in and given its blessing to the attack. Just before the fighting began, Soviet dependents left Egypt and Syria in a hurry. Soon after hostilities commenced Soviet arms were delivered to Egypt in large amounts. But ministry friends averred that the Soviets had opposed Sadat's plan up to the last minute. The weapons deliveries had been agreed upon previously. If the Soviet Union had not fulfilled its obligations at this critical moment, Moscow might have substantially undermined its position in the Arab world. The withdrawal of the wives and children was ordered only when it became obvious that the Egyptians could not be stopped from trying to push Israel out of the occupied territories. Moscow, however, was as uncertain of the exact timing of the assault as it was ineffective in attempting to forestall it.

The day after the war began we received news from Moscow about conversations on the eve of hostilities between the Soviet ambassador in Cairo, Vladimir Vinogradov, and Sadat, and between our ambassador in Damascus, Nuridin Mukhitdinov, and President Hafez al-Assad. Both Sadat and Assad revealed their intentions to go to war shortly; Assad even specified October 6 as the day. Yet the Soviet leadership did not fully believe Assad, and there were doubts about the reliability of the ambassador in Damascus. Mukhitdinov, a disgraced former member of the Presidium of the Central Committee, was notorious for "inventing things." He was also well known for his bad temper and unwillingness to listen to his subordinates' advice.

But even if his reports had been trusted, the Soviets would never have transmitted such secret information to Washington, particularly in view of the fact that Syria was the Soviets' closest ally in the area. And Washington was certainly not forthcoming about its own policy in the Middle East.

In the first phase of the war Malik's instructions amounted to open obstruction of any action proposed by the Security Council. His blunt statement that "no new decision was required" was Moscow's attempt to give Egypt and Syria time to exploit fully their military surprise. In order to help Israel recover from the attack and permit mobilization of its forces, the United States also wanted no action by the UN. As a result, the Security Council, the main UN body responsible for maintenance and restoration of international order, was <u>frozen for many days</u>. Naturally, Kurt Waldheim was preoccupied with the UN's prestige, and I believe that for once he had the sympathy of all his Under Secretaries General. Waldheim's predicament was aggravated by his being almost completely ignored by the Soviets. My advice to Malik to keep the Secretary General at least basically informed about the Soviet position only provoked our ambassador's rage.

When it became clear that the Arabs were losing, there was a drastic change in the Soviet position. To save them from total defeat, Brezhnev invited Kissinger to Moscow to help arrange a cease-fire. A joint Soviet-American position in the UN was agreed upon. Under new instructions, Ambassador Malik now appealed to the Council to adopt urgent measures to halt the fighting. To Malik's chagrin, Moscow's order was accompanied by an injunction not to criticize the United States. He nevertheless found a pretext for venting his anger in public.

When the Chinese representative, Huang Hua, complained about not being allowed enough time to consider the U.S.-Soviet draft resolution, Malik accused China of slandering and blackening the image of the United Nations and of doing nothing constructive in the organization. One should not assume that the U.S.S.R.'s official position is necessarily expressed with exactitude in all Soviet delegates' statements at the UN. While Moscow strictly controls the content of the representatives' speeches to the UN, the actual texts are composed in New York. Moscow's instructions are usually brief, laying down the essence of its policy line. There is great liberty allowed in the wording and style of the speech itself.

The cease-fire resolution sponsored by the United States and the Soviet Union was adopted by the Security Council on October 22, but to no avail. Combat continued and widened. Our communications now indicated that Moscow was eager to stop the fighting by any means possible. We felt that this time something unusual might happen, and it did. Brezhnev wrote to President Nixon urging the United States to join the Soviet Union in dispatching military contingents to Egypt to guarantee the cease-fire. The letter warned that if the United States found it impossible to act in concert, the Soviet Union would consider unilateral action.

Malik was ecstatic; I was concerned. The United States would never accept Brezhnev's proposal, nor would it permit Moscow's military intervention in the war. Once Soviet troops were in Egypt, it would be next to impossible to get them out. History had taught that simple truth.

Exploiting Sadat's desperate situation—Israeli forces were then moving toward Cairo on the west side of the Suez Canal and had encircled the Egyptian Third Army in the Sinai—Moscow was able to force him to agree to its plan. But the Soviet threat was in fact no more than a test of American will, taking advantage of Nixon's domestic difficulties related to Watergate. When the United States responded to Moscow's bluff by putting American military forces on alert, no emergency measures were taken at the Mission. This was a strong enough warning to cool off such attempts to profit from the situation. The Soviet Union was not ready to confront the United States.

Throughout the October war Moscow was preoccupied with its own interests, not with defending the Arab cause. This became clear when the Security Council discussed the question of sending a UN peacekeeping force to ensure implementation of the Council's decisions.

Soviet interpretation of UN Charter provisions concerning the use of international military personnel was narrow and rigid. Moscow recognized only one permissible use of UN member forces: rebuffing aggression (known as enforcement measures under Chapter VI of the UN Charter). According to the Soviets, such action should be undertaken only by the Security Council with the assistance of the Military Staff Committee (the United States, the United Kingdom, China, the U.S.S.R., and France). There should be no command of UN troops vested in the Secretary General. The Security Council itself, through the Military Staff Committee, must exercise the day-to-day direction and administration of any UN military operation. The functioning of this mechanism assumed complete unanimity among the permanent members of the Security Council. Unfortunately, this approach was neither realistic nor practical.

The cold war had made a number of UN Charter provisions dead letters, a situation for which the Soviet Union was largely responsible. But the modern world demanded UN military involvement in situations other than enforcement actions. Soviet objections to UN peacekeeping operations ran counter to the basic notion that conflicts have no single form but could range from war to domestic or intercommunity disputes.

The UN's practical activities—whether the Soviet Union agreed or not—evolved into a number of peacekeeping operations which varied to meet specific needs in each case. Broadly, these fell into two categories: observer missions and military activity carried out with the consent and cooperation of the parties concerned. Its main goals were to bring an end to strife, prevent resumption or expansion of conflict through impartial supervision of cease-fires, truces, or armistice agreements, and oversee troop withdrawals through the stabilizing influence of a UN presence. In Palestine, Kashmir, Cyprus, and other parts of the world, UN observer missions or forces have conducted peacekeeping operations with mixed success.

Ralph Bunche, the Under Secretary General who won the Nobel Peace Prize for his role in negotiating a truce between the Arabs and the Israelis in Palestine in 1949, made perhaps the greatest contribution to practical UN peacekeeping work. Bunche was the best kind of international civil servant. In the late sixties, nearly blind and in failing health, he continued to work long, hard hours on many UN missions.

Soviet insistence on day-to-day supervision of peacekeeping missions by the Security Council was unrealistic. Rejection of the concept of practical management of such operations by the Secretary General—accepted by an absolute majority of the UN membership despite Soviet protests —had only one consequence: Moscow deprived itself of the opportunity to influence the direction of peacekeeping. The move also excluded the Soviet Under Secretary General from direct involvement in this process. My government, ignoring its own interests, did not want its national in this post to be associated with "illegal practice."

I had raised the matter of UN peacekeeping arrangements with Gromyko while I was his adviser. "What kind of so-called peacekeeping operation are we talking about?" he asked. "No mention is made of such things in the UN Charter. They are dangerous and could lead to interference in the internal affairs of states." He always harked back to the Congo as an example. "Remember, in the Congo we saw how UN troops could be used against the progressive forces." Finally, he warned me never to bring up the subject again. I never did.

I thus faced a dilemma when, following the Security Council decision on October 25 to organize a UN Emergency Force to ensure compliance with its resolutions, Waldheim asked me to attend a meeting that evening to work out the plan of action and the terms of reference for the new UN force. It would be hard to refuse Waldheim and equally difficult to depart from the traditional Soviet stance in this matter. I asked Malik what he thought.

He was surprised by Waldheim's gesture and discouraged me from attending. But I told him I was going to participate, even if Waldheim's final recommendation to the Council did not coincide with our position. "Waldheim can't follow the Soviet line," I said. "Besides, he has to report to the Council within twenty-four hours. We don't have much time, and I'm not going to ask Moscow's advice about this." Malik muttered something about the importance of defending our line, but it was a perfunctory reminder. "Well, go on then," he said. "Anyway, we'll soon find out what they're cooking up."

I had been braced for one of his tirades, but it was one of those moments when Malik showed common sense. If, however, Moscow reprimanded me later, Malik would not hesitate to dissociate himself from my decision and condemn me for agreeing to join the meeting.

Waldheim seemed near exhaustion that night. His face was so flushed that at first I thought he was ill. But he was also visibly satisfied that the UN was at last involved in trying to stop the war.

Brian Urquhart of Great Britain, Assistant Secretary General for Special Political Affairs at the time, dominated the discussion. His experience in peacekeeping operations was unparalleled among us, dating back to the mid-fifties. I felt a strong rapport with Urquhart, and I called on him often for information or for his opinion on various matters. Behind his mild appearance there was a man of robust strength and courage. I found his straightforwardness, logic, and practical approach to problems appealing. One could encounter him working at any hour of the day or night; indeed, many people did not think of him in any other setting. When I met him occasionally as he walked his dog in the neighborhood where we both lived, I always felt vaguely surprised at seeing him someplace other than the thirty-eighth floor.

Urquhart's reputation for fairness and integrity seemed almost universal—to everyone but the Soviets. Their prejudice against him was based on two things: he was British and, worse, he had been Dag Hammarskjöld's confidant.

Urquhart told Waldheim at the meeting that it would be logical to follow the general pattern of the first UN Emergency Force (UNEF-I) operation in the Egypt-Israel sector from 1956 until 1967. "What about the total strength of the force?" asked Waldheim. "We still don't know exactly what its scope of actions might be."

It was finally decided to recommend a complement of about 7,000 men, similar to UNEF-I. The numbers could be adjusted according to what might be needed. Other aspects of the operation should also generally follow the previous pattern.

I supported Urquhart's proposal, but I was careful not to say too much, since I could not predict Moscow's reaction to my participation in the meeting. As it turned out, I was not criticized for attending, but I don't believe that Waldheim realized what he had done by inviting me. I heard later that my presence had caused controversy. Many at the UN were astounded that the Secretary General had broken the rule of Soviet exclusion. They were sure that bringing me into peacekeeping operations would be a serious handicap to UN work. I thought they might be proved correct. Moscow had tolerated my initial step, but how would it accept my new role? In the future would I be instructed to behave in an orthodox Soviet fashion? If so, I would probably be forced to erect obstacles that would breed considerable frustration and ill will on all sides.

On October 27 the Security Council approved Waldheim's report and recommendations. The next day the first direct talks in a quarter of a century between Egypt and Israel were arranged under UN auspices at Kilometer 101 on the Cairo-Suez road. Moscow instructed me to send any news I received about these talks. My reports, based largely on Ensio Siilasvuo's cables, turned out to be the best information about the talks. It was no wonder that the KGB kept trying to pirate Siilasvuo's messages before I got them. The Egyptians evidently weren't telling the Soviets everything. But even if they had, Moscow would not have trusted them.

The talks at Kilometer 101 were possible because of American mediation. It became a decisive factor in getting agreement on the cease-fire, Egyptian-Israeli disengagement, and other breakthroughs. Soviet influence in Egypt and the Middle East as a whole declined; it was largely self-inflicted damage.

Political backing of extreme Arab demands and lack of consistency in military support of Egypt and other Arab states had jeopardized Soviet ability to play the role of mediator. And as long as the U.S.S.R. refused to deal with Israel, having broken relations after the 1967 war, the United States was able to exclude Moscow from various initiatives, all unsuccessful, to heal the breach between Arabs and Jews. America was the only superpower that could talk to and be listened to by both sides.

Gromyko and I discussed this problem several times. In 1967, he said, it was too early to consider reversing the Soviet stand toward Israel. By 1970 and 1971, however, I was finally able to get him to say that it had "probably" been an error to break diplomatic relations with Israel or, at least, not to have resumed them after passions had cooled somewhat. Gromyko's view of the proper course to follow would have led him, had he a free hand, to work to restore communication with Israel. A fairly traditional diplomat in many respects, he saw little to be gained from boycotting

346

one party to a dispute. And, while in no way sympathetic to Israel, he distrusted the Arabs.

But Gromyko did not have a free hand. I could perceive that in his evasiveness whenever I raised the question of taking a new tack in the Middle East. It was one of many examples of his refusing to act on the basis of views he knew conflicted with the majority opinion in the Politburo.

What he could do was assign subordinates to maintain contact with Israel on an informal basis. In this role—to Malik's disgust and over his recurrent opposition—I became one of the few intermediaries between the Soviets and the Israelis. Israeli diplomats soon realized that I would give them a hearing and a means of transmitting their views to Moscow. But in my courier's role I was not especially productive. It was a thankless task because Moscow was not interested in changing its policy toward Israel. Occasionally, in fact, it was an uncomfortable part to play.

A year or so later, Yosef Tekoah, then the Israeli permanent representative, asked me to submit to the Soviet Foreign Ministry a lengthy list of Jews seeking permission to emigrate. I tried to evade the chore, saying that emigration matters were outside the ministry's authority. I did not add that they were largely controlled by the KGB, subject to Politburo supervision. I also didn't mention the letter that accused me of taking money to help a Moscow Jew get an exit visa.

Tekoah, however, was insistent. Soviet authorities should review the list to determine if there were injustices to innocent people denied the right to leave. Favorable action on these cases would do much to reduce criticism of Soviet emigration policy and human rights practices in general. Eventually I agreed to transmit the list to Moscow, but I warned him not to expect any response to the communication through me or in any other way. As I had anticipated, none was forthcoming.

Although I discussed Soviet policy on Jewish emigration with many knowledgeable Moscow acquaintances over the years, I found it difficult to predict or influence its course. Foreign Ministry views on the issue were neither sought nor welcomed, although the question became deeply entangled with the broader one of U.S.-Soviet relations.

Inside the Soviet leadership opinion was divided. One camp held that no emigration should be permitted at all. Its members predicted—correctly, as events proved—that to open the door for Jews would invite pressure from other ethnic groups, such as the Armenians and the Germans who had settled along the Volga in the eighteenth century but had been deported to Kazakhstan during World War II. Moreover, a policy favoring Jews would anger ordinary Russians, whose own freedom to travel was severely restricted.

The opposing school held that the Soviet Union would be stronger if it cleaned house. Reflecting Russian anti-Semitism, this second group tended to think of Soviet Jews as inherently hostile to the state. Why keep people who do not want to live in the U.S.S.R.? Good riddance to them.

Foreign policy considerations initially tipped the balance in favor of emigration. During the early seventies, a period of energetic effort to improve East-West relations, Moscow showed a certain sensitivity to Western public opinion and governmental pressure in behalf of Jewish emigration. The first period of outward flow ended in 1974, when the U.S. Congress approved the Jackson-Vanik and Stevenson amendments to American trade legislation, conditioning certain benefits for the Soviet Union on the number of Jews allowed to emigrate. Moscow was determined to show that its policy was not being shaped by such overt outside influence, and it cut back the level of emigration. In 1977, it increased as part of a drive to show compliance with the least offensive human rights aspects of the Helsinki Accords, but the level was sharply reduced after 1979 in the wake of Western criticism of Soviet military intervention in Afghanistan.

What the record showed was a lack of consistency, the absence of a firm policy commitment either for or against eased emigration. In that respect the issue is a typical example of Soviet policymaking. Like many other difficult questions, those relating to Soviet Jews are decided only when external or internal pressures force the Politburo to

348

confront the problem. And the decision made in one set of circumstances can be reversed when the circumstances change. Emigration was difficult to start up. It also has proved difficult to stop entirely. What the shifting practices reveal, however, is the typical preference of the Soviet leadership for avoiding a stand on a prickly subject about which opinion is divided.

The arguments pro and con Jewish emigration remain more or less the same from year to year. At any given moment those who protest the loss of skilled technical manpower may have an edge over those who think it possible to obtain Western concessions by clearing the country of a resented minority. At another time the majority view can change. All that is certain is that the issue is a troublesome one that can generate different responses whenever it is raised.

In my position I was the diplomatic litmus paper on which Israeli envoys could test a proposal in order to obtain an authoritative Soviet reaction. Since my status was unofficial, my opinions could always be disowned. But in the informal consultations that shape much of what is finally decided I was able to play a part which otherwise might have gone unfilled.

In the aftermath of the Yom Kippur War, I was the channel through which Ambassador Tekoah sounded out whether Gromyko would agree to meet with Israeli Foreign Minister Abba Eban at the Peace Conference on the Middle East in Geneva scheduled for December 1973. Gromyko agreed. It became the first Soviet-Israeli encounter at such a high level since the Six-Day War in 1967. Although Gromyko adopted a rather amiable tone, he was tough on substance. He told Eban that in principle it was possible to renew normal diplomatic relations if "important progress" could be made at the Geneva Conference. By "important progress" he meant Israeli agreement to withdraw its forces from all occupied Arab territories. He also expressed willingness to continue the dialogue with Eban within the framework of the Geneva Conference, but it never resumed its work.

* * *

IN APRIL 1975 WALDHEIM APPOINTED ME HIS REPRESEN-
tative to the Geneva Review Conference on the implementation of the Non-Proliferation Treaty. In May I was back in
New York.

A fairly significant cable had arrived at the Soviet Mission. It concerned Vietnam and originated with Ilya Shcherbakov, the Soviet ambassador in Hanoi. Two months after
the fall of Saigon, the message disclosed, Vietnam's leaders
had decided to mount a new offensive, but a peaceful, diplomatic one. They judged that the country's unification had
moved far enough to justify their engaging in a more active
and assertive foreign policy. As a first step, they planned to
seek admission to the UN. Expecting American opposition,
they wanted Soviet assistance and advice in their campaign
to win votes in New York.

Neither the Hanoi decision nor the ministry's order to the
Mission to help them was particularly surprising. Many Soviet Asian experts had long wished for Vietnam to moderate
its negative attitude toward the UN. During the war years
that stand had put Moscow in the illogical position of condemning U.S. policy but blocking efforts to deal with the
conflict in the UN. Bent on complete victory, the North
Vietnamese feared that any solution reached at the UN
would be a compromise benefiting Saigon and the Americans.

Nor was this disagreement on diplomatic tactics the only
source of friction between Vietnam and the U.S.S.R. The
1975 victory, instead of healing these differences, had
opened the way for new ones. In my own view, the United
States had made two mistakes in Vietnam: entering the war
and then losing it. The intervention had obliged Moscow and
Peking to work together in some instances, just when relations between them were deteriorating rapidly. But having
aligned itself with a corrupt regime in Saigon, America had
damaged its prestige by deserting its ally in 1975.

After the fall of Saigon, I and many other Soviets were
deeply surprised at America's acceptance of this final humiliation. Others, especially the Party ideologues, were

elated. They saw in Vietnam the proof of the decay they long claimed was sapping Western strength and will. It seemed a resounding argument for a much tougher line with the capitalist world, especially the United States.

The prospect of disagreement between Moscow and Hanoi arose in the expectation that the Soviets would be pressed to put extensive resources into the reconstruction of Vietnam. The U.S.S.R. could not afford to take on costly new obligations overseas and many in the leadership were troubled by what they thought Hanoi would seek from them. Moscow could not underwrite Castro's bills and Vietnam's as well. Not only is Vietnam bigger than Cuba; the war had left its civilian economy devastated. And the certainty that Hanoi would demand copious aid for reconstruction dimmed some of the pleasure the Soviet rulers took in the American defeat.

"The trouble is," Vasily Makarov said during his stay in New York with Gromyko in September 1975, "we don't see how we can say no. Those bastards are beginning to act as though they had done it all themselves and now we owe them the moon."

Toward the end of 1975, Le Duan, Ho Chi Minh's successor, visited Moscow to try to begin collecting what the Vietnamese thought was their due. From the message sent out to major diplomatic missions after the talks, I judged that neither he nor his hosts had been completely satisfied. Le Duan, it was true, had finally endorsed a range of Soviet policy stands on international questions—on European security, on disarmament, on the Middle East, and even on the advances toward East-West détente which China denounced. But the delegation from Hanoi, the cable noted, "does not consider it expedient for now to take a direct position on the differences" between the Soviet Union and China.

For their part the Soviet leaders had given fulsome pledges of solidarity but restricted promises of practical help. They glorified the heroism of Vietnam's people but committed themselves to assist in reconstruction only "to the extent possible." In practice, Moscow would send out study teams before it bound itself to specific amounts of aid.

351

And the eventual "gifts" would probably consist of weapons and credits to buy Soviet equipment on favorable terms rather than the kind or volume of subsidies that went to Cuba.

One hint of the strain emerged in Brezhnev's formal report to the Twenty-fifth Party Congress in February 1976. He made no mention of helping Vietnam rebuild, for instance, even though the victory and Soviet wartime contributions were given pride of place at the beginning of the speech. In the same passage, however, Brezhnev referred only indirectly to America's role in Vietnam. Speaking of Cuba, he talked of "U.S. imperialism," but as for Vietnam, the outsiders were named only as "imperialist invaders" or "interventionists." Such wording was intentional. It followed the line set in 1972 at the time Brezhnev welcomed President Nixon to Moscow despite the fighting in Vietnam and the mining of Haiphong harbor.

That summit had made the Vietnamese furious because of the way the Soviets dropped the previous denunciations of the United States. Brezhnev was still using the weasel words from 1972, and it was an indication that Moscow's relationship with Hanoi still had its rough edges. Although the Party Congress generally seemed undramatic, there were interesting aspects to the oratory, clues to be found between the lines of the long, self-congratulatory speeches.

The ten-day gathering of the Party elite at the modern Palace of Congresses inside the Kremlin seemed to confirm one trend in Soviet affairs above all others: the increasing dominance of Leonid Brezhnev. His mastery was not complete, but, at least on the surface, it was impressive. The number and length of his ovations were one measure of his stature. But Brezhnev's report sounded a note of anxiety, especially about the state of the Soviet economy.

Brezhnev also signaled considerable disquiet in both what he said and what he omitted about several developments outside the Soviet Union. Perhaps the most notable negative phrase was one composed of only two words: *osobiye vzglyady,* the "particular views" which he noted "a few parties" in other socialist countries have "on a number of questions." Although he claimed an "overall tendency" toward "growing cohesion" between the U.S.S.R. and its Eastern European allies, Brezhnev was actually admitting concern about the independent or heretical attitudes which, in varying degrees, Romania, Poland, and Hungary took toward Soviet economic or foreign policy doctrines.

"Particular views" seems like an innocuous expression. In fact, it is a euphemism for dissent, and to admit in 1976 that Warsaw Pact members had deviated from the Soviet line "on a number of questions" was a significant concession of unease. By that time I had already heard a good deal about the "trouble" in Poland. The Polish Ambassador to the UN, Henryk Jaroszek, had asked me several times to visit his country. But when I was in Moscow in the summer of 1976, Vasily Kuznetsov strongly advised me to find an excuse to decline Jaroszek's invitation.

The most striking formulations in the Brezhnev report's section on foreign affairs dealt with East-West relations in Europe and amounted to a tacit admission that a cherished Soviet diplomatic exercise, once hailed as a personal peacemaking triumph for Brezhnev, had become a potential embarrassment. At issue were the Helsinki Accords, more formally known as the Final Act of the Conference on Security and Cooperation in Europe.

What Moscow had most wanted from the European security talks—an affirmation of the inviolability of existing European frontiers, a formal recognition of the postwar status quo on the continent—it had obtained, but only at a relatively high price. To achieve its goal, the U.S.S.R. had been obliged to accept a number of Western demands, especially pledges of cooperation on human rights and other questions, including freer flow of information and people across East-West borders.

In various meetings of senior Foreign Ministry officials during the years I served as Gromyko's adviser, I heard several colleagues as well as KGB and Central Committee participants in the discussions caution against the trend in East-West negotiations to expand beyond Soviet goals. Their warnings went unheeded. Partly the fault lay in the Soviet decision-making system; it provides few channels for

353

skeptics to use safely in questioning the drift of a basic policy choice.

But even if these caveats had been voiced with greater daring, they would probably have been discounted. The Soviet commitment to the European security talks had been made a matter of Brezhnev's personal prestige.

The doubters reasoned that the U.S.S.R. had already accomplished its basic postwar goals in Europe through bilateral treaties, especially those with West Germany and between the FRG and East Germany and Poland. The division of Germany had in fact been accepted by the West. Other agreements between Moscow and Paris, Moscow and Bonn, Moscow and Rome, provided the necessary foundations for pursuing political, economic, cultural, and other advances in normalizing East-West ties. And the multilateral forum was not likely to add significantly to this basis for the pursuit of détente—at least not without inconvenient side effects.

Against such considerations was a strong set of counterarguments. Given the increasing tension with China, the Soviet Union wanted and needed a maximum of calm and good relations with Europe. The value of the security negotiations with the Europeans rested heavily on the insecurity which marked dealings between Moscow and Peking.

And even though the effort to improve ties with the United States would remain the central focus of Soviet détente policy, Moscow had pursued normalization of East-West relations in Europe. The breakthroughs with France in 1966 and West Germany four years later were immensely valuable. Dealing with the Europeans, the Kremlin could always hope to divide them from their American allies on political questions.

That tactic was not abandoned when U.S.-Soviet relations began to improve. Even at the peak of superpower détente in 1972–73, the Soviets followed one course with America and a different line with its NATO partners. The slow pace of the SALT talks, America's continuing efforts to exclude the Soviet Union from Middle East diplomacy, and, later, the uncertainties and barriers that constricted trade with the United States, all combined to encourage Moscow to keep as many options open in Europe as it could.

Throughout these years—while the Conference on Security and Cooperation in Europe moved through prolonged negotiations—two other factors contrived to allay any uneasiness in the Foreign Ministry or the Central Committee. At the Twenty-fourth Party Congress in 1971, a sweeping peace program formally made the convening of the European conference an article of Communist faith. After that declaration of policy there could be no turning back.

Leonid Brezhnev had come to see himself as the prime mover behind the European security campaign. Always fond of the grandiose gesture, he had increasingly linked his prestige as a peacemaker to the success of the negotiations. His personal commitment had the effect of gagging any lower-level critics. To express doubt about the worth of the conference would be to challenge the wisdom of the leader.

Ironically, however, in 1976 it was the chief negotiator of the Helsinki Accords who was to suffer for the devotion he had shown to Brezhnev's policy. Anatoly Kovalev, a protégé of Gromyko's, was given responsibility for the European talks when consultations leading to the conference were still informal. He heard but discounted some of his colleagues' early warnings. He worked faithfully to carry out Moscow's instructions in the long sessions in Geneva from 1973 through 1975. Already well along in a meteoric career, he expected a significant reward for his efforts at the Twenty-fifth Party Congress. But instead of being awarded membership in the Central Committee, the anticipated promotion he had openly boasted of beforehand, he ended up in a Moscow hospital, the victim of a heart attack and a casualty of the shift in the policy he had so energetically supported.

Kovalev was emotionally shattered when he received no Party post at all at the end of the Congress. Apparently his candidacy was vetoed at the last minute in an inner Party council. His heart attack, an ailment as common among hard-driving Russians as ulcers were among high-powered Americans, was a symptom of shock. While he recovered from it, the European security policy of which he had been the chief executor was permanently altered.

Having committed themselves to the Helsinki process expecting one outcome, the Soviets were unable to maneuver as Western negotiators broadened the scope of the talks to embrace a view of security and cooperation Moscow had never entertained. French, British, and German diplomats at Geneva gradually forced the Soviets to accept language which, if implemented in full, could reduce the obstacles which systematically choked the passage of people from East to West and the communication of information from West to East. NATO and neutral negotiators even obliged the Soviet delegation to agree to the principle that a state's respect for human rights and fundamental freedoms was as valid a test of its peaceful intentions as its respect for another state's sovereign rights and inviolable borders.

Representing the U.S.S.R. in Geneva during two years of bargaining, Kovalev had diligently tried to block evolution of the agreement beyond the limited military and political concept Moscow originally endorsed. Repeatedly, however, his stonewalling tactics were countered by the West. If the Soviets wanted progress toward an accord, the Europeans insisted, they would have to accommodate its expansion. After each delay, Kovalev, on instructions from Moscow, was obliged to concede an inch or two. Cumulatively his position was eroded. Although few Westerners recognized the success their diplomats scored in the relatively unpublicized talks, the Final Act emerged as a notable advance for their ideas and a setback of sorts for the Soviet Union.

It was not Leonid Brezhnev, however, who suffered for the predicament into which his ambition had led his government. For the public record, he continued to claim a measure of victory, although his claim began to sound hollow. And behind the scenes Anatoly Kovalev was made the scapegoat of a policy he had faithfully carried out. Five years later, at the Twenty-sixth Party Congress, Kovalev was still denied a place on the Central Committee despite his having become one of the most important officials in the ministry. Instead, Yuli Vorontsov was rewarded with full membership in the top Party council for having pressed

Moscow's hard-line attack on the Helsinki Accords' human rights provisions at a 1977 follow-up conference of the thirty-five signatories in Belgrade. Kovalev did, it is true, recover to some degree from his disgrace. He appeared in 1981 in Madrid as the leader of the Soviet delegation to yet another follow-up meeting.

Kovalev's case was instructive. In the Soviet system, to be blamed for anything is often cause enough for rejection. Irrespective of one's services or how faithfully they were performed, one could spend one's life making up for that one misstep.

A more ominous aspect of Kremlin behavior regarding the Helsinki Accords was that our leaders once again revealed that they would violate elementary human rights no matter what they might sign, and that the Soviet system itself was intrinsically antithetical to such rights. If democracy is absent, there can be no genuine socialism. The prospect of our society returning to Stalinism, the growing repression of any dissent—more obvious than ever after the trials of Andrei Sinyavsky and Yuli Daniel in 1966—exacerbated my personal frustration with our system. The longer I lived in the United States, the clearer became the difference between our restrictive society and the truly free life in America.

"If democracy is absent, there can be no genuine socialism"

23

AFTER MY INITIAL CONTACT WITH BERT JOHNSON, I HAD resolved not to return to the Soviet Union again. But as the time for my home leave approached in 1976, my determination began to waver. I had not realized that my trial period as a spy would last so long. And now there was a new element.

Gennady had married despite our advice to him to consider such a step carefully. Like most parents, we felt that since he was young, he should establish himself more securely and take more time to make sure of his feelings. But, like most children, Gennady preferred not to wait. Soon, Lina and I became grandparents. As our vacation grew nearer, Lina was excited about seeing our grandson, Alyosha, as well as the rest of our family. She looked forward to the comforts of our home in Moscow and the summer days we would spend at our country house in Valentinovka near Moscow. Her enthusiasm was irresistible. My desire to see my son and grandson and to walk Moscow's streets again overcame my fear of returning to the U.S.S.R.

Why rush the defection? I rationalized. Anna could stay with us in New York for a time yet. I had been collaborating with the Americans and, though I found it hard to believe, I had duped the KGB. Obviously the KGB didn't detect anything wrong, or I would never have returned to New York from Havana.

Furthermore, I was growing used to my new role. It did not disquiet me as it had at first, and I put off the critical confrontations with Lina, Gennady, my mother, with all my previous life. I found it easier to meet with Johnson and tell him about my decision to defect, even to demand that he speed it up, than actually to do it. I knew I was following the path of least resistance, but something tilted my contradictory sentiments in favor of this ultimately useless playing with time. I foolishly hoped a *deus ex machina* would resolve my problems painlessly.

When I told Johnson about my impending vacation, he had ideas about how I should spend it. Weighing the risks—negligible ones, he argued—against the potential benefits, he and his superiors in Washington concluded that I could safely pull off an intelligence coup. In Moscow, by merely following my normal routine I would learn of the latest developments in top-level Soviet thinking and would pick up information about the leaders. I would see Gromyko and other senior officials of the Central Committee and the Foreign Ministry.

All this made sense. Besides, I had already made up my mind to go. Johnson reminded me of the precautionary arrangements we had discussed before my trip to Cuba. This time, I memorized the instructions instead of carrying along an incriminating gadget.

Within a few weeks of my conversation with Johnson, Lina, Anna, and I arrived in Moscow. It was still early morning, but the summer sun had been up for hours as the Aeroflot jet whined down toward Sheremetyevo Airport. No landmark stood out in the flat, forested approach to the international air terminal, but somehow the glint of light off shapeless ponds among the pines and birches signaled a familiar, welcoming landscape. There is no drama to the countryside of northern Russia, only an occasional gentle swell of the land and, even more rare, the bulbous dome of a once-lovely country church. Yet it was my land, my home. Sentimentality suppressed the twinges of fear I might otherwise have felt. The sight of a Mercedes limousine from the UN information center, its blue flag fluttering from a front fender as it pulled up to the plane steps, was reassuring. The KGB was not waiting for me. Behind the Mercedes in a Foreign Ministry sedan sat a functionary who would take care of the passport formalities for Lina, Anna, and me and would stay behind to get the baggage and bring it to our apartment.

There my *teshcha* (mother-in-law) presided over a family reunion. Gennady and his wife, Marina, brought their infant son to greet us, to admire our presents, and to feast with us on the special dishes Lina's mother had prepared. The table was set with smoked sturgeon, my favorite hard sausage, cold salmon, and white mushrooms my mother-in-law had pickled herself. From these *zakuski* (appetizers) we proceeded to a sumptuous dinner.

Conversation was tearful, lively, and warm. Alyosha, a healthy dumpling of a baby, soon fell asleep, completely ignoring his doting grandparents. Gennady was very proud of him, of Marina, and of his work at the Foreign Ministry. I was glad that my son seemed to be so happy. He and his wife had their own apartment and spent most of their free time with her parents. Although I had known about all of this, it was still somehow unsettling to see Gennady so different, engrossed with his new family. He had become, as Russians say, a "slice of bread" cut from the loaf of our family unit. Lina and I of course always knew that this was inevitable, but both of us regretted that Gennady would never be a little boy again. At the same time any hope of talking to him about the idea of leaving the U.S.S.R. had vanished. I felt removed from the festive homecoming. A secret I didn't know how to share with my family was an invisible barrier between us.

The abundance of our table did not reflect the real food situation in the country, which had worsened since our previous vacation. My mother-in-law complained of shortages and the poor quality of consumer goods, the irregularity of supply, and the scarcity of basic foods—milk, butter, and eggs—even in Moscow. She lamented that it had never been as bad before, even in Stalin's or Khrushchev's time. It was true. And the capital, of course, had always been much better off than anyplace else. There is a Russian saying that it lies downhill from the rest of the country—everything flows to Moscow.

"Arkady, you won't believe it," she said indignantly. "My friend told me she paid twelve rubles last week for a chicken at the Central Market [the farmers' free market where prices are not state-controlled]. It's unheard of! That's a quarter of her monthly pension. How can people live?" She shrugged unhappily.

It really was bad for ordinary people with an ordinary income. The chicken my mother-in-law was talking about, although terribly expensive, was unavailable in government-run food stores where the populace shopped. We all knew how lucky we were to have access to the special shops for the privileged class—places that were both well stocked and cheap and were closed to the general public. Whenever I returned to the Soviet Union, this subject was a nagging reminder that coming to Moscow from New York was like entering another world.

I tried to warm up the conversation by asking for the latest political jokes making the rounds in Moscow. My mother-in-law glanced worriedly at the telephone sitting on a small table in the foyer. She began to rise from her chair to close the french doors separating the dining room from the entrance hall.

"Come on, don't worry," I said, pulling her back to her chair. "There's no need to shut the door. The KGB not only monitors our phone, but you can be sure they've bugged every room in the apartment as well." We all knew that it was routine KGB practice to wire the dwellings of "suspicious persons," and that they also monitored the lives of the elite, including its top members, for their "protection." To try to shut the doors against its mechanical ears was futility itself.

Unfortunately, the first story didn't divert us from the subject of food problems. Brezhnev and the failures of Soviet agriculture were current targets. The following was typical:

Brezhnev screamed in his sleep, waking his wife, Victoria.

"Lyonya, what's the matter?" she cried.

"I had a nightmare that we Communized the whole world!" Brezhnev replied in panic.

"So what? That's wonderful!"

"You think so? Well, where are we going to get bread?"

Another one ran: A Soviet citizen walked into Red Square near the Kremlin and shouted, "Brezhnev is an idiot!" He was promptly arrested and sentenced to fifteen days in jail for insulting Brezhnev, and fifteen years at hard labor for divulging a state secret.

Everyone laughed, but since Gennady worked at the Foreign Ministry, I pointedly cautioned him to be careful with anti-Soviet stories. Even though people no longer got ten years' imprisonment for political jokes at the leader's expense, one could still be severely reprimanded. Moreover, in extreme cases, it was possible to lose one's job for telling anti-Soviet anecdotes. Occasionally Brezhnev himself enjoyed some of these stories, but Gromyko would never tolerate them.

AT THE FOREIGN MINISTRY, I FOUND GROMYKO AWAY AND Vasily Kuznetsov in charge of the diplomatic service and, as it turned out, of me. I wanted to rest. He wanted to put me to work.

It wasn't much of a fight. When he asked me to join a group reviewing Soviet policy in Africa, I could make only a halfhearted demurrer. I thought with some amusement that the CIA could not have asked for a better vantage point from which to inspect Soviet policymaking. Kuznetsov told me that the Politburo attached particular significance to elaboration of the "appropriate" policy line in Africa. That continent was in "the concluding phase of colonialism" and the emerging "progressive" states there had become "objects of foreign intervention." It was not unusual for him to begin a private conversation flavored with propaganda slogans. Among the bureaucrats, at least in the Soviet system, such a style was part of a ritual as strong as that of any religion. But I suspected that Kuznetsov, a decent, intelligent man, probably was not fond of the blatant discrepancy between our real goals and the bombastic verbal camouflage in our African policy.

For more than two decades Africa was viewed by Moscow as the most turbulent outpost of the capitalist world, and therefore the weakest. Exploiting local turmoil created opportunities to expand Moscow's zone of control without incurring high costs. Some money and advisers and a supply of relatively cheap weapons could buy disproportionate influence with new and shaky governments or anti-colonialist guerrilla forces.

Beyond expediency, however, Moscow pursued an ideological and political goal, seeking to demonstrate the correctness and applicability of Marxist doctrines in the African setting and the superiority of the Soviet approach over the theories advanced by the Communist Chinese. As a number of African ambassadors to the UN complained, Moscow chose the recipients of its support less and less for their authenticity as liberators-to-be and more and more for their willingness to oppose Peking. What had begun as a contest with the West had developed into a new arena of rivalry between the two Communist powers.

Angola was an obvious example. In a sense, it became a turning point in Moscow's behavior in Africa. Never before had the Soviet Union and Cuba made such a massive military incursion into a Third World country. I wasn't surprised when in 1975 the Soviets began supplying military equipment to Angola to support Agostinho Neto's pro-Moscow faction through the spring and summer of that year, but I was when they began transporting Cuban combat troops and Soviet military advisers in the fall. And I was dismayed by the virtual absence of any strong opposition from the American side.

By the end of the year, despite Soviet-Cuban support, Neto's forces were faring badly in their battles with the opposition movements led by Holden Roberto and Jonas Savimbi. From information received at the Soviet Mission in New York, I knew that Neto had appealed to Moscow for more help. Yakov Malik had been instructed to resist convening the Security Council as long as possible to try to forestall consideration of the situation in Angola. The Soviet Union feared political embarrassment in the UN.

When Malik reported that the American Ambassador to the UN, Daniel Patrick Moynihan, seemed to be pressing Washington and other delegations to take the issue to the Security Council, we could feel the outrage all the way from Moscow. Moynihan displayed greater political foresight than many policymakers in Washington. He understood the consequences of Soviet-Cuban intervention in Angola. He insisted that both the Security Council and the General Assembly begin to deal with the Moscow-Havana actions without delay. Moynihan's advice was not accepted. And on December 19, Congress cut off further military help to Angola.

As a result, there was no U.S. resistance in the UN or effective military countermeasures to curtail or restrain Soviet interference in Angola. Soviet leaders were overjoyed by America's lack of response.

"How did we persuade the Cubans to provide their contingent?" I asked Kuznetsov.

He laughed. After acknowledging that Castro might be playing his own game in sending about 20,000 troops to Angola, Kuznetsov told me that the idea for the large-scale military operation had originated in Havana, not Moscow. It was startling information. As I later discovered, it was also a virtual secret in the Soviet capital. Certainly, Western analysts had assumed that the Soviet Union, which had air-lifted Cuban soldiers to Angola to help Neto defeat the Western and Chinese-supported factions of Savimbi and Roberto, had called on its Caribbean ally for what proved to be crucial assistance.

Why had the Cubans volunteered? First, they badly needed to boost revolutionary fervor at home. More and more Cubans had become disillusioned with Castro's regime and its chronic economic distress. Second, Castro still cherished the idea of himself as a great international figure. His early efforts to spread revolution in Latin America—the obsession of his firebrand comrade Che Guevara—had gone against more conservative Soviet advice to concentrate on first establishing a healthy domestic economy and on mending relations with his country's neighbors.

By 1975, however, Moscow was welcoming and encouraging Cuba's adventurism. Growing Soviet military strength prompted the Kremlin to take a more decisive role in Africa's struggles than had been possible before.

Contrary to the current spirit of Soviet-American relations, the Politburo was determined to push ahead in Africa without taking American opinion into account. Cuban successes had convinced many in Moscow that the United States lacked will in Africa. After its humiliation in Vietnam in 1975, America was increasingly portrayed by Party militants as a diminished rival in the Third World. Although some experts took a more cautious line, the Soviet leaders judged that in addition to the "Vietnam syndrome," the United States now had an "Angola syndrome."

Moreover, 1976 was a presidential election year, a contributing factor in the timing of Soviet offensive actions. The prevailing view within the Foreign Ministry was that America was far more concerned about its internal politics than anything to do with Africa. "Once again the Yankees have handcuffed themselves for most of the year—they won't be looking at us," was a cheerful boast of confidence I heard from more than one Soviet official.

I kept my feelings about Soviet policy in Africa to myself. The ministry officials dealing with that area were among the most conformist, least imaginative diplomats I knew. Only with Kuznetsov could I be a bit more candid.

I told him our diplomats in Angola were so poorly supplied from Moscow that their families at home were shipping them powdered milk, one of the essential foodstuffs they could obtain no other way. Colleagues in the ministry knew that such neglect was common in African posts. As a result, few wanted to take jobs there. The personnel department had great difficulty finding qualified staffers to expand the Soviet presence in Angola, and the ministry cafeteria was full of grumbling diplomats fearful of being ordered into such hardship.

Kuznetsov's assessment of Agostinho Neto was brutally candid: "We only need him for a certain period. We know he's been sick. He's come here a couple of times for treatment. And psychologically he's not all that reliable. But he's completely under our control, and that's what counts now. As for what comes later, we'll handle it."

My curiosity aroused, I began to talk with ministry officers dealing with Angolan affairs. Moscow had never trusted Neto but had hailed him as a hero. Echoing Kuznetsov's thoughts, one African specialist told me frankly that "we needed Neto's prestige as the historic leader of the MPLA." There were better people in the Popular Movement, such as Iko Careira, but without Neto it would be harder to attract Organization of African Unity support for the MPLA. "There were several assassination attempts on Neto before Angolan independence."

"By whom?"

"By his own people, the MPLA," he replied.

"Were these people loyal to us?" I persisted.

"I think so, but who can guarantee it? You know," he added with embarrassment, "these matters are kept under lock and key." Once again I was disgusted to find the Soviet hand behind a crude, gangsterish operation. I did not raise the subject with Kuznetsov.

Regarding my assignment, Kuznetsov spelled out Soviet preoccupation with some specific problems in Africa, particularly territorial disputes among various countries. Potentially, these could complicate achievement of our goals. The most worrisome situations were the disputes between Ethiopia and Somalia over the Ogaden region and between Morocco and Algeria over the Western Sahara. The U.S.S.R. had a special concern in the Ogaden; it had developed close relations with both countries and did not want to jeopardize its influence in the Horn of Africa by having to choose between them. On the other side of the continent, Moscow's approach was colored by its distrust of Algeria and its courtship of Morocco. Algeria was sympathetic to the Polisario Front in its efforts to win control of the former Spanish Sahara, where Morocco claimed a right to rule.

In both cases ideology was secondary to political calculations. The revolutionary regime which had overthrown Ethiopia's Emperor Haile Selassie espoused a strident Marxism, which should, in theory, have made it a Soviet favorite. Soviet, Cuban, and East German military advisers and matériel had become deeply engaged in the Ethiopians' efforts to crush a persistent rebellion in Eritrea. But Somalia also professed a brand of socialism and, more important, had made available for Soviet use the port of Berbera, a strategic outpost on the Indian Ocean. With much to gain in both countries, Moscow had a great deal to lose if they both demanded Soviet backing.

Again theoretically, the Saharan issue should have brought Moscow to the side of Algeria and the Polisario guerrillas. They were socialists, liberators. Morocco was an Islamic monarchy. The ideological merits were clear. But the Soviets had other, practical concerns that inhibited choice. Not wanting to drive Morocco farther into the Western camp, they also resented Algeria's flirtation with Peking and the support the Chinese were giving the Polisario Front's military efforts. As with the Ogaden, conflict endangered Soviet goals instead of serving them. Where troubles had once provided fertile ground for meddling in African affairs, local rivalries now impeded Moscow's purposes.

As my colleagues and I worked on in the early days of July, our task was to produce a plan for extending to Africa the principle of the sanctity of frontiers which had been central to the diplomatic drive for a European security agreement. Even though Africa's boundaries had been set in the nineteenth century by colonial powers oblivious to tribal geography and tradition, the U.S.S.R. wanted no forcible changes made in the often arbitrary lines drawn by European map makers.

At the center of Moscow's concern was an issue that had little meaning for Africa: the unresolved boundary dispute between China and the Soviet Union over territory along the Amur and Ussuri rivers acquired by the tsars at about the same time that England, France, Germany, Spain, and Portugal were parceling out African land among themselves. The Kremlin feared any precedent anywhere in the world which might help the Chinese reclaim the region it once ceded to Russia. Policy toward Africa had to fit this imperative, whether or not it made pragmatic sense.

The review, then, was something of a charade; the outcome had been defined in advance. The specific task set for the Foreign Ministry was the drafting of a message for Leonid Brezhnev to send to all African heads of state, broadly setting out Soviet policy, emphasizing the central principle of the inviolability of frontiers. I was very glad when this tedious exercise came to an end, but by then it was time for us to return to New York.

24

ON A GOLDEN AFTERNOON IN LATE SEPTEMBER 1976, AN isolated corner of New York's Kennedy Airport slowly filled with people eyeing one another to see who belonged and who had intruded. Milling around their cars, idly chatting or nervously checking their appearance, they kept glancing now and then into the haze that shimmered over the distant runway. An Ilyushin 62, a four-engine jet, carrying Soviet Foreign Minister Andrei Gromyko and his delegation to the 1976 session of the UN General Assembly, soon landed on the field.

Waiting to greet him and his fifty or sixty minions were the elite of the Soviet bloc diplomatic community in New York—and some who wished to be regarded as ranking figures in it. From the Soviet Mission there were Ambassador Malik and three deputy permanent representatives, including KGB chief Yuri Drozdov; the secretary of the Soviet Communist Party's New York branch, Aleksandr Podshchekoldin; the Ukrainian and Belorussian ambassadors; and the Mission's top security officer. The UN ambassadors from the Warsaw Pact nations had also turned out for the occasion, as had the envoy from Mongolia.

These dignitaries, at least, had been invited. But almost half of the fidgeting crowd was made up of interlopers: the deputies from the Ukrainian and Belorussian missions, for example, and Boris Prokofiev, a deputy UN Under Secretary General for economic and social affairs, who was constantly currying favor with Soviet higher-ups. The main diversion of these annual greeting ceremonies for Gromyko was to see which ambitious Soviets would manage to push themselves into the receiving line to get a quick, wordless handshake from the Foreign Minister. Since Gromyko wasted almost no time on such courtesies, the uninvited Soviets stood to gain very little from their presence at Kennedy. Nevertheless, in search of fleeting contact with power and celebrity, they always turned up.

The most prominent man in the crowd was not part of the Soviet community in New York. Ambassador Anatoly Dobrynin was the one official whom Gromyko would want to see at this moment.

During my summer home leave I had noted the familiar signs of American-election-year fever within the Foreign Ministry. By late September, I knew from experience, the fever would have become all-consuming. With the presidential vote roughly six weeks away, Moscow policymakers would be burning to know the identity of the winning candidate. Gromyko would be counting on Dobrynin to tell him.

"You'd better be ready," I told Dobrynin in a half-joking greeting. "He's going to squeeze you."

"Not just me," he said. "All of us. The Center has been bombarding Washington for months. We've nearly been squeezed dry already. Now it's your turn."

Dobrynin did not achieve his longevity in the Washington embassy or his exceptional influence in Moscow by making rash predictions, but I asked him if he could pick the winner between President Gerald Ford and Jimmy Carter. He laughed and shrugged. "I wish I did know. No one does."

Tired after the long trip from Moscow—although his forward compartment on the special plane was equipped with beds—Gromyko sped through the airport reception with perfunctory handshakes and no small talk. Over supper with a few of us at the Mission he listened with half an ear to Malik's and my discussion of the General Assembly agenda and the issues he would encounter during the session. His mind was on America, but he wanted to rest before plunging into the subject.

At a senior staff meeting in Malik's office, which the minister made his own while he was in New York, Gromyko lectured the Mission officials and me on his and our responsibilities. While he had come to take part in the General Assembly and to deliver the customary major foreign policy address, Gromyko made it clear that he regarded those duties as routine. His first priority was the relationship with the United States and the talks he would hold with Secretary of State Henry Kissinger.

"For now," he said, "I want all of you to concentrate on the American side of things. All of you. New York isn't just the United Nations. It's a very important *American* city with many well-informed and influential people. You should have contacts with the ones here who know what's going on. Use them. We want all the information you can get."

Trying to turn UN specialists into American political analysts, Gromyko was showing his agitation more than his common sense. Our contributions would be paltry at best.

No unease was apparent, however, in his manner when he finished instructing us and turned to Dobrynin for a forecast of the likely presidential campaign victor. In contrast to his frankness to me at the airport, Dobrynin gave Gromyko a measured but evasive answer. Most of his American contacts, he said, declined to make clear predictions. The situation was still too complicated, the outcome too uncertain. Whereas the incumbent President held a natural advantage and seemed to have the better chance, there was always the possibility that "completely unforeseen circumstances" would make Jimmy Carter the winner.

Knowing what Gromyko wanted to hear—that Ford was the likely winner—Dobrynin tilted his analysis a little to conform to that preference. Most of all, however, he hedged. Weighing the two candidates from the point of view of U.S.-Soviet ties, he also leaned toward Ford, whom Moscow regarded as a follower of Richard Nixon's foreign policies, but did not dismiss the possibility of working productively with Carter.

Characterizing the President as a "football player," Dobrynin presented the view Gromyko shared: Ford was a known quantity and a leader with whom Moscow could continue to do business. Judging by Jimmy Carter's campaign pronouncements, especially on human rights, he was far less likely to continue the policy approach that had fostered U.S.-Soviet rapprochement. But appearances might prove deceiving, Dobrynin cautioned. Election-year rhetoric is often a poor guide to a President's conduct once in office.

Sensible as they were, Dobrynin's words could not appease Gromyko's hunger for certainty. He wanted more definitive answers and had difficulty accepting the fact that they were not available.

Behind his impatience lay an obsession not with American domestic politics but with the United States as both adversary and partner. It has been through this prism, exclusively from the viewpoint of Soviet advantage, that the Kremlin has scrutinized all American Presidents since the October Revolution. Objective assessment is organically alien to the Soviet leadership. It was not important whether or not an American President was good for the Americans. What mattered was how he regarded the Soviet Union and whether he was good for the Soviets. Making use of this "unerring yardstick," as Gromyko liked to call it, the Kremlin has in fact extended "honored" recognition to one extent or another to only three U.S. Presidents since the establishment

370

of Soviet-American diplomatic relations in 1933: Franklin D. Roosevelt for establishing those relations and for the Yalta agreements; John F. Kennedy for the Moscow test-ban treaty and his demonstration of strength during the Cuban missile crisis; and Richard M. Nixon for his Moscow visit, SALT, and détente.

But this measuring rod is not reserved only for American leaders. It is the universal standard Moscow applies. Thus, Winston Churchill was never an outstanding leader but rather an archenemy of the Soviet state and Communism and architect of the cold war. Likewise, after World War II, West Germany had an evil Konrad Adenauer and a good Willy Brandt. General de Gaulle was bad and good—bad before his visit to Moscow in 1966, good afterwards.

Irrespective of the oversimplifications applied to American Presidents, for Gromyko, who had long considered relations with the United States central to Soviet policy abroad, and for Leonid Brezhnev, who had linked many of his domestic programs to the progress of East-West détente, Moscow's ties with Washington were of crucial importance. Relations between the U.S.S.R. and the United States were not just dealings between two powerful states but complex bonds between the two poles of power in the world, between the mightiest forces of two opposite and competing sociopolitical systems. Without abandoning superpower rivalry or the drive for influence in the Third World, the Soviet leadership had tried to improve relations with the United States.

What had been achieved between 1972 and 1976, however, depended considerably on a fragile network of personal and direct contacts between the Kremlin and the White House. President Ford's defeat, Gromyko feared, would interrupt the channel of communication established between Dobrynin and Kissinger. An interruption would be damaging enough; even more worrisome was the possibility that Jimmy Carter might break this special system of contact entirely.

The Kremlin preferred continuity in American leadership. Conservative in many of their attitudes, Soviet leaders dislike abrupt changes or turbulence challenging accepted practices at home or forcing a rearrangement of patterns of conduct abroad they find favorable to them. Working as Gromyko's adviser in 1972, I saw for myself how apprehensive he became as Richard Nixon's reelection campaign drew to a close. Four years later, even though he shared Dobrynin's disparaging view of Ford's intellectual capacities, Gromyko was in the grip of the same kind of tension. Having dealt with seven U.S. administrations, he had no desire to begin again with a new and unpredictable eighth.

Along with most of their people, Soviet leaders are bewitched by the United States of America, but with a mixture of envy and scorn, respect and ridicule. The men in the Kremlin are absorbed by questions of America's military, political, and economic power, and awed by its technological capacity. Ordinary Soviets are enormously curious about the United States. But the U.S.S.R.'s pride has been hurt by a pervasive feeling that the United States does not accord Soviets the recognition and equality they deserve.

Russia and the United States are both among the most populous multiracial countries on the planet, besides being geographical neighbors—a condition not really perceived by many Russians and Americans. But these neighbors are only two miles apart across the Bering Strait from Alaska's Little Diomede Island to Siberia's Big Diomede Island. Both the United States and the Soviet Union occupy large, rich land areas that resemble each other in many respects. Visiting southern Russia in 1867, Mark Twain wrote: "To me the place was like what one sees in the Sierras." In Odessa he wrote: "I have not felt so much at home for a long time."

There are notable psychological and cultural similarities as well between the two peoples. Russians also have a pioneering spirit; their pride and warmheartedness are qualities Americans are known for. There is in the older generation some nostalgic affection for the World War II alliance, exemplified by the friendly relations between Russian and American troops on Germany's Elbe River in 1945. But what is public in America emerges only in private in the Soviet Union. Among friends, liberated by vodka and a sense of security, Russians can be outgoing. Having to suppress this nature most of the time, however, they wistfully admire its expression in Americans to the same degree that they dislike the snobbery or intellectual arrogance they perceive in some other foreigners.

Russian interest in America developed even before the United States came into being, in the course of geographical discoveries and settlement by Russian explorers in the area later called Alaska and even down the Pacific coast into Spanish California. The Russians conquered Siberia very much the way Americans won the West. Siberia was a huge virgin land, hard and wild, but also beautiful and rich.

In the American colonial period, Mikhail Lomonosov and other Russian scholars were acquainted with the works of Benjamin Franklin, who was highly regarded in Russian intellectual society. A prominent representative of the Russian revolutionary tradition, Aleksandr Radishchev, championed the American Revolution and its leader, George Washington. More than a century later V. I. Lenin also praised the American Revolution. And although he called President Woodrow Wilson "a servant of the capitalist sharks" and castigated "bloody American imperialism" for its part in the foreign intervention in Soviet Russia, he stressed that "we are decidedly for economic understanding with America—with all countries but especially with America."* Lenin met with Frank Vanderlip, Armand Hammer, and other American businessmen in order to promote the development of Soviet-U.S. trade. According to him, "economic interests and the economic position of the classes which rule our state lie at the root of both our home and foreign policy."

What commanded Lenin's esteem and the enduring respect of his successors was American economic might, the capacity for technical innovation, the productive strength they wished Soviets could emulate. Although they suppress much of the story in contemporary publications, the leaders remember the prewar collaboration in industry that brought a transfusion of expertise and energy to many Soviet enterprises. Their memories—and hopes of renewed commercial

---

* V. I. Lenin, *Collected Works*, Vol. 30 (1975), p. 51.

relations—figured strongly in Brezhnev's push for rapprochement with President Nixon.

This détente, of course, had its limitations. In various strata of Soviet society, and particularly among the leadership, there is a great deal of hostility toward the United States. Lenin defined American imperialism as "the freshest, strongest, and latest in joining in the worldwide slaughter of nations for the division of capitalist profits." Many still believe that, and it explains why American military power is an overwhelming preoccupation. It is not, however, a mirror image of the U.S. fear of surprise nuclear attack or even vulnerability to such a threat. They abhor American armed strength for what it could do, if properly and consistently directed, to frustrate Soviet expansionism. Furthermore, they understand that it is the main, if not only, barrier to their plans for world domination.

One day, while we were lunching at his dacha at Vnukovo, I asked Gromyko what he saw as the greatest weakness of U.S. foreign policy toward the Soviet Union. "They don't comprehend our final goals," he responded promptly. "And they mistake tactics for strategy. Besides, they have too many doctrines and concepts proclaimed at different times, but the absence of a solid, coherent, and consistent policy is their big flaw."

Gromyko added that "in diplomacy we are superior to the Americans." He was referring to the United States' frequent changes of personnel in important diplomatic positions and delegates to major negotiations. Diplomats at the Foreign Ministry usually have a good laugh over the new round of amateurs and political appointees herded into the American diplomatic service following the installation of an administration.

Gromyko's opinion was shared by other Soviet leaders, who generally see American foreign policy as likely to zigzag even during the term of a single administration. Still, they know that Americans cannot long ignore dealing with the Soviet Union on a business-as-usual basis. "Why not wait until the next presidential election?" is a typical comment of Foreign Ministry officers in charge of American

374

affairs when they confront a difficult situation with the United States.

While intrigued by American freedoms, political pluralism, and cultural diversity, the Soviet leadership is unable to comprehend fully the mechanism of the American political system. Although some understanding of the relationship between Congress and the President has developed recently, there is still little grasp of the relationship of American congressmen to their constituencies, the real role of public opinion, and that worst bugaboo, freedom of information, which they see as a threat to security. The idealism of the American Revolution, carried over into both domestic and foreign policy more than two hundred years later, is perceived by the Soviets as a crippling naïveté. Its manifestations sometimes make them doubt American seriousness. In sum, the Soviets are simply baffled by the American system.

It puzzles them how a complex and little-regulated society can maintain such a high level of production, efficiency, and technological innovation. Many are inclined toward the fantastic notion that there must be a secret control center somewhere in the United States. They themselves, after all, are used to a system ruled by a small group working in secrecy in one place. Moreover, the Soviets continue to chew on Lenin's dogma that bourgeois governments are just the "servants" of monopoly capital. Is that not the secret control center? they reason.

The great gap in Soviet understanding of U.S. policies and practices sometimes means that even experienced message carriers and advisers like Dobrynin do not necessarily convey accurate information. Americans would be astonished if they knew how little Gromyko, who has lived in America and visits regularly, knows about many aspects of day-to-day life in their country. One of Dobrynin's important functions has been as an informal educator trying to correct the limited and distorted picture Soviet rulers have of America. On a visit to New York, Gromyko talked with Dobrynin and me about the U.S. economy, a conversation that began when Gromyko, spooning honey into his tea, remarked that American bees were turning out a distinctly poor product.

The Mission, in fact, had served the Foreign Minister the cheapest available honey, as I explained to him. He immediately wanted to know the price, which he thought was high, and then the cost of other goods—better honey, shirts, Manhattan apartments. As Dobrynin and I answered his questions, Gromyko expressed surprise at the expense of each item. He had never visited American stores and knew barely anything of the costs or real standard of living in the United States.

Dobrynin decided to use this particular conversation to enlighten him in a broader way. To please Gromyko, he agreed that prices were high (although he knew that they were not when compared with the corresponding portion of their salaries that Soviets must spend for food and consumer goods). But he also added that the variety of items available in American markets was extensive.

Gromyko wrinkled his nose in a characteristic gesture of distaste for an inconvenient truth. "Maybe you're right," he admitted, "but they have so many problems too. Poverty. Massive unemployment. Race hatred."

"Of course there are those things. No one denies that." Dobrynin was sugaring the pill he wanted Gromyko to swallow. "But it seems to me that Soviet correspondents tend to overemphasize that side of things. When they focus only or too much on the problems, they create a mistaken impression of the situation here. You know, when I go home to Moscow, people ask me about America as though they thought it was about to fall apart." He laughed loudly but continued seriously. "Our people should think more realistically. They ought to have more accurate information, not just the exaggerations of hack writers."

Gromyko mulled over this advice for a bit before conceding that Soviet propaganda would be sounder if it came closer to reality and that Soviet journalists were too likely to report what they thought Moscow wanted to hear. In practical terms, however, Dobrynin's lesson was wasted. Gromyko made it a point not to interfere in Soviet policy outside his own area. The Soviet press still portrays U.S. society in such unrealistic and contradictory terms that it confuses not only ordinary citizens but also the leaders and the elite. The United States has been described in Soviet media as the richest nation on earth and a country of dying capitalism; as an international robber and a benefactor; as both crumbling and efficient. Highly selective distribution of materials taken out of context, strict controls on foreign travel, narrow limits on contacts with foreigners (even with those from socialist countries), the constant tide of official Soviet views through the mass media and the educational system, leave the people at the mercy of Party propagandists.

As it is in the West, visual information is especially effective. Numerous photographs of the Salvation Army passing out bowls of soup, long lines of the unemployed, men and women sleeping in snow-filled gutters, disfigured bodies of infants poisoned by Americans in Vietnam, plans for nuclear attack on the Soviet Union taken from the American press, with arrows pointing to different Soviet cities—all these things are minutely examined by the population. And the impression made is most favorable to the U.S.S.R. Nevertheless, many Soviets remain fascinated by the material products of American society.

The crowds of young men at the Moscow store which specializes in radios and phonographs could appraise the different makes of U.S. tape recorders or hi-fi equipment as expertly as I could discuss political books. Even into the seventies a late-model American car parked on a Moscow street would draw a knot of onlookers, pretending to be knowledgeable. In a provincial town such a phenomenon might almost stop traffic.

A similar hunger for American literature rather than technology is strong among Soviet intellectuals. They know and cherish Twain, Hemingway, London, and Faulkner, many of whose translated works were only published in Khrushchev's time. Contemporary authors like John Updike, John Cheever, and William Styron also attract a wide readership. Tickets to a semi-private showing of an American movie at the Moscow film union theater, Dom Kino, are prestige items nearly beyond price. Voice of America broadcasts, tape-recorded and circulated, have made American jazz and rock-and-roll a major part of the vast musical underground in the U.S.S.R.

In admiring these and other things about America, however, the Soviets feel that their own achievements are not properly recognized by the Americans. It should be remembered that most Soviets are especially proud of their own culture, and consider it superior to the American. No other nation in the nineteenth century, after all, produced such a pantheon of writers as Tolstoy, Dostoevsky, Chekhov, Turgenev, and Pushkin.

Leonid Brezhnev's policy of détente soon became no less confusing to the Soviet people than most other aspects of relations between the two countries. "International détente," an idea promoted by the Soviet Union as one manifestation of peaceful coexistence, was understood in the United States to mean something other than what it meant to the U.S.S.R. There is no simple answer to why that happened. George F. Kennan wrote that he had never "entirely understood why an impression got about that there was beginning, in our relationship with the Soviet Union, a new period of normalization and relaxation of tensions, to be sharply distinguished from all that had gone before."[*] Henry Kissinger's correct interpretation of détente as "the mitigation of conflict among adversaries, not the cultivation of friendship,"[†] made years after the Moscow summit, does not exactly correspond to President Nixon's characterization of it in 1972. Nixon said that "the new foundation has been laid for a new relationship between the two most powerful nations in the world."[‡] His statement was accompanied by reservations about remaining ideological hostility and compared the principles agreed upon in Moscow by the United States and the U.S.S.R. to a road map each of them had to follow. But when he spoke of the "new foundation," Nixon created a far too optimistic picture of the actual relationship between the superpowers. Brezhnev, for his part,

* George F. Kennan, *The Nuclear Delusion* (Pantheon, 1982), p. 48.

† Henry Kissinger, *Years of Upheaval* (Little, Brown, 1982), p. 753.

‡ *Public Papers of the Presidents of the United States: Richard M. Nixon, 1972* (U.S. Government Printing Office, 1974), p. 661.

although more cautiously, spoke at the end of 1972 about the "substantial new development" in Soviet-American relations.*

It is difficult to explain the true nature of détente in the seventies because it was a corollary to various specific objectives and subjective factors, some of them short-lived, others more long-lasting. There is no question that at the threshold of the seventies the world was substantially different from what it was at the beginning of the cold war. China and numerous Third World nations, as well as other powers, were unwilling to subordinate their policies to Moscow or Washington. The rough strategic parity between the Soviet Union and the United States made the American position-of-strength policy obsolete and forced both sides to search for accommodations in arms control. Changes in relations between the United States and the U.S.S.R. were inevitable and found their implementation in the agreements of the early seventies.

Unfortunately, however, many in the United States and Western Europe drew the wrong conclusions about these moves. The result was a hodgepodge of truth and reality, illusion, hope, misconceptions, and wishful thinking which led to a grandiose notion of détente. But that notion was like a desert mirage; the image is there, but it is not real.

On the surface, the policy of détente appeared attractive and positive. In speeches by Kremlin officials and in negotiations, the Soviets stressed that their desires were to prevent the outbreak of nuclear war, to limit the arms race, to develop normal and mutually beneficial relations on a long-term basis, to seek understanding, to develop economic, scientific, and technological cooperation, and to expand trade. With this comprehensive list, one might well be led to think that the Soviet Union was abandoning its ambition of the final victory of Communism. In fact, Soviet leaders told the West repeatedly what it wanted to hear and lulled many into believing it.

Numerous Americans felt that détente would maximize

* L. I. Brezhnev, *Our Course: Peace and Socialism* (Novosti Press Agency Publishing House, 1975), p. 309.

cooperation while discouraging uncontrolled competition. The Kremlin welcomed a certain amount of cooperation, on its terms, but it never accepted the idea of abandoning competition, either military or ideological. One of the great fallacies of détente was the idea that if the Soviet Union were engaged in economic, trade, cultural, and other agreements, the West would be able to moderate the Soviets' voracious appetite for expansion and promote a shift in the U.S.S.R.'s global aims. Nothing could be further from reality. The Soviet Union has never contemplated agreeing to arrangements that would in any way tie its hands in the pursuit of what it wanted.

In 1970, at a meeting of diplomats in the Foreign Ministry in Moscow, Andrei Gromyko made a statement that was a model of clear intent which has in no way changed over the years: "The foundations of our foreign policy built by Lenin remain fully and totally valid today, and détente in no way has changed our ultimate objectives. But Lenin also taught us to be clever in our dealings with leaders of capitalist countries."

Gromyko pointed out that it was necessary to stress the importance of normal businesslike relations, not to frighten other nations by bluntly revealing Communism's real objectives. No "we will bury you" from Andrei Gromyko. Referring to the guidelines adopted by Lenin in preparing for the 1922 Genoa Conference, the first international meeting in which the Soviet state participated, Gromyko reminded the assembled diplomats of Lenin's teaching that it was advisable to avoid any direct references to "inevitable bloody socialist revolutions" in the capitalist world. He went on to admonish us that such terrifying expressions should not be used because they would "only play into the hands of our enemy. Comrade Brezhnev has obeyed Lenin's advice in this respect." Privately, in conversations at his dacha in Vnukovo, he was even more candid, advising us to pretend in our talks with Americans that we ourselves did not take some Marxist dogmas seriously.

For the West, Leonid Brezhnev defined détente in rosy colors. But it was a different Brezhnev speaking a different language in his major addresses at meetings of the Soviet

Communist Party or to the followers of the world Communist movement. At the Twenty-fifth Party Congress in 1976, he offered an explanation of détente policy: "Détente does not in the slightest abolish, nor can it abolish or alter, the laws of the class struggle. No one should expect that because of détente Communists will reconcile themselves with capitalist exploitation or that monopolists will become followers of the revolution."* In his reports to the more restricted plenary sessions of the Central Committee, he underscored this point in even stronger terms.

Soviet leaders and ideologists have never tried to hide the fact that their policy then and now adheres to the conclusions Lenin articulated soon after the 1917 Revolution in Russia. Lenin's slogan "Who will win?"—a cry of determination to wage a "life-and-death struggle between capitalism and Communism"†—continues as the unchallenged bottom line. At the Twenty-sixth Party Congress in 1981, Brezhnev clearly reconfirmed that position by stressing as his basic thesis that all nations will inevitably become socialist.

Yuri Andropov, speaking in Moscow in April 1982, repeated these words, pointing out that "the future belongs to socialism."** In 1983, Boris Ponomarev, at the festivities accompanying the hundredth anniversary celebration of Marx's death, was more forceful. He recalled the "inevitability of the overthrow of capitalism by revolution of the working people" and declared that although "capitalism [has] managed to buy time and prolong its existence," it "will be liquidated."

In 1981, Konstantin Chernenko declared that "capitalism has discredited itself" and that the peoples will come "sooner or later to socialism."‡

---

* L. I. Brezhnev, "Report of the CPSU Central Committee and the Immediate Tasks of the Party in Home and Foreign Policy," Twenty-fifth Congress of the CPSU, 1976, p. 39.

† V. I. Lenin, *Selected Works*, Vol. 3 (1975), p. 627.

** Y. V. Andropov, *Speeches and Writings* (Pergamon Press, 1983), p. 224.

‡ K. U. Chernenko, *Utverzhdat Leninsky Stil v partynoy rabote* (Moscow, 1983), p. 23.

It is an old message which has been restated at every Party Congress, but perhaps because it is old it does not strike the ear as forcefully or as alarmingly as it did in the century's earlier days. Nevertheless, it is meant today as it was meant in 1917. Some of the methods and styles of implementation have changed, but the underlying desire of the Soviet Union's leaders to dominate the earth remains ever fresh.

Détente was viewed by the U.S.S.R. not only as a temporary measure but also as a selective policy. The Politburo assumed it to be a tactical maneuver for a certain period of time that would in no way supersede the Marxist-Leninist idea of the final victory of the worldwide revolutionary process.

It comes down to this: Détente was a useful means of buying time for the Soviet Union. Moscow knows it cannot immediately subjugate the world and directly govern the people of the earth. Although the Kremlin is committed to the ultimate vision of a world under its control, the leaders are realistic enough to understand that at the present time this is impossible. They know there will be no Communist revolution in the United States in the near future. But they are patient and take the long view. They wait and work toward a clear goal. To be sure, the notion held by some in the West that the Soviet leaders have a secret master plan, a timetable for conquering the world's nations one by one, is pure fiction; but while no such specific plan exists on paper, the idea of expanding Soviet power to the point of world domination is a fundamental long-range aspiration. Whether through ideology, diplomacy, force, or economics, Moscow believes that eventually it will be supreme—not necessarily in this century but certainly in the next—in the competition between socialist and capitalist systems, and that such a struggle will be progressively intensified and is historically inevitable. In other words, those goals cannot be comprehended as the mere continuation of historical Russian imperialist designs or as simple power politics. They are much broader and are deeply ideological.

It is essential to understand the nature of this international struggle that is so central to our time. In order to widen their zone of control or influence, Soviet leaders are focusing their attention on support of various national liberation movements in Asia, Africa, and Latin America while pursuing subversive activities in the West through Communist parties and other organizations. They provide matériel and military help, training, and ideological indoctrination. Although priority is given to those that follow the Soviet model, assistance has also been extended to movements having no Marxist-Leninist base, if their success can weaken the West. Such aid has not always produced auspicious results, as in the cases of Egypt and Indonesia. Moscow, however, is confident that in time the pendulum will eventually swing in its direction.

For the time being, the Soviet Union needs the West. It used détente successfully to get what it wanted: amicable relations with the United States and Europe, credits, and substantial economic aid. The U.S.S.R. realizes that it can obtain that assistance only from the West. How would the leadership provide bread for its citizens if not for American and other nations' grain sales? Where else can the Soviets secure advanced technology that they are incapable of producing in sufficient quantity or quality for themselves? In this connection, it does indeed seem that Lenin was right: capitalists are willing to fight for the privilege of selling Communists the rope with which to hang themselves.

Soviet leaders know well how to pursue their aims. They go slowly, but surely.

I have often been asked whether the Soviet Union would initiate a nuclear war against the United States. I know from numerous Soviet leaders, military and non-military alike, including members of the Politburo, that the answer to this question is an unequivocal no. The Soviet Union does not intend to achieve its goals by means of nuclear world war with the United States and its allies. The old idea of the inevitability of such a struggle was abandoned even before Stalin's death. Soviet leaders are convinced that their victory will come in the course of the development of human society. And if they can speed up the process with a few small, limited conventional wars, so much the better. I know of only one instance when a nuclear strike was even discussed—in 1969 during the time of the Soviet-Chinese border incidents, when the Chinese nuclear capability was no real threat.

As long as the United States' strategic nuclear deterrent is strong enough, nuclear war is something Soviet leaders might contemplate only in the most extreme circumstances, if they were absolutely convinced that the country was in mortal peril and they could see no alternative. They consider the prospect of a worldwide nuclear war unthinkable, to be avoided at all costs, even at the expense of Soviet prestige. All Soviet leaders, the old as well as the new generation, understand perfectly that nuclear world war can bury both Communism and capitalism in the same grave.

Political and military chiefs in Moscow also realize that even if the Soviet Union were to launch a preemptive nuclear strike, the American second-strike capability would be so effective as to virtually wipe out most of the heart and brain of the U.S.S.R. The Soviets cannot accept such a risk. While they are predatory, they are not mad. Like all other human beings, they fear for their own survival. They know that they themselves might well perish along with millions of their more defenseless countrymen.

I never knew whether a nuclear fallout shelter existed in the Foreign Ministry building. I doubt whether Gromyko could find his own way to such a redoubt quickly enough if nuclear war should commence. Of course, he would be escorted to the ministry's bunker or relocation sites outside Moscow by persons whose job it is to carry out such procedures. Given a warning of a few hours, it is possible that many Soviet leaders could survive and continue to function. Whether there would be time to take shelter is another question. However, under military control, the Soviet Union continues to improve its active and passive nationwide defense systems at a cost of more than $2 billion annually. Over 100,000 people work full time in the program. Soviet civil defense could limit damage to the basic political and military structure, protect the strategic command, and ensure continuity of vital government operations. But these measures are not geared to the survival of the population at large.

It would be logical to expect that the pitifully inadequate civil defense systems might have influenced the Soviets to pursue the opportunities provided by détente to slow their military buildup. In addition, the fact that the United States had frozen many of its programs both in strategic weaponry and in conventional forces should have encouraged the Kremlin to do the same. Yet the Soviet leadership has its own logic in the matter.

Instead of easing weapons accumulation after the 1972 Moscow summit, the U.S.S.R. continued to modernize all elements of its arsenal—strategic and conventional—with an increasing flow of missiles, aircraft, tanks, ships, and artillery. At the expense of other sectors of the economy and much beyond its real defense needs, the Soviet Union stepped up its military production by one-third. Its military-industrial base has become the world's largest. The estimated dollar cost of Soviet military investment by far exceeds America's.

Certainly the Soviets have legitimate concerns about defense of their country; the Second World War cost them dearly. Naturally, the U.S.S.R. wants armed forces capable of defending it. But the Kremlin has another goal. Moscow is going to use nuclear military might as a political instrument to pressure, intimidate, and blackmail, if necessary, to get what the Soviets want from West Germany, Japan, or other countries. Soviet rulers still rankle over the memory of their humiliation in the Cuban missile crisis, and they are exerting every effort to prevent any repetition.

Also, the specter of China forces the maintenance of considerable strategic and conventional forces ready for any eventuality on the Soviet-Chinese border.

Further, the refusal to abandon support for national liberation movements as a weapon against the Western powers, and persistent efforts by the Kremlin to penetrate the nations of the Third World for the purpose of luring them into its orbit, imply a willingness to project Soviet military power over the globe and risk, if necessary, conventional wars. Here again, the Soviets are guided by Lenin's formulas, which state that "socialists cannot be opposed to all war," particularly "revolutionary wars" or national wars by "colonial peoples for liberation" or civil wars. Consequently, the Soviet leadership favors and instigates some local conventional wars. In explaining the Soviet military doctrine in 1981, Defense Minister Dmitri Ustinov called attempts to attribute to the U.S.S.R. a willingness to launch the "first nuclear strike" unfounded nonsense, but he said nothing regarding conventional war.

Finally, the Soviet leadership still accepts Lenin's theory that imperialist powers, as they suffer inevitable losses to progressive forces, or as the result of conflicts caused by Soviet pressures on the West, may resort to war against the Soviet Union. Along this line, they also think it possible that the "most adventuristic, reactionary forces of imperialism" might get their hands on the bomb and attack the Soviet Union in a desperate attempt to save capitalism.

Détente's ambiguity increased further in the mid-seventies when Soviet-American relations had been clouded in the aftermath of the upheavals resulting from Watergate and the Jackson-Vanik amendment to the Trade Reform Bill, which tied the Soviet Union's most-favored-nation status to a relaxation of Moscow's emigration policy. That linkage made the leadership's achievement of its goals in economic relations with the United States remote. Furthermore, progress in SALT negotiations stalled after the 1974 Ford-Brezhnev summit in Vladivostok.

Soviet leaders never properly understood the enormous effect of such a "trivial" thing as Watergate. "Watergates" are routine and permanent features of life in the Soviet Union from top to bottom. Bugging, taping, intimidation, bribery, lying, cover-ups—these are all standard measures taken by the KGB, with the leadership's blessing, wherever it wishes and without restriction. Likewise, the Soviets could not comprehend how the United States Congress had the power to block implementation of presidential promises to the U.S.S.R. regarding the coveted most-favored-nation status. Brezhnev, Gromyko, and others truly suspected that the Americans had somehow tricked them in this respect.

Nonetheless, if the Soviet leadership was unable to understand Watergate, what it did realize almost immediately was that presidential authority in the United States had been

386

weakened; and the Kremlin quickly began to exploit the situation. The Politburo decided to deploy the new medium-range SS-20 missiles in the western U.S.S.R. in violation of détente, in an effort to alter the military balance in Europe. There was no fanfare over this; it was all done under the guise of "replacing" old missiles. The peace movements around the world seemed to have missed this move completely. Only later did NATO members fully understand the dimensions of the Soviet threat and take responsive measures.

Under the pressure of events, of purposeful obstruction and unfulfilled promises, the Soviet leadership found the results of its détente policy falling short of the expectations they had aroused. If Richard Nixon oversold the prospective benefits of détente, so did his Kremlin counterparts. The Moscow skeptics who had been stifled or bypassed in 1972 were making themselves heard again by 1976. One important factor contributing to détente's disintegration was not fully realized in the West at that time: Leonid Brezhnev had passed his peak of influence at the Twenty-fifth Party Congress in 1976; thereafter he became more and more immobilized by illness. That fact enhanced the position of the faction within the leadership (Suslov, Andropov, and Ponomarev, among others) that was inclined to push the Americans harder and to engage in more militant activity in Africa and in other parts of the world where U.S. weaknesses could be exploited. Détente began to evaporate.

At détente's inception, the Kremlin made a few concessions to the West. It allowed a certain amount of emigration, permitted an increase in cultural and human exchanges, somewhat moderated the anti-imperialist tone of its propaganda, and even stopped jamming a few foreign radio broadcasts. But after the mid-seventies the flow of emigration from the Soviet Union, never steady or consistent, was reduced; information exchanges, never free of strict censorship, were curtailed to a minimum. And Moscow resumed its old habits, making a noise in every corner of the world, labeling any action by the West in Africa, Asia, the Middle East, or Latin America as neocolonialist and imperialist.

It was that cold current in Soviet-American relations, as

much as the uncertainty over the American voters' choice, which brought Gromyko to New York in September 1976 in such a high state of tension. Soviet leaders simultaneously needed and feared America. American strength was an obstacle to Soviet plans abroad but a useful support of the U.S.S.R.'s economy at home. Gromyko knew that many of his colleagues did not understand America. They cannot find security in unrestrained competition with it, and they cannot —to their disappointment—find the basis for coexistence with it.

25

ON SEPTEMBER 9, 1976, MAO TSE-TUNG DIED. OFFICIAL Soviet reaction was calm, brief, and correct, but the tone of Moscow's instructions to us in New York made it obvious that Mao's departure had stirred a wave of excited expectation. Yakov Malik and I were ordered immediately to visit the Chinese Mission to the UN and sign the book of condolences. Further, we were directed to pass the word in casual conversations with others in the UN that China's friends remembered the good old days of alliance and that it was time to end the bitterness in Soviet-Chinese relations.

Some time later, at an informal dinner at the Mission, Gromyko said that the leadership specifically wanted us to refrain from involvement in anything that might hinder efforts to improve relations with Peking.

"We must avoid anything that would provoke an anti-Soviet response from the Chinese," he stated. Gromyko never glanced directly at Malik while delivering these instructions, but everyone knew they were specifically aimed at him. Sitting on Gromyko's right, Malik kept his eyes fixed on his plate in silence.

Gromyko asked me what I thought of Huang Hua, China's Ambassador to the UN. He particularly wanted to know if I had noted anything unusual in Hua's behavior since Mao's death, but I said there had been no visible change. He then remarked that after so many years of upheaval in China it was still too early to expect any significant shift in Chinese policy.

"Yet," he continued, "in my statement to the General Assembly I've decided to underscore the importance the Soviet Union has attached and continues to attach to normalization of relations with China without any hint of criticism—without any hint."

Moscow's lack of reliable information about China was nothing new. The most valuable part of the Soviet spy network in China—undercover operations—was virtually suspended after the Chinese Communist victory in 1949. Stalin believed there were more than enough pro-Soviet officials at various levels of the Chinese Communist Party who would willingly tell Moscow everything it wanted to know. This proved to be a fantastic blunder.

Since that time the KGB had not been able to mount an effective intelligence apparatus in China. Although there was a Soviet embassy in Peking, its activities were severely restricted. Not only did diplomats have instructions not to speak frankly to the Chinese but their requests to visit most other parts of the country were routinely denied. Therefore Moscow was largely forced to observe what was going on in China as the Americans once did, from Hong Kong and Tokyo. Chinese specialists from the Central Committee, the KGB, and the Foreign Ministry were assigned to Soviet embassies in the countries considered most dependable for this kind of intelligence—Japan, Tanzania, the United States, and a few others—but the data they obtained was generally secondhand.

At a meeting with Bert Johnson, I told him about Gromyko's statements. Johnson was interested in Gromyko's thinking about Soviet-American relations on the eve of the presidential election. But there was nothing new; the Soviets continued to take a wait-and-see approach. Gromyko didn't expect much from his forthcoming meeting with President Ford. Still preferring Ford, the Soviets had begun to watch Carter closely. Gromyko thought it a good sign that Cyrus Vance was becoming influential with Carter, but he deplored the possibility that Zbigniew Brzezinski might play a prominent role in a Democratic administration.

As I was reviewing Gromyko's appointments the morning after his arrival in New York, I discovered a disturbing omission. The schedule did not include Secretary General Waldheim's customary dinner for the Foreign Ministers of the five permanent members of the Security Council. I was surprised. Waldheim had sent Gromyko's invitation well in advance. Since there had been no refusal, Waldheim assumed Gromyko would attend as he had done previously. Nor did the schedule include a personal meeting with the Secretary General, something Waldheim had been counting on. For the Secretary General, as for the American President, it was an election year, and Waldheim badly wanted another term.

I asked Gromyko's assistant, Yuri Fokin, what was wrong. "Arkady Nikolaevich," he snapped, "don't you know what Andrei Andreyevich thinks of Waldheim?" I knew very well, but to express that attitude so crudely would not be in our interest. I decided to take the matter up with Gromyko at Glen Cove, where he was usually in a good mood.

Gromyko's physician had recommended a seven- or eight-kilometer walk around the gardens whenever he was at Glen Cove. The estate provided the isolation he craved. A high fence and thickly wooded terrain stood between him and any offending reminder of the outside world. Yet even there, he was always accompanied by his retinue of advisers and guards. He would pace round and round on his constitutional with his entourage until his physical exercise requirements had been met.

After his walk, lunch was usually served in the dining room for twenty to twenty-five people. Attendance was deemed a special honor. Those who wanted a drink would look hopefully at the small table in the corner of the dining room that served as a bar. Gromyko drank very rarely and did not approve of others indulging in his presence. Without his specific permission, drinks were never served. Nevertheless, Dobrynin, who was always present in New York during Gromyko's stay, usually took what everyone felt was a courageous initiative, saying something like: "Andrei Andreyevich, perhaps we will have a little something to raise our spirits." Lidiya Gromyko nearly always seconded him. Gromyko might fail to react or respond to the suggestion in any way, sitting stonily silent. In that case, drinks would not be served. At other times he would wave a hand and say in his leaden way, "Whoever wants a drink may have it, but I will not." The waitress would then place wine and vodka on the table.

This particular time I sat next to Vasily Makarov, who had brightened considerably at the prospect of getting a glass of vodka. I mentioned to him that I hoped to speak with Gromyko alone after lunch. He became uneasy. "What are you going to discuss with Andrei Andreyevich?"

"Gromyko should accept Waldheim's invitation to dinner with the Big Five, and he should also meet with him alone," I said.

"You're wasting your time," Makarov said. "We discussed that in Moscow. He's against it. If you bring it up, you'll get a blast."

Despite Makarov's warning, I did later raise the matter.

"Shevchenko, whose interests are you defending, Waldheim's or ours?" Gromyko demanded. "Waldheim is not a great power."

I tried to convince him that the majority of UN members would never understand why the Foreign Minister of the Soviet Union had snubbed the Secretary General. It was spitting in the face of the whole UN. Gromyko was unpersuaded.

"What will happen at this dinner? Idle talk. Nothing but empty chatter with a crowd of boring officials and their wives. How can one expect serious conversation in such a situation? It would only be for appearances, nothing else." His face took on a look of distaste as he continued. "Besides, the Chinese will be there. At this point, I don't want to speak to them, but if I'm there, it would also be wrong not to talk. And Waldheim will try to discuss some politics in his silly babbling way. . . . Well, we'll think it over," he said abruptly. When I raised the second question, that of a personal meeting with Waldheim, anger flooded his face. "Enough! I will meet with him at the dinner."

I stressed that the ministers of the major powers always met alone with Waldheim. These sessions were considered important if for no other reason than protocol, even when there was nothing serious to discuss, particularly at the time of the election for Secretary General. Gromyko scowled in silence, indicating clearly that our conversation was over.

Irascible and disgruntled, Gromyko went to Waldheim's dinner. His annoyance was crowned by the fact that Henry Kissinger arrived late by more than an hour. As far as the private meeting with Waldheim was concerned, however, he mulishly dug in his heels. Every day, Waldheim inquired about a time. Every day I avoided an answer, embarrassed at having to offend him with the excuse that Gromyko's schedule was still being reviewed and revised.

With the help of Dobrynin, I finally persuaded Gromyko to meet privately with Waldheim for a few minutes. But Gromyko would not go to Waldheim's office. Instead, he spitefully suggested a humiliating procedure. He would see Waldheim in the Secretary General's small office behind the podium of the General Assembly Hall after a speech by a representative of a Soviet bloc country.

In most respects, the Soviet Union disdained the UN. The one exception resided in the desire to use it to shelter KGB spies and to vent our propaganda. Compounding the UN's weakness was the fact that the United States and other major Western nations had lost confidence in it. On almost any issue they could expect to be opposed by a majority of large and small states of the Third World. Finally, China's attitude toward the UN was, with rare exceptions, indifference.

But the UN has had successes, and Kurt Waldheim played a positive role in some of them. Working with and observing him for more than four years as Under Secretary General, I developed a respect for him. He often appeared stiff and dry, but underneath his formal, buttoned-up exterior Waldheim was a man of strong feelings and determination.

The force which drove him was a mixture of personal ambition and real dedication to the ideals of the United Nations. He saw the organization as more than a last resort for nations in conflict. He meant it to play a role in moderating tensions between East and West, North and South, before they erupted into violence. He conceived of his own mandate in fairly broad terms—behind-the-scenes negotiator and out-front spokesman for a world order built on respect for law and justice.

Waldheim learned the hard way that the office of Secretary General was "the most impossible job in the world," as Trygve Lie, the first incumbent, once called it. Without the cooperation or at least the acquiescence of all five permanent members of the Security Council plus a powerful, large group of non-aligned nations, the UN and the Secretary General are impotent to take any decisive action. To find a common denominator in the enormous complexity of divergent interests is a Sisyphean task. Waldheim tried to retain the favor of all sides—it was his main weakness. Common sense and logic call for the Secretary General to maintain friendly, trustworthy, and businesslike relations with the major powers, but there is a fine line between not desiring to give offense and becoming the prisoner of cordiality.

Waldheim could not be compared with the venturesome and flamboyant Dag Hammarskjöld. Neither could he be likened to his immediate predecessor, U Thant, who spent most of his time twiddling his thumbs. Waldheim's dynamism was always apparent, but a review of the results of his efforts reveals no achievement which could be singled out as a triumph. Nonetheless, some of his initiatives deserve praise. In 1972 he proposed that the General Assembly consider the question of international terrorism. The subject was not new, but Waldheim alerted world public opinion to the issue by laying it before the world council. And in 1976 his action in the Security Council eventually led to a temporary cessation of hostilities in Lebanon.

Waldheim's zeal also expressed itself in a ferocious

schedule of work, often sixteen hours a day spent at his desk or in faithful, alert attendance at Security Council and General Assembly sessions. It was normal to wait thirty to forty-five minutes outside his office beyond the time set for an appointment until the last-minute visitor he had squeezed into his schedule was politely shown out. Waldheim was both too patient with those who importuned him for a discussion and too loath to delegate his authority or the responsibility for seeing the people who crowded his time. I championed the efforts of his charming, intelligent wife, Cissy, when she tried to temper his mania for work. Frequently my colleagues and I urged him to cut back his killing workload. He would agree and inevitably go right on as before.

Waldheim's successor, Perez de Cuellar, a Peruvian who was previously my colleague in the Secretariat, is not as autocratic as Waldheim. He has wisely given more responsibility to his deputies, especially to Brian Urquhart, who deals with Middle East problems, and to Diego Cordovez, to mediate in solving the problems raised by the invasion of Afghanistan.

In some instances Waldheim attempted to imitate Kissinger's "shuttle diplomacy," forgetting his own words that "the holder of this office has great public responsibilities but little or no real power." Yet he persevered through his frustrations and failures. His inexhaustible will to continue was his greatest strength.

Peculiarly, his timidity in challenging the major forces in the UN coexisted with a love of grandeur. He liked to be the center of attention and would accordingly indulge himself in small matters. It was customary for him to keep the Under Secretaries and Assistant Secretaries waiting for half an hour or more before opening his weekly morning meetings with us. Entering his conference room with a quick, firm step, he would take his seat at the table with a self-important expression and at the same time a half-smile on his face. He would always say the same thing: "I apologize. It was a very important telephone call." The members of his "cabinet," as these meetings were unofficially called, were aware that often the reason for the delay was not an "important telephone call" but simply that he had arrived late.

I don't remember that any of these meetings were of particular interest or importance. Nobody took them seriously because Waldheim preferred to make the essential decisions alone with the advice of his few close assistants, his "Austrian Mafia." Nevertheless, he complained of being a solitary man who had to decide almost everything himself. I think he made himself lonely and could have relied on his Under Secretaries more than he did.

I sympathized with his difficulties in that thankless post, particularly those that were generated or exacerbated by the Soviet Union. Neither the Soviet government nor Ambassador Malik informed Waldheim of their real intentions or their basic policy regarding major international problems. They approached him only when his influence was needed in their interests. In contrast, the Americans briefed the Secretary on a wide range of problems. I often heard Waldheim on the telephone with Kissinger or with the United States Ambassador to the UN.

In violation of Soviet secrecy rules, I tried to help Waldheim whenever I could. I informed him in confidence from time to time about Soviet intentions or the instructions of the Soviet government to its Mission on many issues coming before the UN. I know he appreciated my help; perhaps that was why he defended me from attacks which were sometimes richly deserved. He did this not only because of the information I gave him but also just because I was a Soviet and he wished to avoid spoiling relations with Moscow. Waldheim's willingness to help the Soviet Union resulted in substantially increased numbers of Soviet nationals working in the Secretariat. He readily agreed to what both he and Ambassador Malik called the "five-year plan" of filling the Soviet quota of professional posts in the Secretariat. In our last conversation, when Waldheim asked me if it was true that his special assistant, Viktor Lessiovsky, was a KGB professional, I was surprised at his naïveté.

However, Waldheim's cooperation earned him little respect in Moscow. During his campaign for a second term as Secretary General, the Foreign Ministry prepared for the

Politburo an analysis which said that "Waldheim's performance is rather uneven; there are manifestations of his pro-Western convictions. He is flirting with the Americans, the non-aligned countries, and even with the Chinese." Although the analysis conceded that he had permitted the Soviet Union to fill its quota of more than 250 Secretariat jobs, it noted that the key posts around him were held by "functionaries with Western or pro-Western views who exert significant influence on him."

After disparaging Waldheim's susceptibility to flattery by Western leaders, the memorandum also criticized him for pushing "initiatives on important questions contrary to the interests of the U.S.S.R." His attempts to involve himself in the Vietnam Peace Conference, the Geneva Conference on the Middle East, and the European Conference on Security and Cooperation were all seen as intrusive extensions of the UN presence. His idea for a UN-sponsored meeting of concerned parties to prepare for resumed Middle East peace negotiations conflicted with Soviet policy. On Cyprus and South Africa, Waldheim was regarded as too ready to oppose Soviet preferences, but "on so-called human rights questions," the paper commended him for "displaying caution and trying to avoid complications with us."

The Soviets regarded Waldheim as the best they could expect in a Secretary General, but they had little confidence in him. In particular, they resented the authority he managed to retain over peacekeeping operations in the Middle East, fearing the activity of an international force they could not control.

At the same time, however, the analysis stated: "On a number of questions, especially those having great political significance, Waldheim listens to our demands and advice."

In the 1976 UN election, China and the non-aligned countries felt strongly that Europeans had monopolized the post of Secretary General for too long, but they could not agree upon a single candidate from their own ranks. The United States, the United Kingdom, and France supported Waldheim, but Moscow kept its options open. The Soviet delegation was instructed "not to object to the candidacy of Waldheim if another candidate acceptable to us does not have the support of the overwhelming majority." But no other candidacy emerged. Unfortunately, reelection became an obsession with Waldheim, who was willing to pay too high a price for it. The work of the Secretariat slowed to a crawl as a result of the emphasis on electioneering. With all the problems and limitations inherent in his post, if a Secretary General becomes carried away by personal ambition, impartial functioning of the Secretariat is sure to be adversely affected. Ideally, of course, the Secretary General should be free to act in accordance with the UN Charter. But as a practical matter, the position should not be subject to the whim of the major powers who can block a Secretary General's reelection. Perhaps the best way to guarantee the freedom of the office would be to extend the Secretary General's time from five to six or seven years and have it limited to one term.

Waldheim's election was a secondary matter for Moscow compared to what happened across the United States. On November 2, 1976, Jimmy Carter was elected President. Carter's selection of Zbigniew Brzezinski as his National Security Adviser put into the White House a man the Soviets regarded as an unrelenting enemy. The new President's campaign declarations on human rights, including a telegram of support to a noted Jewish activist in Moscow who had been denied permission to emigrate, persuaded the Soviets that Carter sought to promote subversion in the U.S.S.R. Finally, his inaugural address, expressing the hope that "we will move this year a step toward our ultimate goal—the elimination of all nuclear weapons from this earth," was taken as a signal that America's new leader intended to shatter the existing framework of SALT negotiations.

Carter's unpredictability, as much as the substantive shifts in his approach to the superpower relationship, disturbed the Soviets. Americans take change almost for granted. Its rapidity may disturb them briefly but in general they find ways to adjust quickly to new circumstances. Soviets lack such flexibility. It took them time to come to terms with the Carter administration. There was an extended period when the momentum of cooperation diminished further, and misunderstandings accumulated before a working relationship was achieved.

First, the Administration made sweeping changes in American arms control policy. The inaugural address was followed in March by Secretary of State Cyrus Vance's proposals to shelve the 1974 Vladivostok understandings, on which negotiations had stalled, and seek major reductions in strategic nuclear forces. That new position confused and worried the Soviet rulers, but Carter's fresh statements of sympathy and support for Soviet dissenters, including his correspondence with Andrei Sakharov, the 1975 Nobel Peace Prize winner, truly infuriated them. Coming from the Department of State and the White House, these declarations were even more provocative than those made in the presidential campaign. Part of the Soviet response was to arrest prominent activists, accusing one Jewish spokesman, Anatoly Shcharansky, of being a CIA spy.

The atmosphere worsened further after Vance brought two alternative strategic arms control packages to Moscow in March 1977 only to have Brezhnev flatly reject both. Andrei Gromyko went so far as to denounce the American proposals at a press conference and disclosed some of the numbers the Americans had proposed. It was a remarkable breach of the usual secrecy with which both sides had treated the details of SALT bargaining.

I watched these developments from the sidelines at the UN. Not until I traveled to the Soviet Union for summer leave in 1977 did I get a better sense of Moscow's mood. Elsewhere in the policymaking establishment, those who had always doubted the prospects of superpower détente were beginning to press for other policy initiatives. I had but a few days to spend in Moscow, and when I called for an appointment with the ministry's top American affairs expert, Georgy Kornienko, he could only see me at seven in the evening. "It's like a zoo here," he joked on the telephone, and when I came to his eighth-floor office, I saw what he meant.

Six months of experience with the Carter administration had made him more than usually wary. "It's always hard with the Americans," he said, "but with this new crowd we've had a very difficult beginning. We knew what Carter was saying in the election campaign about human rights. We thought his disarmament line would damage the work that had been done on SALT. But we expected that he would change once he got into the White House, once he had to deal with reality. We gave him a couple of months to settle down, but it hasn't happened yet. Instead, the confusion just drags on. We still don't know where they're going."

The situation which so depressed Kornienko gave bitter satisfaction to others in Moscow. Never having dared openly to dispute the Brezhnev line on accommodation with the United States, they could not say, "We told you so." Privately, however, they gloated. And a new militancy, heralding a renewed adventurism in the Third World, could be detected in the Central Committee staff.

Vadim Zagladin, the influential Central Committee propagandist, was ebullient as he assessed the stalemate with Washington. "Look where Gromyko and your fine Americans have gotten us," he said with cheerful sarcasm when we met for supper in Moscow's best Georgian restaurant. "We never could really trust them. It was a mistake to spend so much effort trying. Do we have to go through these somersaults with every new President? I prefer the French. They're tough, but at least they're consistent. Your Americans, they zig and zag, and we end up getting nowhere with them."

"They are not *my* Americans," I protested.

"Oh, come on," he replied. "You've been there so long you've turned into an American yourself."

Zagladin's banter was meaningless. Still, his words gave me a chill. Certainly he did not suspect me, but perhaps he had heard something. There had been some unpleasant signs of tightened security at the ministry. I did not think they were aimed at me, but I wasn't sure. I steered the talk onto safer ground and tried to keep the tone light.

I learned nothing more from him. Back in New York, I could only report to Bob Ellenberg, the new CIA contact who had taken over for Bert Johnson, my impression that time was running short for the Moscow advocates of détente. Kornienko, however, had confirmed to me Gromyko's plans to see President Carter during the 1977 UN General Assembly session. "The meeting with Vance [in March] was useful up to a point," Kornienko had said, "but it left a lot of hard issues unresolved. Things will only be clearer when Andrei Andreyevich can discuss them with the President."

Once again the Soviets would try to restore communications through the "direct way" that Gromyko preferred. Realistically, there was perhaps no other promising means to deal with the problems of superpower dialogue except in face-to-face exploration of the issues by the men with the highest political responsibility. Nonetheless, understandings reached between leaders were not necessarily accepted by their supporters. Brezhnev could still suppress potential opponents in Moscow, but their strength was gathering. And American Presidents could not ensure their own reelection, much less the consistency of policy from one administration to the next.

In the fall of 1977, in any case, Soviets and Americans were not thinking about these long-term problems in their relations. The main objective was restoration of some kind of working understanding that would reanimate the moribund SALT negotiations. Gromyko arrived in America in late September visibly anxious to find a way out of the impasse with the Carter administration. Breaking the normal pattern, he went first to Washington for talks with Vance and Carter.

In New York, his first concern at the Mission was to transmit a detailed report of the White House meetings to Moscow. Gromyko wrote no cables himself, but entrusted the task to his interpreter, Viktor Sukhodrev, to whom he dictated the message from his notes. It ran to forty or fifty pages and covered a wide range of issues—Soviet-American relations, SALT II, and most of the major international problems. He grew impatient as time passed and no manuscript came to him to approve.

"Where is Sukhodrev?" he snarled. "Drinking tea?"

Sukhodrev finally appeared to defend himself. "How can I write in one hour a conversation that lasted for three?" he said in reply to Gromyko's complaints. Gromyko, for once, restrained his temper. Instead of unleashing one of his out-bursts, he retreated into silence and a close reading of Su-khodrev's text.

When I asked him for an assessment of the negotiations with Carter, he was curt. "It's all in the cable. You can read it there," he said as he headed for his bedroom in the Mission apartment. But at the door he turned. A small smile hovered on his lips. "It did not go badly, not as badly as we expected," he said.

Gromyko had been enraged when Carter brought up Anatoly Shcharansky's treatment by the Soviets. "Carter is so ignorant that he can't do any better than to raise a microscopic matter about one man, something which should be of no consequence whatever for relations between our countries," ran one comment. Gromyko concluded, however, that "we can deal with Carter. He is unsophisticated in many matters, and eventually we could probably get him to agree to a lot of things we want."

Gromyko perceived that while Carter was strong on human rights he was painfully naïve about the Soviet Union. From what Gromyko said, Carter appeared to believe that one could work with the Soviet regime as an honest partner, as one would with a Western democracy. Eventually, the controversial SALT II treaty was concluded, and for a while it seemed that détente was blossoming again. But soon enough the Soviet incursion into Afghanistan opened President Carter's eyes to what bear hugs are really worth.

26

Kurt Waldheim's trip to Moscow, part of a round of official visits he paid to key UN members after his 1976 reelection, was something I had worked hard to arrange. I

401

maintained in cables to Moscow that it was important for our standing in the United Nations to show Waldheim the same courtesy and serious treatment he received in Peking or London, Washington or Paris.

When, in the spring of 1977, a formal invitation from the Kremlin finally arrived in New York, Waldheim told me and the Soviet Mission that he would be pleased to make the visit on condition that it include a conversation with Brezhnev. Neither Malik nor I could give such a guarantee, and when we raised the question with Moscow, there was no response. Waldheim chafed as the matter dragged on, forcing a postponement of the trip. Several times he asked me where the matter stood. I had no honest answer for him, so I relied on the story that Brezhnev was ill and could make no commitments as to his schedule.

When Moscow's reply finally came—suggesting dates in either September or November—it included the ambiguous instruction to tell Waldheim that "a meeting with Brezhnev is not excluded." This evasive double negative, so typical a formulation in Soviet diplomatic and bureaucratic parlance, was the nearest thing to a promise I could hope for. After more negotiation on timing, we fixed the visit for early September so that Waldheim could be back in New York for the General Assembly session. In a letter from a friend in Moscow I learned that the Politburo had decided that Brezhnev should meet him. Waldheim was pleased.

I had few illusions about the value of such a session except in a symbolic sense. The Soviets distrusted any man who tried to use the post of Secretary General to intervene actively in international problems. At the same time, they were contemptuous if he contented himself with the role of figurehead statesman.

I also didn't expect the news I was given as Waldheim and I and Roberto Guer, the Argentinian Under Secretary for Special Political Questions, arrived in Moscow. The welcome at Sheremetyevo Airport was properly ceremonious, but only First Deputy Foreign Minister Vasily Kuznetsov was on hand to escort Waldheim along a wide red carpet to his waiting limousine. Gromyko should have done the honors. After we had sped through the city to the Lenin Hills villa where the highest-ranking Soviet guests were housed, the façade of hospitality crumbled further.

Drawing me aside, Kuznetsov whispered, "Arkady, you know, it seems that Leonid Ilyich will probably not be able to receive Waldheim. You are close to him. It would be best if you would tell him the news."

After all the dickering that had preceded the visit, I found Kuznetsov's words nearly incredible. If Brezhnev, at the last minute, were to renege on his agreement, I told Kuznetsov, there was no way of predicting Waldheim's reaction.

Although the Secretary General was patient and deferential to the Soviets, he was, nevertheless, a man of strong pride. He could explode and turn Brezhnev's slight into a major scandal. He could demand to leave the Soviet Union immediately.

Kuznetsov shrugged resignedly. "It's not my decision," he said. "There's nothing I can do about it." He speculated that the change in plan was due to Brezhnev's health and repeated his request that I inform Waldheim.

I blew up. "I've had enough of being put into ridiculous positions over this business. It could very well end the confidence Waldheim has in me and my usefulness at the UN." I suggested that as long as the appointment with Brezhnev was uncertain, it was better to say nothing to the Secretary General, to avert an incident that would turn the visit into a shambles at the start.

Kuznetsov agreed and promised to take up the matter again with Gromyko. There was still no clarification the next day when Gromyko gave a state luncheon for Waldheim in a pre-revolutionary brick mansion in downtown Moscow. A score of cabinet ministers and other high officials feasted on caviar, smoked sturgeon, beef, and Moldavian champagne in a high-ceilinged room with brilliant antique tapestries and massive, brass-encrusted furniture. The pomp, however, was designed to cover the absence of substance.

Gromyko, after a short conversation with Waldheim about the situation at the UN, prepared to return to the ministry. Walking out with me, he proposed that we regard the meal and the chat as satisfying the requirements of official courtesy and that we drop plans for a further meeting between him and Waldheim the next day. I protested: There had been no serious discussion during or after lunch. Waldheim expected a working session with Gromyko and would be insulted if it did not take place. Given the possible cancellation of the appointment with Brezhnev, I told Gromyko it was important that he go through with the schedule.

With characteristic ill grace, he agreed. In his private reception room at the ministry the next afternoon, however, Gromyko was stiff and uninformative in his exposition of Soviet views on world affairs. If he put any nuance into his rote recitation of Moscow's well-known official position, it was so ambiguous as to be meaningless. Waldheim maintained a pretense of polite interest through the performance and even contained his irritation when Gromyko evaded answering a direct question about the meeting with Brezhnev. The timing was "under review," the minister said, advising Waldheim to go ahead with his planned visit to Siberia and Mongolia. When he returned to Moscow, it would be possible to resolve the matter of Brezhnev's availability.

Brezhnev finally met with Waldheim on September 13 in an office where he receives foreign dignitaries in the Kremlin. It was one of the conference rooms used for such purposes, paneled in natural wood without the elaborate boiserie characteristic of much of the gilded, opulent architecture to be found in the rest of the palace. A long conference table covered with dark green cloth stretched down the room before Brezhnev's desk. Chairs for visitors ranged along both its sides. Gromyko, Brezhnev's foreign policy aide, Andrei Aleksandrov-Agentov, Guer, and I participated in the meeting.

The man who rose a little unsteadily from behind a huge, polished, and uncluttered desk to greet us was clearly ill. Stiff and jerky even in the act of shaking hands, the most powerful political figure in the Communist world had a glazed look to his eyes that suggested he was under heavy medication, presumably for the pain said to be caused by the deteriorating condition of his jaw. Nearing his seventy-first birthday, Leonid Brezhnev wore a pacemaker, a hearing aid, and the look of a man on whom age was playing increasingly cruel tricks.

Seated opposite us, Brezhnev was unable to put any spark or forcefulness into his presentation. Haltingly reading from prepared notes, his eyes on the page more often than on his visitor, he recited the Soviet view of the world in flat phrases that were little different from those Gromyko had used to the Secretary General a few days before. The language was stereotypical. His delivery was without inflection, like that of a robot.

The familiar elements of the public Soviet policy agenda were all laid out: the urgency of pursuing détente, advancing disarmament, settling the Middle East conflict, liquidating the remnants of colonialism. Out of deference to his audience, Brezhnev noted the role of the UN in resolving these issues. He even praised Waldheim's performance as Secretary General. He seemed to listen seriously as Waldheim responded by agreeing with the importance of the questions Brezhnev had listed, urging the need for progress in nuclear non-proliferation and emphasizing the value of the UN both in resolving conflict and in easing tension.

As Brezhnev heard out the translation of Waldheim's remarks, however, he showed how weak was his real command of the subjects under discussion. Flanked by Gromyko and Aleksandrov-Agentov, Brezhnev at one point turned to them and asked in a low voice if the treaty on non-proliferation was already in force. I was floored by such a glaring lapse of memory and grateful that Waldheim understood no Russian. The treaty, as Gromyko quietly explained, had gone into effect in 1970.

Another inquiry astonished me even more. When Waldheim suggested that a visit by Brezhnev to the UN would be widely welcomed, the Soviet leader turned to his aides. "May I visit the UN?" he inquired. "Yes, certainly," they replied in chorus, "but not this year, for well-known reasons." They were referring to the scheduled October adoption of a new constitution for the U.S.S.R., an activity that would require Brezhnev's presence. He nodded and mumbled, "Certainly not this year, but maybe I will visit the UN next year."

The discussion of the visit ended the formal conversation. Then Waldheim rose from his chair to say that he wished to present his host the gold UN medal for peace. For the first time in the fifty-minute encounter Brezhnev became animated. He beamed with childlike delight as Waldheim handed him the glittering token, manifesting his long-standing passion for medals, awards, titles, and all sorts of presentation paraphernalia. The number of decorations he collected and wore was so great that Moscow jokesters claimed Kremlin surgeons had given Brezhnev an extra rib to hold all his finery.

As he clucked with pleasure over it, I laughed a little to myself. It was really nothing more than a trinket, a kind of souvenir the Secretary General presented from time to time to statesmen and other notables he wished to flatter. I had told Aleksandrov-Agentov of its relative insignificance, but he had obviously described it to Brezhnev in far more glowing terms.

Leaving the Kremlin, I reflected on what I had seen in Brezhnev's office. It was an antiseptic, lifeless enclosure, removed from both any sense of the enduring, tragic, and inspiring history of my country and any touch with the compelling problems of the modern nation. It was more like the antechamber to a hospital sickroom, a place where an influential patient could be propped up for show before being wheeled back to bed and isolation.

As for the man who occupied this setting, Leonid Ilyich Brezhnev, after thirteen years of steadily expanding power, retained both the limitations of his origins and the cunning which had enabled him to rise above them. A prototypical Party apparatchik, the personification of the bureaucratized politics he had proved so skillful at manipulating, Brezhnev was not an eminent leader. A shrewd intriguer who was open-minded enough to break significant new ground in East-West relations, Brezhnev nevertheless owed his longevity in office first of all to the stability he promised and delivered to the elite.

Its security threatened by Nikita Khrushchev's erratic style, the top rank of Soviet officialdom saw Brezhnev as a welcome relief. He cemented his authority by buttressing the system Khrushchev tried to shake, especially by restoring the security of Party and other officials in their jobs and expanding the budgets of the military. His talents for manipulation and abilities as a middleman in maintaining a balance in the Politburo were expressed more in rewards than in threats or punishment. Favoring most those who were closest to him, he built a network of Party supporters in widening circles of patronage. Corruption reached unbelievable proportions.

Brezhnev was clever enough to listen to those who advocated expansion of military power and Soviet influence in the Third World. Under him, an unprecedented arms buildup made the U.S.S.R a real superpower. But economic stagnation at home had been a heavy price to pay for successes abroad and the mounting of huge military programs.

Yet Brezhnev, despite the poor record of his regime's performance at home, retained and even expanded his personal authority. He too acquired a cult of personality and committed some startling excesses. He carried traditional nepotism to new heights, for example, when he made his son, Yuri, Deputy Minister of Foreign Trade. The younger Brezhnev, an unremarkable engineer whose drunkenness during his service on a foreign trade mission to Sweden some years before had been the talk of Moscow, was given candidate status in the Central Committee in 1981 with no previous record of Party distinction.

His father's immodesty reached offensive proportions when he arranged to have himself awarded the Lenin Prize for Literature, in recognition of his ghost-written memoirs. He also gave himself the title of Marshal of the Soviet Union and decorated himself with the Order of Victory. That ruby-and-diamond-emblazoned medallion on a platinum base is reserved for commanders of major wartime operations. Brezhnev, a political commissar who finished the war as a major general, did not qualify. His action in adding this venerated decoration to his hundreds of others genuinely outraged career military men. Several generals fumed to me that he was not worthy of the honor, that he had debased it by breaking the rules to get it.

Age and illness, of course, greatly diminished his strength and eroded his abilities as an administrator and negotiator. During his last years in power he was a feeble invalid, able to work only a few hours a week, kept alive by sophisticated drugs and modern medical techniques.

How had he continued to remain as leader? The fact was that during his lingering physical and political decline, Brezhnev did not run the country on a day-to-day basis. Real power was exercised by a small group within the Politburo. Friends in the Central Committee had told me years before that the two major contenders for Brezhnev's crown, Chernenko and Andropov, were both—though for different reasons—interested in gaining more time to reinforce their positions and build up their alliances.

I was staying in my own apartment in Moscow during this trip, and in solitary moments I found it very hard to reconcile myself to the idea that I might be at home for the last time in my life. I made a nostalgic inventory of my apartment, lingering by the window for the view our ninth-floor location gave of Gorky Park and the boats plowing the Moscow River. I reexamined my books and icons, inanimate but dear to me.

The same feeling of finality shadowed my walks through the city. Moscow will always occupy a reserved place in my best memories of home. My youth had been spent there; I had met my first love there; my children were born there. Although it is an enormous city, I felt that I knew it so well I could almost sense it breathing.

The familiar route along the river to the Krymsky Bridge and the sooty walls of MGIMO became almost a private processional. On the far side of the river, opposite the Kremlin, I tried to look hard enough so memory would serve me well, at the baroque façades of churches and mansions in what had once been one of Moscow's most beautiful quarters. Again I visited my favorite pictures at the Tretyakov Art Gallery. In the downstairs rooms the great fifteenth-century icons of Andrei Rublev and his followers glowed with mystical vision—the religious passion of Russia's old faith.

Late one afternoon, I went to another favorite retreat, the cemetery in a bend of the Moscow River at the Novodyevi-chii Convent. One of the oldest buildings in Moscow, it is a most interesting historical and architectural monument.

Peter the Great's elder sister, Princess Sophia, was banished there in the seventeenth century for her support of the revolt against the tsar. In a later time, the convent was saved at the last moment despite Napoleon's order to blow it up during the final days of his occupation of Moscow in 1812. The cemetery, now a place usually reserved for interment of senior Party and government bureaucrats or famous people, was located a pleasant walking distance from my apartment.

In the older part of the graveyard, some of my friends were buried alongside famous writers, scholars, scientists, aviators, and Stalin's second wife, Nadezhda Alliluyeva, Svetlana's mother. Lush shrubbery and tall trees give the walks a serene, parklike atmosphere, except toward the new section of the cemetery where, not far from a railroad track, Nikita Khrushchev's family finally obtained permission to put up a monument for him. It is an impressive memorial of stark black-and-white marble with a portrait bust of Khrushchev in bronze by the well-known sculptor Ernst Neizvestny. To me, the artist found the truth: the conflict in Khrushchev's rule, and the dark and bright sides of the man and his career.

On my way out of the cemetery, I passed a group of foreign visitors. I overheard several of them expressing admiration for the famous old convent, which had just been renovated, and its beautiful park. Their comments filled me both with pride for my country's positive contributions to civilization and with sympathy for the suffering and pain it had endured in its long battle to establish itself as a nation. In many wars of independence over the centuries, the Russian people had proven themselves brave in adversity, persevering with the kind of pioneering spirit for which America is famous. But unlike America, which had never suffered the entropy of its body politic experienced universally under Communist regimes around the world, my country had lost its dynamism and creative spirit. Its long slide into economic, cultural, and intellectual squalor had still not ended. No splendor of marble or bronze embellishment over the doors of bureaucracy could hide the fact that our government conducted a funerary homage to a dead philosophy as surely as the cemetery celebrated the physically dead. I felt sorry for those millions who still professed that philosophy and who will, perhaps, continue to do so for a long time into the future.

As I passed graves where others were laying flowers, a rather sardonic recollection came to mind, of a long-ago meeting of the Foreign Ministry's trade union committee. There one self-important functionary rose to make what he called a happy announcement. After great effort, he declared, the union had secured an important benefit for high-ranking diplomats: one hundred places in the prestigious precincts of the Novodyevichii cemetery. The privileges of the elite would be carried over from their lives into death. Recalling the applause his announcement evoked, I felt that, despite the pain I could anticipate from memories of my motherland and people dear to me, I would be able to leave this society without overwhelming regret. Nonetheless, when I left Moscow several weeks later I did so with mixed feelings. For all that I hated, there were still many things I loved.

Soon I was back in New York. Gromyko was there as well, attending the annual General Assembly session. Around this time, another opportunity arose to begin restoration of communications between Soviets and Israelis.

It was an Israeli initiative late in September after Gromyko had finished his Washington talks with President Carter. The day after his arrival in New York, in the late afternoon, Chaim Herzog, the Israeli Ambassador to the UN, called me to ask for an appointment. I went to meet him in the Security Council delegates' lounge.

Herzog, with whom I had developed cordial relations over the years, carried a question from Israeli Foreign Minister Moshe Dayan, then in Washington. Dayan would be coming to the UN in a day or so and might be interested in meeting Gromyko. Without making the matter official, Herzog asked me if I could determine how Gromyko would react to a formal request for such a talk.

At the Soviet Mission I found Gromyko as responsive to the prospect of a meeting as I had hoped he would be. "Only it has to be understood," he said, "that if we are to talk, I will be receiving him in my capacity as co-chairman of the Geneva Conference." Late that evening I gave Herzog Gromyko's reply. Since he did not object to Gromyko's condition, I went to bed hoping that the decade of hostile silence between Moscow and Jerusalem might be coming to an end.

Early the next morning, I left my apartment building through its back entrance, went down a narrow passageway and into a small house on Sixty-fourth Street. On the second floor in a one-room apartment, Bob Ellenberg was waiting. Finally the CIA had set up a perfect meeting place. I could reach it simply by using the service elevator to the garage and crossing a few steps from the exit to the door of the new building. I felt a safety in the arrangement I had never really experienced at the Waldorf-Astoria or the earlier locations. Bob told me that he had rented the apartment so we could have more time to talk than before, but while Gromyko was in New York we had agreed to meet quickly in the mornings so that I could fill him in on the activities of the previous day.

I told him of Herzog's approach to me and Gromyko's response, outlining the potential importance of the encounter with Dayan. For the rest of the day I waited for news that the Israelis had made their request formally. Finally, late in the afternoon, Chaim Herzog asked to see me.

He entered my office looking a bit downcast. Dayan, he said, had decided after all not to seek a talk with Gromyko. Supposedly his schedule at the United Nations had become too crowded and his date for returning to Israel had been advanced. Herzog apologized for inconveniencing me and Gromyko, and left.

I do not know to this day what caused Dayan to change his mind. Herzog's excuse was a flimsy one.

Gromyko received the news without comment, but I felt that he too regretted the opportunity that had been missed. One talk between him and Moshe Dayan would not have changed the course of events in the Middle East, but it might have opened doors that had long been shut and that, unfortunately, still are. The Soviet Union continues to be a mischief-making force in the region, the supporter of extremist

411

Arab groups and nations. There may be no end to conflicts between Israel and its neighbors.

I did not limit my private Middle East diplomacy to Israel. When Esmat Meguid, Egypt's UN representative, suggested in 1976 that a visit by me to his country could be useful, I thought it might help inspire more conventional diplomacy. Gromyko agreed to the visit, although not enthusiastically. A few days later, when I told Meguid that I would accept the invitation, he said that Ismail Fahmi, Egypt's Foreign Minister, was in New York and wanted to talk with me.

In his suite at the Waldorf-Astoria, Fahmi was brutally frank. We had both served as our countries' counselors at the UN a decade before and could speak as friends. He put forward a series of complaints and one remarkable though tentative proposal.

His grievances with the Soviet Union were extensive. Not only was there the familiar story of industrial and military equipment long delayed in shipment, but Fahmi also charged that Moscow was deliberately withholding delivery of vital spare parts for airplanes. Egypt had paid cash in advance for the matériel, but it was still sitting in crates on the Odessa waterfront, a violation of a contract and an open affront.

On top of this treatment, he added, the appointment of Vladimir Polyakov, a junior diplomat, as the Soviet Ambassador to Egypt was a slap in the face. Polyakov, Fahmi said, was "nothing but a mailbox." Moscow's envoy came to the Foreign Ministry only to read out whatever messages he had been instructed to deliver. He answered almost no questions and rarely asked any. "I have no idea what he reports back," Fahmi said, "because he does not try to learn anything about us."

Fahmi said he thought my visit could be helpful. There was a possibility that Leonid Brezhnev would be welcomed in Cairo if he chose to come. "I have not even mentioned this idea to President Sadat," Fahmi confided, "but I am sure his reaction would be positive."

I discounted the first part of his sentence but not the second. Fahmi, Deputy Prime Minister as well as Foreign Minister, was known to be an intimate Sadat adviser. It was unlikely that he would suggest a Brezhnev visit without consulting his chief first, but even if the idea was his own, he had the influence to assure Sadat's acceptance of it. I promised to let Moscow know of our talk; perhaps I would have some sort of answer when I came to Cairo.

After sending a lengthy cable to Gromyko, I arranged with Ambassador Meguid to schedule my trip to Egypt early in January 1977. I received no reply on the subject of a Brezhnev visit, but the silence was not surprising. Nothing so dramatic would be quickly decided in Moscow. Even if it were, another messenger might be chosen to respond to the Egyptians. I was surprised and disappointed, however, when a few days before my departure for Cairo my routine cable notifying the ministry of my travel plans brought a swift reply.

The cable was signed by Gromyko, relatively rare in any event, and his message was blunt. He would prefer that I postpone my trip indefinitely, but if I could not do so at such a late date, I was directed to act in Egypt strictly in my capacity as Under Secretary General. Under no circumstances could I discuss the substance of Soviet policy with my hosts.

There was no way to ignore such explicit instructions and no time either to seek an explanation or to try to get them changed. I went ahead with the trip, but it was a ceremonial affair. Although I talked with Fahmi and a number of his cabinet colleagues, including the Defense Minister, I could not reply to their pointed comments and questions about Soviet policy. To my hosts' and my discomfort, I was as reticent as the Sphinx, as unhelpful as Ambassador Polyakov, whom I also met in Cairo. I found him, as Fahmi had told me, insensitive to Egyptian views and, because of his intellectual limitations, unconcerned about his poor performance. Egypt's decision to order him to leave in 1981 reflected his own failure as much as it did the unhealed breach between Moscow and Cairo.

It was not until more than a year after my Cairo visit that I could report anything significant on Middle Eastern affairs to either Moscow or Bob Ellenberg. By then Sadat had

413

made his dramatic gesture toward peace with Israel, an initiative that brought praise from most Western leaders. Ismail Fahmi, however, quit his post in protest. Militant Arabs denounced Sadat, and the Soviet Union joined the hostile chorus.

27

ALTHOUGH 1977 WAS TO BE A YEAR OF GROWING ANXIETY for me, it began auspiciously enough. A move by Moscow brought me and many other Soviets in New York some relief. Yakov Malik returned to the Foreign Ministry in late 1976 and, just at the turn of the year, Oleg Troyanovsky arrived to replace him.

Gromyko had told me of the impending change before he left New York in October. Lina and I were having a quiet supper with the Gromykos at their apartment in the Mission. I wanted to talk privately to Gromyko about a problem. After the table had been cleared, Lina and Lidiya went into another room to discuss their latest round of shopping.

"Andrei Andreyevich, I would like to discuss a personal matter with you." He looked at me genially and gestured for me to go ahead. I told him that the circumstances under which I had to work in New York were very oppressive. "Malik tries to pressure me all the time. The Party secretary is constantly distracting me from urgent official matters, and the KGB is trying to involve me in its operations. Frankly, I'm not sure how to proceed. I need some guidance about what to do."

"I know Malik's a nasty character. Believe me, you're not the only one to complain about him." He nodded meaningfully. "We're going to replace him soon. Troyanovsky will be our new ambassador."

I wasn't surprised at the choice, but it was an unexpected and agreeable development.

"But as for small-fry Party officials, forget them." Gromyko frowned. He thought for a moment and then went on. "What would you think of being an ambassador to a Western country? Not to some insignificant place, but an important one."

I avoided giving him a direct answer, indicating it would require some time to complete my work in New York.

"There's nothing urgent about it," he replied calmly. "We can talk about it later."

Gromyko had said nothing about the KGB. And my intuition told me that he himself was afraid of it. Lina had more than once reported to me the warnings of Lidiya Gromyko. "Keep as far away as you can from the KGB types," Lidiya Dmitriyevna said. She would stop my wife whenever she began to talk about personal matters. Pointing to the ceiling, she would whisper in Lina's ear, "We'll talk about that somewhere else."

Oleg Troyanovsky, then fifty-seven, was affable, a bon vivant, and a sophisticated diplomat. He was almost a pleasure to work with. In contrast to Malik he was a positive delight.

The son of the first Soviet Ambassador to the United States, Troyanovsky grew up in Washington, attended American schools, and acquired such fluency in English that he was, for many years, Nikita Khrushchev's personal interpreter. From 1962 to 1967, moreover, he served as foreign affairs adviser to two Prime Ministers, Khrushchev and Kosygin. It was a potentially powerful post, but Troyanovsky lost some authority when Khrushchev was ousted and more as Brezhnev edged Kosygin out of the primary role in the making of foreign policy. Troyanovsky went to Japan as ambassador, a post his father had held before him. Leaving in 1975 to make way for an ousted Politburo member, former Agriculture Minister Dmitri Polyansky, he spent about a year in the Foreign Ministry before being named Permanent Representative to the UN.

It was not quite the job he hoped for. His heart was in Washington, a city about whose quiet beauty he reminisced often with me. As Ambassador to the United States, he would complete the pattern of following in his father's footsteps. If he someday realizes this ambition, it will not be because of the forcefulness of his character or the independence of his views. Troyanovsky has learned the virtues of conformism in the Soviet system. He directs his actions in such a way as to make as little fuss as possible, to stay as close as he can to the Moscow mainstream, to bend with the prevailing wind and to smell out any likely change in its direction.

In the Mission he earned more gratitude than respect. Even after a serious automobile accident slowed him down after March 1976, Malik remained an exigent, foul-mouthed, foul-tempered boss. Troyanovsky, a short man with red cheeks and a potato nose in an apple-round face, demanded very little from his subordinates. He had a smile for everyone, an easy courtesy, and a preference for a schedule light enough to leave him time for tennis, more nearly a passion with him than a recreation.

Along with his charm, however, Troyanovsky showed a degree of indecisiveness that bordered on real weakness. It revealed itself in his relations with his wife, Tatyana. Younger than he, she had a determination that extended far beyond their domestic relations. In Moscow she had astonished other diplomats by appearing regularly in the ministry, becoming a real force in her husband's domain and making him the butt of a number of jokes. In New York as well, she was the dominant member of the couple and he, the classic henpecked husband.

Because of his uncertainty about many areas of UN practice and policy, he had a tendency to vacillate on complicated or delicate matters. It grew to be tedious spending long hours going over and over with him aspects of problems more decisive men would have dealt with promptly. But my new colleague put no real strain on me. I had no desire to leave my job, except for freedom in America, and no presentiment of trouble in the offing.

Late in the spring of 1977, however, an unexpected security clampdown, mysterious in its motivation and potentially posing new threats to my safety, dissipated my sense of

416

well-being. The order for it originated in Moscow, but its effect on my life in New York was serious. The first word of it came at a regular staff meeting of senior officials from the Mission and the Secretariat when Troyanovsky told us that the KGB chief had a report to make.

"The special services of the imperialist states are intensifying their campaigns of provocation against Soviet citizens and institutions abroad. It is essential to give a fitting rebuff to these machinations of the enemy. Special vigilance is required of Soviets traveling or living in capitalist countries where, in addition to the subversive activities of Western intelligence forces, hostile émigré organizations are mobilized to . . ."

Yuri Drozdov droned on, reading in a stern, dry monotone from a thick sheaf of papers on the table in front of him. By the looks of the stack of pages, the KGB *resident* was no more than halfway through his speech. I wondered if I could stay awake to the end.

Many of the words could have been lifted from a *Pravda* editorial on security consciousness. They were hackneyed admonitions of the sort everyone in the room had heard hundreds of times before: beware of foreigners; be suspicious of everyone; assume that every Westerner you meet, however casually, is working to undermine Soviet security. The only puzzle in Drozdov's presentation was his reason for making it now. Finally, he got to the point: a requirement that all contacts with foreigners be approved in advance, including contacts of the Soviet nationals who worked for the UN Secretariat. Additionally, wives of Mission and UN personnel were urged not to go around in New York City unaccompanied. And the standing rule that all talks with foreigners be detailed in memoranda written in the Mission —a burdensome regulation that was mostly honored in the breach—was reactivated.

I understood that the KGB intended to enforce old rules often neglected, and to impose new ones as well. This tightening of security standards did not appear aimed at me. It was clear, however, that the new policy would inflict unworkable restrictions on diplomats and their normal procedures. I would be held responsible for the compliance of

Soviets on the Secretariat payroll with a set of rules they would have to break almost every working day.

When my turn came to comment, I tried to get Drozdov to acknowledge the need for exceptions. It was one thing, I pointed out, for members of the Mission to check with their superiors before making appointments with foreign diplomats in New York. But Soviets at the UN saw such people daily as part of their normal duties. Was a Secretariat employee supposed to get written permission before every meeting with his or her superior? If so, from whom? If I spent my time approving and disapproving such requests from my subordinates throughout the Secretariat, I would have almost no time for my regular duties.

Also, I continued, the rule requiring written reports on all conversations with foreigners was one that Mission staffers could handle while those at the UN could not. The reports had to be written inside the Mission, but there was not enough space set aside for the use of Secretariat personnel. Many wasted valuable working time just hunting for a desk to borrow when they came to file a regular report. If they had to produce such memoranda each day but could not draft them in their own offices at the UN, they would lose even more of their working day.

Drozdov gave some ground before my argument, but not much. The regulations applied to all Soviets, he insisted. Those working at the UN would just have to find an efficient way to live with them. But he and Troyanovsky said they would provide space in the Mission for Secretariat personnel. More room was made available, but it was not uncommon for Soviet UN staffers to be waiting for a writing table.

After the meeting I stopped to wonder about the reason behind the imposition of these cumbersome security procedures. It had to be something more than standard Soviet apprehensiveness.

I knew of one major incident in New York, involving the indiscretion of Gerodot Chernushenko, the Belorussian Ambassador to the UN. Oblivious to his driver waiting outside, he stayed all night with a Latin American woman whose parties he often attended. His chauffeur became alarmed in the early hours of the morning when Chernushenko did not appear, and reported to the Mission. Security men alerted Mrs. Chernushenko and were waiting for her husband when he came home for breakfast. A day or so later the Belorussian representative was at Kennedy Airport, morose and under the watchful escort of his wife and the KGB, bound for home. I happened to catch sight of him there while I was seeing off a friend who was taking the same flight, but we were not permitted to talk. Only later did I discover what had caused his abrupt departure. The story made me both angry at his foolishness and disturbed by the KGB's harshness.

Yet I found it hard to believe that it was Chernushenko's misconduct that had provoked Drozdov's draconian response. But if he was the reason for the security crackdown, then unannounced provisions would certainly accompany those the KGB chief had discussed openly, and they would extend to me. In the eyes of the secret police, one ambassador's misstep would make all ambassadors suspect.

My surmise seemed to be confirmed in the days that followed. New surveillance activities included a roster, kept by the Mission guards inside the entrance, in which the comings and goings of senior officials were recorded as we entered or left the building. Inside the Mission also I sensed that I was under added scrutiny. At the UN, KGB agents routinely appeared in my path, but now I frequently spotted them near me in the Mission, riding the elevators with me, noting whom I spoke with, where I went.

If the secret police had paid me this sort of special attention in the first months of my collaboration with the CIA, I might have found it intolerable. Now I felt more curious about the cause of the new controls than concerned that they might endanger me.

The intensified security measures did not affect me personally, and I continued to have unlimited access to all secret documents and to meet with whom I chose. Ellenberg and I agreed that whatever had prompted the KGB to act, I was in no greater jeopardy than before.

In the summer of 1977 I even relished the chance to take my home leave again in the Soviet Union. Sensing no particular threat of detection, I had none of the forebodings I had carried to Cuba and the U.S.S.R. the year before. The KGB trusted no one completely, but it did not seem to distrust me more than anyone else.

But as I traveled to the Crimea to visit my mother and then later to the mountain resort of Kislovodsk, I became aware that I was the focus of secret police observation. I was shadowed and scrutinized more than before. At first I was only irritated, but by the end of my leave I could not help being worried. Anxiety returned and the old frustrations mounted to new heights of impatience.

My first direct exposure to the changed atmosphere came when I reported to the Foreign Ministry the day after my arrival in Moscow. Following long habit, I went to the office of the chief of the International Organizations Department, where I had begun my diplomatic career and where typists and senior officials alike greeted me on a first-name basis, treating me as part of their professional family. But my welcome chilled when I asked the head clerk to bring me the back files of code cables so that I could "read in," as I did on every trip home.

"I can't," she said apologetically. "There are new regulations. You have to get special permission unless you are on the *razmetka* [access list], and you're not."

I was amazed by the severity of the new rules. They were stricter than anything I had experienced before in the ministry, almost a throwback to the secrecy of Stalin's time. Most interesting of all was that the procedures had been put into effect at the same time that Drozdov was beginning to enforce similar restrictions in New York. Obviously, the crackdown was a general one. But even with that knowledge, I was still not sure how my own access might be affected. And I did not know what had prompted the extra security mania.

My first question was soon answered: my status was unchanged. Viktor Israelyan, the department chief, was quick to open his safe and hand me some cables he had stored there. I had further confirmation of normality in talking with another senior official. He had no time for conversation in his office but invited me to visit him at home. I went there the next evening for supper and the usual long, informal dissection of all our colleagues, their latest missteps, their next promotions. He and I had worked together in New York in the 1960s, and we had become friends although his career was only tangentially connected with diplomacy. He volunteered the information no one else had given me—the source of the security restrictions.

"You know," he said, "we had a ChehPeh in the ministry." The initials stood for *chrezviychainnoye proisshestviye,* literally, an "extraordinary incident." What my friend meant by the acronym, however, was an act of subversion.

According to him, the KGB had begun to suspect the loyalty of a secretary in a Soviet embassy in Latin America. While keeping track of his contacts with the CIA, the security men did nothing precipitous until they could arrange for what seemed to be a routine transfer back to Moscow. There the game continued. The young diplomat was assigned to the ministry's Policy Planning Department, an office with wide access to coded cable traffic. For a few months he was closely watched until he was seen passing documents to an American agent. Arrested, he killed himself with a cyanide capsule before he could be interrogated.

If any other Foreign Ministry official had told me the same story, I might have doubted its accuracy. But coming from someone whose responsibilities over the years had given him excellent working relations with the KGB, the detailed account rang ominously true. I grimaced with concern—for myself rather than the ministry. "We'll all be under suspicion just because one man was a traitor."

"It's not just the one case," he continued. "There have been incidents in other countries—attempts to recruit our people, quite a number of them. And we always have the problem of drunkenness and people sleeping around." He launched into the tale I already knew of Ambassador Chernushenko.

"I never would have thought he would end up in trouble. He seemed the most orthodox, straitlaced man in New York," I said.

"Oh, but he drank heavily," he observed.

I did not try to correct that impression, although I had never seen Chernushenko disabled by alcohol. He was punctual at Security Council meetings and scrupulous about the relatively limited duties he was given to perform. Boris Solomatin, the former KGB *rezident,* was just the opposite. After a weekend binge at Glen Cove, he was often too hung over to keep his official appointments. But no one reported on him; the KGB protected its own.

The story of the young diplomat preyed on my mind. I felt I could understand what had impelled him and I was deeply sorry for him. At the same time I was relieved at knowing the impetus behind the increased security at the Mission and in the ministry. It sprang from a real event, one far from New York. But I found it all too easy to picture the KGB manipulating me into the same trap it had set for the young diplomat quietly summoned home from South America, shadowed, and finally brought to bay. He had been desperate enough to make preparations for suicide, to choose death. I desired no such end. I had to revive the hypersensitivity I had managed to dull. I had to become more aware of danger. I did not want to live in fear, but I saw that to deny it would be to lose my best shield against discovery.

Fortunately, the KGB helped me rebuild my defenses. Unusual incidents began to nag at my consciousness, occurrences which taken separately seemed only minor oddities. The episodes that alerted me started almost immediately after the talk with my ministry acquaintance. The next night I boarded an express train at the Kursk station for an overnight trip to the Crimea and a reunion with my mother. Before its midnight departure, I found that I was sharing the compartment with a woman, not an unusual situation on Soviet railroads, which assign sleeping space without regard to sex. (There was no special car for the elite on this train.) She and I were both privileged enough to get reserved space on a southbound train at the height of the summer vacation season.

To permit her the privacy to change into her nightclothes, I stepped out into the corridor for a cigarette, noticing as I gazed idly into the darkness outside that another man, one whom I had seen earlier in the Kursk station waiting room, was in the corridor, not smoking, just standing as though on guard. He was there the next morning when I went out to

422

let my traveling companion dress, and he was seated in the dining car when I came for breakfast.

I did not give the man much thought, simply registering the coincidence of his presence as slightly peculiar but not alarming. There was nothing menacing in his looks or behavior, just a perceptible interest in me that was a level above normal curiosity. When I stepped off the train in Yevpatoriya, into the bright sunshine and velvet air of the Crimean shore, however, I forgot all about him. My mother, cheerful in her seventy-sixth year, was there to greet me. She had remarried after my father's death in 1949 and led her own life in the Crimea. To my regret, she and Lina had never liked each other and had not been on speaking terms for a long time. This was the reason I was alone on the trip. Nevertheless, she was my mother and I felt strongly about seeing her, my last link to childhood. I somehow needed to return to earlier days, to give her my unspoken farewell, hoping she would forgive me my decision to leave my homeland without telling her.

As I left Yevpatoriya for the return trip to Moscow a few days later, I was given a demonstration of KGB omnipresence. When I handed my ticket to a train guard, he asked me to wait a minute before boarding, and another official hurried up to explain that my reservation had been changed. I was given a bunk in a different sleeping car, one that turned out to be relatively empty. That was strange in itself. At the peak of the summer vacation period there were rarely any last-minute places to be had on the northbound trains from the Crimea. A car with empty berths was a rarity bordering on mystery.

I began to suspect that the KGB might have arranged the last-minute switch in my reservation and the unusual extra space in the car. As on the trip south, I was being shadowed. Again a silent, watchful man was always in the corridor whenever I stepped out of my compartment. He also managed to be in the dining car when I ate supper and breakfast. And although the traveler to Moscow was not the same man who had accompanied me to the Crimea, they resembled each other in the cool professionalism with which they held me under observation.

To keep watch on me, I concluded, the KGB had had me moved into a car where it had reserved a number of compartments for its own use. Foreign journalists and diplomats, when they travel by rail, are routinely placed in these KGB precincts. Learning only at the last minute of my return to Moscow, the Yevpatoriya agents had to act quickly to supersede the station manager's arrangements and put me where I could most easily be kept in sight.

I was not so much surprised by this demonstration of the KGB's reach and authority as I was disquieted at being its cause. Andrei Gromyko and everyone below him in the Foreign Ministry had treated me completely normally. But the secret police, it seemed, took another and possibly ominous attitude.

As long as I remained in the Soviet Union, I had to live with and adjust my actions to the KGB's apparent doubts about me. But there was nothing I needed or wished to do that would create added distrust. A day after returning from Yevpatoriya, I was again at the Kursk station, this time with Lina, boarding another train headed south. Our destination was the mountain resort of Kislovodsk on the northern edge of the Caucasus, a spa I loved, not for its foul-smelling, supposedly health-giving mineral water, but for the luxury of a complete rest and change of scene.

Krasnye Kamni (Red Stones), the sanatorium where we were to spend twenty-four days, represented the peak of Soviet privilege. In the guise of a clinic and under the management of the Health Ministry's Fourth Department, which treated only elite patients, the facility was actually one of the finest resort hotels in the Soviet Union. Just to be admitted confirmed one's status. The opulent suites in the main building and several luxurious dachas below it were patronized even by Politburo members. One of the maids told us that the well-appointed apartment to which Lina and I were assigned in 1977 had been regularly used by Premier Aleksei Kosygin. That fact explained the special secured telephones in the foyer and bedroom and direct hookups to the *Vertushka* switchboard in Moscow. The view from our porch over the mountain-ringed town of Kislovodsk was incredibly beautiful. Lina and I watched the morning mists

424

burn off the slopes and at the end of languid days saw the shadows from one peak slowly eclipse thick stands of pine and spruce on its neighbors.

What brought Lina and me back to Krasnye Kamni on each summer leave was not the confirmation of our social position but the rejuvenating tranquillity of the setting. It was an island separated from the outside world by brick walls and iron gates, armed guards and dogs. No ordinary mortal could make a reservation; no one was allowed to enter without a pass or an invitation. No one was supposed to encroach upon the playground of his *nachalstvo* (masters) or to see how we spent our free time.

Except for taking progressively longer baths every other day in the sulfurous Narzan water piped into the basement of the lodge, we limited the medicinal side of our rest cure mostly to long walks on the forested mountain above us and excursions on foot to the small town of Kislovodsk and the surrounding countryside. In the clean, charming little town, I had a queer sensation passing the shopwindows in which a familiar, smiling image was prominently displayed—Joseph Stalin. In Kislovodsk, his picture had solidly occupied its accustomed places long before it began reappearing on Moscow's streets, taped to the windshields of taxicabs. Whenever I spotted one of these memorials in a shopwindow, I could not help but feel a dread that was almost fatigue at the thought of a possible resurrection of a new form of Stalinism. After what my country had suffered at the hands of one of modern history's greatest mass killers, when confronted with the easy, routine acceptance of him in the shopwindows of Kislovodsk, I remembered the old saw that people often cling to the stones that crush them. My memories of the war and later, of friends and relatives who had suffered or who had simply disappeared under Stalin's rule, strengthened my resolve to leave.

We were supposedly at the resort sanatorium on doctor's orders, but most of us were fit enough. Paying only a third of the already low standard fee of 220 rubles for twenty-four days, Lina and I devised our own schedule. We told the doctors not to wake us on their morning rounds beginning at eight o'clock, slept until at least nine, breakfasted in our room as often as not, took an invigorating bath and massage or a swim in the enclosed pool, and finished with a long walk before lunch. We avoided the fully equipped gymnasium and the tennis and volleyball courts, preferring to take our exercise by following one of the winding, uphill paths fifteen hundred feet above the main building to the hilltop plateau and its splendid vistas of the Caucasus range to the south.

Most of the other healthy guests paid as little attention as we did to the medical staff and its regulations for keeping the country's ruling class in governing trim. Few of us attended the afternoon political lectures that were compulsory for the doctors. But the evening movies, concerts, and dances were generally crowded. The bar also was well attended. Open before the midday and evening meals, it was fully stocked with vodka and Western brands of whiskey and wine, none of which was served in the dining room next door. It was no problem, however, to empty out a glass of the Narzan mineral water we were supposed to drink, refill it with clear vodka, and carry it with healthy hypocrisy to the dining table. Both the waitresses and the medical watchdogs looked the other way.

Being at Kislovodsk always gave Lina and me a breathing spell in our growing periods of tension. We were friends; we made love; we slept well. Both of us liked to spend time with each other; equally, we did not want to be completely isolated. It was possible to eat or entertain in our suite, but Lina and I preferred to take most of our meals in the common dining room. Our favorite table in an alcove afforded both privacy and an excellent view of the gardens and the mountains. The vista remained, but privacy dissolved as we sat down for our first luncheon and found two men sitting only a few feet away.

One, who introduced himself as Nikolai Petrov, a functionary of one of the research institutes of the Ministry of Health, was short, bouncy, and talkative. His companion, Aleksei Prokudin, was tall and taciturn. They were inseparable. They were also, obviously, determined to attach themselves to us. After finding them several times next to us in the movie theater or just setting out for a walk when we did, I was forced to agree with Lina's instinctive feeling

426

about them. Petrov was KGB. Prokudin, Lina guessed from his erect bearing and clipped speech, was GRU.

I had told Lina about the security campaign in the Foreign Ministry and the reasons for it, so she was not alarmed by the counterintelligence agents' interest in us. We worked out various stratagems to shake our protectors—varying our eating hours, even slipping into the dining room just as it was due to close, or taking off for day-long picnics and walks on distant hillsides. Still, all too often, Petrov and Prokudin managed to find and join us. I noticed that there were sanatorium staff members watching other vacationers too, but it seemed that they were neither as overt nor as diligent as Petrov and Prokudin were in my case.

In their company I behaved as I normally did with Soviet colleagues in New York, sticking to safe topics of conversation and keeping my own remarks either orthodox or flippant. With other guests at the resort, however, I did not have to watch my tongue so closely. Usually without any prodding from me these top officials, after a drink or two, would unburden themselves of views more nearly seditious than anything I let slip to the KGB. Russians like to talk. The resort was beautiful, but the routine of the days there was inevitably dull. On walks in the woods or over drinks before and after the evening show, we got to know each other quickly.

What I heard at Kislovodsk in the summer of 1977 from Party bureaucrats and cabinet ministers alike was a familiar litany of shortcomings in the planning and management of the economy and agriculture; how they were all doing their best to improve the situation and would, of course, achieve success in time. But they talked of palliatives, not of real reforms or substantial changes. No one criticized the system itself. Only a few were truly bitter.

"We can tinker here and there and make one part of the chain function a little better for a while," said one of our companions, "but nothing really changes. Some other part of the machinery goes wrong and the deliveries we were counting on to make our sector produce properly don't come through. I'll be glad when I can retire and forget about it."

He was among the more conscientious. He also displayed a self-appraising candor rare in such circles. Most of the others, fattened on their special privileges, were indifferent. If they knew how poorly average Soviets fared under their rule, they remained confident, at least, that no popular unrest would force them to change or lose their status. Their wives shopped in stores only the elite could enter. Their children went to schools where the parents' jobs, not the youngsters' aptitudes, were the criteria for admission and promotion. They traveled in comfort, certain that places would be found for them on trains and planes. Chauffeured cars carried them to and from work, met them at the resorts they visited or the installations they might be sent to inspect. They or friends of theirs brought luxuries home from trips to the West. Expert doctors, equipped with the best imported drugs and instruments, stood by to care for their health. And fawning subordinates assured them of their competence, their value to the state, their position.

The cocoon of privilege in which they and I lived was warm, comfortable, and crippling. Most of those inside never looked out. The worst they could imagine would be to fall from their perch, and the only thing that might endanger their hold would be some action on their part—protest or an overly zealous effort to institute reforms or corruption too blatant for the authorities to ignore. Few of them were possessed by any such suicidal drives.

One almost daily occurrence on the hillside above the main sanatorium building illustrated how insensitive the men in high positions in government had become. Regularly, as Lina and I walked up the mountain on a road restricted to foot traffic, a blare of sirens would mount behind us and a cavalcade of cars, with a local police vehicle at the front and back, would speed past us and the other hikers, forcing everyone off the road and covering us with clouds of dust. "Who is that?" I heard an angry pedestrian ask a companion.

"Didn't you know? It's Yuri Andropov. He's staying in one of the dachas at Krasnye Kamni."

The KGB chief, a member of the Politburo and one of the most powerful men in the Soviet Union, suffered from a weak heart and had to be driven to the fine fresh air of the plateau. But instead of the longer route other cars used, his chauffeur took a shortcut, turning a hiker's path into a highway. If his passage inconvenienced or enraged lesser mortals, their discomfort was of no consequence.

Andropov's behavior in the elite preserve was in striking contrast to the noisy show put on by his cavalcade up the mountain. Unlike other prominent officials who frequented the resort, he and his wife kept strictly to themselves in seclusion in an extra-heavily guarded dacha. Andropov did not care to mingle even with his own class, declining to take his meals in the dining room and shunning encounters with anyone but those who were invited to visit him.

Seeing Andropov's convoy plowing its way through the clumps of wild roses on the Kislovodsk mountainside, I realized once again how irrelevant individual traits are to the collective behavior of the Soviet rulers. Whether or not he sought it, Andropov had achieved a numbing isolation. He and his Politburo colleagues had lost touch with the reality of the society they directed. Unwilling to understand it, they were unable to inspire it. They could still generate fear but not sympathy, command obedience but not enthusiasm. And sheltered as they were, they would not venture to change their course.

Having come to Krasnye Kamni to refresh my spirits, I left the resort gloomy and tense. The persistent attention of Petrov and Prokudin irritated me more than it scared me, but their nagging questions about my attitudes toward the West and my views of the Soviet system suggested that they were trying not just to test me but perhaps to trap me.

Stopping in Moscow for a few days before returning to New York, I was able to confirm the assumption Lina and I made about our companion-interrogators at the sanatorium. Over dinner with an old friend, a high official in the Health Ministry, I casually mentioned Nikolai Petrov and the Moscow medical center where he claimed to occupy a senior post. He had never heard the man's name. I moved the conversation quickly to other subjects, my suspicion transformed to certainty.

The only question that remained in my mind was the degree of the KGB's distrust. It was possible that all diplomats of my rank were being put under the police microscope, but it was also conceivable that I had been singled out. I had only one safe course: to assume the worst and behave as normally as I could until the danger either passed or forced me to act.

With the passage of time it was more and more difficult to act. Anna now had to stay in Moscow to attend high school. I could always arrange for her to come to the United States for summer or winter vacations, but the fact that she was in Moscow, in conjunction with Lina's unwillingness to consider life beyond the Soviet elite, was a potent deterrent which kept me waiting and dragging, limiting even my ability to choose the right time to break with the regime.

I HAD HAD A SERIES OF DISAGREEMENTS WITH ALEKSANDR Podshchekoldin, the local New York Party boss, on different matters and on different occasions. After one of them in early 1978, a Soviet national working at the Secretariat stopped me in a UN corridor to whisper a warning. "I'm surprised at how furious Aleksandr Nikolaevich [Podshchekoldin] has become," my friend said. "I know you're doing a good job, but you may have more trouble from him."

Podshchekoldin had told him: "Shevchenko has been here long enough. He should go home." Lina had picked up similar vibrations from talks with other Mission wives. According to her, Podshchekoldin had been heard more than once observing that "Arkady is a big figure here. He should be more active in guiding the community. He should participate more in the life of the collective and the Party."

I paid little attention when I first became aware of the criticism, but my UN colleague's advice sank in. I had not sought a collision with Podshchekoldin. I would do my best to avoid provoking another one by staying away from him. When the next regular Party committee meeting was called in mid-February, I pleaded illness and did not attend. That proved to be a mistake.

One Saturday early in 1978, I slept late, exhausted from

the strain of my double life and worried about my daughter. Lina had flown to Moscow, summoned there by her mother to deal with Anna. She was having, or making, trouble at her school. The teachers had complained. Her grandmother was having no success in disciplining her, so Lina went home to try to work out the problem.

The night before, I had had difficulty sleeping. I had put a pillow over the telephone to muffle it and taken one of Lina's tranquilizers. Still under its effect the next morning, I dimly heard a noise at the apartment door. Half conscious, I recognized the sound of insistent knocking, but I refused to get up. I pulled the covers over my head and went back to sleep.

When I went out for a walk later, I asked the building doorman whether he had noticed anyone coming to my apartment that morning. He told me that my driver had been in the building with two other men, but he did not know where they had gone, only that they had stayed just a short time. I went back upstairs and telephoned Nikitin.

"Ambassador Troyanovsky was worried about you," he said. "He sent me over to find out where you were and what you were doing."

"And who came with you?"

"The doctor and Yuri Shcherbakov." Shcherbakov was KGB, the Mission security officer.

"Why?" I asked. "What are they worried about? Why did the security man come?"

"I don't know," Nikitin answered. "It wasn't my idea. He just came along."

For the rest of the weekend the incident bothered me. It was unusual, a warning I could not ignore. Monday morning I went to the Mission to confront Troyanovsky.

"What the devil do you mean sending the KGB after me?"

"We've been concerned about you, Arkady Nikolaev-ch," he replied. "There's no reason to be upset." He smiled as though we were sharing a small joke.

To me the KGB was no joke. The secret police at my door reawakened too many familiar anxieties. When I called El-enberg to ask for a meeting that night, I imagine that he

431

thought I had acquired some new information. The convenience of having him almost at my back door enabled me to spend more time at each session, to go deeper into whatever subject we explored. Ellenberg welcomed the detailed picture I was able to give him of the Soviet position on preparations for a special UN session on disarmament in May. And there was Anatoly Dobrynin's assessment of the Carter administration after its first year in office.

Dobrynin's annual report on the Washington embassy's work was a document running to more than two hundred pages and full of trivia as well as substance. There were the dutiful listings of the number of staff and Party meetings held in 1977, the themes which had been examined in Party lecture series, the propaganda accents used in material disseminated to the American public and government officials.

What chiefly interested Ellenberg, however, were the ambassador's comments on the political and economic situation in the United States, his judgments on American military programs and posture, and his forecast for U.S.-Soviet relations. President Carter, Dobrynin wrote, was fundamentally unpredictable. He had gone back and forth on the questions of importance to Moscow and still could not be said to be firmly committed to any consistent approach. One element of Carter's thinking, the human rights concerns which the Soviets had hoped were mostly campaign rhetoric, had emerged instead as a central element of U.S. foreign policy. This troublesome development meant that Moscow could expect no move to repeal the restrictions which linked trade concessions to the emigration of Soviet Jews.

I had read the Dobrynin report carefully and made notes. It gave me an opportunity to assess his thinking since many of his cables from Washington did not reach the UN Mission. His comments on the U.S. Communist Party were interesting. Party leader Gus Hall was considering a change in tactics. Until then, Hall's approach had only diminished Communist influence in the United States. Dobrynin endorsed Hall's proposal to make a fresh effort to break out of political isolation, to broaden the Party's contacts with "democratic and progressive forces" in America with a view to building something like a popular front.

I found it hard to take the proposal seriously. Although I had no direct contacts with American Communists, I knew that their activities were so unsuccessful that Moscow had to subsidize the Party through a variety of stratagems. The Soviet Mission had to take out a large number of subscriptions to the Party paper, the *Daily World*. Almost as soon as the copies arrived, however, they were tossed into the Mission wastebaskets. Not even Soviet diplomats found the paper worth reading. *

After my first review of Dobrynin's report, I told Ellenberg the highlights and promised to provide a more complete account later. But I had nothing to add when I met him after the incident on Saturday. I was concerned not only about Drozdov and Podshchekoldin's behavior but also about Lina. I wanted to tell her of my intention to break with the Soviet government, and to try to get her to come with me, but I was still not sure what her reaction would be. I wanted Anna to come for her summer vacation so I could try to persuade her to join me and to help me influence her mother.

My biggest problem was to convince Lina that I could be a success in a new life in the West. The sticking point, of course, was that I didn't know myself whether I would be a success or not. I might never be able to offer Lina the things she loved and already had. What I had achieved in the Soviet Union would be gone forever. If I was a success in the United States, it would have to be on a different basis. I was afraid she wouldn't be willing to gamble on a new future.

When I called Ellenberg and told him and Carl McMillan, the FBI agent who became the other half of the team working with me in mid-1977, what had happened on Saturday, they understood my concern.

"It's not usual procedure," I said. "Along with Podshchekoldin's behavior toward me, this KGB business looks like part of something bigger. It worries me, and it ought to worry you."

---

* Since the FBI reportedly also takes a substantial number of subscriptions, one wonders how many ordinary Americans actually read the paper.

Although they had observed nothing out of the ordinary in their own surveillance of the KGB, this was not necessarily reassuring. They agreed that the situation was abnormal, possibly dangerous, but perhaps did not require urgent action. Ellenberg realized I was deeply disturbed. He began to give ground, but only a little. He hoped I would stay on the job a few months more. Gromyko was coming to the special session on disarmament in May, only two months away. Couldn't I hold on until then?

Finally, he pledged that I could complete my work early in the summer of 1978. "When your daughter gets out of school," he said, "you can bring her to New York, and we'll have everything ready. If you move now, while she's still in Moscow, you know how hard it'll be to get her out."

That was exactly what I wanted, of course. I had decided that telling my wife and daughter together about my plans for our future would be the most persuasive approach. But then an abrupt and ominous call to return to Moscow changed everything.

In the first months of 1978, I was busy with problems and activities relating to the special session of the General Assembly devoted to disarmament, scheduled for May and June of 1978. The preparatory committee for the session was laboring over various documents and my department was responsible for helping the committee with its work. Waldheim delegated to me almost exclusive authority to deal with the support that the Secretariat provided the committee. Western and non-aligned countries complained that I was promoting Soviet ideas while distorting their positions.

In the midst of these events my hidden career came to an end. On the last day of March 1978, a Friday, I received a late-afternoon call from Oleg Troyanovsky. His tone was normal, routine, cryptic only because all our conversations were cautious on lines that could be tapped.

Could I come to the Mission this evening? Expecting nothing out of the ordinary, I promised to be there within an hour or two and went back to the pile of documents on my desk. Later, at the Mission, the ambassador was in a hurry to get away. "There's a cable from Moscow waiting for you upstairs," he told me, but before he could say anything more, the telephone rang. Tatyana, his wife, was on the line and out of sorts.

"What's holding you up?" I could hear her, loud and impatient. "The car is waiting. Close up that sweatshop"— she used an untranslatable bit of underworld slang—"and let's go."

Troyanovsky promised to join her right away. Standing up, he stuck out his hand with an apologetic smile. "I'm sorry. I have to go. Why don't you read the message and we can talk about it tomorrow. Will you be coming out to Glen Cove?" I told him I would see him on Long Island, and I went up to the seventh-floor code room. What I read there shook me profoundly.

The message was a summons home. The pretext was thin —"for several days of consultations in connection with the forthcoming special session of the UN General Assembly on disarmament"—and vague enough to be ominous—"as well as for a discussion of certain other questions." I was almost certain there were no consultations scheduled on the special session itself. From the delegates who had come from Moscow to the preparatory committee I knew that the basic Soviet position was set. I had already passed on its details to the CIA. Why should there be consultations on a matter that was virtually settled? And why hold them now, when the work of the preparatory committee had raised no unanticipated questions for Moscow to deal with?

Moreover, what were the "certain other questions" Moscow wanted to discuss? My UN contract had been renewed in February. Gromyko and I had gone over my plans as long ago as the General Assembly session in September 1976, and he had been pleased at my promise to stay on in New York to help Troyanovsky settle into his job. Knowing Gromyko, I was almost sure he had not suddenly found a new assignment for me. If that was one of the "other questions," he would save it to discuss during the disarmament session in May. What could be so pressing as to require a trip now? In the rare cases when ambassadors are called home, the reasons are precise and clearly stated. This cable gave no such reasons.

Moscow may have thought that referring to the consultations on disarmament alone wouldn't be convincing enough —in fact it probably would have been—so someone decided to add the unusual phrase "certain other questions." This was a mistake; it put me on alert. I don't understand how such a lapse could have occurred, but I am very glad that it did.

Beyond that, the timing was most awkward. Waldheim was in Europe, and in his absence all the Under Secretaries exercised final control over the areas of their responsibility. Logically, my presence in New York supervising the work of the preparatory committee was much more important for the Soviets than going to Moscow for some unspecified consultations.

But if I had been discovered, the cable could be a death sentence. It ordered me to "advise when it would be convenient" to fly to the Soviet Union. I realized it would never be "convenient." I did not intend to face whatever was waiting for me. I could not take the risk. Instead, I had to stall, to buy some time, to hold my own consultations with the Americans, and to make absolutely certain that my instinct was right—that there was no innocent reason for the summons.

Fortunately, I had a few days to play with. Troyanovsky had said he wanted to discuss the message with me, but I managed to postpone that talk. When I arrived at Glen Cove on Saturday, he was on the tennis court. The rest of that day I made certain our paths did not cross, and on Sunday I rose late and, telling Lina that I faced an overload of work, headed back to the UN while my colleague was again working up a sweat.

The UN was deserted on Sunday afternoon. I picked up the telephone in an unlocked office down the corridor from my own and dialed the familiar number. "This is Andy. It's urgent. I need to meet him as soon as possible." I hung up the telephone feeling as if I were standing in the aftermath of a thunderclap.

PART THREE

THE END OF THE GAME

436
190
12⟌246
20 pages.

28

As I waited in my UN office that Sunday afternoon, I tried to read some of the material on my desk, but I could not concentrate. The Americans had assured me repeatedly that there had been no leaks, but could they be certain? Washington was full of fast talkers who too often spoke before they thought. Had I been given away accidentally?

Or had I compromised myself? Had I been too arrogant with the Party hacks and the KGB in New York? In our brief talk Friday night, Troyanovsky had given no indication of alarm or distrust, but he might not be aware of anything; it would be unusual for the KGB to tell an ambassador what it knew or suspected.

If it really was all over, if time had run out, what could I do to hold my family together? Again I searched for ways to keep Lina with me, to get Anna out of Moscow. I had one trump card: my position as Under Secretary General and the two-year contract that would formally oblige the UN to keep me on no matter what the Soviets said. Could I bargain my job for my daughter, a quiet resignation for her freedom?

Staring out over the East River, watching the shadow of my own building creep across the water into Queens, I realized that the moment I had been waiting for and dreading had come and caught me unprepared.

In turmoil I drove to my apartment, barely remembering to call Nikitin and tell him to pick up Lina at Glen Cove. Then I hurried to the elevators, through the garage, to the building in the rear.

Bob and Carl were both waiting for me in the CIA apartment. They seemed worried, but also a bit irritated. They were, after all, husbands and fathers whose Sunday I had interrupted. What I told them erased their impatience and transformed it to concern.

I repeated the text of the cable and gave them my reading of what it meant. "I think this is it; I can't wait any longer," I said. "I'll tell them I can't come immediately. I'll say that with Waldheim away and preparing the special session there's too much work to do. I'll get a delay. But even if Moscow is willing to wait that's going to give us only a few weeks at most. I must have official word now from your government that it will accept me."

There was no argument. In March, Bob had talked me into going along through the special session. Now he did not try to reassure me or remind me how useful I was. He and Carl agreed to act right away. We set our next meeting for Monday night, and I told them I would try to call and confirm it. There was little more to say.

When Lina arrived from Glen Cove, loaded with grocery bags from her regular weekend shopping expedition, I casually mentioned that I would be going to Moscow for consultations. The news made her cheerful, a mood I tried to match. Together we planned the gifts I would take to family and friends. She was pleased at the chance to shop for bargains in New York that could be resold at a profit in the Soviet Union. I agreed to all her plans even as I knew I would never see Moscow again, perhaps never be with Lina . . . or Anna . . . or Gennady. A wave of uncertainty came over me, a surge of love and doubt.

I fought it down with difficulty. I knew there was no turning back, and yet part of me wanted a second chance, some miracle that would restore youthful hopes for Lina and me, for my country, for the ideals I had once believed in. I did not feel like a traitor to my country and my people. The Soviet regime had betrayed them; it had betrayed me. But if I went to Moscow as ordered, I would get no second chance.

I slept poorly, but the next morning I was in control of myself when I went to the Mission. I told Oleg Troyanovsky that because of my heavy workload at the UN, I was going to have to ask the Foreign Ministry for a delay of at least a few weeks. I said that the preparatory committee needed my full attention.

"I think I should stay until the committee finishes. Besides, how would I explain to Waldheim why I had to leave suddenly?"

"I wouldn't advise you to do it that way," Troyanovsky replied. "It's none of my business, but when the Center makes a request like this, it's best to go and be quick about it."

There seemed to be something other than cordiality in his tone. Was he giving me honest advice or a warning? Whichever it was, I decided not to ignore it. "Well, I just can't go today or tomorrow," I said. "I've got a ton of work, but I'll tell Waldheim's assistants my mother-in-law is seriously ill and I have to go look after her. I'll cable Moscow that I'll be on the Sunday flight."

Troyanovsky looked displeased. He had obviously wanted me to take the flight on Thursday. But he probably couldn't insist without provoking questions he didn't want to answer. He shrugged. "It's up to you. Just let the Center know."

I sent the cable and made the arrangements for my departure. I then went to the morning meeting of the preparatory committee and took my place on the podium next to Carlos de Rozas, the chairman. De Rozas, a senior Argentine diplomat whom I liked and respected, greeted me with a quip about the last committee session, but he soon noticed that I was subdued. "Is something the matter?" he asked.

"I'm not sure," I answered. "I've had word that my mother-in-law in Moscow is ill. I may have to go to her." De Rozas was sympathetic. My final deception had begun.

When the morning session ended, I stopped at the section reserved for the Soviet delegation and invited an old friend to join me for a meal at the Golden Dragon, a Chinese restaurant on Second Avenue.

We talked shop: the work of the preparatory committee, the continual personnel intrigues at the Foreign Ministry. Finally I broached the subject about which I knew he would be thoroughly informed, the "consultations" in Moscow. I did not tell him I had been called home.

"What's new from the Center on the committee?" I asked. "Is anything brewing there?"

"Nothing new," he said instantly. "Just the opposite. I got

a letter last week telling me not even to send in a report until after the committee finishes its work. The big boys don't want to be bothered. They've already made their decisions.''

"So you don't think there's any need for me to go over, just to wrap up any loose ends.''

"Absolutely not. Don't even suggest it. They'll think you just want a chance to nose around Moscow.''

There it was; the summons home was a deception. After we finished lunch I phoned the Americans from the restaurant and confirmed the appointment for that night. At our meeting I asked that we set Thursday as the date. It was only three days away, but it would give the Soviets less time to try to stop me.

"We can do it all by Thursday," Bob agreed. I took his words as an indirect form of the official acceptance I had asked for. We also went over the escape plan, since we didn't want to risk another contact before Thursday.

On Thursday night I would work very late at the UN, come home briefly to my apartment, and then meet them and a getaway car as soon as Lina was asleep and I could safely leave. The car would be a four-door white sedan parked on the far corner of Sixty-fourth Street and Third Avenue. Lookouts would be posted around my building to watch for any sign of KGB surveillance. If there was anything unusual, the automobile's signal lights would be flashing, warning me to stay away.

In that case I was to pretend that I was out for a late-night stroll. I was to walk up Third Avenue and go into a neighborhood bar. From there I would call and arrange for another team to pick me up.

The plan was simple and it seemed workable. But it covered only the actual escape, none of the questions we would have to deal with later: arrangements for Lina, with the UN, with the Soviets for the rest of my family, for my future. The Americans ticked off the details of the basic procedures, and I took a measure of confidence from their competence and calm.

I tried to hide my nervousness, but I made a bad job of it. It was hard to concentrate on the details we were discussing. All I could think of was my wife and daughter. What on earth could I say to Lina? She had a hot temper and very often blew up before listening to explanations. It was courting disaster to ask her directly to defect with me. First, she would never agree to it without Anna; second, she had no idea that I was working with the U.S. government. I was afraid to tell her—I had let it go too long already, sure in my heart that she would object so violently she might shut off our chance at freedom —if only involuntarily—by the scene she was sure to make. In her fury and confusion she might very well call the Mission to have the KGB come and get both of us. My life would be over. For Lina or my children it would be no better in Moscow with me dead. I hoped I could make her realize that in our confrontation. I saw again, as at the beginning of this venture, that I was trapped. Also as before, the only way I could see out was to present Lina with a *fait accompli* before actually discussing it with her. Going over and over all this was a nightmare.

I put all my concentration into a letter I intended to leave for Lina in our apartment after she was asleep on the night I went to the Americans. I also planned to leave her a large amount of cash, in case of any emergency that might occur before I could reach her by phone. I had in my bank account a considerable amount of money accumulated from my UN salary that I had held back from the Soviets.

Looking back, knowing how frantic I was over all this, I don't know how I kept Lina and others from noticing the strain I was under. Every time I entered the Mission I would be gauging the chances that I might not walk out of it. In every talk with Lina I would worry about a slip of the tongue. Every time I got into my car, I would expect to find KGB agents inside, waiting to shut off my freedom.

I needed release and I took it in tranquilizers. Since the blow-up with Podshchekoldin I had been using them heavily. Under their influence I sleepwalked through my work. Tuesday morning I had to present a statement for the Secretary General to a meeting on apartheid. My subordinates drafted it for me, and after a perfunctory clearance with Waldheim's senior assistant, I droned through the four-page text and promptly forgot every word of it.

The hours blurred as I went through the motions of work

and my bogus preparations for the trip to Moscow. Lina was meanwhile absorbed in buying presents for relatives and friends at home. She too wanted to go to Moscow. I told her I wished we could travel together but it would be a very short trip and we would have to pay for her tickets ourselves. I reminded her that it would soon be summer, when we could go home for our long vacation. From my bank account at the UN I withdrew the large sum of money I planned to leave with Lina, and stored it in my office safe. I also sorted out personal papers I kept there. Finally, Thursday came.

Near the end of the day I called Lina to tell her to have supper without me; I would be working very late. Then, as my office emptied out, I began to put the finishing touches on the life I was leaving. I gathered together a number of personal files and dumped them into my briefcase. On top went a few photographs from my desk and shelves—Anna, a snapshot of Lina and Lidiya Gromyko taken at the Soviet Mission with the Polaroid camera I had given the Foreign Minister, of Kurt Waldheim and me in his office, of Waldheim and me across the table from Brezhnev and Gromyko in the Kremlin.

I stopped. My briefcase was beginning to bulge, and my head had begun to throb. What if, after all, I had become paranoid? What if the strain of my double life had finally forced me into a trap of my own making? Maybe I was not suspected. Was I wrong to think there was anything but concern about my health? Was that the real explanation for the summons home? Perhaps they were worried about my nerves, not my loyalty.

The bout of indecision was wrenching, but it was also short. I had answered these questions before. I had answered the real question in the letter to Lina . . . the letter to Lina . . . I had to reread it and probably rewrite it.

I took the envelope from my safe, slit it open, and again read the familiar words. As I did so, I found I wasn't satisfied. I sat down and began again.

"I am desperate," I wrote. "I can neither live nor work with people I hate, whether in New York or in Moscow." I described the mounting pressures of the last months, the increased tension between me and Podshchekoldin over Party matters, the constant hounding by Drozdov and the KGB.

I said that I intended to ask for political asylum in the United States. I did not reveal that I had been working with the Americans, but I told her I had conclusive evidence that my call to Moscow was a trap. I wrote that I believed we would never be permitted to leave the country again, and that it was very likely I would be dismissed from the ministry. "Please come with me," I begged. "It will be a much better life here, and I will try to move the earth to get Annushka out of the Soviet Union. We can begin a new and free life abroad where people are not persecuted and afraid." I pleaded with her to trust me, reminding her that I had never let her down. I told her that to return to the Soviet Union would be dangerous, perhaps fatal, for both of us. I promised to explain everything when we met, and urged her not to be hasty even though I knew she would be terribly upset by this letter. I asked her specifically not to call anyone at the Mission or to go there. I told her that I would call early the next morning for her decision.

I put down my pen in despair. Even if I had possessed more eloquence, I doubted that my arguments would bring Lina over to me. When we were poor, struggling, miserable in that awful communal apartment with Gennady sick and crying, then we had been truly happy. But over the years, I had been absorbed in my work. We had grown apart. Lina also had been obsessed with my getting to the top. Was it my success that had spoiled everything? Or was it Lina's preoccupation with security? Perhaps it was only the weight of years.

Whatever it was, I was demolishing the rock she stood on. She would never forgive me. She would probably not risk a new adventure, starting over in America with me. I had written the truth without being able to tell her all of it. If she decided to leave me, at least the letter would prove that she was not my accomplice. The Soviets might leave her and the children alone.

I folded the pages and put them into a new envelope along with the money. That, too, went into the briefcase. I looked at my watch. Nearly midnight. Time to go.

I telephoned the Mission to ask that my driver pick me up. I tried to hear in the duty officer's voice any nuance of suspicion, any false note. But his manner was dry, ordinary, bored.

The car would be sent immediately. Perhaps ten minutes later, Nikitin rang me from the guard desk at the entrance to the Secretariat. Did I need him to come up? No, I would be right down.

Nikitin held the back door of the black Oldsmobile for me and got behind the wheel with nothing more than a perfunctory "Good evening." Normally we chatted easily, exchanging small talk about the Mission or New York. But in the last few weeks he had seemed unusually reserved. I knew he liked me, knew he was grateful because I helped him to get a third tour in America. But now I wondered if he sensed that I was in trouble.

I did not believe he was a KGB agent. But like all Soviets abroad, he was obliged to cooperate with them. I assumed that as a routine matter he had to report my comings and goings. Lately, perhaps, they had been more inquisitive and pressed him harder. Maybe he had detected the tension. Maybe the other drivers had said something about me. Whatever, he was silent.

Nikitin pulled the car out into the nearly empty thoroughfare of First Avenue and headed north. At first I sank back in the seat, but then I began to look around, to check the traffic behind us. There were very few cars on the avenue and most of them were a block or more behind us. One pair of headlights, however, seemed to me to have picked us up as we left the UN.

They stayed behind us as we drove north through the Forties and Fifties. I grew nervous. Would I ever make it to Bob and Carl? The Soviets might be waiting for me inside my apartment. Did I dare go home?

However, when Nikitin turned left in the Sixties, the car that had seemed to be following us kept straight on up First Avenue. I relaxed again. In front of the apartment building Nikitin helped me out of the car.

"Please pick me up at the usual time tomorrow," I told him, stressing the final phrase, the continuity of my routine. "Sleep well," I added. "Good night."

"Good night, Arkady Nikolaevich," he said. *"Do svidaniya."*

446

"*Do svidaniya*, Anatoly," I replied. We were never to meet again.

As I had hoped, Lina was asleep. Still, I had to hurry. I took an overnight bag from the living-room closet and jammed a few shirts and some socks and underwear into it. I did not dare make any noise. If Lina were to wake, it might be hours before she went to sleep again.

What else would I need? My mind was a blank. I tried to focus but could not. Nothing was real except the threat of discovery, the chance of escape. I was living from minute to minute, moving through a kind of trance in which I could act but not calculate. Nervous energy, not rational thought, kept me going.

I tiptoed to our bedroom door, took a last look at my sleeping wife, slid the envelope just inside the door, and then left the apartment. I started to head for the service elevator and stopped abruptly.

It didn't run after midnight. I could not take one of the regular elevators either. There was always the chance that I would meet one of the other Soviet officials who lived in the building. And I would have no ready explanation for the bags I was carrying, no answer for the obvious questions about what I was doing, where I was going so late at night.

I had not worked out this part of my plan with Bob and Carl. For a minute I didn't know what to do. Then I remembered the fire stairs at the end of the hallway. I could walk down, although it was twenty flights. The staircase went to the ground floor at the back of the building. I would be able to get out without being seen by the night clerk at the front desk.

Grasping bag and briefcase in one hand, I opened the exit door. The staircase was dimly lit, the concrete steps a dark gray, the metal rail cold and slippery under my sweaty hand. After the first six floors I had to stop and shift my briefcase and bag from one hand to the other. My clenched fingers had begun to ache. The briefcase kept bumping against my knee or my shin, making me stumble occasionally. Five flights further I stopped again and rested. I had been taking silent, almost mincing steps and now my calf muscles were trembling from the unusual strain. My heart seemed to be throbbing, booming out the alarm I felt.

I rested twice more before I reached the ground floor. Gingerly I pushed open the heavy door and peered around it. There was no one in sight. I walked the few steps to the service entrance and let myself out into the narrow passage that led to Sixty-fourth Street. A chill drizzle hit me, and with my free hand I tugged my dark blue raincoat closed. On the sidewalk I looked anxiously to my left. I could see the white car parked on the other side of Sixty-fourth Street. The signal lights were not flashing. Everything was all right.

It was some fifty yards to the car, but the distance seemed enormous, perilous. There could be a KGB agent waiting in a dark doorway, invisible to me, unseen by the Americans, with orders to stop me and a knife or gun to execute the command. What if the Americans had discovered danger but were waiting until I appeared to turn on their warning lights? How could I pretend to be out for a walk with my overnight bag and briefcase?

The escape plan suddenly seemed irrelevant: I ran. I dashed along Sixty-fourth Street and barely paused to glance at the empty stretch of Third Avenue before rushing across it toward the car and safety. By the time I reached it, Bob was on the pavement holding the back door open for me. He took my cases and tossed them into the front seat, squeezed in beside me, and snapped: "Let's go."

Carl was on my other side. We sat in silence as the driver pulled away from the curb and began a circuitous trip across Manhattan, downtown to the Lincoln Tunnel. The city streets were nearly empty, but the tension I had felt an hour before, leaving the United Nations, rose in me again each time headlights from behind lit up the interior of our car. Bob and Carl obviously felt the strain too, and it was not until we had crossed into New Jersey that I broke the silence with a question.

"Where are we going?"

"Pennsylvania. We have a safe house in the Poconos, about two hours from the city."

There was no further conversation. My friends were nervous. I was exhausted. As we sped through the dark, I blanked out. My mind was numb and empty, too tired to be elated, too tense to feel safe.

29

IT MUST HAVE BEEN CLOSE TO THREE IN THE MORNING WHEN we left the highway and began to slow down on winding back roads, stopping at last outside a heavy wooden gate that swung open quickly to let us through. Tires crunched on a gravel driveway as we pulled up at a large red brick house with lights on in the downstairs windows. Inside, Bob and Carl introduced me to four or five men, obviously guards, whose names I did not register.

"There's a bedroom for you upstairs," one of them said.

I went up to the second floor, used the bathroom, and came down again to find a plate of sandwiches laid out in the living room. "There's a lot to do in the morning," Carl said. "You ought to get some rest now."

I took a sandwich and headed back to my room. In the hall outside my door a stocky Oriental was unfolding a cot. "I'll be here." He smiled. "Just in case."

I did not find his presence reassuring. Was the safe house not so safe after all? But I was too tired to ask any questions. I was also too nervous to sleep. After the familiar rumble of New York, the countryside seemed ominously quiet. Each sound stood out in the silence, bringing me to a strained alert. I took a couple of tranquilizers, but they did not work.

Would I ever be safe anywhere? Had the KGB already started to hunt for me? Once they began, would they ever stop? Another voice within countered: Don't lose control. You're free, free.

But now that I'm free, now what? I admired America. I liked Americans. But I realized it would not be easy to adjust to life here. I knew it would take time, a long time, to establish myself, to make friends.

And where would I find them? I couldn't go back to my New York neighborhood, right under the nose of the KGB. But New York was my only home in America. Where would I settle if I had to leave it? To whom would I go if Lina refused to stay, if Anna were kept in Moscow?

Before dawn I gave up trying to sleep. I washed, dressed, and came downstairs. Bert Johnson had arrived during the night, and the mere sight of him heartened me. I suddenly realized how much I had relied on his steady calm, how much I had missed him in the last hectic days.

Even though the sun was just coming up, everyone in the house was awake. Perhaps they had also been too keyed up to sleep. Over coffee, we started to discuss our next moves.

One thing had to be done right away. To forestall any Soviet charge that I had been coerced, the Americans wanted me to demonstrate my freedom of action by registering under my own name at a nearby hotel and renting a car as well. They were not suggesting that I stay in the hotel, only that I show I was on my own, independent.

Since it was too early to go into town, however, I suggested that we take a walk. New leaves caught the early light in a calm that lifted my spirits. As we walked through the grounds around the house, it was as though an enormous weight on me was dissolving. The morning gave me the first real sense that I was free and that freedom was welcome, invigorating. Johnson broke into my silence. "Are you sure you don't want to just disappear?" he asked. "It would be easier. It could save a lot of complications."

I knew that Bert and the others were accustomed to defectors who preferred to hide themselves, who wanted money, protection, a new identity, safety in anonymity. But we had been over that before. I wanted independence and a chance to speak out.

"Look, I made all that clear from the start, and I haven't changed my mind," I said roughly. Half joking, to remove the sting, I added: "And you guys have to respect my wishes. After all, I'm still Under Secretary General."

I smiled, but I was serious. I felt it was my best hold on

both the Soviets and the Americans, as well as on myself. I still hoped it would be the key to bringing my family to me or, at least, win me guarantees of their security.

By this time we had come to the main gate of what I saw was a high wooden fence surrounding the property. "Let's go out," I suggested. "I'd like to look around some more."

My escorts exchanged quick glances, then shrugged and opened the gate onto a narrow lane. On the far side, unplowed fields stretched away to rolling, forested slopes. The landscape was quiet and clear, and again I felt a surge of freedom that made me want to run like a boy. But after we had walked a few hundred yards, I sensed that the Americans were on edge. Bob, who was a few paces ahead, stopped and turned around. "I think we ought to head back," he said.

"Why?" I asked, falling into step. "What are you worried about here?"

"Well, we're pretty sure that everything's okay, but it's always better to be cautious. You never know." He hesitated. "Andy, this is the critical stage. The KGB is going crazy, assuming they're aware you're gone. Drozdov has to realize he'll never be forgiven for letting this happen. God knows what they might be willing to do to get you back. Or just to get you. You're still fresh, as far as they know. They'll think you've only been with us a few hours, not enough time to give much away. They've got to try to stop you before it's too late."

We were near the house. Carl broke in: "What do you think?" he asked. "You know them better than we do. Don't you feel they'll try to come after you? How long will they keep it up? For Christ's sake, do you really believe you can live openly?"

There it was again. I was angry.

"Yes, I know them. I know what they've done and what they can do." I was thinking of Leon Trotsky, supposedly safe in Mexico, of the prewar kidnappings and executions staged in Europe by the near-legendary NKVD agent Lev Manevich, of Walter Krivitsky's assassination, of other deaths and disappearances since. "I told you that in the beginning I'd have to have protection.

"But I don't want it forever. Being a public figure will be

451

the safest thing for me in the long run. Sure, I'm scared, but the more visible I am, after a while, if something violent happens to me, everybody will think the Soviets did it. They might still seek revenge, but I want it to cost them plenty.

"I intend to run my own life. I'm not going to have plastic surgery, and I'm not going to hide. That doesn't do any good anyhow. If they found me after hiding ten years and killed me then, it wouldn't make a hell of a lot of noise. If they kill me, I want them to hurt for it." I suddenly felt bitterly depressed. "Besides, living underground is only changing one prison for another. Rather than live like that, I would have gone back to Moscow, gotten out of politics, and spent the rest of my life reading in my garden."

But I knew that even that option was not really possible. In my country no one would have understood such a move. I would be thought crazy to give up my position and privileges, and might well have been placed under indefinite psychiatric supervision.

"Look, I'm grateful to you. I really am. I know the danger, and I know it'll last a long time. I need protection, and I'll do whatever you think is necessary for my safety."

I had cleared the air, but I was exhausted again. Johnson checked his watch and decided it was time to perform our charade in town. I brought my overnight bag down from the upstairs bedroom, and we drove five or six miles of narrow country roads into the resort town of White Haven. At a Howard Johnson lodge I crossed an empty lobby, filled in a registration form for an incurious clerk, took a key to a second-floor room, and left my "luggage." Another quick stop to rent a car, and I had established my presence as a free man. I drove the hired car a few blocks and then handed over the keys to one of my guards while Bob took Carl, Bert, and me back to the safe house.

On the way, Johnson raised a complication. As long as I remained Under Secretary General, he explained, Washington could not formally act on a request for political asylum. My status as an international civil servant meant that officially I was not entitled to refuge in the United States. "Do you really intend to try to stay on at the UN?"

"I'm not going to run like a criminal," I said. "My position is my one weapon to help my family. Besides, to live independently, I need the money from the UN.

"Most of all, I want to put the Soviets in a corner, to make them swallow the reality of the UN Charter and the staff rules. They pretend to respect them when it's to their advantage. Well, I'd like to see them do it when it's galling."

"We understand that," Johnson replied. "But they'll make Waldheim knuckle under and dismiss you. He'll never ruin his relations with a superpower for one man, no matter how much he likes you."

He was right. But I was going to play out the string as far as it would go.

"Well, this is America," Carl said, "and in a situation like yours, Americans would go to a lawyer. You'll need one to deal with the UN for sure, but you'll probably need one for a lot of things. We can't be intermediaries for you, not with the Soviets, and not even with the American government. You'll have to have your own means of communication. In case you want some names, I've got a list of three or four lawyers in New York back at the house."

At the house, I went over the things I had to do that morning. Call Lina. Call the United Nations to arrange for my office to be sealed and to advise Waldheim's assistants that I would be away briefly. Write the Soviets to state my reasons for breaking with them and make my demands concerning my family. Call a lawyer.

Around 8:30 a.m. I reached the officer in charge of security at the UN and explained that I would be away for a few days because of illness. He agreed to seal my office until I returned, a routine measure at the UN. In the Secretary General's office I spoke with his personal assistant, Ferdinand Mayrhofer, an Austrian diplomat with whom I was friendly.

"I'm not feeling well and the doctor has told me to take a complete rest. I'll need a few days off. I know this is a bad time, but I can't help it."

"Is it anything serious?" he asked.

"No. I don't think so. But I'll have to take some leave. I'll get you a request in writing so you can advise Waldheim."

"That's fine," Mayrhofer said. "He hasn't called in yet

from Europe, but I'll be talking to him today, probably more than once."

"I'll call you back later then, when I can tell you more."

"More? Is there something more?"

"Well, there's a little. I'll phone again soon."

A few minutes after nine o'clock, I called Lina. Even though I needed to hear her voice, I dreaded the turn our talk might take. On the one hand, I wished her awake, waiting for me to call as my letter promised, but, on the other, I half hoped she was still asleep with the bedroom telephone turned off. Then I could postpone the confrontation, the better to be calm, persuasive, convincing.

I was not prepared for what actually happened. After one ring the telephone was answered.

"Da?" It was a man's voice. Russian.

"Lina?" I was puzzled at first.

"Yeeyo nyet doma." ("She's not at home.") The voice was that of a stranger. It was not even Nikitin, our driver.

I dropped the receiver as though it had burned me. I could only imagine what had really happened. I was suddenly struck with the possibilities.

She must have awakened early, read my letter, and panicked. She called someone at the Mission. They took her away and left a KGB man in her place. She had acted like a lamb asking the wolves to help her. And she put herself beyond any help from me.

I raged at her and at myself. I should have risked confiding in her. Why didn't I make a better plan? Why hadn't I asked the CIA to watch her? Why didn't she wait?

Like a man emerging from a fever dream, I forced myself to face reality. My anger could change nothing. There was no point in pretending that I would get her back. I would probably never even be able to speak to her again. I might never be able to see Anna either, since Lina could not and probably would not help me.

The Americans were right about my prospects at the UN. Sooner rather than later, I would be cut off from the work that had been my life. I was already separated from my family; Lina's disappearance had snapped the last threads. I had my

454

freedom, but at that instant, it didn't seem worth the price. Dazed, I sat looking at the telephone.

Johnson saw my distress. When I told him that Lina had gone or been taken to the Mission, he was not completely surprised. He knew from our talks that my letter had been a long shot at best, that she was more likely to cast her lot with the Soviets than with me. His reaction helped to cool my own, to make me admit that my expectations had not really been far from his. Nevertheless, I still had a responsibility to my family.

I sat down to write, to attempt to strike a bargain for my family's security. I could do so only by dealing from strength and only with the highest Soviet authority: Leonid Brezhnev. I would resign from the Communist Party, but keep my Soviet citizenship as long as I could remain in my post at the UN. I would refuse to carry out any orders from Moscow, but would insist—for negotiating purposes—on remaining Under Secretary General. Troyanovsky was going to be my messenger.

There were typewriters with both English and Cyrillic keyboards at the safe house, but I decided to write these letters in my own hand. The first one was addressed to Brezhnev. In stiff, official Russian I wrote:

> The betrayal of the ideals of the October Revolution which is taking place now in the U.S.S.R. and the monstrous abuses carried on by the KGB compel me to take the decision to renounce my membership in the CPSU [Soviet Communist Party], of which I wish officially to notify you by this letter.
>
> I also inform you that it is not my intention to resign from the post of Under Secretary General until certain questions regarding my family are resolved. I write of this in a separate note which is attached. I will await an official reply from the U.S.S.R. Mission to the UN on this matter.

In the attachment I proposed a quiet resignation, with Waldheim's concurrence, on condition that I receive a written, signed, and sealed guarantee of my family's immunity from "repressive measures of any sort" and of my wife's right both to retain our apartment and dacha and to receive regular hard-currency payments from me for her and our children. I pointed out that UN staff rules prohibited any government

455

from instructing a Secretariat employee on any matter, but offered "not to make a dramatic scene in this regard" if the Soviets gave me the written pledge of my family's well-being.

In a note to Troyanovsky, I requested that he transmit my letter to Brezhnev along with my official refusal to return to Moscow as ordered. I stated my "categorical refusal to take any instructions whatever from the Soviet Mission." I also told him of my intention to ask the Secretary General for a leave of absence "for a certain time," during which I would remain in "necessary and constant contact" with Waldheim's staff.

Finally, in English, I wrote Waldheim a note asking his help in obtaining the guarantees I sought from the Soviets so that I could resign quietly from the Secretariat. "For the present time, I ask your approval for a leave in order to rest and think," I concluded.

As I composed these drafts at a table in the corner of the living room, I half expected the Americans to look over my shoulder, to suggest the wording to me. But they left me alone until I was finished. Afterward I asked them to help me correct the grammar in my letter to Kurt Waldheim and to translate accurately the two Russian notes into English, as I wanted to attach them to my letter to Waldheim. Although the Soviets later accused me of putting my signature to CIA clichés, the language was my own. It was nearly noon before I was done. I asked Johnson if he could have the letters delivered for me.

He shook his head. "No. We can't act as intermediaries for you either with the Soviets or with the UN. That's one of the things you'll need a lawyer for, to preserve your independence."

Carl handed the list to me. "We've been in touch with all of them," he said. "They know who you are and are willing to help." There were only four names on the sheet of paper, but I recognized one immediately: Ernest Gross, a former U.S. representative to the United Nations.

"I know Gross," I exclaimed. "Well, I've never met him, but I studied his books on international law years ago. What's he doing now?"

Carl said he was a corporate attorney with a successful practice in New York. "He works on Wall Street," he added.

"Good," I joked. "That means he's dependable. The Soviets will be impressed. I'll call him now."

Bert suggested an alternative. It was almost lunchtime and they judged it would be safe—and effective—for me to eat in the hotel restaurant in town. I could telephone Gross from my room and call Mayrhofer again. Using the car I had rented, we drove to town. Bob went to the dining room to get a table for us, while Bert, Carl, and I went up to my room.

On the telephone Ernest Gross was enthusiastically supportive. He approved of holding on to my UN position and said he would draw on both his UN expertise and his experience of past negotiations with the Soviets. He agreed to deliver my letters to the Soviet Mission, and Johnson promised they would be taken to Wall Street that afternoon. By the end of our talk we were on first-name terms and Gross was ready to start researching the UN regulations that would apply to my case. I was buoyed by his warmth and his combativeness.

Ferdinand Mayrhofer was more troubled. I read him the letters, and when I had finished he was silent. "But how are you, Arkady?" he finally blurted. "Where are you? You're not in trouble, are you?"

"Ferdinand," I replied, "I'm fine; I'm safe. I'll be calling you regularly." I also told him that Ernest Gross would be representing me. As our conversation ended I heard Mayrhofer exclaiming, almost to himself, "Oh, Lord, this is going to be quite something, quite something." I knew he was thinking of Soviet pressure on Waldheim.

Over lunch at a corner table in the restaurant, we talked cheerfully. Bert toasted my escape, my freedom, my future. I drank to my protectors. I told them that Mayrhofer did not expect Waldheim to return to New York for ten days or so. And I did not intend to leave the UN without meeting and talking with him.

"So it looks like we're stuck with each other for quite a while," I said.

Back at the safe house they had already anticipated our enforced togetherness and had produced a portable chess-

457

playing computer, Boris. I wasn't surprised when I lost the first two rounds, though I managed to win a third game.

Bob asked me if I felt like doing some work, and I agreed, glad to end my contest with the computer. What he had in mind was to complete our examination of Dobrynin's annual report to the Foreign Ministry. We had discussed the main points, Dobrynin's assessment of the state of U.S.-Soviet relations, the American political situation, military posture, and other matters. They had not had time to turn their notes into a full report, and I had promised to look over their draft and help flesh it out. There were a lot of details missing. I had finished about three pages when Ernest Gross phoned.

The Soviets were demanding that the U.S. government produce me for a meeting over the weekend. The Americans, in turn, disclaimed any control over me and referred them to my attorney. What did I want to do?

My strongest wish—not to meet the Soviets at all—could not be honored. As long as I was a Soviet citizen, Gross pointed out, my government's representatives had the right to assure themselves that I was well, that I was not being coerced. It would put the American government in a difficult diplomatic position if I refused such an encounter. Moreover, a meeting might give me a chance to find out more about Lina, to discuss the guarantees I wanted for her and my children.

I accepted. "But I want you to make them understand that I'm still Under Secretary General," I told Gross. "This isn't a consular matter between them and the Americans. It's between them and me, and if we have to meet, I'll see only Troyanovsky. No one else. No consuls, no KGB, no one."

"They'll be mad as hell," Gross predicted.

"That's tough," I replied. "Either it's the ambassador or there's no meeting."

Johnson approved my condition, agreeing with Gross that I could not avoid a face-to-face session at some point. "But we'll need some time to make arrangements," he added, thinking about the security problems involved in bringing me into range of the KGB.

I called Gross to tell him of Johnson's concern. We decided that he and I should meet before confronting the Soviets, and

I would come to New York the next day, Saturday, to his home.

The prospect of meeting the Soviets worried me. I could no longer concentrate on the work I was doing for Bob. To keep occupied, however, I offered to cook our dinner that night. I said I would make borscht, something that takes hours to prepare. Concentrating on the soup helped me relax again. Once the pot was simmering I proposed that we play cards and that I teach them my favorite game, preference, a complicated variation of whist. We settled down to the game with drinks and snacks until the soup was ready.

Some of the men around the table knew only vaguely who I was. They were full of questions about the Soviet Union, my motives, my plans. Finally, one of them raised the issue I had already faced twice that day: my insistence on a future in the open. I replied as I had before.

"But aren't you afraid?" one of the agents persisted. "It's one thing for an artist to defect and go on with his career, but the politicals don't do that. They never have."

"Sure, I'm afraid. I'd have to be crazy not to be," I said. "But you guys are the experts. Is there any evidence that the KGB death squad might be operating in the United States? Have any other Soviet defectors been killed recently?"

"No, none. But they're all still in hiding."

"And that's just it. I won't live like a rabbit in a hole in the Arizona desert for the rest of my life."

"Okay, Andy," Bob intervened. "We know how you feel. We're with you all the way. But once you're on your own, the KGB could show up at any time. What would you do if Drozdov walked through that door right now with a gun on you?"

I answered with a bravado I didn't feel. "I'd try to kill him first."

Bob exploded in a laugh. He motioned to a guard to pull out his pistol and passed it across the table to me. "It's yours. We'll back you up, if we don't starve first. When is that stew of yours going to be ready, anyway?"

The tension was broken. The borscht was served and pronounced a success. The others cleaned up, and I went to bed. Again, the folding cot was in the hallway in front of my room.

I tried to read one of the Russian books that had been provided for me, Aleksandr Nekrich's *June 22, 1941*, an indictment of Stalin's failure to prepare the Red Army for Hitler's invasion. The work had been officially published in the Soviet Union in 1965, but was quickly withdrawn. I had never been able to get a copy before, but I couldn't concentrate on it. My mind kept racing ahead to my meeting with Troyanovsky. I tossed and turned for a long time before I finally fell asleep.

But the fear I had pretended not to feel surfaced in my nightmares. I was alone in a room. Drozdov came in with a pistol leveled at me. I reached for the gun. It wasn't there.

I woke in a sweat, and for the rest of the night I managed only fitful tossing. I was up and dressed before sunrise. The house was quiet. I pulled a chair over to the window and watched the brilliant spring dawn.

30

ON SATURDAY MORNING I CALLED FERDINAND MAYRHOFER at his home. He had talked with Waldheim, who at first had been shocked at my defection, and then, cautious as ever, had declined to discuss the matter over a transatlantic telephone. Mayrhofer also said that some sort of UN announcement would have to be made early in the week, but that no preliminary text had been prepared.

"I can't dictate the wording, Ferdinand," I said, "but want it to make clear that I have only asked for temporary leave, that I remain Under Secretary General." Mayrhofer promised to advise Waldheim of my wishes.

This time I was more aware of my surroundings as the Pennsylvania countryside and the New Jersey Turnpike flashed by on our route into New York, but I saw only the view through the windshield. Johnson had asked me to sit in the back seat of the heavy automobile, where the windows were curtained. Shortly before noon Johnson and I arrived at Ernest Gross's residence, a comfortable upper East Side apartment, where he and his wife greeted me with warm hospitality. He produced a chilled bottle of Russian vodka to toast our collaboration. After some pleasant conversation, we got down to business. Soviet pressure, he reported, was intense. They wanted the meeting as soon as possible, and they didn't like the idea of Troyanovsky's coming alone.

"They don't even trust their own ambassador," I said, savoring their dilemma. "But they'll think up something."

We ruled out a variety of possible meeting places. The Soviet Mission was out of the question. To use the American Mission would lend credence to the Soviet claim that I was under U.S. government control. A conference at the UN would be complicated to arrange, for political as well as security reasons; my CIA and FBI guards could not accompany me there. The Gross apartment would be too informal a setting. We decided on his Wall Street office. Johnson approved the choice, and suggested that we time it for Sunday evening, when the building and surrounding streets would be empty. He also urged that Gross give the Soviets minimum information about our plans. "Once they agree to the conditions, all we have to do is tell them that it will be eight o'clock Sunday. We'll supply the address later."

Gross and I then talked about my status at the UN. His research had turned up a regulation that gave the Secretary General authority to dismiss someone like me in "extraordinary circumstances." However, Waldheim would have to observe a number of contractual obligations.

"I feel sorry for Kurt," I said. "The Soviets will probably make it hell for him. But it's a real matter of principle, and he'll have to respect the regulations or face a revolt from the staff for letting one country dictate to him." The UN Charter provides that UN personnel "shall not seek or receive instructions from any government" and demands that each member of the UN respect the exclusively international character of the Secretary General and his staff. It gave me some satisfaction to think that by trying to force me from the post, the

Soviets would clearly illustrate to the world how little regard they have for their obligations under the Charter.

But it was neither my intention nor my desire to make Waldheim's situation intolerable for long. I told Gross that I might be prepared to resign eventually on honorable terms, but for the time being we should not make such an offer. First, we had to exhaust all avenues regarding the guarantees for my family.

As an initial step, he would talk with the UN administrative and personnel chief to see what separation payment I was entitled to under my contract. I was pleased to learn that he already knew George Davidson, the man he would be dealing with. Davidson, a Canadian diplomat, and my colleague as Under Secretary General, was certain to be no pushover in any bargaining.

Finally, Gross and I discussed what he should say once my defection became known to the press. I told him it was important to make the same point I had insisted on with Mayrhofer: my remaining as Under Secretary General. Beyond that, if there had been a meeting with the Soviets, he could confirm it but say nothing about my motivations or plans.

We closed our talk as friends. I felt I was fortunate to have him representing me. He radiated competence as well as zest for the case. His enthusiasm was infectious. It gave me a new, welcome dose of confidence.

I was further reassured when a doctor, whom the CIA suggested I see, gave me a brief medical checkup back at the safe house and pronounced me healthy. My blood pressure was up, but not dangerously.

On Sunday, Gross said the Soviets were still insisting on having a number of their people at the meeting. From their hints, however, he expected them to accept our conditions, with the proviso that Anatoly Dobrynin could attend to back up Troyanovsky. I had no objection to Dobrynin's presence, or to having a State Department official attend as an observer.

In contrast to Gross, who seemed to relish the imminent face-off, I dreaded it. I knew that Troyanovsky and Dobrynin would try to play on our years of acquaintanceship and on my most intimate concerns.

I could deal with normal diplomatic negotiations; I had been doing it all my life. But this was different; the stakes were personal, not political. The emotional challenges would be hard to handle.

On Sunday evening I found a veritable flotilla of cars in the driveway, including a long, heavy limousine, toward which Johnson steered me. Until then we had used ordinary sedans, but this car was full of radio communications equipment and was to be preceded and followed by chase cars full of agents.

The precautions intensified as we neared New York. At the New Jersey entrance to the Holland Tunnel a state police car cut in ahead of our cavalcade while a second temporarily halted all traffic behind us. No one following the convoy could see the path it took once it entered New York.

From the tunnel we drove around the southern tip of Manhattan and headed north, up the East Side, before doubling back to 100 Wall Street. Johnson explained that our round-about route was designed to suggest to observers that we had come to New York from Long Island or Connecticut rather than from the west. I only half listened. I was distracted by the scene outside the car.

On my earliest trip to the United States in 1958, Wall Street was the first "sight" I had visited in New York. I arrived there during the lunch hour, and had to push my way through the mass of people thronging the narrow pavement. I was amazed—revolted, actually—by the frantic spectacle of the floor traders I saw from the Stock Exchange's visitors' gallery. Later on, as almost a New Yorker myself, I had brought other Soviet tourists to witness the same clamor. I had not imagined the street any other way.

But in the gathering dark of that Sunday night, New York's financial heart was eerily at rest. Energy conservation measures had cut the lighting, and the streets were echoing, shadowy, a ghost town. It was as though some catastrophe had wiped out all human life, leaving only great, hollow architectural monuments. The sensation of passing through an underworld toward a meeting I did not want intensified my unease.

But in front of 100 Wall Street there was plenty of activity. As the limousine pulled to a stop, I saw about twenty somber-looking men quickly form a double column from the edge of the sidewalk to the lobby entrance. Johnson left the car but ordered me to stay inside. He checked the arrangements and then returned, opened the back door, and said urgently, "Now."

With Johnson in the lead I hurried through the human corridor into the empty building to an elevator being held for me. It shot upward and opened to a waiting Ernest Gross.

"I won." He was beaming. "They've agreed. Just Troyanovsky and Dobrynin, but they'll be a few minutes late."

"Fine." I tried to share his pleasure, but all I really felt was a small measure of satisfaction. "At least they made one concession."

I did not anticipate that there would be more. Before the ambassadors arrived, Gross and I went over the points we wanted to discuss and the order in which we would present them. Central was my absolute refusal to return to Moscow or to take any further instructions from the Soviet government. I would begin by making that statement, the same one I had put in the letters two days before. I would repeat my demand for assurances about Lina, Gennady, and Anna. Then we would hear the Soviets' response. The conference room was arranged for formal negotiating. We would be seated on opposite sides of a long table with a tape recorder in the middle of it.

It was 8:15 when an agent telephoned from the lobby to say that the ambassadors had arrived and were on their way up. Ernest Gross, Mark Garrison (the State Department Soviet specialist who acted as the observer), and I sat down at the table with Gross in the middle. A door leading to Gross's private office was at our back. Dobrynin and Troyanovsky entered through another door. Knowing them both well, I saw the tension behind their pretended affability. Their hands were extended, but their eyes were hard.

As Gross spoke, I watched them for some sign of their real feelings. Troyanovsky and I had not been close, but Dobrynin was a man whom I liked and respected. He had always shown friendship to me—not intimacy, but still something more than a professional relationship. Although we were suddenly adversaries, I felt a twinge of sympathy for him. He could probably understand my decision better than almost any other Soviet. He would never openly display that understanding, of course, but he is too honest not to have felt himself much of the terrible disillusionment which had motivated me.

Both ambassadors were professionals, and they easily assumed their official personalities, shrewd negotiators in a situation where a show of human instincts would have undermined their bargaining position. When Ernest Gross presented the "problem" as one of securing the guarantees for my family's safety mentioned in my letters to Brezhnev and Troyanovsky, they pretended surprise. They claimed they had not received the letters.

Angry, I whispered to Gross, "The letters were sent, weren't they?" He assured me that they had been. He told me the ambassadors were shamming, and their manner made it obvious. To cut the tension, he made a joke about New York's terrible postal service. Then he offered to give the Soviets copies of the English translations of the letters.

At first, they refused to read them. "We just want to have a heart-to-heart talk and find out what really happened," Troyanovsky insisted. This was not what I had wanted, but with Mark Garrison providing a running translation for Gross, we began a conversation in Russian.

I repeated almost the exact words I had used in my letter to Troyanovsky, but as soon as I mentioned the guarantees I wanted for Lina and my family, Dobrynin interrupted.

"By the way, we saw to her departure just now."

"Yes," Troyanovsky added. "She sent her regards."

I was startled, thrown off balance. I stammered something ridiculous. "That is completely wrong. . . . I don't agree to that. . . . It isn't serious . . . two ambassadors seeing my wife off . . ." A frightening image flashed through my mind: Lina, probably heavily drugged, with these two men holding her up, surrounded by KGB guards, propelled onto the Aeroflot flight which I had been scheduled to take. The scene I had so often pictured for myself had come true, but Lina had been taken in my place.

I tried to recover, to go back to the subject of the written guarantees for my family's well-being. Dobrynin, however, took a different tack. "We've both known Shevchenko for fifteen to twenty years," he told Gross in English. "He enjoyed the complete trust of the Soviet government, of the

465

leadership of the Soviet Foreign Ministry, and our trust as a colleague in our common work."

Then he turned to me. Employing the intimate form of "you" that Russian friends normally use with one another, he expressed only concern for me, bewilderment at my action. "Arkady, we have known each other for many years. I don't believe that all these years you have acted contrary to your convictions. . . . How can it be explained?"

"I was an idiot," I snapped, "believing in idiocies."

The hypocrisy in Dobrynin's question was tiresomely familiar to the three of us. We realized that millions upon millions of Soviet citizens conceal their true feelings about the Party line and policy. I knew that many officials—Party, government, even KGB—held deviant opinions, hidden for years, lifetimes. Anyone foolish enough to voice such thoughts risked losing not only his position and privileges but perhaps his life. One false step could mean disaster, personally or professionally, or both. Nearly everyone in the Soviet Union must be at all times alert and cautious. It was second nature for most Soviets, and I was no exception. Dobrynin and Troyanovsky knew all this better than I, for they were older and had lived longer under the Soviet regime. Still, it was no surprise that they were peddling the same threadbare goods.

In the course of the conversation Dobrynin continued to press for details, for the immediate cause of my decision. I mentioned the attempt to break into my apartment. Troyanovsky dismissed it. "You were ill . . . we were worried about you."

"It was not the only incident," I said, "just one of the last."

The KGB had mounted an intensive surveillance of me, shadowing me in the corridors and elevators of the UN, at the Mission, on the streets of New York. Dobrynin and Troyanovsky denied this; it was all a misunderstanding. But I was not going to take orders from Moscow anymore, I said, and would not go back to the Soviet Union, not "for anything."

Ernest Gross, seeing my agitation, put a hand on my arm in an attempt to bring me back to a diplomatic posture. It was too late.

"This is empty talk," I exploded. "My disagreement is total . . . but it is my private affair. . . . The letters develop my thoughts. I do not see why we should discuss any questions before you read the letters." Twice more I asked for an end to this "fruitless talk" before Dobrynin took the letters with a theatrical gesture and, together with Troyanovsky, began to read.

In the several minutes of silence that followed, I tried again to get myself under control. I failed. I was sure that they knew the contents of the letters and probably my letter to Lina too. And now they were pretending incredulity, twisting everything to make me seem an American pawn, and the whole business nothing but a devious, provocative game.

I was also roiling with frustration over Lina's flight. Or, rather, her abduction. And when Dobrynin put down the letters and smirked that they seemed marked by "signs of American clichés," I jumped to my feet.

"Mr. Gross," I said in English, "I don't want to continue this insulting conversation." To Dobrynin and Troyanovsky I said the same thing in Russian: "Stop the conversation."

"Don't get upset. There's no need," Dobrynin soothed. "Let's talk. Let's talk."

But I had had enough of such talk. I turned and left the room, stumbling in sickened fury into Gross's private office. Alone, I tried to restore my shattered composure, but it was useless. I held my head in my hands and broke down, choking on my outrage, my bitterness, my sense of loss.

For another half-hour the talk continued in the conference room, but it went nowhere. Dobrynin and Troyanovsky repeated their concern about my welfare and their inability to understand my decision. Gross pressed them to talk business: the issue of the guarantees. The Soviets would dwell only on the past. They refused to accept the finality of my action or to deal with demands for my family's future. The talk ended with Gross's offer to pursue the discussion at another time.

Gross found me in his office and began to sum up the impasse. He quickly realized, however, that I was in no shape to consider its details or to think ahead. We deferred further discussion until the following day. As I started to leave, he handed me two envelopes the Soviets had given him.

One contained a letter from Lina, arguing that I had made a mistake, urging me to come home to Moscow. It was in her handwriting, but not her language. The other was supposedly from Gennady, typed, unsigned, and transparently false in its repetition of the ritual phrases that also marked his mother's letter. I saw now that I had lost Gennady long ago. For his own security, I had never encouraged him to be critical of the Soviet system and had not shared my true feelings about it with him or with Anna. I had not revealed myself fully even to Lina. The years had taught me the danger for the whole family if we were to discuss Soviet flaws and shortcomings frankly among ourselves. One could too easily give oneself away in other environments. Furthermore, not only was Gennady young and inexperienced, he wanted a career at the Foreign Ministry, where any breath of criticism of our system could ruin him forever. But, having protected him from my own dissenting opinions, I now had to pay for it by separation from my son for the rest of my life. I scanned the letters and put them in my pocket.

Both, I realized, were KGB concoctions. Lina had accepted their false account of my conduct, had been tricked into believing that I was a CIA captive but that the Soviets would free me so I could follow her home. She had dismissed what I wrote to her and had swallowed the KGB-manufactured tales. She had very likely taken a heavy dose of tranquilizers also, for at the airport, the Americans informed me later, she seemed confused, nearly incoherent. She told U.S. officials she was voluntarily taking the flight to Moscow, but she was closely and continuously escorted by a large group of KGB agents, in addition to Dobrynin and Troyanovsky. Exactly as I had imagined, the KGB accompanied her right onto the plane. Neither in the waiting room nor in her letter was she able to speak freely.

By the time I perused the two letters, I was beyond emotion The confrontation with Dobrynin and Troyanovsky had drained me of all feeling. In the three days since my escape I had been running on a reservoir of nervous energy. Suddenly it ran dry. We left the building through the basement garage. (I was told later that there were KGB agents in the streets, trying to observe the comings and goings, but keeping their distance

468

from American security personnel.) I was driven back to the safe house without registering the route, my companions, even my own thoughts. I sank into an emotional torpor from which I roused myself only when events required some response from me.

However, the events came quickly enough. On Monday, a United Nations spokesman announced at the regular noon press briefing that I had taken a sudden leave of absence. Exhausted by the events of Sunday night, I had gone back to bed after breakfast. Johnson woke me with the news and the language of the statement: "Mr. Shevchenko has informed the Secretary General that he is absenting himself from the office and in this connection he mentioned differences with his government. Efforts are now being made to clarify the matter and for the time being, therefore, Mr. Shevchenko is considered to be on leave."

I had not expected anything to be released so soon, but the statement affirmed, if indirectly, my continued status as Under Secretary General. It also gave the public enough information to conclude that I had broken with the Soviets.

It was the news story of the moment, first on the TV network shows and then, Tuesday, in the newspapers. True to the tradition of the American press, the reporting quickly became sensational.

"Soviet Citizen, Waldheim Aide, Defects at UN," read the *New York Times* headline on April 11. Journalists proclaimed it one of the biggest U.S. intelligence coups ever, and speculated on my motivations.

Almost all the reports highlighted my colleagues' shock. I had been regarded as an orthodox Soviet functionary, obedient, loyal, a hard-line Communist. The fact that I was one of the U.S.S.R.'s youngest ambassadors was cited, along with my service as adviser to Gromyko, as proof not only of my "brilliant career" but also of my political reliability. Some reporters suggested that I had been in line to become a Deputy Foreign Minister. In trying to find the rationale for my action, they seemed to project ever-higher positions for me.

On Tuesday, while making a formal protest to the State Department, the Soviets issued their own explanation from the Mission. There was "no doubt," the official statement claimed, that I was the "victim of a premeditated provocation and that the U.S. intelligence services have been directly involved in this detestable frame-up." They demanded that I be returned to the Soviet Union.

Ernest Gross responded with a denial of the Soviets' charge and a rejection of their demands. He also confirmed that I had met with Soviet officials, whom he did not name, to prove to them that I was acting freely. But *Pravda* (the Russian word for "truth," so incredibly misapplied as the name of the Communist Party's official newspaper) printed its version of the affair on Thursday, in a few lines at the back of the newspaper, describing me as a "Soviet citizen who worked in the UN Secretariat." It was said that "the propaganda campaign being conducted in the American press over the Shevchenko case has the clear aim of covering up the unseemly activities of [the U.S.] special services."

Actually, the only propaganda campaign was the one the Soviets instigated. It was a classic piece of KGB disinformation technique. Whenever a defector embarrasses Moscow, every effort is made to smear the miscreant. Usually one of five motives is cited: greed for Western money, woman trouble, alcoholism, coercion, or criminal activity. My case seemed to call for extreme measures. Soviets at the UN began a whispering campaign about me in which four of the charges were liberally applied.

Some journalists uncritically picked up the KGB line. One press account had me romantically involved with an American woman. According to a *New York Times* story, "Soviet and other Eastern bloc diplomats appear to be especially eager . . . to call attention to Mr. Shevchenko's alleged drinking problem as a means of explaining his defection."

Tad Szulc, writing in the Washington *Post,* was one of the few who understood what was going on. "The initial Soviet charge that Shevchenko had been 'coerced' by American intelligence," he wrote, "is patent nonsense. Heavy hints dropped by Communist sources in New York that he had a 'drinking problem' seem to fit under the heading of character assassination. The defection obviously was an acute political and propaganda embarrassment for the Kremlin." Throughout the journalistic barrage I remained silent. As a UN official, I could not speak to the press without special permission, and as a defector in hiding I could not invite reporters to meet me.

But the press nearly caught up with me. On Tuesday afternoon Johnson burst into the living room of the safe house. I had never seen him so agitated. "We've got to get out of here! The goddamn clerk at the hotel saw your picture in the local paper and remembered you. He blabbed about your registering there. The press is all over the place. We're blown. If they've got it, the KGB has it."

Although the safe house was several miles outside of White Haven, Johnson believed its location was no longer secure. While I packed my few belongings, he arranged for other agents to return the hired car, pay the hotel bill, and collect my overnight bag. Within a few hours he and I and the guards were installed in a Marriott hotel in New Jersey, not far from New York City. We took a series of adjoining rooms, rented in the name of one of the agents, anonymous, claustrophobic cubicles to which all our food was brought. It was depressing enough to make me think that this was the way the rest of my life might pass.

My room looked out over the hotel parking lot, where the intermittent clangor of delivery trucks, trash collectors, and guests' cars seemed orchestrated to interfere with my efforts to sleep. I dozed and woke, dozed and woke, unable to order my thoughts and energy in either condition. I had no will to return to the unfinished summary of Dobrynin's report. I could not concentrate sufficiently to read or play chess. I managed a few card games and watched television for hours. I was like a hibernating animal under armed guard, waiting for Kurt Waldheim's return to New York to set in motion the final arrangements which could be made only with him.

My protectors and companions tried to bring me around, but it was not until Ernest Gross called to propose a meeting that I shook off my depression, at least briefly. He wanted to bring me up to date on his discussions with UN officials, but he and Johnson also thought I should make a quick, unexpected appearance in public to disprove conclusively the Soviet portrayal of me as a CIA captive. I agreed, and met Gross at his apartment on Thursday.

On the financial side, he reported, UN officials were taking a

471

helpful, businesslike attitude. No actual terms had been set, but the rules were likely to be interpreted generously enough to give me a substantial settlement if I chose to resign. Johnson wanted to move quickly, to close out the affair soon.

"It's going to be harder and harder for you to maintain your position as Under Secretary General when you're under our complete protection," said Johnson. "This isn't a normal way for a UN official to act."

I couldn't deny it, but I wasn't ready to surrender outright. "It doesn't depend on me," I said. "I can't do anything until Waldheim gets back. It has to be settled between him and me, face to face."

They accepted my position. Gross suggested that we go to the Century Association, a pleasant club where we could have a drink and make a display of casual, everyday behavior that the other members could report to journalists. Our contrivance proved successful.

We walked into the club and sat down at a table next to one occupied by Francis Plimpton, a distinguished American lawyer and diplomat whom I had known when he represented the United States at the UN in the sixties. Plimpton recognized me and joined us, remarking how surprised he had been by my defection.

"What I remember about you," he said, "was how tough you were in the Security Council. We figured you were always pushing Fedorenko to take a harder line, just when we thought we had him ready to compromise."

"You misunderstood what was really going on," I explained with a laugh. "The problem was that Fedorenko often forgot his instructions. It was my job to remind him, and to keep him on track. And if I hadn't done it, I would have been in trouble —with him, first of all."

We reminisced about a few other things. Gross introduced me to other members and friends, and after a suitably convivial interlude we left.

In the days that followed, I learned from Ferdinand Mayrhofer and others that the Soviets were pressuring Waldheim to dismiss me. Soviet diplomats had raised the issue with the Secretary General in London and Dublin and had taken a very tough stand. From Gross I learned that Troyanovsky was demanding another meeting with me.

The first encounter had been difficult enough. I did not relish the prospect of a second. But Johnson urged me to do it. "I understand your feelings," he said, "but you shouldn't be too rigid. You need to show them once and for all that your mind is made up and that you are acting freely."

I respected Bert. He was a friend, and I was accustomed to relying on his advice, which was usually in my own interest. On this occasion I believe he was also, understandably, an advocate of official U.S. thinking. Another round of SALT negotiations between the Americans and the Soviets was scheduled for May, and the State Department may have thought my defection might damage the climate for the talks unless the Soviets came to understand that my action had been my own, free and uncoerced. In any case, I agreed to see Troyanovsky one last time, to try to gain from him the thing that remained uppermost in my mind, the guarantees I wanted for my family's future.

Again, we set the encounter for Sunday night in Ernest Gross's office. For a second time a convoy swept us through the vacant streets of Manhattan's business district to the empty skyscraper and the law firm's conference room. This time, only Oleg Troyanovsky sat across the table.

His face was flushed and he was obviously on edge, but he kept his composure. Thanks to Gross, who repeatedly nudged me and whispered urgings of restraint, I maintained a semblance of calm as well. But when Troyanovsky spoke of my "unfortunate . . . accidental decision," I bristled. It was still not too late to "reconsider" and come back to the Soviet Union, Troyanovsky purred, "with no repercussions." I told him I would never return.

He pressed me with a veiled threat: "With every passing day" the possibility of my being taken back "will recede." Again, I said I would not change my mind.

What I wanted from him in writing—guarantees on behalf of Lina, Gennady, and Anna—he would give only orally, only indirectly.

"No one is going to enter into any deals," he said, "because

473

no one will prosecute your family. Your family has nothing to do with your decision."

I looked at him in disgust when he referred to the protection my family could count on under Soviet law. That law, I knew, could always be twisted to serve political ends or ignored by KGB decree. But Gross wisely defined Troyanovsky's statements as sounding "like an assurance . . . in my lawyer's ears." Troyanovsky coldly replied that it was "a statement of fact," but his implicit pledge that Lina could keep our property and be safe from reprisal was on the record. I recognized that it was the only assurance I could get. I had to be content with it, and with the tape recording which preserved it.

I also had to be content with a further wait for the final act of my life as a diplomat. Like the others that month, it was played out late at night in a nearly empty building in an atmosphere of uncertainty and tension.

On April 25, nine days after my meeting with Troyanovsky, Gross called to tell me that Waldheim had returned from Europe, had asked to see me, and had agreed, as well, to my request that we use his office in recognition of my official status. I went that same night to the UN building, leaving my American guards outside as I entered through the basement garage, to be escorted by UN security men to the Secretary General's thirty-eighth-floor office. Except for the uniformed men who guided me, Ferdinand Mayrhofer, who welcomed me, and Waldheim himself, the huge headquarters was empty. The hum and bustle that had been so welcome to me over so many years was stilled. The void was depressing.

Waldheim, rising from behind his desk to greet me, was noticeably tense. His first question showed his uncertainty. "No one pressured you into this, did they?" he asked.

"Kurt," I answered, "if there had been any pressure, do you think I would be here?" I went on to assure him that I did not want to create difficulties for him by insisting on remaining at the UN. "I don't want to hurt the organization," I said. "I know it's best for it and for me to have an amicable separation."

Waldheim took his chair with obvious relief. Although my lawyer and UN officials had prepared an agreement on a settlement that gave me a little more than $76,000 in deferred retirement, accrued pension, unused annual leave, and termination pay, I had not yet confirmed my willingness to accept the arrangement. My words ended the suspense.

"I knew you would behave decently," he said. "I never doubted you."

There was one more matter to discuss. I reminded Waldheim that I had lost contact with my family and might need his help in my effort to protect them at long distance.

"I'll do what I can, Arkady," he said, "but you, better than anyone else, know that it's doubtful that anything I can do would really be effective."

As we talked, he signed the separation papers and handed them to me for my signature. With that exchange and a handshake, our talk and my work were over. I tried to thank him for the privilege I had felt in working for him and for the UN, but my words were poor, choked with sentiments I found I could not express.

Taking my leave of Waldheim, I glanced for the last time around the rather small but tastefully furnished office of the Secretary General. Looking at the blue flag of the UN standing in the corner, at the round coffee table and comfortable sofa where I had so often sat with him during my five years as his deputy, I thought how odd it was that my career should end this way. I liked my job and I liked Waldheim. Regretting that I would no longer be part of the UN, I left Waldheim's office and went with Ferdinand Mayrhofer to my own.

There I designated the books and files which belonged to me, and watched as guards separated my possessions into piles that would be packed later. As they worked, I stood in front of my desk looking out the windows and around the walls, from the lights of New York to the map of the world, from my busy past, now being dismantled, into my uncertain future. In this building, I thought, I had made many friends, men and women who had gone on to great distinction in their own countries. We had worked together in difficult times, on sensitive issues, trying to improve the planet's chances for survival. Too often we had been able to do very little. Yet our effort was worthwhile, the work of peace.

I felt unfinished, unhappy to be leaving it. I had never foreseen making such a surreptitious departure.

Mayrhofer interrupted my melancholy. "We're ready. We'll

475

do the packing later," he said. "Where do you want us to send the boxes?"

I looked around as though an answer might materialize from the familiar furniture. "I don't know," I said after a long pause.

Mayrhofer understood my dilemma. "Don't worry," he said. "We'll keep them safe until you send for them. Good luck."

I rode back to the garage in an empty elevator and walked out again into the empty city streets to be driven to an empty hotel room in New Jersey. I was profoundly dispirited. I was beginning to realize that I might be that way for a long time. I had cut myself off from the two worlds I knew and belonged to —my homeland and the United Nations. Already I missed them both, and the friends who lived in them and were now sealed off from me. I would have to find a new world—but how? I would have to make new friends—but where? I was only forty-seven, but suddenly I felt old and alone.

Epilogue

ON APRIL 20 I WAS DRIVEN TO WASHINGTON, D.C. THE move made it easier for me and various government officials to hold lengthy discussions, but it was also another step away from familiar ground. I was anxious about Lina, worried about whether I would ever see Anna and Gennady again, whether I could cope with life in a strange city.

When we arrived in Washington, Bob and Carl, both of whom were based in New York, introduced their replacements, Lee Andrews of the CIA and Sandy Greenfield of the FBI. They had arranged to move me into a CIA safe house in the suburbs.

"But why should I go to a safe house?" I asked. "You know I'm not going to live in hiding."

They replied that it was only temporary, and reminded me that the first weeks after my defection would be the most dangerous ones.

As it turned out, the house was very nice. To all appearances it was just another well-kept suburban home, surrounded by the blooming trees and azaleas for which springtime in Washington is justifiably famous. A bedroom and a small study had been set aside for my use. A housekeeper born in Eastern Europe knew the Russian dishes I loved. No one rushed me to do anything. I had time to myself, time to recuperate.

I had arrived in Washington with the clothes on my back and a few changes of shirts and underwear. One night, before I left New York, Bob Ellenberg and I returned to my 65th Street apartment building through a rear door only to find, as the Americans had expected, that the Soviets had removed all my belongings. The rooms were stripped. Clothes, books, furniture, mementoes, pots and pans, everything had been taken away, like Lina, as though it were the property of the Soviet state.

I told Greenfield I needed some clothes. "Wait a minute, Arkady," he responded. "We have to do a few things before we can go." He explained that it wouldn't be wise to appear in public without a disguise, at least for a while. "But why the masquerade? You'll be with me all the time," I protested. He insisted that at least I had to wear dark glasses and a false mustache. Finally, I agreed. Although there was some joking as they fitted me out in my disguise, I was acutely aware of what was on their minds. I was a potential target for assassination or kidnapping by KGB agents, many of whom are based in Washington.

On the shopping excursion I felt a little silly and self-conscious, and as we drove back to the safe house I decided I would no longer be camouflaged. I hadn't gone through my years as an American spy only to wind up timorously incognito. I knew, although I didn't like to think about it, that living openly in the United States carried a certain risk, but that risk was always part of the price of my freedom.

I had never stopped thinking about my family and wondering if there were any possibility of reunion. Not long after I settled down at the safe house, I received the materials forwarded to me from the UN, as Mayrhofer had promised. They included some family photographs I had kept in my office, and I spent a good deal of time looking at them. I wanted to take steps to reestablish contact with Lina and the children, but learned that the U.S. government would not be able to help me in this task. I would have to get outside help. There were many other practical matters for which I would need assistance. I decided to engage a local lawyer.

The government agents provided me with a list of some half-dozen Washington attorneys. One was William Geimer, who had served in a high position in the State Department. It seemed to me that his background would enable him to comprehend my situation.

I had intended to interview several of the attorneys on the list, but changed my mind during my meeting with Geimer. His relaxed but professional attitude impressed me. I felt in

478

stinctively that I could trust him; that he would not only give me good counsel but that we could become friends. As I look back, I see now that I needed friendship as much as I needed advice. I wanted an attorney who would not only represent me personally but also care about my general well-being.

I began to feel a little more confident about my future, but my improved spirits were cut short. Early on May 11, Lee Andrews knocked on my bedroom door. "Arkady, can you come downstairs right away?" he called. "We've got some bad news."

I wondered what could have happened. Of the several possibilities which ran through my mind as I descended the stairs, none approached the truth.

Sandy Greenfield was waiting in the living room. Both men looked tense and solemn.

"Arkady, Lina is dead."

I was stunned. The news was not just bad; it was devastating. Lina, *dead?* I could not bring myself to believe the news report they handed me. It was datelined Moscow and had been published in the London *Evening News*, under the byline of Victor Louis, a Soviet citizen whose ties to the KGB have made him a wealthy tipster for the Western press. He wrote only when and what Moscow authorized him. A news story of his in October 1964 had been the first announcement of Nikita Khrushchev's ouster.

According to his article, my wife had committed suicide. That she was dead I could believe; that she had taken her own life, never. Lina had been moody at times, occasionally even depressed, but she never dealt with these emotions by letting them grow within her. Her standard reaction was anger. She would lash out and then would seem to feel better. She was a strong woman, determined to overcome obstacles and to get the best out of life. She would have been the last person to give in to suicidal impulses, to surrender.

But what could have happened? My surmise is that she had been tricked into going back to Moscow, most likely with the promise that the Soviet government would get me back. When she later realized that I was not returning to the Soviet Union, and that she would never be allowed to return to the United States, she may have lashed out at the wrong people. It would

479

not surprise me if she had threatened to reveal many of the sordid secrets she knew about the lives of top Soviet officials. Thereby she would have made herself a threat to several careers, and thereby, in turn, a candidate for extermination by the KGB. Could they have murdered her to protect themselves, and perhaps at the same time punish me? Knowing them as I do, I'm inclined to think that that is what happened.

Over the years, I had heard many times that the KGB used medical assassinations to eliminate "undesirable" politicians and others. A neat, clean solution. There had been frequent gossip about such remedies. Stories about Maxim Gorky's death in that manner, for instance, and those of such leading political figures as Andrei Zhdanov in Stalin's time, persisted in Moscow circles. There had been other tales about such things happening to less celebrated but potentially troublesome people.

Still dazed with a mixture of fury and anguish the day after I heard the news, I telephoned the Soviet Embassy in Washington and got through to Anatoly Dobrynin. "Tell me the truth," I pleaded. "What happened to my wife?"

"I know nothing more than you do," he replied coolly. "The only information I have is what I read in the American press."

I thought of my children. What had happened to them? Were they safe? What must they be thinking? I felt fairly secure about Gennady; he was independent, he had a good job and a well-connected wife. But what about Anna, living in our apartment with her grandmother? I sent telegrams and letters to them, but got no answer; they were probably never received. Gennady replied toward the end of May in a dry, stiff letter written not for me but for the Soviet officials who would scan it for any hint of sympathy.

On May 23, I wrote Gromyko requesting that the Soviet government allow me to meet with my daughter. No answer. I yearned desperately to contact Anna, to establish communication with her, to determine if she wanted to join me in the United States, and, if so, to find a way to bring her here. My government companions steered clear of this problem, so I turned to Bill Geimer. He helped me draft pleas to President Carter and to Secretary of State Cyrus Vance for help. The responses were polite and sympathetic: they believed in the reunification of families; they wished me well; but there was nothing they could do.

I decided to act on my own. Geimer volunteered to go to the U.S.S.R. and try to talk with Anna. He went to the Soviet Embassy to request a visa, and to assure the Soviets that we were not interested in creating trouble or publicity. He promised that if he were allowed to meet with Anna he would not put any pressure on her. He would simply assure her that I was well, and ask if she would like to come to the United States for a visit. We never received an answer to his request.

I still have not given up hope of seeing Anna again someday. At the same time I realize that the surest, cruelest way the Soviets can punish me is to keep us separated.

It was some time before I could settle down enough to begin what became many, many months of debriefing. (Why they call this process "*de*briefing" has always been a mystery to me. As far as I could see, *I* was doing the briefing.)

The talks were both more extensive and more satisfying than any I experienced in New York. There I was usually hurried, sometimes nervous, never quite certain of how much background Johnson or Ellenberg needed to make them understand the significance of a seemingly minor policy development or personnel shift in Moscow. But the Washington experts had the time and the desire to discuss Soviet affairs in depth, the knowledge to ask the right questions and understand my answers without a lot of background explanation, the command of Russian to help me find the precise phrases to describe nuances and to recollect many things stored deep in my memory. Our talks, whether on Soviet foreign policy, arms control, or the Kremlin's global ambitions and the personalities and maneuverings of the top leaders, were stimulating for me.

The people with whom I dealt were courteous and patient. I say patient because I tend to ramble on at length. My only complaint about the briefing process was that it seemed to go on forever. What a contrast it was to KGB stories I and other Soviets had been told about pressures and tests to which defectors were subjected by the CIA and FBI. I was never

481

"grilled" or hooked up to lie detectors or other machines or harassed in any way.

While the briefings were in progress, I also began to go out in Washington with Andrews and Greenfield and other FBI agents assigned to me. I particularly wanted to restore my library. It was not only necessary for my future livelihood but also the sole activity during those days of upheaval and grief that gave me any contentment. Book-hunting has been my lifelong passion and hobby. I soon learned the location of good Washington bookstores and in so doing, became more familiar with the city's neighborhoods, and felt increasingly at home there.

I had also begun to search for an apartment, but it was quite a while before I found a suitable one. I have always liked the familiar comfort of my own place, and the atmosphere of the safe house had begun to wear on me. It was not that the Americans were unfeeling. In fact, they gave me steady support and understanding through my bursts of anger and periods of depression, and the constant listlessness of grief. I relied on them, appreciated their help and concern, liked them —and yet came to resent their presence. They were companions and advisers, but they were also guards and hindrances. I had wanted always to be free; now I also wanted to be free of them. No matter how well-intentioned the surveillance, I still somehow felt a captive.

As the months passed, I also realized that I longed for emotional support of a kind they could not provide. With CIA and FBI agents I would always be, first of all, a ward, a property for which they were responsible. I was lonely. I wanted to talk to women, to be in their company, to have them notice me and care about me. When I told Andrews and Greenfield how I felt, they seemed at a loss. Whatever the many resources of the CIA and FBI, ladies-in-waiting were not among them. We discussed my loneliness, but at first found no obvious solution. I didn't like the idea of singles bars, although we had begun to go to restaurants in the city, sometimes staying overnight at a hotel in the area where I thought I was most likely to find an apartment. But I did not see myself picking up a girl in a bar. There were no groups or clubs I could join without revealing my identity, and I could hardly place a personal ad in the *New York Review of Books:* "Soviet defector, 47, seeks female help in making new life."

Finally, the FBI agents suggested trying an escort service. They would not make any phone calls themselves, but they would give me some numbers from the phone book and look the other way. That was how I met Judy Chavez.

At first, I was quite taken with her. I asked that she give up her other patrons and be my companion exclusively. She agreed, but with several conditions. She had lawyers' bills to pay both for a divorce she was seeking and for her defense against a marijuana possession charge in New Jersey. She needed money and wanted freedom. One marriage had left her determined to make no new permanent ties. She also had a sick sister to help and a mother with whom she spent her weekends. I offered to support her. I could afford it with my UN severance payment and some other money of my own.

For several weeks I believed she was keeping her promise. She helped me settle into my new apartment, where I lived under an assumed name. Something so small as merely going in and out of the building without a CIA or FBI guard gave me a surge of pride and joy each time it happened. I began to feel new energy and self-confidence. The neighborhood I had chosen turned out, fortuitously, to be fairly close to several Connecticut Avenue bookstores where I could rummage around, building my new library.

I kept the apartment myself, cooked for myself, and did whatever I felt like in my free time. The novelty of liberty made the smallest chore seem a pleasure.

Soon, however, my adjustment was interrupted. I had been mistaken and naïve in trusting Chavez's sincerity and good intentions. She sold the story of our relationship to the news media, and, more important, revealed my identity as well as my address. She embellished her story with the claim that I had paid her with money furnished by the CIA, although she knew very well that I had used my own funds. The media had a field day. I wanted to sue her, but Bill Geimer, who flew back from European business trip to deal with the clamor, joined CIA and FBI officials to persuade me to forget the damage she had tried to cause. To go to court would only prolong the sensation without giving me any satisfaction. They were right, and the episode faded from public attention despite a paperback that Judy Chavez published.

Looking back, I feel fortunate that that period of stress, confusion, and bad judgment was relatively brief. The presence of steadying friends and strong support ameliorated the anger and humiliation I felt. I do not believe that what I went through during this period is all that different from other defectors' experiences. The important thing is that a person in this situation should never be left to fend for himself or to keep his feelings and emotions pent up inside. I know this is easier said than done, for friends who will go through such an ordeal with one are hard to find. Government officials, with all their good intentions and assistance in the settlement process, simply cannot replace someone personally close to you. I think that this is the reason why some Soviet defectors who have had no financial problems or difficulties in finding suitable jobs have still been unable to adjust to life in the West, and in a moment of desperate loneliness and despair have thrown their hopes away by returning to the Soviet Union. These unfortunates will never be forgiven, if they are even allowed—in some cases for propaganda reasons—to return to their previous jobs, and they will never have a chance to regain freedom.

I was one of the lucky ones. I found loving friends and I found Elaine, my wife, who loves me and to whom my success and happiness are important. I found Bill Geimer, who also cared and gave me countless hours, days, years of himself, to bring me into a new life.

I have lived in the United States for nearly seven years now and for nearly all that time Elaine has been with me through disappointment and success and sometimes the comedy that only another immigrant could fully appreciate. Both my wife and I feel strongly about our private lives, but since this is a memoir I feel I should say a few things. Bill Geimer inadvertently became our matchmaker. He and his wife, Maureen, invited me to dinner at their home with some friends—one of whom was Elaine. She and I took to each other immediately. A slender, red-haired southerner, well educated and intelligent, she captivated me. We found that we had many interests in common, from art to politics. Usually our views coincided, but even when they differed, I liked the outspoken way in which she defended her opinions. Our strong mutual attraction led to our marriage at the end of December 1978, and it brought me a lucky bonus in the form of a mother-in-law with whom I am best friends. It was wonderful having a family again. A year of turmoil had ended with the promise of peace and growth.

In a few months Elaine and I moved from my apartment into our own house. Here was another new experience, one that involved a lot of complicated and unfamiliar problems for me. I found the ramifications of this very ordinary—to most Americans—procedure simply mind-boggling. Again, Bill Geimer saw us through the arcane and sometimes comic process of becoming home owners. We celebrated its conclusion in a restaurant where I used my newly acquired credit card. As I pulled it out of my wallet, Bill joked that now I was "becoming a true American."

There were still many lessons to learn. I had had no idea that to get myself into shape to begin working effectively again could take so long. I was not prepared for the many difficulties —large and small—that this process entailed.

There was, to begin with, a deluge of confusing but necessary paper procedures for taxes, Social Security, an automobile, all kinds of insurance, and information and instructions about how life is lived in the United States. There is no comparable process in the Soviet Union for the complete management of one's life. As the years went by, however, the forms became less formidable and the pace more natural. I have even taken to griping about mowing the lawn and the price of garage repairs, along with millions of others who I hope will soon be my fellow citizens.

Elaine had been a court reporter when we met, but when we began to work on this book together, she left her job to assist me. To this day I cannot get over the real satisfaction of being able to say something freely for the first time in my life, without the necessity of remembering constraints on what was politically or ideologically acceptable.

I have a full work schedule—lecturing regularly at the Foreign Service Institute of the U.S. State Department and before university and business groups, and writing for various journals and newspapers. I still consult with the government on a variety of subjects. I will continue to pursue academic interests. In short, my life has become more and more what I had longed for over the years, lived openly and with no master other than myself.

My initial lecture abroad took place in Toronto, Canada, early in 1983. It was on this occasion that I experienced the first threat made against me by the KGB or their sympathizers: the organization sponsoring my talk received an anonymous telephone call saying there would be "big trouble if Shevchenko spoke." I had made up my mind, however, that the Soviets would never again dictate to me in any matter, and the engagement proceeded without incident.

I have been asked many times whether the KGB poses a real threat to my life. From the beginning, of course, I have realized that this would always be a possibility. But it is a risk I have reconciled myself to, because I refuse to be driven underground. Since my defection, I have learned that I was sentenced to death in absentia in Moscow. I have also been told that some KGB defectors since my time have said that I was suspected of working for the CIA in the spring of 1978. I am glad that my intuition did not fail me over that fateful cable of recall to Moscow for "consultations."

The best way for me to meet any potential risk from the KGB is to remain publicly active. I do not seek danger; life is precious to me. But to hide myself away just to cling to it is not living. I have continued to follow Soviet policy closely. I read Soviet newspapers, magazines, and books and talk with other defectors in situations similar to my own. I intend to follow these pursuits as well as new areas of interest fostered by freedom for the rest of my life.

AFTER THE DEATHS OF LEONID BREZHNEV, YURI ANDROPOV and Konstantin Chernenko, it was no longer possible for the Kremlin's old oligarchs to resist selecting a younger leader. Mikhail Gorbachev won the toss and now leads the Politburo. Whether or not his stewardship will open a new era for the Soviet Union remains to be seen. Gorbachev has definitely initiated a new style; he is dynamic and bold at least, and barring unforseen crises he should have enough time to develop and implement his line.

As one who once belonged to the stratum from which possible future leaders are chosen, I agree with William Hyland that "the younger generation, which had been shut out of the top leadership for years as the Brezhnev collegium tenaciously held on to power, may push to accelerate the implementation of new policy initiatives." But it is very important, as he has also rightly said, to understand the built-in continuity and momentum of the Soviet system, and the considerable influence the ghosts of the past will exert over whoever occupies the Kremlin. Even modest attempts at reforms will likely meet vigorous opposition from both younger and older members of the elite who will prefer the old order to any other because they may not be able to perceive any other that would be so beneficial to them personally.

The Brezhnev generation—well defined by Robert Ford, the veteran Canadian Ambassador to Moscow, as "mostly anti-intellectual, quickly and often sloppily educated"*—is fading away. Its place is being taken by men of Mikhail Gorbachev's generation, who have neither endured the immediate post-Revolutionary period nor participated in the Second World War. Most of them are better educated and have, in general, a deeper understanding of the complexities and realities of Soviet society. I do not think they will be more aggressive for not having personally experienced the calamity of war. I tend to believe that they will be more thoughtful about the need to overcome economic and social stagnation within the country—and, most especially in this regard, that they will comprehend the necessity of a significant reallocation of resources from the military to the civilian sector; the present military buildup has created structural economic imbalances that effectively preclude the growth and development of industry, agriculture, and technological innovation. In sum, they might begin to pay some attention to one notable Marxist-Leninist idea: that socialism should serve as an inspiring example of domestic performance to other peoples, which is certainly not the case now.

One general qualification needs to be entered here, however. The Soviet economy has been depicted in gloomy hues

* Robert Ford, "The Soviet Union: The Next Decade," *Foreign Affairs*, Summer 1984, p. 1136.

for years, and every new setback seems to call forth predictions about the system's longevity and future viability. But the faltering economy and other afflictions should not mislead anyone about the durability of the regime. There is no doubt that the U.S.S.R. is experiencing serious domestic and other difficulties. But it has overcome worse troubles in the past. It has both tremendous natural wealth and vast human resources. In their ability to withstand centuries—not decades—of hardship and privation and yet persevere, the Soviet people are unmatched by any nation on earth, with the possible exception of the Chinese.

The West, therefore, should not delude itself by focusing its attention exclusively on Soviet flaws and shortcomings. There have also been successes. It is premature to predict the imminent decline of the U.S.S.R. and its empire; matters must worsen considerably before this idea can be entertained realistically.

The Soviet Union neither will begin to reshape itself into a free-enterprise society nor will it soon disintegrate. Neither do I believe that the Soviet challenge to the free world is ideologically now less threatening, or that it has simply turned into a "fairly conventional geopolitical challenge," as some analysts suggest. They exaggerate the loss of ideological faith among the population and underestimate Soviet ideological appeal in Central and Latin America, Africa, Asia, and other parts of the world. A fresh impression from Richard Harwood of the Washington *Post*, derived from a recent visit to the Soviet Union, states the case rather well. He noted that in effect a new religion has emerged in the U.S.S.R., a religion that flourishes as did the old Orthodox faith in times past. The new religion, of course, is Leninism. "It is a religion," Harwood writes, "sustained by a profound faith in a beneficent Father, Vladimir Ilyich Lenin. As Christ [is] to Christians, a Muhammad [is] to Moslems, Lenin to this society is a holy prophet and guide, not divine perhaps, but more than mortal. To believe otherwise—to dissent from Leninist orthodoxy—is the new heresy." *

* Washington *Post*, September 23, 1984.

I remember how difficult it was for me to free myself from the veneration of Lenin, so deeply implanted in me from childhood on.

Mikhail Gorbachev is as doctrinaire in his convictions and beliefs as his predecessors. He is a product of the Soviet system, or to be more precise, of the party apparatus. One would be absolutely wrong to entertain the idea that he would want to alter substantially the existing system or ease ideological indoctrination of the population or allow the Soviet people more liberty in the area of human rights. In fact, changes in Moscow's top leadership have had a rather marginal effect on the essential character of the Kremlin's power structure and on its policy direction. The leadership under Gorbachev is pursuing basically the same ultimate global and domestic aims of the Soviet Communist Party.

As regards Soviet threats to world peace today and tomorrow, I think Richard Pipes has got succinctly to the root of the problem: "As long as the *nomenklatura* remains what it is, as long as the Soviet Union lives in a state of lawlessness, as long as the energies of its peoples are not allowed to express themselves creatively, so long there can be no security for anyone else in the world."* It seems to me very doubtful that the *nomenklatura* class will disappear any time soon under the coming generations of Kremlin leaders.

For years the Kremlin has shown itself to be internally conservative to the point of ossification, working only to preserve the status quo in the Soviet Union. It has been a different story in the world arena. Under détente, the U.S.S.R. has increased its military forces at an alarming rate, and much beyond any reasonable defense needs. It has tried to project its power and influence all over the world. In 1979, it took a step unprecedented since the Second World War by invading and using its own combat troops in a state outside the Soviet bloc: Afghanistan. In its treatment of its own citizens, it systematically violates the human rights provisions of the Helsinki Accords. The suppression of the Solidarity movement in Poland provoked great indignation from the international com-

* *Foreign Affairs*, "Can the Soviet Union Reform?," Fall 1984, p. 59.

munity, as did the killing of 269 civilian passengers on a Korean Air Lines jet.

Such behavior has put into sharp focus some important and far-reaching issues pertinent to the nuclear age. Could the Kremlin be as adventurous with its nuclear arsenal as it has been with its conventional forces? Is there a conflict of interest between the Soviet political and Soviet military leadership? If so, is the military getting the upper hand and turning the Politburo toward a kind of Bonapartism, as some observers have suggested? One cannot overemphasize, in this connection, that there is *no* disagreement among Soviet leaders —political or military, young or old—as far as their ultimate goals are concerned. They view world development in terms of a continuing struggle between two opposing social and political systems. They believe in the inevitable, if long-forthcoming, victory of Soviet-style socialism in the course of what they call "the objective development" of human society. But they do not intend to achieve this victory by resorting to nuclear war.

Nuclear war could only be a last resort, to be initiated solely if the Soviets were fully convinced that the very existence of the nation was at stake, and if there appeared to be no alternative. At the same time, by projecting its military might over the globe more and more aggressively, Moscow invites the risk that conventional conflicts and confrontations with the West could escalate out of control. Among the militant ideologues and the military, there are those who are willing to take such a risk.

Yet, I do not see how military or security men—influential as they are—could usurp the primacy of the Party. Ultimate power in the U.S.S.R. unquestionably belongs to the Party with the Central Committee and Politburo at the top. Any real Bonapartist tendency on the part of a present or would-be leader would immediately recall to those high in Party ranks the cases of Georgy K. Zhukov and Lavrenty P. Beria, who attempted to put the army or the security apparatus above the Party and failed. The military and security forces are, in the final analysis, instruments of the Party; it will not permit a change in that arrangement.

The West must deal with the Soviet Union, like it or not,

There is more than enough rationale for this: both the Soviet Union and the United States occupy unique positions of power which will inevitably affect mankind's future. Although East and West apply different rules of the game in competition, it is imperative, if we are to avoid cataclysm, to maintain a dialogue with the U.S.S.R., to seek reasonable and practical accommodation, even cooperation where our interests are in alignment. This cooperation is essential to resolve global problems such as preventing accidental nuclear war and nuclear proliferation, reducing the level of military threat, and achieving progress in arms control. It is required to handle crisis situations that will inevitably appear from time to time, irrespective of the status of Soviet-American relations.

The U.S. sometimes lacks the steadiness needed to deal persuasively with the Soviets. Its policy toward the Soviet Union seems to jump from extreme to extreme. Yet I have never doubted that America's strength makes it the one power capable of forcing Moscow to restrain itself. This is something that can be achieved if American leaders do not forget an old and still true lesson: what the men in the Kremlin understand best is military and economic might; energetic political conviction; strength of will. If the West cannot confront the Soviets with equal determination, Moscow will continue to play the bully around the globe.

Plain truth is the most effective weapon against the falsehoods on which the Soviet system is built, the myths about itself it has been all too successful in spreading around the world. Truth is also the one force that can dispel the secrecy behind which the Soviet leaders hide the reality of their system and their intentions.

I have tried to tell the truth. I have searched for the truth about myself, about the country I grew up to love, and the regime I learned to know and hate. I hope I have contributed to exposing the lies, to weakening their appeal, and to bringing nearer the day when the people to whom I still belong will be free as well to speak the truth openly for all the world to hear.

Index

Real life espionage from novelist and foreign correspondent...

WILLIAM STEVENSON